Hong Kong

Directed by Hans Johannes Hoefer
Produced, Edited and Designed by Leonard Lueras and R. Ian Lloyd
Editor in Hong Kong, Saul Lockhart

APA PUBLICATIONS

TABLE OF CONTENTS

TABLE OF CONTENTS

THE INSIGHT GUIDES SERIES RECEIVED SPECIAL AWARDS FOR EXCELLENCE FROM THE PACIFIC AREA TRAVEL ASSOCIATION.

HONG KONG

Sixth Edition

APA PUBLICATIONS

Publisher: Hans Johannes Hoefer
Managing Director: Julian Sale
General Manager: Henry Lee
Marketing Director: Aileen Lau
Editorial Director: Geoffrey Eu
Editorial Manager: Vivien Kim
Editorial Consultants: Brian Bell (Europe)
                    Heinz Vestner (German Editions)
Updating Coordinator: Hilary Cunningham (N. America)

Project Editors

Helen Abbott, Diana Ackland, Mohamed Amin, Ravindralal Anthonis, Roy Bailet, Louisa Cambell, Jon Carroll, Hilary Cunningham, John Eames, Janie Freeburg, Bikram Grewal, Virginia Hopkins, Samuel Israel, Jay Itzkowitz, Phil Jaratt, Tracy Johnson, Ben Kalb, Wilhelm Klein, Saul Lockhart, Sylvia Mayuga, Gordon McLauchlan, Kal Müller, Eric Oey, Daniel P. Reid, Kim Robinson, Ronn Ronck, Robert Seidenberg, Rolf Steinberg, Sriyani Tidball, Lisa Van Gruisen, Merin Wexler.

Contributing Writers

A.D. Aird, Ruth Armstrong, T. Terence Barrow, F. Lisa Beebe, Bruce Berger, Dor Bahadur Bista, Clinton V. Black, Star Black, Frena Bloomfield, John Borthwick, Roger Boschman, Tom Brosnahan, Jerry Carroll, Tom Chaffin, Nedra Chung, Tom Cole, Orman Day, Kunda Dixit, Richard Erdoes, Guillermo Gar-Oropeza, Ted Giannoulas, Barbara Gloudon, Harka Gurung, Sharifah Hamzah, Willard A. Hanna, Elizabeth Hawley, Sir Edmund Hillary, Tony Hillerman, Jerry Hopkins, Peter Hutton, Neil Jameson, Michael King, Michele Kort, Thomas Lucey, Leonard Lueras, Michael E. Macmillan, Derek Maitland, Buddy Mays, Craig McGregor, Reinhold Messner, Julie Michaels, M.R. Priya Rangsit, Al Read, Elizabeth V. Reyes, Victor Stafford Reid, Harry Rolnick, E.R. Sarachandra, Uli Schmetzer, Ilsa Sharp, Norman Sibley, Peter Spiro, Harold Stephens, Keith Stevens, Michael Stone, Desmond Tate, Colin Taylor, Deanna L. Thompson, Randy Udall, James Wade, Mallika Wanigasundara, William Warren, Cynthia Wee, Tony Wheeler, Linda White, H. Taft Wireback, Alfred A. Yuson, Paul Zach.

Contributing Photographers

Carole Allen, Ping Amranand, Tony Arruza, Marcello Bertinetti, Alberto Cassio, Pat Canova, Alain Compost, Ray Cranbourne, Alain Evrard, Ricardo Ferro, Lee Foster, Manfred Gottschalk, Werner Hahn, Dallas and John Heaton, Brent Hesselyn, Hans Hoefer, Luca Invernizzi, Ingo Jezierski, Wilhelm Klein, Dennis Lane, Max Lawrence, Lyle Lawson, Philip Little, Guy Marche, Antonio Martinelli, David Messent, Ben Nakayama, Vautier de Nanxe, Kal Müller, Günter Pfannmuller, Van Philips, Ronni Pinsler, Fitz Prenzel, G.P. Reichelt, Dan Rocovits, David Ryan, Frank Salmoiraghi, Thomas Schollhammer, Blair Seitz, David Stahl, Bill Wassman, Rendo Yap, Hisham Youssef.

While contributions to Insight Guides are very welcome, the publisher cannot assume responsibility for the care and return of unsolicited manuscripts or photographs. Return postage and/or a self-addressed envelope must accompany unsolicited material if it is to be returned. Please address all editorial contributions to Apa Photo Agency, P.O. Box 219, Orchard Point Post Office, Singapore 9123.

Distributors

Australia and New Zealand: Prentice Hall of Australia, 7 Grosvenor Place, Brookvale, NSW 2100, Australia. **Benelux:** Utigeverij Cambium, Naarderstraat 11, 1251 AW Laren, The Netherlands. **Brazil and Portugal:** Cedibra Editora Brasileira Ltda, Rua Leonidia, 2-Rio de Janeiro, Brazil. **Denmark:** Copenhagen Book Centre Aps, Roskildeveji 338, DK-2630 Tastrup, Denmark. **Germany:** RV Reise-und Verkehrsuerlag Gmbh, Neumarkter Strasse 18, 8000 Munchen 80, West Germany. **Hawaii:** Pacific Trade Group Inc., P.O. Box 1227, Kailua, Oahu, Hawaii 96734, U.S.A. **Hong Kong:** Far East Media Ltd., Vita Tower, 7th Floor, Block B, 29 Wong Chuk Hang Road, Hong Kong. **India and Nepal:** India Book Distributors, 107/108 Arcadia Building, 195 Narima Point, Bombay-400-021, India. **Indonesia:** Java Books, Box 55 J.K.C.P., Jakarta, Indonesia. **Israel:** Steimatzky Ltd., P.O. Box 628, Tel Aviv 61006, Israel (Israel title only). **Italy:** Zanfi Editori SRL. Via Ganaceto 121, 41100 Modena, Italy. **Jamaica:** Novelty Trading Co., P.O. Box 80, 53 Hanover Street, Kingston, Jamaica. **Japan:** Charles E. Tuttle Co. Inc., 2-6 Suido 1-Chome, Bunkyo-ku, Tokyo 112, Japan. **Kenya:** Camerapix Publishers International Ltd., P.O. Box 45048, Nairobi, Kenya. **Korea:** Kyobo Book Centre Co., Ltd., P.O. Box Kwang Hwa Moon 1 658, Seoul, Korea. **Philippines:** National Book Store, 701 Rizal Avenue, Manila, Philippines. **Singapore:** MPH Distributors (S) Pte. Ltd., 601 Sims Drive #03-21 Pan-I Warehouse and Office Complex, S'pore 1438, Singapore. **Switzerland:** M.P.A. Agencies-Import SA, CH. du Croset 9, CH-1024, Ecublens, Switzerland. **Taiwan:** Caves Books Ltd., 103 Chungshan N. Road, Sec. 2, Taipei, Taiwan, Republic of China. **Thailand:** Far East Publications Ltd., 117/3 Soi Samahan, Sukhumvit 4 (South Nana), Bangkok, Thailand. **United Kingdom, Ireland and Europe (others):** Harrap Ltd., 19-23 Ludgate Hill, London EC4M 7PD, England, United Kingdom. **Mainland United States and Canada:** Graphic Arts Center Publishing, 3019 N.W. Yeon, P.O. Box 10306, Portland OR 97210, U.S.A. (The Pacific Northwest title only); Prentice Hall Press, Gulf & Western Building, One Gulf & Western Plaza, New York, NY 10023, U.S.A. (all other titles).

Chinese editions: Formosan Magazine Press Ltd., 6 Fl. No. 189, Yen Pin S. Road, Taipei, Taiwan, R.O.C. **French editions:** Editions Gallimard, 5 rue Sébastien-Bottin, F-75007 Paris, France. **German editions:** Nelles Verlag GmbH, Schleissheirner Str. 371b, 8000 Munich 45, West Germany **Italian editions:** Zanfi Editori SLR. Via Ganaceto 121 41100 Modena, Italy. **Portuguese editions:** Cedibra Editora Brasileira Ltda, Rua Leonidia, 2-Rio de Janeiro, Brazil.

Advertising and Special Sales Representatives

Advertising carried in Insight Guides gives readers direct access to quality merchandise and travel-related services. These advertisements are inserted in the Guide in Brief section of each book. Advertisers are requested to contact their nearest representatives, listed below.

Special sales, for promotion purposes within the international travel industry and for educational purposes, are also available. The advertising representatives listed here also handle special sales. Alternatively, interested parties can contact Apa Publications, P.O. Box 219, Orchard Point Post Office, Singapore 9123.

Australia and New Zealand: Harve and Gullifer Pty. Ltd. 1 Fawkner St. Kilda 3181, Australia. Tel: (3) 525 3422; Tlx: 523259; Fax: (89) 4312837.
Canada: The Pacific Rim Agency, 6900 Cote Saint Luc Road, Suite 303, Montreal, Quebec, Canada H4V 2Y9. Tel: (514) 9311299; Tlx: 0525134 MTL; Fax: (514) 8615571.
Hawaii: HawaiianLMedia Sales; 1750 Kalakaua Ave., Suite 3-243, Honolulu, Hawaii 96826, U.S.A. Tel: (808) 9464483.
Hong Kong: C Cheney & Associates, 17th Floor, D'Aguilar Place, 1-30 D'Aguilar Street, Central, Hong Kong. Tel: 5-213671; Tlx: 63079 CCAL HX.
India and Nepal, Pakistan and Bangladesh: Universal Media, CHA 2/718, 719 Kantipath, Lazimpat, Kathmandu-2, Nepal. Tel: 412911/414502; Tlx: 2229 KAJI NP ATTN MEDIA.
Indonesia: Media Investment Services, Setiabudi Bldg. 2, 4th Floor, Suite 407, Jl. Hr. Rasuna Said, Kuningan, Jakarta Selatan 12920, Indonesia. Tel: 5782723/5782752; Tlx: 62418 MEDIANETIA; Mata Graphic Design, Batujimbar, Sanur, Bali, Indonesia. Tel: (0361) 8073. (for Bali only)
Korea: Kaya Ad Inc., Rm. 402 Kunshin Annex B/D, 251-1 Dohwa Dong, Mapo-Ku, Seoul, Korea (121). Tel: (2) 7196906; Tlx: K 32144 KAYAAD; Fax: (2) 7199816.
Philippines: Torres Media Sales Inc., 21 Warbler St., Greenmeadows 1, Murphy, Quezon City, Metro Manila, Philippines. Tel: 722-02-43; Tlx: 23312 RHP PH.
Taiwan: Cheney Tan & Van Associates, 7th Floor, 10 Alley 4, Lane 545 Tun Hua South Road, Taipei, Taiwan. Tel: (2) 7002963; Tlx: 11491 FOROSAN; Fax: (2) 3821270.
Thailand: Cheney, Tan & Van Outrive, 17th Fl. Rajapark Bldg., 163 Asoke Rd., Bangkok 10110, Thailand. Tel: 2583244/2583259; Tlx: 20666 RAJAPAK TH.
Singapore and Malaysia: Cheney Tan Associates, 1 Goldhill Plaza, #02-01, Newton Rd., Singapore 1130, Singapore. Tel: 2549522; Tlx: RS 35983 CTAL.
Sri Lanka: Spectrum Lanka Advertising Ltd., 56 1/2 Ward Place, Colombo 7, Sr Lanka. Tel: 5984648/596227; Tlx: 21439 SPECTRM CE.
U.K., Ireland and Europe: Brian Taplin Associates, 32 Fishery Road, Boxmoor, Hemel Hempstead, Herts HP 1ND, U.K. Tel: (2)215635; Tlx: 825454 CHARMAN.

APA PHOTO AGENCY PTE. LTD.

The Apa Photo Agency is S.E. Asia's leading stock photo archive, representing the work of professional photographers from all over the world. More than 150,000 original color transparencies are available for advertising, editorial and educational uses. We are linked with Tony Stone Worldwide, one of Europe's leading stock agencies, and their associate offices around the world:
Singapore: Apa Photo Agency Pte. Ltd., P.O. Box 219, Orchard Point Post Office, Singapore 9123, Singapore. **London:** Tony Stone Worldwide, 28 Finchley Rd., St. John's Wood, London NW8 6ES, England. **North America & Canada:** Masterfile Inc., 415 Yonge St., Suite 200, Toronto M5B 2E7, Canada. **Paris:** Fotogram-Stone Agence Photographique, 45 rue de Richelieu, 75001 Paris, France. **Barcelona:** Fototec Torre Dels Pardais, 7 Barcelona 08026, Spain. **Johannesburg:** Color Library (Pty.) Ltd., P.O. Box 1659, Johannesburg, South Africa 2000. **Sydney:** The Photographic Library of Australia Pty. Ltd., 7 Ridge Street, North Sydney, New South Wales 2050, Australia. **Tokyo:** Orion Press, 55-1 Kanda Jimbocho, Chiyoda-ku, Tokyo 101, Japan.

E F G

Indeed, readers, even as *Hong Kong*, the book, was being hand-carried to Singapore printing presses for final production, Hong Kong, the British Crown Colony, was experiencing regular and monumental changes to her improbable Chinese-

Hoefer

Lueras

Communist-British-capitalist character. Not "normal" changes, mind you, but the kind that made for a lot of fancy publishing footwork and backpedaling in the final weeks of this book's creation.

Hong Kong is the ninth title in the award-winning Insight Guides series by Apa Productions. It was originally meant to be the sixth of Apa's books about Asia-Pacific destinations, but the more Apa's team of writers, photographers and artists dug into this compact colony, the more complicated the place became. The sheer dynamism of this misplaced megalopolis on China's derrière both fascinated and frustrated anybody who attempted to accurately capture the mood of the place.

Lloyd

However, more than five years after Apa's publisher, Hans Hoefer, began serious efforts to produce *Hong Kong*, it has abruptly come to life. You are now reading the product of numerous last-minute design lurches, a series of unforeseen editorial burnouts, and untold other human intrigues that bounce off and cling to one another in the ironic process called bookmaking.

Meanwhile, Hong Kong, the colony, continues, "like an Atlantis in reverse," to rise above a once "barren rock" in the South China Sea. As *taipan* and refugees exchange places with every surge of an economic tidal wave, "Honkers," as oldtimers affectionately call it, reaches higher into the sky. Massive construction dominoes continue their high-rising march through the New Territories and on to the nearby Chinese border and Kwangtung Province. Its unpredictable and impetuous face-

Maitland

Lockhart

Rolnick

lifts are sometimes rather shocking in their odd East-West design, but, as a young female visitor from England remarked recently, "If all goes well, Hong Kong should

be a really nice place when they finish building it."

Quite.

Indeed, readers, during the single month before our press time, not just quaint Chinese-Victorian homesites and upstairs-downstairs storefronts were disappearing, but even colonial "institutions" such as the lion-guarded Hongkong and Shanghai Banking Corporation building on Des Voeux Road and the prim high tea palace long known as *the* Hong Kong Club were being wrought extinct by the wrecker's ball (they are now both rebuilt) and Hong Kong's unofficial national bird, the construction crane. In other urban quarters, nostalgia-minded folks were heard sighing as the colony's old Supreme Court building now the Legislative Council's Chambers

Huang

began buckling and "falling" into Mass Transit Railway excavations also long completed. And when word was received that the grand Murray Barracks were to be dismantled, tsk-tsks filled Mid-Levels salons and Wanchai watering holes.

Even Hong Kong Island's southside chic were not spared. From Shek O to Stanley and all the way to Kowloon Peak on "the other side of the harbour," sentimentalists bemoaned a recent revelation that the venerable Repulse Bay Hotel—its rooms included—would soon be kissed away by demolition crews —to be replaced, developers say, by three 50-storey towers on a massive concrete podium.

This "changes" list grows with every passing lunar moon: The old China Fleet Club site was due for redevelopment (now finished); the busy and personable "Poor Man's Nightclub" shopping bazaar opposite the Macau Ferry Pier Carpark will soon be made to disappear; and already gone is the old Tsimshatsui Railway Station, long the last stop on the *real* Orient Express. Only a lone Victorian clocktower winks across the harbour at sleek Central District as a reminder of pre-747 days when one could ride multiethnic rails all the way from Kowloon to Paris.

Bloomfield

Chalkley

Lawrence

As aforementioned, all of the above made for a flurry of last-minute editorial exercises. Consider, would-be editors, that not one week before we put this book to bed, one of our correspondents frantically advised us to leave out an entire paragraph in the Western District travel section because not only did a favourite cafe he described there disappear, but so did the entire surrounding block of antique buildings around it that he had described as particularly beautiful and worthy of touring time.

The headaches that come from revising this book were hardly soothed by the secrecy surrounding the Sino-British negotiations on the future of Hong Kong.

Despite that, the pages that follow have managed to keep pace with the colony's fast-changing times.

Stay tuned.

Hong Kong, the book, was more than five years in the making, but what is more important is what the book represents. What you are actually looking at is an anthology and time capsule of old and new Hong Kong images and words created by on and off-island folks with more than 200 years of combined editorial and graphics experiences in and about the colony.

Publisher **Hoefer**, who initiated the Insight Guides concept in 1970 with a landmark "new generation" travel book about the island of Bali in Indonesia, has been exploring this place off and on since 1973. During his visits to the colony, Hoefer has captured many of the fine photographic images you'll see here and there throughout the book.

Hoefer had long entertained the idea of producing this particular book, but the reality remained a fantasy at the back of his publisher's mind during an extremely productive decade in which his publishing house, Apa Productions, produced other Insight Guides, including *Bali, Java, Singapore, Malaysia, Thailand,* the *Philippines, Korea, Burma, Nepal, Sri Lanka, Taiwan,* and on destinations outside Asia such as *Hawaii, Florida, Mexico,* and *Jamaica.*

Hoefer was also creatively preoccupied by other "personal" photographic projects, such as the "coffee table" book about Malaysia, titled *Jalan-Jalan,* which he shot entirely with an old-fashioned 8 by 10 field camera. That book has been unanimously praised by both photographic critics and travel book reviewers as yet another new and exciting genre of travel books.

Bits and pieces of *Hong Kong* had been completed by the fall of 1980, but the book actually went into final editorial production when *Leonard Lueras,* then Apa's editorial director, and *Ian Lloyd,* then director of Apa's international photo library, teamed up with Hong Kong author-editor-habitué Saul Lockhart to push *Hong Kong* through its final birth pains.

Lueras, who joined Apa in 1977 and proceeded to produce a best-selling Insight Guide about Hawaii is a Honolulu-based journalist who first arrived in Hong Kong in 1970 as a roving correspondent for *The Honolulu Advertiser,* Hawaii's major morning daily. During and after his nearly 10

Boschman

Cranbourne

(continued)

years as a reporter for *The Advertiser*, Lueras has written and edited a half-dozen books on Aisa-Pacific subjects, and has contributed articles and photographs to numerous publications in the United States and Asia. He was also an editor-at-large for Pacific Magazine, the prestigious, award-winning travel and culture magazine formerly published by Emphasis Inc. of Tokyo and Hong Kong.

Lloyd, who with Lueras, coordinated the final production, editing, photographing and design of this book, is a native of Midland, Canada, who first joined Apa Productions in early 1980. By the time Lloyd completed his three-year service as Apa Photo Agency's managing director in 1983, the agency has grown to be one of Asia's most modern photographic production centres and certainly the most extensive photo archive and stock house in Southeast Asia.

Llyod, a master of the use of both available and unavailable light sources, made a final photographic foray into the colony to "get" several final photographs that were needed to round out the book's visual impact and balance its editorial structure. The results of his search and enjoy missions into inner Hong Kong are obvious throughout *Hong Kong*.

Lockhart, meanwhile, has performed yeoman labours as Apa's local media master and "man in Hong Kong." He was responsible for, among the other things, the writing of the book's introductory essay, the Macau travel section, most of the lively essays in the book's feature section, and nearly all of the Guide In Brief section. He also co-edited, with Lueras, all preliminary and final textual materials.

Lockhart is a well-known freelance writer, editor, photographer and sometime movie-dubber who has been based in the Orient since 1966. After a stint as a freelance correspondent in Vietnam, he moved to Hong Kong in 1967 to establish a permanent home base at Repulse Bay. In addition to covering all aspects of the colony, his assignments have taken him from high in the Himalayas to the bottom of Truk Lagoon, and from the Canadian Arctic to the jungles of Papua New Guinea. While corresponding for scores of news, feature and travel publications, Lockhart has also managed over the years to author the *Complete Guide to the*

Philippines and Manila By Night, and co-author *A Diver's Guide to Asian Waters* and the *Hong Kong Good Food Guide*. In 1984, Lockhart was awarded the Pacific Area Travel Association's Gold Award for his story on Kandy's (in Sri Lanka) magnificient Perahera Festival.

Meanwhile, far below the Foreign Correspondents' Club, author **Harry Rolnick** takes us on a non-format tour of Hong Kong Island. Rolnick, a native New Yorker, studied music for many years before settling into the writing game. He played many instruments, composed, conducted and wrote songs for several off-off-Broadway productions (including Tennessee Williams' *The Purification*) and singing commercials.

Rolnick's current writing career began with film reviews for the *Bangkok Post*, a position which led to the editing of an entertainment magazine there, and the writing of a few books on restaurants and travel in Thailand. A sojourn as a tourist guide writer for the Libyan Tourist Association was then followed by a move to Hong Kong, where he has existed ever since as a freelance writer. Rolnick has had more than a dozen books published, including a restaurant guide to the People's Republic of China, a history of Macau and assorted books of humour. He has also written feature articles for numerous international publications, including *Geo*, *New West*, *New York*, *Diversions*, *Pacific* (on which he served as a contributing editor), *The Asian Wall Street Journal*, *The Wall Street Journal*, *The International Herald-Tribune*, the London *Guardian*, *Orientations* and others. His latest book is titled Connisseur's Guide to Hong Kong and Macau.

Nearly as peripatetic and prolific is **Roger Boschman**, Kowloon resident, who has written for us about the wonders of Kowloon and the New Territories. Boschman, who was born in Carrot River, Saskatchewan, Canada, began a lifetime of travelling and writing at the age of 12 when he collected a first paycheck from a New Zealand publication. After spending later years in Canada "starving in an attic, doing non-profit writing," he left for warmer climes—first in Australia, where he became (so he was told) the second person ever to ride a motorcycle from Cairns to Cape York (long before roads went through); then in Papua New Guinea, where he stayed for eight years, walking the famous Kokoda Trail twice, joining several patrols into the Papuan Highlands, and, for three years, serving as manager of Papua New Guinea's National Literature Bureau and editor of the bureau's literary journal, *Papua New Guinea Writing.* Boschman moved to Hong Kong in 1974 and has since freelanced for several regional and international publications. He has also completed three novels, each "ready for sale."

Another freelance wonder is author **Derek Maitland,** who contributed articles on Hong Kong urbanity in the book's introductory section. Maitland, a British born Australian novelist, moved to Hong Kong in 1976 to complete work on an Asian and Pacific literary fellowship he received from the Australian Council. As he notes in an introduction to a book, *Firecracker Suite,* made possible by that grant, "he has put that grant to good use—combining his flair for comic writing with a study of the cultural cataclysms that can erupt when East meets West in an Oriental setting." Maitland authored a second book, *Breaking Out,* and served for a while as a freelance correspondent in Vietnam (an experience which inspired a third novel, *The Only War We've Got*).

Alan Chalkley, who analyzes—in post-Freudian and fiscal terms—Hong Kong's penchant for making money, is an economic journalist who has spent 30 years, on and off, in the Asian region, with occasional side trips to North and South America and his native Britain. Chalkley manages to work on many newspapers and magazines and aggressively indulges in the sheer joy of living in Hong Kong, a place he describes as "the most exciting city on the globe."

Frena Bloomfield did double-duty for *Hong Kong.* She first considers the scheming and dreaming that permeate all life in Hong Kong, then takes us on a strange collection of ferry boats to the far reaches of the colony's lovely outlying islands.

Bloomfield was born and educated in London. She qualified as a librarian but escaped into journalism by joining the Croydon Advertiser Group of newspapers. She later became a freelance writer and has had three novels. *The Dragon Paths, The Sky-fleet of Atlantis,* published in London and *The Tantrik Warriors.* She lived in Asia for nearly a decade, part of the time in Nepal where she was the NBC radio correspondent, and most of the rest of her Aisa time in Hong Kong. As a freelance writer, she has contributed to the *Guardian, New Society, The Far Eastern Economic Review, Asia*

Magazine, Aisaweek and the British Broadcasting Corporation (BBC), among others. Her books include *The Occult World of Hong Kong* (Hong Kong Publishing, 1980).

Other writers who have contributed to our editorial spaces are **Veronica Huang,** formerly a reporter for *The Asian Wall Street Journal* and Hong Kong food and festivals experts **Lesley Nelson** and **Linda Wong**.

Two other editorial hands that we would like to thank for their important early-on contributions and conceptual groundwork are **Jane Ram,** whose early editorial advice was most helpful, and **Spencer Reiss,** then a *Time* magazine correspondent and now a *Newsweek* magazine writer-editor who very much set the initial editorial "tone" of this book.

Very special editorial thanks also to journalists **David Watts, Paul Maidment** and **Nedra Chung,** whose copy-editing eyes and pencils proved important and invaluable at various stages of production. Watts, former staff correspondent in Southeast Asia for *The Times* of London, contributed much-appreciated editorial advice and assistance, as did Maidment, formerly opinion page editor of *The Asian Wall Street Journal.* Chung, meanwhile, served as a conscientious copy editor, critic and editorial troubleshooter throughout the *Hong Kong* bookmaking process. Chung and Apa would like to acknowledge the assistance of **Kathy McClure** in the preparation of the book's index and in the translation of travel and other sectional materials into Chinese, and the kind help of Hong Kong journalist **Stephen Siu,** who wrote and edited our Guide In Brief guide to "Survival Cantonese."

This edition is also very much the efforts of free-lance journalist **Rolf Steinberg.** A graduate of the Columbia School of Journalism, Steinberg coordinated production of this edition while on a visit to **Apa** headquarters from Berlin. Likewise, Apa Research Editor **Linda Carlock** offered assistance in removing editorial and textual inconsistencies.

The highly graphical character of *Hong Kong* owes its existence to several senior and new Hong Kong creative hands.

Responsible for the Happy Valley cover shot and numerous spectacular and poignant photographs sprinkled throughout the book was **Max Lawrence,** a native of New Zealand and sometimes Singapore resident who has been working with Apa Productions and the Apa Photo Agency since 1978.

Also important were a series of pictures, many of them of rare occurrences in the colony, captured by senior photographer **Ray Cranbourne.** Cranbourne, who has been working in Hong Kong since 1968, is currently taking pictures for the Hong Kong Tourist Association, Cathay Pacific Airways and other publications and institutions. After leaving his native Melbourne in the early 1960s, Cranbourne began an international odyssey as a freelance photographer for his hometown newspaper, *The Melbourne Sun.* While touring Europe and the United States on the back of a Vespa motor-scooter, he covered, among other news events, the Rome Olympics of 1960. During 1966 to 1968 he photographed the war in Vietnam for *Newsweek, Fortune* and other leading American publications. Cranbourne has won several awards from the Art Directors' Club of New York for his creative photography, and in 1980 he was awarded the Pacific Area Travel Association's (PATA) Excellence Award for photography in Asia.´

Also from Melbourne is **Bob Davis,** who began his photographic career with Tasmania's Department of Film Production. Davis, who has had his work published in numerous international books, journals and magazines, is a longtime roving journalist who is now based in Hong Kong where he manages The Stock House, one of Hong Kong's most complete and creative stock photo agencies.

Other photographers whose works appear here and there throughout *Hong Kong* are **Frank Fischbeck,** who shuns publicity but is respected as one of Hong Kong's best senior photographers; **Dean Barrett,** Hong Kong's roving and resident expert on Thai women (recent research has produced the book *Girls of Thailand*), who is known in Hong Kong's thin social satire circle as "Uncle Yum Char"; **Werner Hahn,** an award-winning designer and photographer who has long been a member of the Apa family; and

Jan Whiting, an American who lives in Australia and regularly contributes fine Asia images to the Apa Photo Agency's fast-growing archive. Other photographs were captured by Asia-based photographers **Irwin Kelaart, Marcus Brooke, Blair Seitz, Richard House** and former and present staff members of *The South China Morning Post.*

Other graphics were rendered by Hong Kong artist **Bill Yim,** creative director of Yimages of Hong Kong, and by Apa in-house designers-artists **Molly Wee** and **Galen Song.** Maps were prepared by **Tony Khoo** and **Noianie Jantan.**

"Amazing" credit is also due **Leo Haks,** Apa Productions' former managing director. Leo has stirred much of his own creative magic into this production by allowing us to include special feature images of several re-productions of rare pieces in his superb collection of Chinese folk art. He has also offered massive doses of good spirit and constructive criticism to this effort. Thank you, lah.

Other institutions and persons who contributed to *Hong Kong* in one or many ways were Hong Kong's Urban Council, the Hong Kong Art Museum, the Hong Kong Tourist Association, the Macau Tourist Information Bureau, the Hongkong and Shanghai Bank, Pan American airways and Cathay Pacific airlines, Jonathan Cape Limited (London), the London Public Record Office, Hong Kong Publishing Company, *Discovery* Magazine, *Pacific* Magazine (Emphasis Inc.), *The South China Morning Post*, The Academy of Motion Pictures Arts and Sciences (Los Angeles), Raymond Boey, Sam Chan, Vivien Loo, Alice Ng, Ivy Tan, Diana Tan, Joan Cunningham, Derek Davies, Lis Lau, Wendy Hughes, Molley Wee, Brian Cuthbertson, Mary Lee, Hugh Van Es, Dean Le Cain, Sapurodin B. Shahir, Eric Cavaliero and Brian Forsgate.

—APA PUBLICATIONS

OTHER INSIGHT GUIDES TITLES

COUNTRY/REGION

ASIA
Bali
Burma
Hong Kong
India
Indonesia
Korea
Malaysia
Nepal
Philippines
Rajasthan
Singapore
Sri Lanka
Taiwan
Thailand
Turkey

PACIFIC
Hawaii
New Zealand

NORTH AMERICA
Alaska
American Southwest
Northern California
Southern California
Florida
Mexico
New England
New York State
The Pacific Northwest
The Rockies
Texas

SOUTH AMERICA
Brazil
Argentina

CARIBBEAN
Bahamas
Barbados
Jamaica
Puerto Rico
Trinidad and Tobago

EUROPE
Channel Islands
France
Germany
Great Britain
Greece
Ireland
Italy
Portugal
Scotland
Spain

MIDDLE EAST
Egypt
Israel

AFRICA
Kenya

GRAND TOURS
Australia
California
Canada
Continental Europe
Crossing America
East Asia
South Asia

GREAT ADVENTURE
Indian Wildlife

CITYGUIDES
Bangkok
Berlin
Buenos Aires
Dublin
Istanbul
Lisbon
London
Paris
Rio de Janeiro
Rome
San Francisco
Venice
Vienna

PASSAGE TO DESTINY

When George Orwell bestowed such ominous significance on the year 1984, so many years ago, the tiny colonial outpost of Hong Kong had no idea it would be its own year of destiny. Nineteen-eighty-four was the year Hong Kong's future was decided—in the form of an agreement between Great Britain and the People's Republic of China, initialled on September 26 in Peking and signed on December 19 in the same city.

Hong Kong's destiny was shaped by two powers only; their agreement was arrived at without Hong Kong's official participation and with public consultation only after the fact when change was impossible. At midnight, June 30, 1997—the moment the 99-year lease on the New Territories (90 per cent of the colony) expires—the British Crown Colony, including the two areas (Hong Kong Island and the Kowloon Peninsula) "ceded in perpetuity," in 1841 and 1856, will be returned to China.

During the often-acrimonious negotiations over almost two years, Britain, which clearly came out second best, managed to extract a 50-year guarantee from China (beginning in 1997) which, on paper, insures Hong Kong's basic freedoms. Hong Kong will become a Special Administrative Region of China on July 1, 1997. That arrangement is conveniently accommodated by the official Peking stance of "one government—two systems." Hong Kong's "Hobson's Choice" was to accept the Chinese takeover with the guarantees as promised in the Sino-British agreement or to accept the same Chinese takeover without any guarantees. In refugee-minded Hong Kong, where almost half the 5.5-million population has fled from turbulent upheavals in China, trusting the Middle Kingdom for the 50 years after 1997, and the time remaining before then, is more than a moot point of academic interest. It remains to be seen whether the promise of China's paramount leader, the ageing Deng Xiaoping, will be kept until midway through the next century. In other words, will Deng's policies survive his demise.

"Borrowed time, borrowed place," is the perfect description, coined by novelist Han Suyin, of Hong Kong. Historically, the colony's citizens have tried to ignore the perpetual uncertainty of their future—their "borrowed time"—and have preferred to make their pile quickly. During the brief, but anxious, two-year period of the negotiations, those same citizens could only peek into an uncertain future like youngsters eavesdropping on their parents discussing the children's long-term educational and career plans. Since then, Hong Kong has surged forward, more fatalistically than optimistically, but still looking with characteristic myopia at the near future in the fervent hope that destiny will unfold without severe or permanent disruptions. Hong Kong is reassuming the very real Chinese self that always lay just below the modern urbane facade; it believes its destiny is in the hands of fate, influenced perhaps by hefty doses of good joss (Luck).

Preceding pages: Hong Kong as seen from the old Kowloon train station; British Ambassador Sir Richard Evans and Chinese Assistant Foreign Minister Zhou Nan initial the historic agreement on the future of Hong Kong. Right: the agreement in the form of a British government White Paper. Following pages: signatories page followed by the text of the Treaty of Nanking, 1842.

**A Draft Agreement
between the Government of the
United Kingdom of Great Britain and Northern Ireland
and the
Government of the People's Republic of China
on the Future of Hong Kong**

26 September 1984

Sealed by the Plenipotentiaries on board
Her Britannic Majesty's Ship —
"Cornwallis" this twenty ninth day of August
1842, corresponding with the Chinese
date, twenty fourth day of the seventh month
in the twenty second year of Taoukwang.

Henry Pottinger
Hr. Ms. Plenipotentiary

大清欽差便宜行事大臣等

大英欽奉全權公使大臣各為

君上定事蓋用關防印信各執一冊為據俾即日按照和約開載之條施行妥辦無礙矣要至和

約者

道光二十二年七月二十四日即

大英國記年之

一千八百四十二年 八月 二十九 由江寧省會行

大英君主汗華帥之鈐關防

Hsung Pottinger

11

Treaty

Her Majesty the Queen of the United Kingdom of Great Britain and Ireland, and His Majesty the Emperor of China, being desirous of putting an end to the misunderstandings, and consequent Hostilities, which have arisen between the two Countries, have resolved to conclude a Treaty for that purpose, and have therefore named as their Plenipotentiaries, That is to say:—Her Majesty the Queen of Great Britain and Ireland, Sir Henry Pottinger, Bart, a Major General in the Service of the East Company, &c.; And His Imperial Majesty the Emperor of China, The High Commissioners Cheying, a Member of the Imperial House a Guardian of the Crown Prince and, General of the Garrisson of Canton: and Elepoo, of the Imperial Kindred, Graciously permitted to wear the insignia of the first rank and the distinction of a Peacock's feather, lately Minister and Governor General and now Lieutenant General Commanding at Chapoo: Who after having communicated to each other their respective Full Powers, and found them to be in good and due form, have agreed upon, and concluded, the following Articles:—

Article 1

There shall henceforward be Peace and Friendship between Her Majesty the Queen of the United Kingdom of Great Britain and Ireland, and His Majesty the Emperor of China, and between their respective Subjects, who shall enjoy full security and protection for their persons and property within the Dominions of the other.

Article 2

His Majesty the Emperor of China agrees, that British Subjects with their families and establishments shall be allowed to reside, for the purpose of carrying on their mercantile pursuits, without molestation, or restraint, at the Cities and Towns of Canton, Amoy, Foochowfoo, Ningpo and Shanghai; and Her Majesty the Queen of Great Britain will appoint Superintendents, or Consular Officers, to reside at each of the above named Cities, or Towns, to be the medium of communication between the Chinese Authorities and the said Merchants, and to see, that the just Duties and other dues of the Chinese Government as hereafter provided for are duly discharged by Her Brittanic Majesty's Subjects.

Article 3

It being obviously necessary and desirable, that British Subjects should have some Port whereat they may careen and refit their Ships. when required, and keep Stores for that purpose, His Majesty The Emperor of China cedes to Her Majesty the Queen of Great Britain the Island of Hong Kong to be possessed in perpetuity by Her Britannic Majesty. Her Heirs, and Successors and to be governed by such Laws and Regulations as Her Majesty the Queen of Great Britain shall see fit to direct.

Article 4

The Emperor of China agrees to pay the sum of Six Millions of Dollars as the value of the opium which was delivered up at Canton in the month of March 1839, as a Ransom for the lives of Her Britannic Majesty's Superintendent and Subjects who had been imprisoned and threatened with death by the Chinese High Officers.

Article 5

The Government of China having compelled the British Merchants trading at Canton to deal exclusively with certain Chinese Merchants called Hong Merchants (or Cohong) who had been licensed by the Chinese Government for that purpose, the Emperor of China agrees to abolish that practice in future at all Ports where British Merchants may reside, and to permit them to carry on their mercantile transactions with whatever Persons they please, and His Imperial Majesty further agrees to pay to the British Government the sum of Three Millions of Dollars on account of Debts due to British Subjects by some of the said Hong Merchants, or Cohong, who have become insolvent, and who owe very large sums of money to Subjects of Her Britannic Majesty.

Article 6

The Government of Her Britannic Majesty having been obliged to send out an Expedition to demand and obtain redress for the violent and unjust Proceedings of the Chinese High Authorities towards Her Britannic Majesty's Officer and Subjects, the Emperor of China agrees to pay the sum of Twelve Millions of Dollars on account of the Expenses incurred and Her Britannic Majesty's Plenipotentiary voluntarily agrees, on behalf of Her Majesty, to deduct from the said amount of Twelve Millions of Dollars, any sums which may have been received by Her Majesty's Combined Forces as Ransom for Cities and Towns in China subsequent to the 1st day of August 1841.

Article 7

It is agreed that the Total amount of Twenty one Millions of Dollars described in the three preceding Articles shall be paid as follows

Six   Millions immediately
Six   Millions in 1843. That is: Three Millions on or before the 30th of the month of June, and Three Millions on or before the 31st of December.
Five   Millions in 1844. That is: Two Millions and a half, on or before the 30th of June, and two Millions and a half on or before the 31st of December.
Four   Millions in 1845. That is: Two Millions on or before the 30th of June, and two Millions on or before the 31st of December.

And it is further stipulated, that Interest at the rate of 5 per cent per annum, shall be paid by the Government of China on any portion of the above sums that are not punctually discharged at the periods fixed.

Article 8

The Emperor of China agrees to release unconditionally all Subjects of Her Brittanic Majesty (whether Natives of Europe or India) who may be in confinement at this moment, in any part of the Chinese Empire.

Article 9

The Emperor of China agrees to publish and promulgate, under His Imperial Sign Manual and Seal, a full and entire amnesty, and act of indemnity, to all Subjects of China on account of their having resided under or having had dealings and intercourse with, or having entered the Service of Her Brittanic Majesty, or of Her Majesty's Officers; and His Imperial Majesty further engages to release all Chinese Subjects who may be at this moment in confinement for similar reasons.

Article 10

His Majesty the Emperor of China agrees to establish at all the Ports which are by the 2nd Article of this Treaty to be thrown open for the resort of British Merchants, a fair and regular Tariff of Export and Import Customs and other Dues, which Tariff shall be publicly notified and promulgated for general information, and the Emperor further engages, that when British Merchandise shall have once paid at any of the said Ports, the regulated Customs and Dues, agreeable to the Tariff to be hereafter fixed, such Merchandise may be conveyed by Chinese Merchants, to any Province or City in the interior of the Empire of China, on paying a further amount as Transit Duties which shall not exceed 5 per cent on the Tariff value of such Goods.

Article 11

It is agreed that, Her Britannic Majesty's Chief High Officers in China shall correspond with the Chinese High Officers, both at the capital and in the Provinces, under the terms "Communication" 照會 The Subordinate British Officers and Chinese High Officers in the Provinces under the terms "Statement" 申陳 on the part of the former, and on the part of the latter. "Declaration" 箚行 and the Subordinates of both Countries, on a footing of perfect equality. Merchants and others not holding Official situations, and therefore not included in the above on both sides, to use the term "Representation" 稟明 in all Papers addressed to, or intended for the notice of the respective Governments.

Article 12

On the assent of the Emperor of China to this Treaty being received and the discharge of the first instalment of money, Her Britannic Majesty's Forces will retire from Nanking and the Grand Canal, and will no longer molest, or stop, the Trade of China. The Military Post at Chinhai will also be withdrawn, but the Islands of Koolangsoo and that of Chusan will continue to be held by Her Majesty's Forces until the money payments, and the arrangements for opening the Ports to British Merchants be completed.

Article 13

The Ratification of this Treaty by Her Majesty The Queen of Great Britain and His Majesty the Emperor of China, shall be exchanged as soon as the great distance which separates England from China will admit, but in the meantime counterpart copies of it signed and Sealed by the Plenipotentiaries on behalf of their respective Sovereigns, shall be mutually delivered, and all its provisions and arrangements shall take effect.

Done at Nanking and Signed and Sealed by the Plenipotentiaries on board Her Britannic Majesty's Ship "Cornwallis" this twenty-ninth day of August 1842, corresponding with the Chinese date, twenty-fourth day of the seventh month in the twenty-second year of Taoukwang,

(signed)
Henry Pottinger
Her Majesty's Plenipotentiary
(and)
Elepoo
Newchien
Cheying

Translation of Chinese characters:
The Emissaries representing both the Emperor of the Great Ching Empire and Her Majesty of The British Empire have agreed to the terms of the above mentioned treaty. To formalize the Treaty, please seal with the official defence chop; each party concerned should retain one copy of the treaty. The treaty is effective as of this day and should be carried out without regrets.
Signed By: Elepoo
              Newchien
              Cheying
Recorded on this 24th day of the 7th month, Taou Kuang Year 22; English Calendar; 29th of August, 1842 on Board Her Majestys' Royal Ship "Cornwallis" in the Jurisdiction of Chiang Ning Province.

大清欽差便宜行事大臣等
大英欽奉全權公使大臣各爲
君上定事蓋用關防印信各執一册爲據俾即日
按照和約開載之條施行妥辦無礙矣要至和
約者
道光二十二年七月二十四日即英國記年之
一千八百四十二年八月二十九日由江寧省會行
大英君主汗華船上鈐關防

A 'THREE-LEGGED STOOL'

The Hong Kong Chinese always reckoned this British Crown Colony to be a "three-legged stool," with one leg in Peking, another in London and the third in Hong Kong. That idea was immediately coshed by the Chinese in the opening rounds of their protracted negotiations with Britian over the territory's future after July 1, 1997, the day the 99-year lease on the New Territories (90 per cent of the colony) expires.

But that metaphor still suggests Hong Kong's historically unique balancing act. If

thousands of chests of British opium confiscated earlier at Canton, and to redeem a bent British pride. Six days later, Commodore Sir J.J. Gordon Bremer led a British naval force onto Possession Point for the ritual planting of Her Majesty's flag. It was all grand imperial theatre, but this annexation was instantly unpopular with higher-ups in London and Peking — so much so that both Elliot and his Chinese counterpart, Kishen, were reprimanded by their superiors and given huge boots in their lower-ranking bums.

WENCHLOW TRADER

one leg is chopped off just a wee bit, the stool is askew. If the legs are of even more unequal length, the stool tilts crazily and doesn't fulfill its original (and stabilizing) function. And if a leg is accidentally broken, or deliberately lopped off, it will topple.

From the moment of its controversial 19th Century birth, Hong Kong has been at centre-ring, delicately resting its fate on that improbable set of legs.

This fragile tripod arrangement officially began on Jan. 20, 1841, when Britain's sole remaining plenipotentiary in China — Trade Superintendant Captain Charles Elliot, RN, annexed Hong Kong Island on his own volition, and by force of arms, to obtain trade concessions, to recover compensation for

Hong Kong's Founding Fathers:
One Went to Tibet, the Other to Texas

Kishen, the Chinese negotiator (who was Viceroy of the metropolitan province of Chihli), was roundly taken to task by his superiors for capitulating and giving away a bit of the Middle Kingdom to red-bearded British barbarians. He bowed, withdrew into his robes, quietly lost face, and was banished to Tibet.

Elliot, who, like Kishen, meant well, suffered similar ignominy. The opium traders — for whom Elliot blockaded Canton and occupied three forts in order to secure "one of the islands ... conveniently situated for commerce intercourse" — attacked Elliot after the fact because in their opinion his Convention of Chuen Pi was too conciliatory; indeed, the "foreign mud" merchants *still* had to pay customs charges to the Chinese, even though trading from desolate Hong Kong was less convenient than trading at Whampoa (their traditional entrepôt at Canton).

London was livid. Lord Palmerston, Queen Victoria's Foreign Secretary, dismissed Hong Kong by calling it a "barren island with hardly a house upon it." It would never become a trading centre, he harrumphed. Victoria her-

fail" to gain a more formidable concession from the Chinese. This upbraiding effectively ended Elliot's professional career. His next posting was as Britain's Consul General to Texas.

A Thorn in the Lion's Paw

Today, nearly a century and a half later, Elliot's name is still not honoured in massively successful Hong Kong — not even by a street, sandbar or park bench. The names of his successors, however (whether middle or senior-

Victoria, Hong Kong, 1860, artist unknown.

self clucked about the deal: "*All* we wanted might have been got if it had not been for the unaccountably strange conduct of Chas. Elliot ... He tried to obtain the *lowest* terms from the Chinese."

Poor Elliot was recalled to Whitehall, probably by fast return clipper, and another chap, Sir Henry Pottinger, was given the dubious honour of being the first governor (1843-1844) of this Victorian White Elephant. The dishonoured captain was chastised for negotiating a dud settlement and for not using "the full employment of that force which was sent to you expressly for the purpose of enabling you to use compulsion, if persuasion should

ranking civil servants), adorn highways, buildings and waterways throughout the colony.

Perhaps Elliot is still a non-person because Hong Kong has not yet fully proven its worth to Britain. It certainly cannot be called a "barren island" any more, but maybe it needs to do more penance. Or perhaps, in the insular view of Whitehall, Hong Kong is not really worth all the hassles it has caused the British Lion.

Is it really worth Britain's time and energy to cope with and be responsible for Hong Kong's 5.5 million Chinese? Mother England periodically attacks the Hong Kong immigration "problem" with controversial and restrictive Nationality Bills. She growls even louder when Hong Kong's British civil servants lead movements against their own countrymen to argue the colony's case against trade restrictions imposed by the United Kingdom and the European Economic Community.

Even though more than half the population have British Dependent Territory Passports (the latest bureaucratic name, under the latest British Nationality Bill, for a Hong Kong Passport), there will be a safe haven in Britain come July 1st, 1997 (when the Chinese take over) for only a few Chinese civil servants and community leaders.

There must have been many times during the Sino-British negotiations from 1982 to 1984 when British civil servants wished Hong Kong would just slink away and leave London alone. Do those same people today rue the day Elliot occupied this "barren" place?

Royal Navy Ships and a squadron of vintage Royal Air Force and Army helicopters on hand to "defend" this 400 square mile territory, its 22 miles of contiguous land border with China and thousands of miles of coastline spread over 235 islands. (The cost of defence agreements negotiated only for a part of this decade was HK$1.4 billion!)

Ironically, as any Army cook or Hong Kong factory worker can tell you, these defence agreements don't mean much because China, if it wished, could take the colony back without a shot — with only that proverbial phone to call to Her Majesty. So, the local troops are really here only for "internal security," usually to assist the police and to "protect" the colony from periodic invasions by illegal immigrants (II's).

Hong Kong is still the world's 15th largest trading entity (excluding **OPEC** and **COMECON**) and the world's third largest port; it is, in short, an economic force to be reckoned with.

High-rise Hong Kong has proven its "viability," but despite its successes—evidenced by recent economic recoveries under political uncertainty—the colony still has to negotiate financially with Mother England just for the privilege of having a token contingent of British troops stationed here to show the flag. Indeed, economically depressed Britain is so short of troops and funds that Hong Kong has been paying 75 percent of the colony's defence costs just to keep a few battalions of British and Gurkha troops, a few

Managing in a 'Borrowed Place'

The Hong Kong government now has near complete internal self-government (see article on "Who Rules Hong Kong") and even has the power to conclude certain negotiations with sovereign powers. The colony, for example, regularly negotiates its own economic treaties with other countries and belongs to international financial institutions such as the Asian Development Bank. When it cannot "belong" to something directly, it joins a

In the past century Hong Kong's suburbs have risen from the sea. Old Causeway Bay, 1846, above, and New Causeway Bay, right.

British delegation. Whether Hong Kong will have this autonomy under China after 1997 remains to be seen.

But for all its apparent strength, Hong Kong constantly would balance its very existence by catering to colonial masters in London and impulsive Communist Party mandarins in Peking. Hong Kong has no real power. Hong Kong can only make money for every party concerned and exhibit a marvellous capacity to be flexible and bend with every problem that blows its way.

Problems here are tackled with stop-gap measures (which may inadvertently survive the test of time), but such a system has weaknesses because the colony's administrators can never enjoy the luxury of long-term planning. That problem is expected to be exacerbated with

Ironically, that controversial Convention of Chuen Pi, negotiated by Kishen and Elliot was never signed, but that minor legal detail did not stop the occupation and settlement of Hong Kong Island.

The first governor, Pottinger, felt Hong Kong should be retained, but during subsequent fighting in 1841 and 1842, Hong Kong was just regarded as another pawn in ongoing negotiations with the Chinese — until subsequent instructions issued by Palmerston on June 5, 1841 arrived and reversed his earlier decision.

In spite of the fact that the "home country" had been a bit lax in declaring sovereignty over its newest acquisition, Pottinger felt so strongly about Hong Kong's potential future

the countdown to 1997.

Unfortunately this bodes for an uncertain future. As Chinese author Han Su-yin has described this dilemma, the colony, though "squeezed between giant antagonists crunching huge bones of contention . . . has achieved within its own narrow territories a co-existence which is baffling, infuriating, incomprehensible and works splendidly— on borrowed time in a borrowed place."

With more than nine-tenths of the colony leased from China, the vibrant economic entity that is Hong Kong today would not exist without the New Territories. The "borrowed time in a borrowed place" is to be returned at midnight June 30, 1997, and the "loan" will presumably be marked "paid-in-full."

that he encouraged permanent building and awarded land grants. These practices he ordered stopped when he went north to take part in renewed hostilities against the stubborn Chinese. A long round of fighting ended at Nanking — on Aug. 29, 1842 with the signing of a Treaty of Nanking — when the Chinese capitulated to the "Outer Barbarians" just as Pottinger's forces were preparing to attack that city. At the time, Pottinger, like Elliot, —was being politically chastised for spending too much public money on "useless" Hong Kong development projects. With the Treaty of Nanking, however, those arguments ended and London gladly accepted the Island of Hong Kong in perpetuity, so that Britain could have "a Port whereat they may careen and refit their Ships, when required, and keep Stores for that purpose..."

Previous to this time, Macau and Whampoa were the major China trade ports. But with the eventual silting of Macau's harbour — located adjacent the Pearl River Estuary — and the weakening of Portuguese power in Asia (and the growing strength of England), British traders wanted a place of their own to build godowns and process and sell profitable "foreign mud," as opium was nicknamed by the Chinese. Hong Kong was also a well-sheltered (from typhoons) harbour near enough to China to facilitate trade, but far enough from the Middle Kingdom so the British could conveniently manage private

concessions with a minimum of interference.

By fortuitous accident, Hong Kong Island became England's China port, and proceeded to become both a swashbuckling embarrassment and lucrative money machine for England. Hong Kong was taken for trade and continues to exist *only* for that commercial reason. Everything else in life was, and still is, secondary to this business of earning profits.

Chinese authorities such as Jui-Lin, above, the Viceroy of Kwangtung and Kwangsi province (photographed in 1870 at age 65), marvelled at the prim Victorian look of *gweilo* ladies, above.

Biting the Dragon

As Dr. Norman Miners of the Political Science Department of the University of Hong Kong expresses it, the Treaty of Nanking was the first of three "indefensible bites" the British Lion took out of the Chinese Dragon's rear.

During the six months Pottinger had been away from the colony fighting, much progress had been made in settling this barren island. Though there was confusion over land sales, astute British traders instantly recognized that if Hong Kong did indeed become a prosperous colony, the key to success here would be land. And of course the local Chinese were always — as they are today — one speculative step ahead of the "barbarians"; they readily sold land whether they had title to it or not. Good *joss* (luck) apparently was with the traders, because on June 26, 1843, Hong Kong was officially declared a British Crown Colony.

The second of England's three bites occurred as a result of the Arrow War (also called the Second Opium War) when a Hong Kong-registered *lorcha* (a junk-rigged schooner with a foreign hull) named the *Arrow* was boarded off Canton in October 1856 by Chinese sailors. The *Arrow's* crew was detained, and this impropriety properly irritated the British.

Hong Kong's Consul General, Harry Parkes, retaliated in force, hoping to use this *casus belli* to force the Chinese to allow foreigners back into Canton. (Entrance into

Canton was guaranteed by the 1842 Treaty of Nanking, but had never been asserted.) The local British fleet sailed up the Pearl River, breached Canton's city walls and forced their way to the Chinese Viceroy. Immediate British demands inspired by the *Arrow* incident were quickly met, but the key question of access to Canton was not. The Viceroy said he could not guarantee the safety of foreigners if they were allowed in the city.

Shortly thereafter, guerilla warfare broke out and foreign-held factories in Canton were attacked. Until that time, Hong Kong had been only a minor commercial dependence of Canton. The *hong* (the original trading houses, some of which still do business in Hong Kong today) at this time transferred their headquarters to the security of the new

agreements, foreigners now gained the rights to station diplomats in Peking and travel at will throughout China. On March 26, 1860 under a subsequent Convention of Peking, Kowloon Point (Tsimshatsui) was leased in perpetuity from the Chinese. In October of that same year, another battle took place in the north and the Emperor's Summer Palace in Peking was sacked by the allies. Lord Elgin, the British plenipotentiary who negotiated for the British this time, secured on Oct. 24 and 25, 1860, the cession of an additional three and three quarter square miles of new territory consisting of Kowloon Point (on which the British had built a harbour defence fort in 1842) and Stonecutters Island (in the harbour) with the signing of two Conventions of Peking.

British colony at Hong Kong and that trading situation was reversed. Hong Kong took its first step forward towards becoming a full-fledged Asia entrepôt.

Tsimshatsui in Perpetuity

Increasingly, local acts of terrorism continued to occur in Hong Kong, Canton and along the vital Pearl River. British forces, this time joined by French allies, fought back, and in December 1857 captured Canton yet again. By the summer of 1858, allied forces had moved to the far north, where they eventually forced another Chinese capitulation and negotiated stronger concessions known as the Treaties of Tientsin. Under the terms of these

With that second British "bite," Hong Kong now consisted of nearly 36 square miles of sovereign territory. The colony's harbour could now be defended on both sides and the colony's British residents had a convenient haven across the water where they could engage in nefarious — mostly sexual — intercourse with Kowloon's natives.

Hong Kong's 20th Century *laissez-faire* image and beliefs were shaped in those early days. However, Hong Kong's perennial population problems also began during those days. During that century's long Taiping rebellions

The mandarin lady, left, wore her courtly best for this 1870s portrait, as did Sir Richard Macdonnell, Governor (1866–1872), above.

in China, the colony's population increased from about 90,000 in 1859 — of which only a few thousand were Europeans — to 150,000 by 1865. Hong Kong began its long history of "bursting at the seams."

Hong Kong's Inscrutable Landlord

England's third and last "nibble" of the Middle Kingdom occurred in 1898 — and it is this final morsel which now keeps Hong Kong nourished and economically alive. By the mid 1880s, the colony's powers were concerned about the territory's security. What pushed Britain to force China's hand once again was a coaling station grant to France on the South China Coast opposite Hainan Island. After expressing Her Majesty's displeasure re-

non-recognition, China inexplicably accepts the annual rental fee. Britain feels that the New Territories lease is a valid contract being legally fulfilled. The Chinese say there is no contract, or the contract is null and void, but they inscrutably accept and thank the British for their annual donation.

In that third bite, the Crown Colony gained about 350 square miles spread over the mainland and 234 outlying islands. They also inherited a late 20th Century headache — an uncertain Hong Kong future.

Though the constant question in Hong Kong's collective psyche—what will happen in 1997?—was always deeply buried, in spite of bitter riots in the Fifties and Sixties, it bubbled to the surface with a vengence in mid-1982 with the lead up to Prime Minister

garding this grant, Britain duly informed Peking that for defence purposes (nothing was said about "balance of power with France") the colony would require additional territory. Eventually a demarcation line was drawn from Deep Bay to Mirs Bay and Britain forced China to lease it additional New Territories for 99 years from July 1, 1898.

Britain recognizes that piece of paper promptly every year by paying HK$5,000 in rent. The People's Republic of China refuses to recognize Imperial treaties signed under the duress of gunboat diplomacy, but despite this

The Hong Kong "look' is as varied as the four local folks on these pages. As of 1983 more than 5.5 million such people were living here.

Margaret Thatcher's visit to Peking (end of September/early October, 1982).

That question, though officially answered with the signing of the Sino-British Agreement in December 1984, has of course spawned two additional questions: What will happen when Hong Kong reverts China as a Special Administrative Region in July 1997 *and* what is going to happen in the "lameduck" time in between?

It was in the Seventies that the peaceful economic and diplomatic upswings began, racing head-long into "modernization."

Meanwhile, the Chinese Dragon turned its back on a former ally, the Russian Bear, and overtly embraced the capitalistic West. Western businessmen and tourists have since flocked to China. Mao's death in 1976, and the subsequent arrest of the "gang of four," cleared the way for the more practical leadership of Vice Premier Deng Xiaoping. In 1978, Hong Kong received its first "official" visitor from north of the border since 1949. Significantly, the caller was Li Chiang, China's Minister of Trade. The following year, Hong Kong's Governor, Sir Murray MacLehose, was invited to Peking where he met with Deng, who advised Hong Kong investors "to put their hearts at ease." That assurance's effect in Hong Kong and other international boardrooms was ecstasy. It was as if Deng had personally signed a 1997 New Territories lease waiver in blood.

MacLehose belatedly reported publicly during the oftimes acrimonious negotiations

sands of refugees. The PLA gladly accepted the tens of thousands of these illegal immigrants (II's) caught by Hong Kong forces.

A Communist Country Club

On the economic side, a Special Economic Zone established on the Chinese side of the border at Shenzhen (Shum Chun) had embraced more than 1000 local co-ventures — of Hong Kong expertise and money, and Chinese land and labour — by the end of 1983. Some of these ventures were resorts, golf clubs and amusement parks, to help the average Hong Kong worker part with his money (only Hong Kong dollars are used).

China-controlled companies have actively, and for the most part openly, participated in

in 1983 and 1984 that Deng also stated China would take back Hong Kong. He said the comment passed back to Whitehall and No. 10 Downing Street — something the British government never has acknowledged — privately, though it was hidden from the population at large.)

The end of the Seventies and beginning of the Eighties also ushered in even closer cooperation between Hong Kong and Chinese authorities. British and Gurkha troops on this side of the border worked closely with units of the People's Liberation Army (PLA) to stop the flow of hundreds of thou-

Hong Kong's subsequent property boom by investing billions of Hong Kong dollars in local enterprises.

The new capitalistic Communists get along just fine with Hong Kong's very astute property barons; both exult in the regular increase of the value of their joint property shares. Even the big British *hongs* formed joint ventures with "China-controlled companies" (as they are identified in Hong Kong's press).

China, however, does not completely ignore the political workings of the colony in favour of quick money-making. The Chinese took a long and serious look at the Hong Kong government's very modest plan to create district advisory boards throughout the colony in

A cheerful but superstitious chap above wears jade amulets; right, a jade-eyed Englishwoman.

21

1981. But the plan went through.

It looked closely at the partially elected Regional Council, a New Territories' council which mirrors the Urban Council, formerly the colony's only partially elected body; a politically toothless group charged with rubbish collection, beaches and recreation.

With the advent of the Sino-British Draft Agreement and a white paper on representative government, the colonial government commited itself not only to elections but also to training a leadership and an administration to take over the decision-making and running of the colony from July 1st, 1997—the date the lease on the New Territories expires and the entire British Crown Colony of Hong Kong reverts to China in the form of a Special Administrative Region. The agreement was signed in Peking on Dec. 19, 1984 by Britain's Prime Minister Margaret Thatcher and China' Premier Zhao Ziyang.

Increased elective representation in the District Boards and the Urban and Regional Councils are in the offing. The biggest electoral change came with the advent of a partially-elected (albeit indirectly via functional constituencies) Legislative Council.

Of the few political options available to Hong Kong, full independence—a common goal of most colonies—was not a viable option. Previously, even tiny steps towards more representative and democratic government here were taken only with due consideration of Peking's authoritarian views.

But during the two-year negotiating period, as Hong Kong rocked with anxiety, it was the Chinese, specifically Premier Zhao Ziyang, who announced the colony's 50-year (from 1997) guarantee, forcing the British to scramble for plans to give the local citizens more say in goverment in order to prepare them for a time during which they will, for the most part, be self-governing.

So it is indeed ironic that the Chinese are now directly responsible for the British instigating political reforms when successive British and Hong Kong governments used the same Chinese government as an excuse not to reform.

Both Labour and Conservative British governments there have found it difficult to find a replacement for Sir Murray MacLehose, who was appointed to his post in 1971 and has had four extensions to his gubernatorial posting which terminated in April 1982. Sir Murray was the first governor to be appointed from the diplomatic corps. His successor is another diplomat Sir Edward Youde, who came from the Foreign and Commonwealth Affairs desk in Whitehall, but was a former diplomat in Peking.

He proved his diplomatic skills by not only being a major part of Britain's negotiating team, but also in putting Hong Kong's occasionally divergent (from Britain's) points of view to the Prime Minister Mrs. Thatcher and is credited with influencing and changing some of the British positions.

Ironically, Hong Kong's continuing prosperity, which is partially nourished by China's modernization is at the same time the colony's greatest weakness and strength. It is common sense here to say that China only tolerates Hong Kong's and Macau's existence because they act as convenient foreign exchange windows to the outer world—to the cash register and abacus tune of about US$5.85 billion in 1985, up 121% on 1984. Investments from Hong Kong and Macau unbelieveably represented a staggering 80% of that foreign investment.

Hong Kong also serves as a transhipment centre for China export goods because China's own such transport infrastructure is lacking. Besides, Hong Kong is, literally, China's window on the world. Its excellent trading, communications, and transportation facilities help China to gain greater access to international markets. It has a large reservoir of management skills and modern technology which China taps regularly. With the combination of its Western style economy, free and open marketplace and Chinese culture, Hong Kong serves as a "commercial laboratory" for China's own venture into modernization, which includes modern management. It is a place where China can buy or borrow nearly all the know-how the capitalist world has to offer. Many Chinese trade organizations have set up representative offices in Hong Kong, including those from the Special Economic Zones, open cities, provinces and municipalities. As an international business and financial centre, Hong Kong provides a venue where Chinese enterprises can seek out business opportunities, engage in joint ventures with foreign concerns and find an access to the international financial market.

Hong Kong could become China's centre for international trade and investment, if promises concerning the Special Administrative Region (due to be set up when sovereignty is handed back at midnight on June 30, 1997) and, most important, the lead up time to 1997, are kept.

However, as China's economic prosperity grows, so grows the Chinese infrastructure, a development process which means that one day China may catch up or even surpass Hong Kong—a potential reality which would more and more dilute Hong Kong's role as the country's only good entrepot.

Mutual ventures across the Sino-British border, for example, are bringing prosperity to many Hong Kong companies and people because they allow businessmen to keep land (Hong Kong's most expensive commodity) and labour costs under control (thus enabling local manufacturers to undercut competitors in Singapore, Taiwan, Japan and Korea).

But most of these venture agreements are for a specific time period—five or 10 years in most cases—and when these contracts expire, the factories and technology revert to China. China will eventually use this new expertise and hardware to compete directly with Hong Kong, and given present economic inflationary trends, Hong Kong may not be able to compete with the mainland for business when the contracts close.

Seductive Neon

The still booming economy also exposes another Hong Kong weakness: people. The very bright neon lights of this glamorous colony are reflected in the sky for many miles. More tempting are Hong Kong television stations, which during every broadcast minute emphasize on mainland TV screens the differences between living standards and life-styles here and in China.

During Sir Murray's visit with Deng in 1979, the Governor discussed the subject of illegal immigration. Sir Murray wanted Deng's help in stemming this human floodtide. Deng promised to do what he could and he eventually sent another battalion of PLA troops to police the border. He also made a very astute appraisal of the refugee situation. The Vice Premier, noting that the real cause of this problem was the obvious discrepancy in Hong Kong and Chinese living standards, suggested that the only way to combat the refugee situation was to "equalize" these two disparate living standards. At first interpretation, China-watchers and men-on-the-street here thought this was a reference to Deng's modernization programme. But following Deng's comment, there was a great surge of even more illegal immigrants across the border. There were unspoken fears here that Deng was again flooding Hong Kong in order to lower the colony's standard of living, a move that would "equalize" standards of living in another way. Eventually this most recent flood of refugees was dammed, and once again Hong Kong gasped and wondered aloud what the next subtle swish of the Dragon's tail would *really* mean.

End-of-the-Lease Days

No one can really predict what will happen in Hong Kong's near of far future, but the government has not backed off its commitments due to the 1997 lease expiration or the increased population which is expected to reach almost 7 million by 1996.

At the end of 1984 it was estimated that total outstanding public sector expenditures in construction were near HK$30 billion and that total expenditure in the next decade would top HK$100 billion.

The dreaded question of "What will happen to Hong Kong in 1997 when the lease on the New Territories runs out?" had always been around, but only discussed by government officials discreetly, never in public or for quotation—until the negotiations began in 1982.

British Prime Minister Margaret Thatcher's visit to the Middle Kingdom and Hong Kong in September 1982 brought the dreaded question from a closet off stage to a centre stage. The initialling of the Sino-British Agreement in September 1984 (and its subsequent signing in December 1984) answered many questions about Hong Kong's future— and created many new ones.

If Hong Kong is to continue to survive as one of the world's top 20 trading entities, as a source of more than half of China's foreign exchange and as a living symbol of China's modernization and political aims, there will have to be more giving and understanding on China's side, or Hong Kong will deteriorate into a burden well before the "50-year guarantee" from 1997 expires in 2047.

The first inkling of what would happen came from no less an authority than Hong Kong's former governor Lord Murray MacLehose, who said in London in December 1982 that some sort of special status situation would be worked out. He was the first one on the British side to state the obvious.

Ironically, Lord MacLehose also stated in London that the Chinese had announced their intention to him in 1979 to take over sovereignty when the time was ripe. This was never released publically—though he says he passed it onto the British government. The only public statement to come from his historic meeting with China's paramount leader, Deng Xiaoping, was Deng's widely hailed advice to Hong Kong investors to "put their hearts at ease." The remark was widely interpreted at that time to mean China would let the *status quo* remain.

Though Mrs. Thatcher reiterated her moral responsibility for the 5.5. million souls while she was in the colony, the Hong Kong

23

Chinese population is under no illusions what she and her party really think. Britain's new nationality law, which took effect Jan. 1, 1983, makes it quite plain. Hong Kong people have had their worthless Hong Kong British passport diluted even further as it is now a British Dependent Territory passport.

The BNO (British Nationality Ordinance) passport are to be issued only to Chinese citizens of the new Hong Kong Special Administrative Region, and cannot be passed on to subsequent generations. Another sticky problem for Britain is the 15,000 or so non-Chinese residents of Hong Kong. China refuses to recognize them because they are non-Chinese and Britian will not take them in because they were born outside the United Kingdom to non-Britons.

Hong Kong suffered badly from an acute case of the S&P syndrome which stands for stability and prosperity — during the Sino-British negotiations. And it continues to have relapses frequently, depending on the political and economic climate. They were the key words in the Sino-British communique and have since echoed forth at every pronouncement from either side.

China's 13th National People's Congress ended in December 1982. It approved a new constitution which, under Article 31, allows for the creation of Special Administrative Regions, a political entity aimed directly at Hong Kong, Macau and Taiwan.

Perhaps more significant, the sixth Five Year Plan launched by the same Congress restructured China's economy quite drastically. An example: State companies will now pay taxes to the government and are allowed to keep profits. Does that not sound suspiciously like capitalistic Hong Kong?

Hong Kong has taken a severe drubbing in the international press since Prime Minister Thatcher's visit. In addition, wordwide recession which really hit the colony in 1982 (exacerbated by the negotiations with China) has affected the liquidity of the over-extended property companies and Deposit Taking Companies (the local version of Savings & Loan Associations).

The backlash of the drop in property prices has affected Hong Kong government revenues because they represented more than 50 percent of the government's income. Hence, the first deficit in a decade because land sales have fallen dramatically.

Business is still being conducted. By the end of 1983, there were more than a dozen contracts with payment schedules beyond 1997. There are many more now, including mortages. One of the biggest deals contemplated is a nuclear power station in Kwantung province, which will supply electricity for both the province and Hong Kong. China Light & Power will supply part of the finance and the expertise in this massive project which will run right pass 1997.

In 1983, China signed her largest deal — a US$3.5 billion nuclear power station in Daya Bay (30 miles northeast of Hong Kong). The station expects to sell 70 percent of its output — about 10 percent of the estimated demand by 1990 — to Hong Kong, earning hundreds of millions of dollars in foreign exchange. The Hong Kong Government formed the Hong Kong Nuclear Investment Co. for a 25 per cent joint-venture stake with the Guangdong Power Co. to build, commission and operate the plant. Due to negotiating delays, the construction contracts were only signed with British and French firms in 1986.

China for her part, is still investing directly in Hong Kong with property, construction and stock investments worth about US$5 billion by 1985. Also in 1985, China went into the commercial money market for the first time to float a loan worth HK$300 million.

The Hong Kong dollar took a beating in 1983 due to the political uncertainty surrounding the Sino-British negotiations; just before Mrs. Thatcher's visit to Peking in Sept. 1982, the Hong Kong dollar dropped from HK$5.60 to HK$9.60 for every US dollar. It was finally pegged by the government to HK$7.80 in September 1983. In spite of severe political problems which Hong Kong faced in 1984, it was business as usual. Exports surged more than 30% over the calendar year 1983 and the G.D.P. grew by 8%— almost double the predicted figure. In spite of downturns in major Western markets and severe threats from Western protectionism against imports, particularly textiles, export grew by 37.8% in 1984 and 6.2% in 1985. The GDP increased by 9.4% in 1984 and 4% in 1985. Hong Kong also played host to nearly 3.5 million visitors in 1985, (up from 3.1 million 1984) who filled up new hotels and created room shortages, in spite of predictions to the contrary.

So where does all this leave Hong Kong? For a moment, she sits here—economically viable, frustrated at times, but somehow coping with the problems caused by her long and improbable existence on a three-legged stool.

Every October 1st, until the Hong Kong Cricket Club moved in 1975, Chairman Mao's visage would smile down from Central's festive and Communist Bank of China.

Ancient 'Cathay'

61 A.D.: A Roman envoy, perhaps the first western tourist in the Orient, follows the Silk Road east to somewhere that may have been China. His account of an enormous, civilized empire is dismissed as fantasy.

100: Wandering monks bring the teaching of Buddha, already nearly 1,000 years old, across the Himalaya from India. In concert with China's native Taoism, this new "Way" spreads quickly during an era of disaster and discontent. By 589, with the ascendance of the first "alien" dynasty from Western Mongolia, Buddhism becomes China's official state religion.

758: Sea-going Arab traders burn and loot Canton, then, as now, South China's principal city. To the north and west, after two centuries' vogue, Nestorian Christianity vanishes from China, leaving behind a few stone tablets.

1100: Pressed by "Northern Barbarians" — known and feared along the Danube as the Mongol Horde — gentry farmers from central China flee south to fertile valleys in today's New Territories. Among them are the Tangs, Hong Kong's oldest family, whose descendants still live as a clan in Kam Tin.

1279: While Kublai Khan treats Marco Polo to a 20-year Far East tour, his horsemen rout the last Sung emperor — a 12-year-old boy — from a rough hide-out near present-day Kowloon Bay. Polo's account of "Cathay," published in Europe at the turn of the century, is widely dismissed as fantasy.

1405: Commanding 62 ships and 28,000 men, imperial court eunuch Cheng Ho sails through the straits of Malacca to India and the Persian Gulf. Ho's later expeditions reach east Africa and even Mecca, but the Emperor remains unimpressed and in 1431 bans further forays into the barbarian West.

1498: Vasco da Gama, with four ships and less than 100 men, leads Portugal's "Age of Discovery" around Africa to Mozambique and India. Over the next 10 years, the Portuguese seize Goa and Malacca, building forts and replacing the Arabs in control of the lucrative East Indies spice trade.

1513: Connecting Malacca's "Chin" merchants with Marco Polo's fabled "Cathay," Portuguese officials send Jorge Alvares east in a junk to investigate. Though refused entry to Canton, he does some small trading at Namtao (a coastal town north of Castle Peak) and returns with the news that a great — and fabulously wealthy — Chinese empire indeed appears to exist.

1517: Uncertain where or what "Portugal" is, Peking officials spend two years pondering Alvares' successor, envoy Tomé Pires. Though finally brought before the Dragon Throne itself, Pires' request for a trade agreement is judged insufficiently humble, and he returns to Canton empty-handed. Greeted there by news of an unsuccessful Portuguese naval assault, ever-hopeful envoy Pires is jailed, and dies shortly after in captivity. Eschewing revenge — or diplomatic nicety — his countrymen finally find their profits smuggling silk, tea and porcelain from small ports up and down the coast.

1540: Encouraged by local merchants, Portuguese privateer-traders pull in for the winter at Liampo, a small island south of Shanghai. Never more than a rude group of waterside huts, creative mapmakers quickly make Liampo a city — "Europe's first settlement in China." En route there two years later, storm-blown adventurer Fernão Mendes Pinto by accident discovers Japan — and a friendly, lucrative new market.

1549: Chinese troops, ordered to suppress the burgeoning Japan trade, set upon and destroy Liampo. Undeterred, Portuguese survivors regroup 90 miles south of Canton on windswept Sanchuang, where three years later St. Francis Xavier expires — having visited Japan but denied his dream of converting China. Undeterred still, smuggling operations move in 1553 to Lampakkau, a larger island nearer the mouth of the Pearl River. By 1556, the place boasts of 400 matshed huts and thriving Chinese supporters.

Rich Macau Middlemen

1557: "The mandarins of Canton, at the request of the local inhabitants, have given us this port of Macao," writes Japan-finder Mendes Pinto. The concession is a reward — albeit tacit and grudging — for driving off "dwarf-robber" pirates. But with the port comes a richer plum: permission — in fact, a monopoly — for regular trade in Canton. The Japanese and the Chinese make the Portuguese their middlemen in the lucrative trade between the two countries, and Macau becomes a winter stopping point for an "Annual Royal Japan Voyage" originating in Goa.

Moving quickly to shore up their gains, the Portuguese by 1665 have warehouses, churches and stone-walled villas on the hills that surround this old fishing village.

A Fé O Império
For Faith and Empire

1600: Macao (commonly spelled Macau) hits its zenith, *A Fé o Império* — "For Faith and Empire" — not necessarily in that order. Macanese carracks rule the Far East waves, trading Chinese silk for Nagasaki silver, bringing Indies pepper, Indian cotton and European manufacturers to Canton, then sending back to Malacca and Lisbon silk, porcelain, pearls, silver and tea. Two hundred

1601: Having been bested by the Portuguese, Spain, Holland and England form India companies and send their own ships east. The Macanese do not view competition kindly: the first Dutch arrivals, sailing from a new base in Java, are attacked, beaten and publicly hanged. Later skirmishes — culminating in 1607 with a naval battle off present-day Lantau Island — spur Macau to fortify and the Dutch to build an outpost on Taiwan. In 1627, the Dutch invade Macau, only to be repulsed by a lucky cannon shot fired by a Jesuit father.

1637: Captain John Weddell's four armed merchant ships shoot their way into the Pearl River Estuary. Though turned back short of Canton, they demolish a fort, burn several

percent profits make a disappointing voyage, and the now solid town of 6,000 — complete already with its Praia Grande — is said to rival Venice in the richness of its trade. For Faith, scarcely a street lacks some sort of church, and a Jesuit seminary tops the highest hill. Missionaries following St. Francis Xavier convert 150,000 Japanese, while in Peking, Father Matteo Ricci wears mandarin robes and lives as a court philosopher.

Marco Polo's book about his wanderings told of exotic lands previously known only in dreams. Polo and his friends spent 20 years on their big tour of the Far East.

villages and establish the English in Chinese eyes as the "most ferocious of all the Western Barbarians." Blamed for allowing these "red beards" through, the Portuguese forfeit their 80-year-old trading rights at Canton. Shogun Iemitsu in 1639 closes Japan — in the process crucifying Christian missionaries and exterminating tens of thousands of converts. The Dutch two years later take Malacca. Portugal's Far East commercial empire effectively vanishes.

1685: Emperor K'ang Hsi, a noted patron of Jesuit scholars, reopens trade in Canton on a limited basis. After HMS *Macclesfield's* profitable visit in 1699, British ships begin arriving annually from East India Company "stations" on the Indian coast. Fifteen years later, already the world's largest commercial organization, the company asks for — and receives — permission to build a warehouse (a "factory") near Canton.

A Celestial Illusion

1687: The ancient Confucian Classics are published in Latin at Paris, sparking the Enlightenment's China craze. For writers from Leibnitz to Voltaire, against strifetorn, bigoted Europe the Celestial Empire seems a model of order and reason: just laws, a learned bureaucracy, and above all a benevolent philosopher-king. Chinese porcelain and backs, bribes and fees: The Emperor appoints (and squeezes) Hong merchants, who govern (and squeeze) barbarian traders. Terms of business for foreigners are severe: they may reside in Canton from September to March only; may not bring arms, warships or women; must pay for everything in hard cash, normally silver; and except for special occasions must stay within the carefully marked confines of their waterfront factory district. Trade, despite all this, prospers, and even impoverished Macau has a minor renaissance, swallowing its pride and supplying the new merchant princes with sumptuous off-season retreats.

1773: While "Indian" revolutionaries dump East India Company tea into Boston Harbour, British traders at Canton unload

CHINESE MERCHANTS, &c.
1 in their Summer Dress .... 2 in the Winter Dress .... 3 a Merchant's Wife ....

furnishings, mock-Chinese landscapes and architecture rise to the height of fashion, topped off in 1763 by a 10-storey pagoda built in London's Kew Gardens. The illusion lasts just about a century, then dims when Europe reads more current reports of Chinese corruption, vice and tyranny.

The Imperial 'Squeeze'

1757: By Imperial edict, a Canton merchant's guild — the "Co-Hong" — gains exclusive rights to China's foreign trade. The privilege is paid for with "squeeze," an old, notably Oriental system of royalties, kick- 1,000 chests of Bengal opium containing 150 pounds each and together worth a million silver dollars. The two events are not unconnected: with its tea trade expanding worldwide, the Company hits on Indian opium to balance — and, later, more than balance — purchases of Chinese tea. A decade later, as trade in both directions booms, 13 foreign-devil factories line the Canton waterfront, the larger belonging to the E.I.C. In 1784, Canton sees its first American ship, the *Empress of China,* and a novel cargo of Turkish opium

Early British sketches of Chinese aristocrats, above, inspired a China rage in Europe.

carried all the way from Smyrna.

1793: Lord Macartney, fresh from successful negotiations with the Russian Czar, arrives at Peking's Court of Heaven seeking new ports to open for trade. In a flush of high British honour, his lordship evades the *kowtow* (crawling in on all fours, then performing "The Three Kneelings and Nine Prostrations" at the Emperor's feet) by insisting that a mandarin of comparable rank do the same before a portrait of King George III. During breakfast with the Lord of the World & Dispenser of Light, however, the clever envoy gets an undiplomatic goodbye: "We possess all things in abundance," says the Imperial Dragon, "and have no need of the manufacturers of outside Barbarians."

'Foreign Mud'

1800: Despite the Emperor's boast, China's taste for "foreign mud" (opium) tops 2,000 chests a year. Alarmed at the drain of silver — and the growing horde of addict-subjects — Peking thunders an edict totally banning the drug trade. But Canton has other ideas, and with everyone's connivance, lured by profits and squeeze, the high days of open smuggling begin. To keep its own hands officially clean, the East India Company holds auctions in Calcutta, where private, usually British "country" traders load swift and heavily armed "opium clippers" for the two-to-three-

week voyage east. Though the dealing is done at Canton, the chests stay safely out of sight of Lintin, the "Solitary Nail," as the Chinese call it, that stands in the mouth of the Pearl River. Squeeze takes care of official complaints — in 1804, the *Hoppo* alone nets some £200,000 — and from Lintin oared "crab boats" run the drug on its final leg to quiet coves around the delta. By 1816, when Macartney's successor, Lord Amherst, is rebuffed from even entering Peking, yearly imports total 5,000 chests — three quarters of a million pounds.

1802: British warships move to invade Macau as France invades Portugal. Fearing a Portuguese accommodation with the invading French armies, Lord Wellesley, Britain's Governor-General in India, sends an expeditionary force. Word reaches the fleet of the Peace of Amiens before troops disembark and Macau is saved from an invasion. But a couple of years later, the Portuguese colony is not so lucky. Again, France is the enemy in Europe and after taking Goa, Britain sends a force to occupy Macau. This time the British troops occupy three forts. British traders in the Portuguese colony are delighted until they realize they have misjudged the Chinese reaction. Portugal relies on negotiation, instead of force of arms, for its strength in China. Now the East India Company faces the possibility of a Chinese army crossing into Macau to throw them out. Trade stops and the merchants persuade the British admiral to leave. Afterward the Chinese enter Macau to verify the situation. Trade continues again.

1833: The East India Company's monopoly hold on the opium trade with China is broken and Queen Victoria's Foreign Secretary, Lord Palmerston, appoints Lord Napier of the Royal Navy, Chief Superintendent of Trade. Palmerston instructs Napier to induce British subjects to obey Chinese laws, which of course would be the end of the lucrative but illegal opium trade. Unfortunately for his lordship, the Foreign Secretary also instructs him to proceed to Canton and deliver a letter to the ruling Viceroy. Napier has no right under Chinese law to enter Canton because only merchants are so privileged. Furthermore, under the very Chinese laws he is charged with upholding, he has no right to pass a "letter" to the Viceroy; only a "petition." His lordship haughtily refuses to pass his "petition" through an intermediary. Deadlocked, Napier returns to Macau whilst the Viceroy orders the cessation of all trade with the British bar-

Though "official" approval was, well, unofficial, Her Majesty's East India Company dealt sticky opium by the clipper-full all along the South China Coast. Drugs are now a no-no.

barians. Before dying three weeks later, Napier sends two frigates up the Pearl River to force passage past the forts, but the ships are cut off and hopelessly stranded.

1839: Opium is still *the key* to British commerce in the East and Palmerston writes Napier that "it is not desirable you should encourage such adventures, but you must never lose sight of the fact you have no authority to interfere or prevent them." A strong anti-opium viceroy, Lin Tse-Hsu, is appointed by the Dragon Throne to clean up Canton. He orders all foreign merchants to obey the laws and confiscates their opium — some 20,291 chests in all. Additional British forces begin to arrive to force Lin's hand in opening Canton once again to the opium trade. Lin exerts his

time, Elliot becomes Her Majesty's sole plenipotentiary in China due to the illness of another more senior naval officer. When negotiations break down with Lin's representative, Kishen, Elliot's fleet attacks Canton and occupies the city's protecting forts. Three days later, on Jan. 20, the Convention of Chuen Pi is to be signed. Its terms include the annexation of the island of Hong Kong, a point of land included at Elliot's request.

The fact that the treaty is never actually signed does not bother Commodore Sir J.J. Gordon Bremer, who leads a contingent of naval men ashore on Jan. 26 at Possession Point to plant the Union Jack. Both Kishen and Elliot displease their superiors with this deal and are recalled. Hostilities break out

authority over foreigners by making an "official" visit to Macau.

Hong Kong -- 'In Perpetuity'

1841: To Captain Charles Elliot, Royal Navy, the fourth Superintendent of Trade in China, fell the thankless job of trying to protect the interests of British merchantmen and sort out the political mess in Canton. He is under instructions from Palmerston to not only solve the trade problem, but also to find a "conveniently situated" island to "afford natural facilities for defence and be easily provisioned." By a quirk of fate at this moment in

again and this time Hong Kong's first governor, Sir Henry Pottinger, who replaced the discredited Elliot in August 1841, marches his troops as far as Nanking before the Chinese capitulate on Aug. 29, 1842. The Treaty of Nanking cedes (amongst other things) Hong Kong Island "in perpetuity."

1845: Macau is freed of rule from Goa after nearly 300 years and joins with Timor and Solor as part of a single provincial region. Inspired by Hong Kong's forced British annexation, the Portuguese Territory rebels at

The Imperial Dragon frowned on the use of "foreign mud," *the* Chinese drug of choice.

paying rent. A British Protestant religious teacher refuses to remove his hat during a Corpus Christi procession and is arrested, only to be freed by a contingent of British Royal Marines who cause the death of a Portuguese soldier.

1849: The governor of Macau is assassinated by rebellious Cantonese who have learned that the Portuguese territory is not under British protection. The Portuguese blow up a Chinese border fort which had peppered the Portas do Cerco (border gate) with gunfire. Macau reasserts its independence from the Chinese with that assault.

The Second Opium War

1856: On March 26, the Chinese cede Kowloon Point (Tsimshatsui) and Stonecutter Island "in perpetuity" to the British colonials. By 1864 the Taiping Rebellion is crushed, and by 1878 the Dragon Throne has dispatched its first ambassadors to the world of outer Barbarians.

1860: An unprovoked attack on a British-registered *lorcha* (a junk-rigged schooner) by Chinese soldiers triggers the Second Opium War (or the "Arrow War," after the name of the *lorcha*). Attacks on the East India Company headquarters in Canton forces the British to regroup in Hong Kong. In retaliation, Britain takes Canton yet again in 1857, and Peking in 1858.

1862: A Sino-Portuguese treaty is signed, granting Macau a colonial status similar to Hong Kong's. A second treaty in 1887 confirms Macau's Portuguese status in perpetuity and defines the colony as the old town and two off-shore islands, Taipa and Coloane.

1898: In an effort to strengthen its defences, Britain forces China to lease it another 350 square miles of territory, including 233 more islands, for a period of 99 years, beginning July 1, 1898. (The lease expires three days before June 30, 1997.) The opium trade now has more breathing room and the Hong Kong government naturally collects increased revenues on profits. By the turn of the century, the Home Office is pressing Hong Kong to decrease opium consumption. (Note: opium use was not completely banned in the colony until after World War II.)

1900: The Boxer Rebellion begins and Chinese prejudice against foreigners surfaces all over the country.

1905: Dr. Sun Yat-sen leads an anti-Manchu movement that works to topple the Dowager Empress' Ching Dynasty. That same year Japan is victorious in the Russo-Japanese War. In Hong Kong, meanwhile, workers lay 28 miles of railway track for the new Kowloon-Canton Railway.

1911: Dr. Sun succeeds in overthrowing the Dragon Throne, and the Republic of China is born.

1912: The 85-mile railway link between Hong Kong and Canton is completed.

1914: Despite an exodus this year of 60,000 Chinese fearing an attack on the colony after the outbreak of World War I, Hong Kong's population begins its evermore claustrophobic climb — from 530,000 in 1916, 630,000 in 1921, 725,000 in 1925, 800,000 in 1930, and 1 million in 1937 to 1.6 million by 1941.

1918: A "Derby Day" fire envelops the racing stands at Happy Valley and thousands of race fans are killed.

The Chinese Civil War
And a Guerilla Named Mao

1922: Hong Kong experiences its first seamen's strike, a walkout which cripples the colony. China, meanwhile, had already coped with its first general strike two years earlier when Manchurian Railways workers quit their jobs. Like the strikes in China, Hong Kong's are directed against foreigners and inequitable treaties.

1925: A Bolshevik agitator, Borodin, organizes a Communist boycott of British and Japanese goods.

1927: General Chiang Kai-shek's Kuomintang troops escalate their Nationalist campaign to rid the country of Communists. The Chinese Civil War divides the country.

1928: Mao Tse-tung establishes his first guerilla base. The Japanese occupy Manchuria in 1931 and the following year the Communists declare war on them.

1935: Mao gains control of the Communist Party and the following year Chiang Kai-shek is kidnapped during what becomes known as the Sian Incident.

1937: The Sino-Japanese War erupts, so Kuomintang and Communist armies "unite" temporarily to fight a common foreign enemy.

The Japanese Occupation

1941: On Dec. 8 (Dec. 7 in Hawaii), the Japanese Imperial Fleet attacks Pearl Harbour and commits America to another World War. British, French, American and Dutch colonies fall before advancing Japanese like so many bowling pins. Japan occupies this colony on Christmas Day. As Hong Kong's Europeans are herded into Stanley Fort, Japan recognizes Portugal's neutrality and tiny Macau becomes the only "neutral pocket" in China. Macau becomes a refuge for escapees who successfully run through Japan's military gauntlet.

1945: On Aug. 6, an American atom bomb drops on Hiroshima. That same month, Sir Cecil Harcourt steams into "Fragrant Harbour" at the head of the British fleet to re-establish Her Majesty's presence in the war-ravaged British Crown Colony of Hong Kong.

1946: The Bretton Woods Agreement is signed, thereby forbidding the importation of gold for private purposes. Britain signs. Portugal does not. Thus begins a Macau-to-Hong Kong gold-smuggling operation which lasts until 1974 when Hong Kong abolishes a law which requires special licenses to import gold. Tiny Macau becomes one of the world's greatest importers of gold (which then usually

colony's residents now number nearly two million. This time, however, many of the new refugees are affluent Shanghai entrepreneurs, and proprietors some arriving in the colony with complete factories.

1951: Hong Kong's lucrative China trade dries up as a UN embargo on the export of strategic goods to China takes effect. Hong Kong is forced to change overnight from a mere transshipment depot for Chinese goods to a manufacturing centre.

Kowloon Riots

1952: In March, riots break out in Kowloon when the government refuses permission for a mission from Canton to enter to provide com-

finds its shiny way to Hong Kong — where it is then sold on the open market). China's civil war rages on.

1948: Hong's Kong's first skyjacking took place on July 16 as a Macau Airways' catalina flying boat en route to Macau from the colony is taken. The pilot was shot by the lone hijacker and the plane crashed, killing all but one of the 27 passengers and crew.

1949: Routed Kuomintang forces flee to Taiwan. Communist Chinese troops stop at the British border and a heavy Red Bamboo Curtain seals off the Middle Kingdom. While China's civil war was being fought, Hong Kong's refugee population swelled, and the

fort to victims of a squatter fire. In Macau, waves of immigrants threaten to swamp the tiny territory. Macau signs an agreement with China pledging co-operation with the Communist regime.

1953: On Christmas Day, Hong Kong's Shek Kip Mei squatter area bursts into flames leaving 53,000 homeless. After the debris is cleared on Boxing Day, Hong Kong begins an emergency housing programme. By the end of 1980, one out of every two people in the

Chairman Mao inspired a socially realistic school of art with visions of the Great Helmsman and his people, above.

colony will be living in public housing.

1954: Dien Bien Phu falls and the French lose Vietnam. A conference in Geneva is called to guarantee Indochina's neutrality and John Foster Dulles, the American Secretary of State, snubs Chinese Prime Minister Chou En-lai by refusing to shake hands.

1955: China, in a show of force, blocks Macau's plans for a 400th birthday celebration; in a genuflection to diplomacy China later frees American prisoners-of-war captured during the Korean War.

1956: Another wave of immigrants hits the colony — pushing the population above 2.5 million. Squatter huts spring up everywhere and rioting between Nationalists and Communists explodes in the streets. Khrushchev denounces Stalin and invades Hungary. French, British and Israeli forces take the Suez Canal to prevent its nationalization by Egypt's Nassar. At on-going Geneva peace talks, China proposes cultural exchanges with the United States. Hong Kong gets cable television in time to catch some of this year's political and military action.

1962: Yet another wave of immigrants — estimated to be between 60,000-100,000 — crosses the border, but this time they are shunted back and forth like ping pong balls as Chinese border troops herd them towards Hong Kong while colonial forces try desperately to keep them out. The deluge stops as quickly as it began — when Mao orders it to stop.

1964: Legal gambling begins at Macau, turning this somnolent territory into a "Las Vegas of the East." Hong Kong makes history by being the only city in the world in which Britain's famed mopheads — the Beatles — lose money.

1965: The war escalates in Vietnam with the first U.S. air strikes against North Vietnam. Marines land at Danang and a "protracted" ground war is on. Hong Kong braces for an American invasion. R & R troops slowly begin trickling into the colony on leave from the war, and during the next 10 years this trickle expands to more than 3,000 GIs a month. U.S. Navy vessels become as familiar a sight in the harbour as do servicemen from all three of the United States' armed services do in the bars and nightclubs of Wanchai and across the harbour in Tsimshatsui restaurants.

1966: Rioting flares up again, this time over a price rise in the first class Star Ferry fares. Peking, however, remains mute. Mao starts his great proletarian "cultural revolution" to regain control of the country. Young intellectuals take over the ancient Middle Kingdom, and traditionally revered elders are cast aside, sometimes with brute force.

The chaos in China spills over into Macau as Red Guards plaster the tiny Portuguese territory with posters. Portuguese troops fire on rampaging Red Guards, killing eight. Macau's governor, Brigadier Nobre de Carvalho, negotiates from a position of weakness because Portugal cannot come to its aid and Macau's tiny police force and garrison is helpless. In Hong Kong, Chief Superintendent John Tsang of Special Branch, one of colony's highest ranking Chinese policemen, is unmasked as a Communist spy and disappears across the border, only to become the chief of security for Kwangtuong Province. By this act he establishes himself as a character in all subsequent fiction written about the colony.

1967: Brigadier de Carvalho plays a last trump and suggests that the Portuguese leave Macau. Peking pulls back its Red Guards. China doesn't want either Portugal or Britain to pull out at this point in time due to economic considerations. On Jan. 29, the Portuguese make a public apology for the Red Guard killings and pay China HK$2 million in compensation. The Hong Kong government is shocked at this Portuguese capitulation. Meanwhile the British Embassy in Peking is sacked and Red Guards take to Hong Kong's streets. The government fights back, but just about all aspects of the economy are paralyzed — except R & R nightlife business. Stories circulate that special "triads" are keeping Wanchai free of Communist cadres so that police can concentrate on protecting other districts. Peking responds vociferously when bigger Hong Kong riots break out and tension is mounting. By the end of this year, the "disturbances," as they are referred to locally, are quelled and Hong Kong and Macau are still Western-run colonies.

Hong Kong's first vehicle tunnel, the Lion Rock Tunnel, opens as a symbol of the government's regard for the future. A water shortage forces the colony to ration that precious liquid.

The pound sterling is devalued — an unexpected financial shock — and Hong Kong loses a third of its sterling reserves. Hong Kong devalues, revalues in the same week and then pegs its currency to the U.S. dollar.

1969: The Hong Kong government stages its first Festival of Hong Kong to say thank you to "residents" who have tolerated the past few years of the cultural revolution across the border with nervous patience, aware of the potential danger to the colony.

1970: Prince Noradom Sihanouk of Cambodia is deposed in a coup backed by Americans and Field Marshall Lon Nol takes over. The war in Vietnam spreads to that former Khmer kingdom.

The U.S. dollar is realigned against other currencies, and Pope Paul VI visits Hong Kong, the first Roman pontiff to do so. A first "Jumbo Jet" arrives at Kai Tak Airport.

1971: The United States cannot muster enough support for Taiwan in the United Nations General Assembly and the People's Republic of China is eventually recognized as the "real China" and takes Taiwan's place in that world body.

Sir Murray MacLehose, the first Hong Kong governor to be appointed from the British diplomatic corps, arrives to assume his post. This is a signal to China that Britain is concerned about Hong Kong's future. Shortly after MacLehose's arrival a new

teriously catches fire and rolls over in Hong Kong's harbour.

Severe rain causes the horrors everyone here expected. On Po Shan Road apartment buildings slip down the steep mountain slopes above Central, one level of flats collapsing into another. Across the harbour in Kowloon, a mud slide in Saumoping buries hundreds alive.

1973: Britain floats the pound sterling because it cannot afford to artificially prop up that currency any longer. But Hong Kong is prepared this time and has long since diversified its cash reserves.

The first of the "spiraling" OPEC oil price rises hits Hong Kong; de-energising effects are felt immediately.

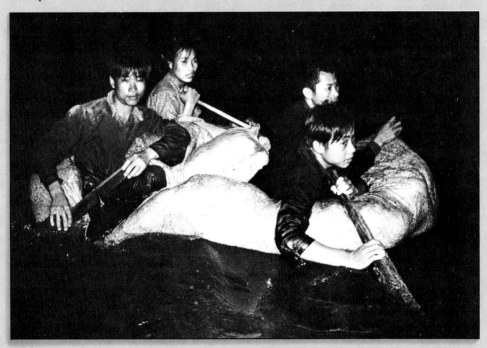

Jumbo Floating Restaurant at Aberdeen catches fire.

1972: The entire world is caught off guard by the once unthinkable sight of U.S. President Richard Nixon visiting China. He has audiences with the aging Mao Tse-tung and Chou En-lai, and treats the Middle Kingdom to a Western-style media circus as the world's press flocks into the Forbidden City and other Chinese places.

In Hong Kong the cross-harbour tunnel opens and motorists bid farewell to the colony's time-consuming, but pleasant, cross-harbour vehicular ferry cruises.

The cruise liner *Queen Elizabeth*, bought by shipping magnate C. Y. Tung to be converted into a Seawise Floating University, mys-

The United States officially "recognizes" China, sets up a Peking liaison office, closes its Taipei embassy, and creates a China institute to handle consular matters. Britain joins the European Economic Community, Mother England vows to protect Hong Kong interests, but doesn't.

Hong Kong's stock market collapses and the Hong Kong government holds its last Festival of Hong Kong, backing instead a new Arts Festival, a month long orgy of high-class "culture" held annually.

More problems for Hong Kong: above, a group of illegal immigrants is spot-lighted by a patrol boat just off the shore; right, a restaurant at Aberdeen erupts in flames in 1971.

36

The colony's first "new town," Tuen Mun, is opened in the New Territories and will eventually house 200,000.

During this shocking year, senior police officer Peter Godber slips out of Hong Kong to escape arrest, taking with him more than HK$4.6 million, six times the amount he officially earned during his Hong Kong police career. Hong Kong's rampant police corruption — previously dismissed or minimized by the government and the police anti-corruption bureau — is now common knowledge.

Meanwhile, back in China, Deng Xiaoping is rehabilitated for a second time and becomes a deputy premier — second in power only to Chou En-lai.

The Macau-Taipa bridge is completed.

1975: The police bust a Mr. Big in the local heroine trade — Ng Sik-ho — and his assistant, Ng Chun-kwan, who were sentenced to 30 and 25 years in prison respectively. This narcotics crackdown on big drug syndicates involved law enforcement agents from Britain, Thailand and the United States, in addition to Hong Kong police.

The infamous Peter Godber is extradited from England, stands trial and gets four years. He is convicted partly on the testimony of another copper, Taffy Hunt, who was given judicial immunity in exchange for fingering Godber. Hunt later bragged to reporters at his home in Spain that he made more than a mil-

1974: In response to public outcry — and pointed nudging from an embarrassed governor and Whitehall — Hong Kong sets up an Independent Commission Against Corruption (the ICAC) with a wide mandate to stamp corruption out. The police force is the first government department on the commission's check list.

Following this year's revolution in Portugal, Macau's governor, Brigadier Nobre de Carvalho, is called back to Lisbon and ordered to resign from the Portuguese army. A young technocrat, Lt. Col. Garcia Leandro, replaces him. Since China refuses to take back Macau, the colony's status was changed to a "Chinese territory under Portuguese Administration."

lion U.S. dollars working for the Royal Hong Kong Police.

Her Majesty Queen Elizabeth II and H.R.H. the Duke of Edinburgh arrive for a royal visit; they are the first reigning British royalty ever to set foot in their colony.

The U.S. Embassy in Phnom Penh is evacuated on April 12 and that Cambodian capital city falls on April 17. Pol Pot takes over in Cambodia. Saigon falls 13 days later and the long war in Vietnam ends.

1976: A big Tangshan earthquake kills 240,000 in China and a trembling Hong Kong experiences scary aftershocks in the middle of the night.

After a mass demonstration by off-duty policemen on Queensway in Central, the

Governor orders an amnesty for all crimes of corruption committed before Jan. 1, 1977. With hundreds of staff assigned the ICAC drive against corruption becomes one of the world's most effective.

Both Chou En-lai and Mao Tse-tung die and China begins "a new era" under Deng Xiaoping and Hua Guofeng, the "new" Celestial Kingdom's Vice-Chairman and Chairman respectively. And in a conscience-cleaning move which shocks the world, Mao's widow, Chiang Ching, (Jiang Qing) and three other zealous revolutionaries — the infamous

in Southeast Asia. Eventually, 70,000 of these "boat people" put into Hong Kong.

The gigantic High Island Reservoir opens and begins quenching Hong Kong water problems, while in China the Bamboo Curtain opens wide and for the first time in many moons tourists are allowed to visit the People's Republic.

1979: Deng Xiaoping goes a-calling on Jimmy Carter, then struts around Houston in a cowboy hat. Weeks later China invades Vietnam "to teach them a lesson."

Back in the Royal Crown Colony life rolls

"gang of four" — are arrested.

1977: Rumours hit Macau that Portugal is trying to give the colony away, but the Chinese will not take it back. The Deputy Prime Minister of Portugal visits the 400-year-old colony in a show of faith.

London continually pressures the Hong Kong government for more social services, but the colony's conservatives resist. Fears grow that Whitehall, under a Labour government, will turn the ultra-capitalistic colony into a welfare state.

New Refugees

1978: Peking and Lisbon exchange diplomatic niceties and Col. Garcia Leandro, Macau's governor, visits Macau's old landlord, China. As a sign of improved relations, China approves in principal a Hong Kong-Macau helicopter service.

Vietnamese refugees fleeing the south (after buying their way out with gold) start piling up

on. Hong Kong's US$1 billion Mass Transit Railway (MTR) opens; the rusty freighter *Huey Fong* brings 3,000 more Vietnamese boat people to the colony for Christmas; and in Kowloon a Sung Dynasty Village opens, offering visitors an easy journey into ancient Chinese "living" culture.

1980: In October Hong Kong ends its "touch base" immigration policy which previously allowed Chinese refugees to remain in the colony if they reached an urban area safely. Such illegal immigrants (II's) will no longer be home free here.

The colony's longest running sideshow — an enquiry into the alleged suicide of Inspector John MacLennan (who according to official police reports shot himself in the chest five times) — reveals sordid details about police

Chou En-lai and giggling comrades on a 1977 People's Republic stamp commemorating the first anniversary of his death, above. Right, Prince Charles in his bachelor days.

undercover agents who stalk after homosexuals. Chinese, who regard homosexuality as a "white man's disease" are exposed to an unseemly side of life in a big city.

1981: Hong Kong's perennial problems of fire and water plague the colony. Fifty fires in different squatter areas leave more than 30,000 homeless, but luckily there is little loss of life because of speedy action by firemen and police. By the end of the year, the Housing Department admits that more than 1.2 million people in a quarter of a million households — 20% of the population — still live in "unsatisfactory conditions."

Rumours of property prices leveling off are proved false with new land sales. The Peninsula Group pays a world-record HK$36,174.40 a square foot for the 10,090 square feet Merlin Hotel site in Kowloon. The colony also sets another world record for the largest single real estate deal when HK$2.8 billion is paid for the 85,960 square feet old wing of the Miramar Hotel, which comes to a mere HK$32,573 per square foot.

In Macau, a new administration led by governor Commander Vasco Almeida e Costa takes office.

1982: The highpoint of the year is the visit of the British Prime Minister, Mrs. Margaret Thatcher, to Peking and Hong Kong in September. During this visit, the first talks on Hong Kong's future (the 99 year lease on the New Territories, nine-tenths of the Colony, expires in 1997) began. The negotiations and subsequent jitters thus generated overshadow the departure of Sir Murray MacLehose from his office as the 25th governor for more than a decade. He was replaced by Sir Edward Youde, another Mandarin-speaking, old China-hand diplomat (instead of a colonial administrator).

Hong Kong's stock market takes a dive on Thatcher's visit which also acts as a catalyst to bring down the soaring property market, already in decline. Carrian Investments Ltd. and Eda Investment Ltd., two of the largest property companies are bailed out by their creditors, the former to the tune of HK$250 million by the Hongkong and Shanghai Banking Corporation.

China's 13th National People's Congress meets and releases the sixth five year plan which completely restructures the economy. The Chinese also announce they are putting in US$100 million in infrastructure construction into the Shenzhen Special Economic Zone on Hong Kong's border.

China and the US continue their arguments over arms sales to Taiwan, resulting in another Shanghai Communique earlier in the year which pleased neither party.

With an eye on the date when most of Hongkong's land area reverts to China, a restaurant named "1997" opened its doors for diners-out in the British colony.

1983: The Sino-British negotiations on Hong Kong's future continue to hold headlines, affecting every facet of the colony's existence.

Property market continues to fall, pulling with it a number of deposit-taking and real-estate companies. The largest to fall is the Carrian Group which owes HK$10 billion to the banks when the plug was pulled on the year-long rescue effort.

In July, the Chinese tip their plans for Hong Kong to a group of university students — Hong Kong will become a Special Administrative Region, will keep its own capitalistic system, judiciary and police, but the future head will be a Hong Kong Chinese.

In September, as confidence in the negotiations erodes, the Hong Kong dollar drops to HK $9.55: US$1 (from HK $5.60 before Mrs. Thatcher's visit in September 1982). The government pegs the currency to the US dollar at HK$7.80 and stability is resumed.

The tone of the negotiations changes for the better around autumn after China leader Deng Xiaoping reportedly receives a letter from Mrs. Thatcher in which she concedes Hong Kong's sovereignty to China.

1984: Hong Kong's most important day, September 26th equal in significance to the day the colony was founded in 1841, is added to the calendar. On that day the British Ambassador to China and the Chinese Vice Foreign Minister initial *A Draft Agreement on the Future of Hong Kong*, ending two years of often acrimonious negotiations between the two countries on Hong Kong's fate.

(At the start of talks in 1982, China cut Britain off at the pass by declaring that she would resume sovereignty over the entire territory. Britain's position that she held sovereignty over Hong Kong Island and the 3½ square mile Kowloon peninsula by right of two 19th Century treaties ceding the land, was demolished by China's paramount leader, Deng Xiaoping, even before British Prime Minister Margaret Thatcher brought up the subject. However, it took the Iron Lady until the summer of 1983 before she saw the futility of Britain's negotiating stance and gave in by announcing the British withdrawal in 1997. After that, negotiations proceeded in a much friendlier atmosphere.)

The government sets up an Assessment Office to gather opinions on the Draft Agreement, as promised by Mrs Thatcher. (Opinions collected are sent to London to assist Members of Parliament in their debate on the matter.) "Catch 22" is that both the Chinese and British governments announced after the initialling that "no changes could be made." The real choice for Hong Kong's population is to accept China's take-over in 1997 with the agreement as writ (including safeguards therein) or to accept China's take-over in 1997 period.

Almost as important as the agreement itself are the government's plans for Hong Kong's administration in the years running up to 1997. Key points include elections (something the government usually shied away from due to "the geo-political situation," as the phrase went) to the Legislative

precedent setting move, the Legislative Council—normally a tame rubber-stamp assembly—votes down the government's taxi tax package, acceding to petitions from thousands of taxi drivers.

Hong Kong-appointed Legislative and Executive Councillors, who have been left out of the Sino-British talks, gain strength and stature as the they fly to London several times passing on Hong Kong's anxieties and arguing forcibly—sometimes publically—with various British Members of Parliament and politicians.

For the second year running, Hong Kong's accounts go into the red with a planned deficit for 1984/85. The government

Council (totally appointed now), the District Boards (partially elected now) and new Regional Councils. The government has stated its intent to train local decision-makers in the intervening years to 1997 to prepare the territory for its semi-autonomous, almost-self-governing role as a Special Administrative Region of the People's Republic of China.

A brief period of tension descends upon Hong Kong in February when hooligans turn a taxi "park-in" strike into a full-fledged riot involving 5,000 people. The fear comes not because of the riot itself, but because of one of China's early statements that they will not resume control over Hong Kong until 1997 unless the British cannot control avents. In a

raises profits tax to 18½ per cent from 16½ per cent and salaries tax to 17 per cent from 15 per cent, to raise revenue. But Hong Kong's export-led economy surges ahead with a 25 per cent growth in exports and a 6.8 per cent increase in GDP, in spite of the political anxiety of the previous two years.

In a shock announcement in March, Jardine Matheson & Co., the colony's oldest *hong* (European trading company), states its intention to move its corporate headquarters from Hong Kong to Bermuda. No other international companies follow suit.

British Prime Minister Margaret Thatcher takes tea in a tiny and crowded resettlement estate flat during her visit in September 1982.

41

MONEY MADNE$$—IN-REAL CASH TERMS

On first landing in Hong Kong, visitors may well get the impression that they are participating in a *kung fu* movie; later, that the whole territory is a giant stage-set, being built for a block-buster Hollywood epic entitled "The Tower of Babel." And later still that it is an "anti-health clinic," where people go to get ulcers, fill up on cholesterol and melt down their adrenalin glands.

Hong Kong is, of course, all three. It is also the world's biggest exporter of watches (in quantity terms) and toys, the world's largest drinker of brandy (and nearly all

Asia, but many of them are massed misery; Hong Kong's crowds are massed energy. They have a reputation of being the rudest people in the world. There are some, however, who believe that the rudeness tag has more to do with centuries of Chinese superstitions.

It has a government, but nobody knows quite what or where or who it is, or who really "controls" it; and the reality probably is that no one does. Hongkongians do have a vote sometimes, for a few members of the Urban Council, but very few people register to vote, and even fewer actually vote.

swank brands), one of the fastest-growing · economies in the world in real terms, the world's biggest collection of refugees for its size, the world's biggest user of telex machines — and, it has the world's biggest public housing programme per capita.

That's just for starters. It had until recently the world's largest water de-salting plant (water is quite a problem in Hong Kong, because they mix some of it with all that brandy, you see). It has two large and computerized race-tracks, in a place where gambling is illegal except on their hallowed grounds, and the money they take in rivals the government's budget. Some parts of Hong Kong are so crowded, they look like (and are) wall-to-wall people. There are other crowded places in

There is even confusion over the name of the place. Well before the beginning of the Sino-British talks drew attention to Hong Kong's precarious status, the word "colony" went out of style; the words "country" or "nation" were too dignified; "territory," though that sounds as if it should be full of Red Indians, is the official designation for most purposes. Hong Kong legally remains a British Crown Colony until midnight on June 30, 1997. It has an executive council assisting the governor and has the power to negotiate international trading pacts.

The gold exchange, above, has been frenetic in recent years, but Jardine, Matheson & Co's board room, right, is usually composed.

Virtue As Vice
And Vice-Versa

You see, Hong Kong is a "vice-versa" place. That is, all vices elsewhere are virtues here. The visitor should be warned that the accepted description of Hong Kong by some of the "old hands" is quite misleading. They will take a visitor to a great meal, with great wines, and solemnly tell him that Hong Kong is "sheer materialism, old man," a money-grubbing joint with no soul. They will say that it "pulls down all its fine old buildings and erects dead

• *Luxury:* What you enjoy from hard work and shrewd bargaining. Most of the rich in Hong Kong, a generation or less ago, were beggars, duck-farmers, tailors, dispossessed bourgeoisie and sundry malcontents from all round the region; among the Westerners, a lot were and are night-school students from Peckham and Peebles and Manhattan and Melbourne. They are "self-selected" — that is, they are all refugees of one kind or another, from the bloodthirsty cruelties of politics, or from the greediness and incapabilities of governments, from Peking to Pittsburgh.

eyesores in their place." Well, the old buildings were not that good, mostly pastiche and fake — neo-Romano-Graeco stuff, Brighton Victorian, and poorly finished. The new buildings are not bad — not bad at all; take a look into some of them.

Yes, Hong Kong has a soul, believe it or not. But it helps if you remember the vice-virtues of Hong Kong. A short guide to them:
• *Materialism:* Another word for hard work, and the ability of individuals and families to take their lumps, accept trouble and fight their way out of it, find new jobs, new incomes, share poverty and prosperity, eat well, drink well, and make do with small pleasures. Materialism means self-reliance and solvency, both public and private.

They came because they wanted to try things out; Hong Kong is a collection of ragged-trousered volunteers.
• *Anarchy:* Another word for freedom. See the description of "government" above. This government of Hong Kong, if it can be identified at all, gives almost no incentives for either work or capital — but, more important by far, it doesn't get in your way, either. You can set up a company within a week; there are no ownership rules, no currency controls, and precious little registration necessary. If you join the anarchy, then you can take all the credit for your successes, but you must take all the blame for your failures. Fair enough?
• *Greed:* Another name for "consumer demand," which is a leading economic virtue.

Consumer demand is extremely buoyant and elastic in Hong Kong. Income earners in Hong Kong, somehow, manage to do the impossible — they spend a lot of what they get, and they save a lot, too. See a good economic theorist. Or better still, work in Hong Kong. Taxes are low, by the way.

Overtaking the Wongs

• *Envy:* Another name for what the economists call the "demonstration effect." Hongkongians work in the faith that if the other guy can make it up to the Mercedes level, then they can, too. It isn't a question of "keeping up with the Wongs"; the name of the game is overtaking them.

• *Gluttony:* Another name for good taste and enjoyment, the final consumer demand that drives economies forward. All those yachts you see in the Hong Kong marinas, all those television sets, all those cars on the ridiculously crowded roads, all those packed restaurants — the people devouring those things have not got their money from rich aunts, privileges and sinecures; they have got it from screwing the last cent out of every second of time. Here it would be appropriate to quote from Dr. Samuel Johnson, the great guru of the rationalist revolution of the 18th Century:

> There are few ways in which a man
> can be more innocently employed
> than in getting money.

• *Avarice:* Another name for savings, the accretion of capital, which in previous eras has been highly regarded as a virtue. In this cen-

tury, somehow or other, it seems to have been condemned by a vocal minority of envious people (usually in very comfortable jobs) who talk about "materialism."

• *Pride:* This is sometimes a virtue, sometimes a vice. Hong Kong has no pride in its "traditions" especially — maybe a few in its memories. It has no jingo chauvinism; it has no national anthem (it sings that British one when people from the Royal Family come to call). It has no bloodthirsty harangues about its armed forces and their invincibility — the "armed forces" are a few Ghurkas, a flight of helicopters and a couple of small gunboats.

Instead, Hong Kong has pride (which at times comes close to arrogance) in its professionalism, its craft, its flexibility, its incredible cosmopolitan clout. Its academic record is almost nil, but its practical record is rivalled only by one or two other small nations, most of which are — guess where? — here on the east side of Asia. When you visit Hong Kong, you are in the middle of a set of countries which have taken their economic fortunes by the scruff of the neck and shaken them into prosperity. No mean feat.

Commerce, Sweet Commerce

Materialist? Cruelly capitalist? Unthinking, uncaring? No, it's not really like that at all. Oh sure, Hong Kong is no massive government "welfare state" — but there is that housing programme, one of the biggest in the wide world; there are hundreds of private and public charitable bodies, and a lively voluntary Community Chest. The Hongkongian may seem rude and rough when he jostles you on the packed sidewalks; in private, he is generous, cooperative and much given to self-help and clan-help and much quiet mutual support.

Oh sure, the city is a busy and sometimes cold place to the newcomer. You have to make your own way, form your own society, bit by bit. But when you have done that, you will find that you have a warm, helpful circle — and what is more, if you want to, it can be composed of all the races on earth. There *is* a Hong Kong society, and it is not the fly-by-night, make-the-money-and-run affair that it is often dubbed; it is complex, and fascinating, and competitive-cooperative, and is based on all

ment of the total society and economy, the tackier side of drugs, hawking and prostitution. It is negligible in the government as such, except perhaps in the field of public works and other construction (and some say the police have weak moments). As for corruption in private-sector commercial life, it boils down to "secret commissions," "finders' fees" and all that jive; commerce is what Hong Kong lives by, and if you think that commerce is a sweet, soft slush fund, then don't come to Hong Kong to do it. Take the corruption stories, like the brandy, with a splosh of water. Remember only one thing — Hong Kong lives by its wits.

Maybe, one day, the giant stage-set of Hong Kong will be dismantled, and this Dallas-by-

those vice-virtues given above.

Corruption? Alas, yes. Although the big syndicates are said by the Independent Commission Against Corruption (a much embattled permanent official body) to have been broken up, corruption still exists.

On The Tacky Side

A lot of the corruption is still organized and exploited by Europeans, too, you know. It is sad, therefore, but it affects only a tiny seg-

Every safe deposit box in the vault at the Hong Kong and Shanghai Banking Corporation (left) has a good story to tell. Above, a gold merchant admires the soft and rich feel of his bullion.

the-sea will disappear or disintegrate. Which would be a pity. Along with only a few other places, like Singapore and Seoul and Taipei, Hong Kong exemplifies the solution to the world's energy problem. No, not all that hassle over oil and coal and solar heating and nuclear fission — but the energy potential in man, how he makes his way in the world.

Take all those "vices" listed above. They come from old feudal societies, and are designed to keep most people in their societal places, and to keep all the goodies for the rich and powerful.

Well, Hong Kong's vice-virtues look set to be the parameters of the future . . . though of course no one can say for sure. To look at Hong Kong in all its frenetic variety is to witness what Alvin Toffler, presciently enough, called "future shock."

WHERE BUSINESS WORKS

Having no raw materials worth very much, except the most valuable raw material of all, energetic people, Hong Kong lives by trading and organizing, and turning other countries' raw materials and components into final goods; its typical exports are garments, watches, toys, electrical gadgets and a host of plastic items. But it also exports some boats and ships, and some components for the other countries to work up into *their* final goods. Finally, it is China's main trading port, handling a large and rising proportion of that giant country's rising trade, together

with most of the trade of the Portuguese territory of Macau next door.

Since it has little local produce, it imports huge amounts of consumer goods — foodstuffs, French wines, Scandinavian furniture, you name it, and a whole raft of Japanese consumer whatsits, as well as capital goods like machinery and equipment, and all the raw materials it needs. It is therefore a very good customer for a hundred other countries, on all the continents. Hong Kong makes its income from "value added," in the form of processing, assembly, financing, communications and all the myriad paper-shuffling of commerce, insurance, documentation, shipping, air freight, fees, commissions, accountancy, etc., etc.

Hong Kong's First Commandment: Know How to Make Money

The economy is extremely flexible, thanks to a general policy on the part of the government to intervene as little as possible in the business process. The establishment of a business is easy and cheap; money and staff are freely moved in and out; there are a few government incentives for industry, chiefly involving the leasing of land and the building of specialized accommodation for "flatted factories." There are few disincentives, in the form of controls or niggling regulations. The government assumes that when you start a business in Hong Kong, you know how to make money at it, and that you will be honest enough to declare the taxable income (at the low rates of tax on private and corporate income, it is barely worth spending time and money on avoiding it); so it leaves you alone. There are many chambers of commerce, a Trade Development Council which organizes overseas promotions, many lively trade commissions from many countries, and a lot of legal and accountancy help.

The connections with China are very close, and Hong Kong is Peking's main source of foreign exchange earnings. In very recent times, China has changed its economic philosophy a great deal, introducing free enterprise elements and a more open economy; some of the Chinese provinces have been given a measure of independent action, and two of these are near Hong Kong — Kwangtung (Gwangdong) and Fukien (Fujian). Both trading and financial links between China and Hong Kong have therefore increased enormously in importance very recently.

Hong Kong has no import or export duties, only some domestic "excises" on petroleum products, tobacco products, wines and spirits and a few other things; these are directed at the domestic consumer for revenue purposes. There are duties and licences on vehicles, of course (these have been steeply raised from time to time, in an attempt to moderate vehicular traffic, but they have totally failed to do so). There are health and agricultural products regulations on imports and exports, controls to suppress the narcotics trade, and controls on firearms and ammunition.

In Hong Kong, all but the infirm or dishonourable work, whether at a pipeworks, left, or at the Kwai Chung container terminal, right.

Hong Kong is thus a free trade area. Attracted by its success, China has now started to develop its own free trade export zones nearby, just across the border from both Hong Kong and Macau. These are designed especially as sites for mutual ventures, which usually take the form of businesses in which China supplies the land, buildings and labour, while the foreign partner supplies foreign exchange, equipment and know-how. An interesting arrangement is the "compensation trade" method of financing — the foreign partner does not receive profits or interest on

reached over 4 per cent a year. The place is therefore very crowded. With a land area of only 1,050 square kilometers, the density is 4,828 people per square kilometer; but fully 70 percent of the land area is mountains and uninhabited islands, so the true "livable-area" density is over 16,000 people per square kilometer. One corner of Kowloon called Mongkok is alleged to be the tightest-packed mass of humanity anywhere on earth. But with every mouth, there comes a pair of hands, and Hong Kong hands work well ...

The main task of the Hong Kong govern-

the money he puts in, but supplies of the product or service which the joint venture produces (a foreign firm which helps to build a hotel, for instance, gets to sell a proportion of the rooms on its own account, or in the case of a factory producing textiles, the foreigner gets a proportion of the output).

Affluence as a Problem

Hong Kong had about 5.5 million people as of 1983; the population is growing at about 1.5 per cent a year as far as natural increase is concerned, but there has been a very large and almost unaccountable number of illegal immigrants from China in recent years, so the total population increase at times may well have

ment is a very obvious one: to arrange and encourage the housing, feeding and employing of this large and accelerating mass of people. In addition to a continuous programme of public housing, the government is building four complete new industrial town areas in the New Territories which were "leased" from China in the last century and will be handed back (with the rest of the place) in 1997. When completed, these new urban areas will contain 2-3 million people, and will help to take up a great deal of the population.

In such a crowded place, with a busy people always on the move (as you will discover the first time you are jostled on the pavements), a lot of government and private expenditure goes into the "infrastructure" — especially modes of travel. The road system is perpetually being extended and improved and the Hong Kong government is committed to spend more than HK$100 billion in public sector construction over the next decade, much of it will be on roads, including a coastal highway along Hong Kong traffic-choked north shore. A US$2.2 billion air-conditioned underground railway (the MTR) stretches from Kowloon and the New Territories under the harbour to Central District — some 25 stations spread over 26.1 kilometers. A US$1.2 billion Hong Kong Island extension with 14 stations (two were already in existence) spread over 12.5 kilometers opened in 1985.

There is a vehicular traffic tunnel under the harbour (and another HK$3 billion one

around US$6,574 by the end of the year 1985, and has been growing at an average rate of 9½ percent in real terms. This is one of the highest growth rates in the world. The GDP per person is about the same as Singapore's, 20 times that of India and about a quarter of that of the United States. The incomes are skewed, with a few rich and a lot of poor — but a large and increasingly aspiring middle-class. It is from this class that Hong Kong, like all capitalist countries, gets its prosperity; the place is driven by ambitious small proprietors and professionals, shrewed brokers and bankers and middlemen.

In very recent times, Hong Kong's problem has become that of affluence, because of those high growth rates. Money supply has been soaring; consumption expenditure ditto; con-

is scheduled to open in 1989 or 1990), in addition to a cat's-cradle of ferries in all directions round the waters of the territory — from island to island. Hong Kong's airport has got to be unique in the world now — it is in the middle of residential Kowloon! Hong Kong also squeezes in a container port, which is so busy that it ranks third in the world in container throughput (after New York and Rotterdam). When its expansion plan is completed in 1988, the port will be number two in the world with a capacity of some 2.2 million TEUs (20-foot units).

The Gross Domestic Product per capita (the total value of goods and services produced in the place divided by the population) was

struction and property development ditto. Hong Kong receives more than three million foreign visitors every year, but one million Hongkongians now travel abroad each year, despite the fact that most of them hold only a shaky document called a Certificate of Identity (which means they must have a visa to go to the bathroom). The explosion of real incomes threatens to price Hong Kong's goods out of export markets — and *that* would be catastrophic. But the people have a record of being ingenious and flexible in their business, and their challenge is to continuously switch the pattern of their capital and consumption spending around to meet the new demands of each arising situation, to avoid the worst dangers of damaging domestic inflation.

Fiscally, Hong Kong is very conservative indeed. The government has had a surplus on every annual budget since the mild recession of the early Seventies. The reasons for the overflow of money are the buoyant tax and land sale revenues, the latter making up some 60 percent of government revenues. But Hong Kong's markets are particularly cyclical and with so much money coming from the over-inflated property values, the government went into a rare fiscal deficit in the 83/84, 84/85 and 85/86 financial years, reflecting the dramatic fall in the property market. But Hong Kong is a crowded place and there are limits to what a government can do in the way of spending — budget expenditures run up against sheer barriers of work-space and workers. And another point; a number of

Hong Kong lives by foreign trade, of course. Its importance may be judged by the fact that total trade (exports plus imports plus re-exports) is estimated at US$59.01 billion for 1985 with a Gross Domestic Product of US$39.6 billion (+4% on 1984). That was the "visible" trade alone; if the "invisibles" were added in, the income from commerce and communications, then in balance of payment terms the total foreign activity would be likely be three times the GDP.

Hong Kong has no central bank, partly because the public debt has been negligible, and partly because a group of big banks plus the government Banking Commissioner's Office seem to have looked after the currency with little difficulty. Key interest rates

government departments are so efficient that they cover their costs with their income — the Post Office, for instance.

As a percentage of Gross Domestic Product, however, government expenditure is very high, amounting to some 19 percent in the 1983/84 financial year, having doubled in the last decade. More than half the public spending is on public works, schools, housing, health service facilities, etc. In Hong Kong, the utilities are all in the private sector, except the water supply (and that is because a proportion of the water comes by pipeline from China).

Whether you fancy a flawless porcelain piece, left, or blue jeans faded to taste, above, all are here within a coin's toss of one another.

were set for years by a tiny sub-committee of the Hong Kong Exchange Banks Association. But in 1981, the statutory Hong Kong Association of Banks took over. It has obligatory membership for all banks and its chairmanship will alternate between the two note issuing banks, The Hong Kong and Shanghai Banking Corporation and the Chartered Bank.

The Association has to consider not only the domestic money flows, but also the general trend of rates elsewhere, because money flows into and out of the place, being subject to no controls, can be considerable. The banknotes are issued by two leading banks (under the guidance of the government, of course) and the coins are issued by the government — a

53

typical "mixed economy" arrangement.

The money supply grows by fluctuating percentages each year, depending on the foreign and domestic trade fortunes of Hong Kong — it shrank in two years (1971 and 1973), but has tended to rise steeply again in recent years, by more than 20 percent in 12 months. Nevertheless, the cost of living has not risen to the same degree; even in the grossly inflationary years 1979 and 1980, consumer price indexes rose between 12 and 16 percent a year, depending on the income-level. The sharpest increases have been in rents for all sorts of accomodations, and the government bowed to pressure in 1973 to impose limits on rents for residential property, which were lessened in 1980 and again in 1983, 1984 and 1985.

the savings "habit" goes deep in the society, and at the counters of the lordly banks who accept longer-term deposits you will see many very modestly-dressed people like hawkers and fishermen. Total time and savings deposits have recently been approaching HK$10,000 per person on the average. Gross domestic savings as a ratio to domestic product are well over 20 percent, which level is taken by economists as a sign of good, capitalist take-off into sustained growth. These figures also indicate confidence in the local economy — otherwise those millions would be fleeing abroad.

The taxation system is very simple, with low rates on both individual and corporate incomes, and with the minimum of rules, allowances, exemptions and all that clutter of cal-

Hong Kong is extremely well-banked, to put it mildly. To give numbers of commercial and merchant banks and their branches at this point would be to invite a swift overtaking of events; suffice it to say that as of 1985 there were 143 commercial banks licensed to operate over the counter in Hong Kong, and 131 representative offices. Demand deposits and time deposits in commercial banks have risen to five times their size in the period 1969-1979. And Hong Kong banks are so liquid that when there was a run on the Hang Lung Bank in 1982 (due to false rumours of the bank's connection with a faltering property giant) the Chartered Bank transferred HK$1 billion in cash overnight. Savings deposits alone have risen 10 times —

culation that appears on most countries' schedules. Offshore income is, in general, exempted from local taxation, although in the case of some banking activities, where a loan borrowed and lent offshore is actually organized in Hong Kong, part of the income is taken into the tax net.

If you are an employer, all you have to do regarding staff pay is to account to the authorities for the total pay of any employee who receives more than the personal allowance; there is no "Pay As You Earn" or withholding tax on individual incomes, but some forms of interest receivable are taxed at source. You can buy tax certificates if you want to pile up your taxes in advance, and get a so-so rate of interest on them.

Licences, where needed, are obtained swiftly and usually without corruption; government offices are helpful and efficient. You should register a business name, for a small fee; formation of a private limited company is swift and cheap; licences and permissions are required, for instance, to sell the goods subject to excises, to run a restaurant, to build a new building and to occupy it. All land is Crown Land, on various long leases; when a lease falls through, the government usually auctions off the new one (and prices for leases of prime sites in Hong Kong have now become the highest in the world).

Harnessing of the Hong

A description of the Hong Kong economy would be incomplete without mention of the big trading houses called *hong*. The four leading hong are of British foundation, including Jardine Matheson, Wheelock Marden, Hutchison Whampoa and the Swire Group. There are also two big conglomerates whose bases are elsewhere in the world, Sime Darby and Inchcape, which hold significant interests in Hong Kong. But recently, thanks to a very active takeover bid market, mergers and other financial arrangements, British control of the hong is waning. New and energetic Chinese groups, based on shipping and property and the textile industry, are beginning to build new "empires" and have even taken over one of the old British-founded concerns (Hutchison Whampoa). These new entrepreneurs bring to the Hong Kong economy the same businesslike, even buccaneering, spirit that the British once did. They enjoy the same cooperation of the government that their predecessors did, plus the trust and cooperation of the new administration in Peking. Their arrival on the scene changes a few names on the roll of chairmen and directors of Hong Kong Inc., but it does not change the system — the system under which both public and private enterprise vie to expand and rebuild the economy at an almost frightening speed, but deftly and skillfully.

What is the secret of Hong Kong's fiscal and banking and commercial success? No one is quite sure. Because of this, and because so many businessmen and administrators are somewhat inarticulate on the subject, you will hear some people complain that the "system" is all wrong, and that everything should be done some other way. Experts

sometimes come to Hong Kong, intending to teach the Hongkongians how to run a society; they go away sadder and more confused than ever.

It all looks like chaos on the outside, but perhaps it is the chaos of the new jigsaw puzzle, freshly stirred on the table-top. Somewhere, every piece fits. But the trouble is that by the time you have fitted all the pieces neatly together, the whole economy has changed, and a fresh box of pieces arrives. Hong Kong is an "organic" entity; it grows from its internal pressures and needs, and is at the mercy of the world of trade and the shifting winds of history. It has to seek a perpetual state of dynamic balance, in a nastily fluctuating world. It abhors rigidity. Flexibility is all.

A patient lady in a cashier's cage quietly waits for dollars to roll into her lair, left; above, construction workers vibrate through yet another structure. Hong Kong does work.

WHO RULES? THE LION OR THE DRAGON?

Hong Kong investors should put their hearts at ease.
-- Deng Xiaoping

When those reassuring words from China's Vice Chairman were spoken during a face-to-face meeting with this British Crown Colony's Governor, Sir Murray MacLehose, in March, 1979, Hong Kong's business and financial community heaved a collective sigh of relief. Like men on death row, another reprieve had stayed the colony's precarious life yet again.

Those words were enough to push any thought of Sino-British Agreement into the background. And they were interpreted as an indication that China wanted to continue the lucrative *status quo* under the British. (A solution not without precedent since China did not take Macau back when it was offered in 1974. Rather it retained sovereignty and became a "Chinese territory under Portuguese administration," complete with a Portuguese governor and flag.)

Deng also told Sir Murray that China intended to take over Hong Kong's sovereignty when the time was ripe. He never publicised that remark until December 1982 at which time China and Britain were in acrimonious negotiations over Hong Kong's fate.

Just who ruled Hong Kong is probably no longer a moot point. There was no doubt the British governed this 400-sq-mile capitalist enclave, having secured that lease-holder's right by virtue of three 19th Century treaties. But since the advent of China's Communist government in 1949, the ruling British and the ruled Cantonese have accepted that Hong Kong's existence is China's whim.

Peking Calling

The Chinese had always called the three treaties "unequal" but were happy to leave things alone, calling the question of Hong Kong an internal one to be settled at China's convenience. That's the way things stood until British Prime Minister Margaret Thatcher's visit to China in September 1982. The Chinese reiterated their stand that they have sovereignty over the colony because they never recognised the "unequal"

Sir Edward Youde, Hong Kong's 26th governor arrives in May 1982.

treaties. To the sovereignty question, the British, fresh from a victorious battle in the Falkland Islands, responded that treaties are contracts under international law and all discussions must start from there. Talks began on what would happen when the lease on the New Territories expires in 1997. Since the land under lease comprises nine-tenths of the territory and Hong Kong would never be able to live without it, the talks were really about the fate of the colony as an entrepôt.

The stale cliché, oft repeated and much believed, was that Peking could at any time

reclaim Hong Kong with a single phone call to London.

The Sino-British talks touched off a run on the stock-market, acted as a catalyst to nudge the property-market balloon downward and caused the Hong Kong dollar to move in the same unfortunate direction. But judging from the various post-Mao transfers of power, China seems to have re-gained stability. China's cultural revolution is hopefully gone forever—its Maoist social blueprint having been modified to suit a more realistic view of China's global position. Hong Kong will be passing through another period of uncertainty as the years dwindle away to 1997 when Hong Kong becomes a Special Administrative Region of China—

ostensibly autonomous in most things—under a 50-year one-government-two-systems guarantee. The year 2047 is a long way away, however.

Pampering the Dragon

If logic were the only guideline, Hong Kong's future, as a Special Administrative Region of China, would be secure as long as it remained an entrepôt, China's window to the commercial world. Under Maoist leadership in particular, Hong Kong had been regarded as less a political entity than a commercial necessity, a sort of wily handmaiden to Communist Peking; running errands and handling business deals with ideologically abhorrent "Outer Barbarians." But

as an offshore base because of its harbour by British's squabbling trade-infatuated "merchant princes" in the mid 1800s, neither China nor the British really wanted it.

The man who "possessed" the island for Queen Victoria, the intrepid Captain Charles Elliot, Royal Navy, was told to leave it alone and concentrate on spearheading Britain's trading interests in China's mainland ports. Lord Palmerston, the Foreign Secretary at the time, contemptuously dismissed it as "a barren island with hardly a house upon it." Its first administrator, Sir Henry Pottinger, was forced to take his subordinates to task for planning roads, allocating land and generally launching development against the home government's wishes, while he was away fighting the first Opium War against the Chinese.

chauvinism and nationalism also played an important part in the negotiations on Hong Kong; hence the prolonged uncertainty. There was also China's basic underlying mistrust in its refuge-minded population.

Viewing the Middle Kingdom's turbulent history, the uneasiness that pervades the territory is understandable. Will Hong Kong enjoy another half century of freedom and capitalism under Chinese sovereignty? Will the current Hong Kong government turn into a lame-duck administration as the clock ticks on to 1997? This immediate worry is of greater concern at the moment to the people of Hong Kong than the larger question of their future from 1997 to 2047 and beyond.

When Hong Kong Island was first claimed

It took two years for the British Government to actually grant Hong Kong official status as a Crown Colony, and even then the recognition was given with the sort of jaundiced eye with which Westminster has regarded Hong Kong ever since.

The truth is that Hong Kong has never been the Empire's showplace, the "Jewel of the East," that its own administrators and supporters in Britain would liked have. It had always been something of a colonial embarrassment, a disreputable black sheep located sufficiently east of Suez to be largely ignored and left to its devices.

As a trading post it was an immediate failure. Pottinger, the colony's first governor, prophesied that it would become a "vast emporium of commerce and wealth." In fact, it could not compete with the rich mainland treaty ports like Shanghai and languished for many years as a backwater retreat, opium depot, and a haunt for pirates, smugglers and other less illustrious characters of the British Empire. Its early administrations were peppered with the sort of scandalous characters who have been a familiar blot on successive Hong Kong governments up to the present day — incompetents, exploiters, distressed judiciary, corrupt police and civil servants, and more than a few con-men and outright criminals. 'Tis no wonder that descriptions like "detestable society" and "grotesque anomaly" were pinned to Hong Kong in its early days.

Right into the late 1920s, when piracy was

such that no real attempt was made to defend it and it fell quickly to the Japanese on Christmas Day, 1941, after a token, but desperate fight by Hong Kong volunteers, British and Indian Army regulars and a raw, untested expeditionary unit from Canada.

Yet for all its inauspicious history, Hong Kong has survived and indeed flourished. It has outlived the old Treaty Ports and remained a British-administered outpost in the wake of global decolonization, and survives incongruously as a capitalist bastion on the very edge of a gigantic Communist society.

Today it is listed among the top **20** trading nations in the world and is a manufacturing giant in its own right. It has confounded everyone, even the British, by fulfilling Sir Henry Pottinger's dream of a vast, wealthy Eastern

still rife, the colony's main role was that of a staging point for British troops rushed out here to protect the Shanghai concession (where the real political and commercial wheeling and dealing was going on). During the 1930s the colony had something of a strategic importance as a cross-roads for shipping and travel within the eastern sphere of Britain's empire. Other than that, it was simply a haven of British rule, and therefore British law, for Britons who found themselves in an otherwise alien and often troubled region.

In World War II, Hong Kong's value was

Chinese paper money, left, isn't worth much in the colony, but the colony isn't worth much without Chinese blessings. Above, Gurkhas.

emporium. And it did this not through any real determined struggle of its own, but because the Chinese ultimately wanted it that way.

After China's Communist Revolution of 1949 and the lowering of the so-called "Bamboo Curtain" on the world-at-large, both Hong Kong, and the nearby Portuguese-ruled enclave of Macau, were left intact by the Chinese leadership as convenient windows to the world. They became offshore venues in which the Communists could indulge in capitalist dealings without the danger of tainting their domestic ideology or exposing their people to harmful influences. Hong Kong's status hinged (and still hinges) upon just how useful it could be to Peking.

Milking the Money Machine

Hong Kong served Peking well. It was soon acting as its main intake and clearing house, evading Western trade embargoes to the point where China earns about US$6 billion in foreign exchange annually, an estimated 35 to 40 percent of its hard currency which it sorely needs to pay for its current "modernization" programme.

At the same time the colony became a dumping ground for Chinese undesirables and was flooded with refugees and immigrants, largely southern Cantonese, who obviously weren't going to slot peacefully into the Maoist revolutionary scheme. This influx swelled Hong Kong's population from its 1946 level of a mere 600,000 to well over 3.5 million by 1966.

creaking, strife-torn, tax-riddled old pensioner on the other side of Suez.

But unlike the British motherland, Hong Kong is not a democracy. It's a contemporary anachronism, a living museum piece of colonial power and economics. A working model of the perfect corporate state. A benevolent dictatorship, if you like.

Parameters of the Pyramid

Hong Kong is now ruled by an administrative pyramid topped by a governor appointed by Whitehall in the name of the Sovereign. Below is a 21-member Executive Council of civil servants, the Commander of British Forces which includes 10 "unofficial" members of the public sector, normally

It also gave the colony a large pool of cheap, exploitable labour with which to develop its industrial infrastructure based on textiles and electronics. The bamboo floodgate remained open and another 500,000 illegal immigrants from China arrived here between 1978 and 1980 alone. Recent stern legislation, however, has curbed that deluge.

Today, Hong Kong's existence rests entirely upon its ability to *make a fast buck*. It is a well-milked money-making machine, and as such is looked upon with favour by Peking — especially since China itself is now turning its dragon's head in a running dog direction. Meanwhile, Hong Kong's own business leaders and colonial administrators now cock their affluent noses at Mother England, that

taken from the business or financial community, each of whom is appointed by the governor. It is the governor alone who decides what matters the council (which meets *camera*) can discuss.

Policy is passed into law by the 56-member Legislative Council which in 1985 met, for the first time in its long history, with elected, instead of appointed, members (albeit only 24 members and they were indirectly elected through functional constituencies).

Toothless Council

The people of Hong Kong have a direct vote for half the representatives to the colony's 30-member Urban Council, the politically toothless equivalent of a municipal authority in the West. The Council is responsible for keeping the twin cities of Hong Kong and Kowloon running smoothly, that is, collecting garbage, running parks, recreation and culture, and licensing restaurants.

Hong Kongites can also vote for about half the members of the District Boards, which the name implies, deal with grass roots problems by area. Another council is the newer Regional Council, a 36-member group with 12 directly elected members and another 9 chosen by the 9 District Boards in the New Territories. This council is similar to the Urban Council, but has, as its bailiwick, the New Territories. All these political activities are aimed at preparing Hong Kong for whatever government it may be that runs the colony after the expiration of the New Territory's lease in June 1997.

The government has promised a review of the election activities — particularly the ones for the Legislative Council — in 1987 in order to fine tune the process. However, they have run into trouble with the Chinese whose ranking member in Hong Kong Xu Jiatun, head of the New China News Agency (his is a political/diplomatic post, not a journalist one), who attacked the government in late 1985 for not following the Draft Agreement. Their distrust of the British was rekindled with these elections even though representative government is specifically mentioned in the Agreement.

The head of the Hong Kong and Macau Affairs Office in Beijing, State Councillor Ji Pengfei (the highest ranking PRC government official ever to visit Hong Kong) tried to play down Xu's remarks during his December 1985 visit, but his deputy, Lu Ping, who arrived in early 1986 for a visit, reiterated Beijing's displeasure with the way the British are preparing local Hong Kong people for self-government. The Hong Kong government has stated it will consult with the Chinese government in 1987 before subsequent steps in the process are taken.

The Hong Kong government solicits its population's opinions through some 400 statutory advisory groups and officially recognized bodies such as trade groups and traditional Chinese welfare organizations called *kaifong*. This system of opinion-seeking,

Left, ceramic dragon wall mural in Peking's Forbidden City. Queen Elizabeth's likeness, above, appears on the colony's charming one cent currency notes.

however, has been criticized as being inadequate because public feeling is, on occasion, only half-heartedly assessed. In 1984, for example initial attempts to introduce legislation on registration fees for taxis were met with fierce opposition by taxi-drivers and criticism by others that not enough consultation had taken place. In 1985, the government and the unofficial consultative process was again taken to task by an outraged public which succeeded in stopping a bill which would do away with juries in commercial trials and managed to modify a "Powers & Privileges Bill" for the expanded Legislative Council which would have affected the freedom of Hong Kong's very free press.

Twin Pressures

So far, this archaic system of *laissez faire* government has meant continuing prosperity; the colony's wealth is plainly visible. Unfortunately, it is bureaucratically top-heavy. Constant overt changes in policy have regularly forced Hong Kong administrators to increase social spending on health, education and medicine. More than HK$100 billion is budgeted for construction in the public sector in the Eighties and roads and low cost housing estates are the biggest budgeted priorities along with schools, hospitals, clinics, and recreational facilities. Sadly, there never seems to be enough money available. The twin pressures of an overheated economy (which regularly forces a cut-back in government spending) and the untimely arrival of probably a half million more immigrants in the late seventies combined to set various housing, medical and educational programs back by five years or more, in spite of official promises.

"How Much Money Do You Have?"

Socially, Hong Kong will suffer. Economically, the colony will succeed. The influx of people has again given Hong Kong industrialists a new supply of cheap labour and has effectively reversed a labour shortage trend of the late Seventies. Though they are banned, restricted and distrusted by most countries in the world, especially by Asian neighurs, Hong Kong's Chinese population faces a grim austerity not unlike that from which most fled. Live here they must, regardless of politics, competition and crowding.

Their only hope is to acquire enough wealth to make their stay pleasant, and to find a future opportunity, somehow, to get out.

ON HONG KONG ROCK, 'ANYTHING GOES'

There are two diametrically opposed catch-phrases by which people in Hong Kong live their everyday lives. One is *Anything Goes* and the other is *Don't Rock the Boat*.

Anything goes so far as business and much of one's personal life are concerned. The colony was established on the twin principles of free trade and *laissez faire*, both of which were noble philosophies in an age in which Britain's foreign trade had been monopolized for two centuries by the East India Company.

In the present age, Hong Kong is still, to a great extent, faithful to its founding creeds.

18.5 percent for limited companies — and there's no limit on the amount of money that can be transferred in and out of the colony. Hong Kong is cosmopolitan, but only in the sense that many people of many different nationalities come here to make money, make it fast, and then get out.

Quick Gratification

Hong Kong offers quick gratification, normally a return on investment after five years within a framework of minimal government

Virtually anyone from any part of the capitalist and some of the Communist world, can hang a business shingle here and engage in any business that's not harmful to human life.

The average Hong Kong industrial worker, and that means Chinese worker, earns under HK$3,000 a month, works six days a week, and gets as little as seven days of annual paid leave a year, plus 17 public holidays in addition to a weekly rest day. That's high by Asian standards, but an embarrassment to anyone who is aware that this is, after all, a British colony where British law and ethics presumably apply.

However, both profit and taxable salaries are low — a flat rate of 17 percent for wage-earners and unincorporated businesses and

intervention. In one sense, that's all it really does have to offer. Long-term security is still a question mark even with the Chinese Dragon taking over, though a short-term boom is expected as local and overseas investment and business try to get in before the magic year of 1997

This impermanence has given Hong Kong the continuing holler and ring of a frontier town, a place for the gambling man. With four seething stock exchanges and as many commodities exchanges, it's a place where the "rugged individualist" can "do business" with

"Hong Kong offers quick gratification and minimal government intervention" — on Connaught Road, above, and at Gucci's, right.

62

the freedom of a Victorian mill-owner, free of any real interfering trade unionism or colonial government restrictions.

It's a place where business takes precedence over every other human pursuit, where success is measured by the number of cars, furs, Oriental antiques and diamonds one owns, and by the height at which one lives on The Peak.

It's a high-rolling heaven where expatriates tend to look at life as a series of three-year banking plans (three years being the usual "tour" of employment or duty), where shops always seem to be open, bars never seem to

patriate and Chinese, communicate with one another. Both sides work equally hard at it — Hong Kong's got no real idle aristocracy — but otherwise they stay aloof from each other, the one returning home each night to a standard of living that, at the bottom line, costs nearly three times that of the other.

Expatriate Perks

An expatriate office worker at the bottom end of the expatriate scale will not work here for less than HK$10,000 a month plus perks

close, private clubs abound, and servants are an accepted necessity in any household. Acting as a cushion to all this affluence and privilege, there are more than five million people working damn hard to provide just about anything, *anything,* that one's acquisitive heart desires. In that respect it is an awfully exciting city.

Whilst business is the predominant full-time hobby in Hong Kong, so is it largely the level upon which the colony's two populations, ex-

"The expatriate can cope . . . while the 'local' has to make do." A quartet of Her Majesty's finest, above, cruise into the imperial past.

(perquisites). A Chinese office worker, classed as "locally hired," is eligible for public low-cost housing, in which half the colony lives and can retire at the age of 60 after 25 years of service on a monthly salary of HK$2,500 to 5,000.

In the government, the biggest single employer in Hong Kong, an expatriate civil servant signs on for 2½ years, is expected to pay only 7½ percent of his salary as rent and can look forward to leaving — or taking his accrued holiday — before his next tour begins. Added to this is a gratuity of 25 per cent of his total earnings plus three months' full-paid leave and travel expenses. These expatriate terms, which are of course topped by the private sector, are denied to most Chinese

employees; only those who fight their way into the upper echelons of the bureaucracy are thus rewarded.

With his accommodation paid for, the expatriate can cope with Hong Kong's grotesquely inflated rents — and help push them up — while the "local" has to make do in cheaper, tightly packed urban tenements or gigantic, industrial-design public housing estates with floor-space allocations that would be considered scandalous and unlivable in the West.

The expatriate, including one who is

Laissez faire, or non-boat-rocking, reached its prosperous zenith in the late Sixties when much money was salted away in London banks and little was spent locally on housing, health or education. In response to this British habit of saving money for a rainy London day, Hong Kong's Chinese suddenly and violently rocked the boat. Inspired by the fervour of mainland China's Red Guard rampage, a local campaign of riots, strikes and bombings erupted here and hit the colony where it hurt most — its confidence in the colony's future. Money and people fled until Peking, by con-

"temporarily" here for a lifetime, knows that he's eventually going to leave — returning to his home country with a considerable bankroll and, if he is philanthropic enough, a Royal Honour on the Birthday Honours List for "services to the community." Conversely, the Hong Kong Chinese knows that he is here to stay and has few places to go back to -- except, perhaps, Communist China from where he probably came. He must be happy with what he gets.

This glaring division between the two populations invites consideration of the second of Hong Kong's catch-phrases, *Don't Rock The Boat.* Hong Kong's very survival depends on cheap labour, one is told. Also, *laissez-faire* must reign if investment is to continue.

firming again the value it places on this foreign exchange window, helped quell Red Guard passions and restored peace in the colony.

Though the gulf between typical expatriate and Chinese lives is still wide, Hong Kong is now beginning to move into a new phase of social development in which *almost* anything goes. The romantic "China Coast" life with its "World of Suzie Wong" mystique and lure of instant wealth is gradually giving way to an understanding that Hong Kong can no longer be just a money machine masquerading as a legitimate society.

"The expatriate here knows that he's eventually going to leave." Expatriate pleasure-junkies, above, frolic in Hong Kong's harbour.

THE URBAN BEEHIVE

Atlantis In Reverse

Hong Kong's largely mountainous topography has had much to do with the manner in which the colony's administrators have miraculously squeezed a population of more than five million people into little more than one-tenth of the colony's land space.

Within the twin urban beehives of Hong Kong Island's harbour foreshores and mainland Kowloon live half the colony's people. They have less than nine square feet of living space each, and the Kowloon district of Shamshuipo has a population density of 165,000 people per square kilometer — the highest ever experienced by mankind.

Ramshackle development has been another reason for this big squeeze. Lack of planning, decentralization and housing in past decades forced thousands upon thousands of refugees and immigrants from China straight to the source of Hong Kong's life-blood, the harbour.

In those times of rampant *laissez faire,* Hong Kong solved part of the problem — the scarcity of new commercial space — by simply creating land where none existed, reclaiming it from the harbour.

Nowadays, so much of this reclaimed land exists — approximately 10 sqaure miles has been created since the colony was established — that the entire business district on the island harbour-front, from Queen's Road down to the water's edge, now stands where junks, East Indiamen and tea clippers once rode at anchor. That includes the General Post Office, City Hall, British Forces Headquarters, the Mandarin Hotel, the soaring 52-storey Connaught Centre and the adjacent Exchange Square.

On the mainland side, Kai Tak Airport runway, the Kowloon-Canton Railway terminus, the Kwai Chung Container Port and the entire Tsimshatsui East development (which includes four luxury hotels and a dozen commercial centres) have all virtually risen like an Atlantis in reverse from the seabed.

In the late 1950s, the extent of the reclamation works began to worry the colony's planners. So much of the harbour was slated

Residential high-rises like particular one at left contribute to that Kowloon district's density of 165,000 persons per square kilometer.

for reclamation that engineers feared that tidal currents might be affected by the changing configuration of the shoreline. A hydraulic research station in England settled the question by constructing a 75-foot scale model of the harbour with electronically controlled weirs at either end simulating the tides. Tests showed that only a few minor modifications were needed to avoid damaging the colony's most vital asset.

This harbour reclamation is still going on, mainly along the Wanchai and North Point-Quarry Bay waterfronts on the island, but otherwise the colony has removed its blinkers and taken a new look at itself, discovering hinterland areas suitable for large-scale development in the New Territories.

Three sites at Tuen Mun (Castle Peak), Tsuen Wan and Shatin are currently being turned into vast "new towns," or satellite cities, which will eventually house more than two million people, most of them from the densely populated concrete jungles of Kowloon. A new site in Junk Bay has been designated as another new town and people started moving in in 1986. To give an idea of the new residential pressure cookers that will replace the urban tenements, one public housing complex at Tuen Mun will accomodate no less than 90,000 people.

Overcrowding — too little land and too many people — is put forward as a reason for many of the inequities of Hong Kong's society. What it means is that there's not enough *flat* land where immense industrial-residential estates can be built. In fact, Hong Kong has a great deal of unused land, hilly though it is, in the backwaters of the New Territories and on the island itself.

Luxurious Speculation

A trip from Central District ·to the South side of the island, Repulse Bay and then on to Stanley and Shek O reveals large areas of empty, and very scenic landscape — rolling and tumbling hillsides framing some of Asia's prettiest beaches. Towering luxury apartment blocks have been placed in hillside niches, meticulously cut out of the mountain. But genuine fears of landslides have stopped construction of towering flats in Mid-Levels, above Central District, after the disastrous landslides of 1972.

There is certainly pressure on this land, but not from the industry of the population.

The Crown, which owns all land in Hong Kong, is leasing it bit by bit to private developers for luxury, high-rent residential development — and at a pace which keeps the demand for it at such a fierce pitch that the rents are among the most ridiculous, and pitiless, anywhere in the world. On the one side government is attacked for its piecemeal land policies which drive up land prices, but on the government create surplus budgets, keeping taxes low. A no-win situation.

Stanley, for example, a former fishing village on the island's southern coast, now a

developers for luxury residential use.

Another example of this is Lantau, Hong Kong's little-known "sister" island. Lantau is one-and-a-half times the size of Hong Kong Island. It's beautiful. And it's comparatively untouched. Yet the first priority of development has gone to local and international consortiums who have been given the island's best locations to develop luxury residential and holiday resorts, the facilities of which only the wealthier citizens of Hong Kong will be able to enjoy.

People pressure is undoubtedly something

fashionable residential enclave for expatriates trying to escape the Central District and Mid-Levels rat race, illustrates the general pattern of development in Hong Kong. Luxury apartments there (*luxury* by Hong Kong standards) have recently been offered for rent at a staggering HK$10,000 to $30,000 a month. The village is earmarked for redevelopment sometime in the next five years. The government's plans call for the resettlement of a Chinese squatter village — which dates back hundreds of years — that nestles in a picturesque valley and climbs up into the hillsides around the bay. The squatters will be moved into high-rise public housing estates built on land reclaimed from the bay. Then old homesites will be offered to private

of a nightmare for Hong Kong's planners, as anyone standing in the middle of the island's Causeway Bay area, or Mongkok and Shamshuipo on the Kowloon side, will quickly agree. But within the principle of *laissez faire* that insists on ruling most of what goes on in Hong Kong, the main bulk of the people are simply being crammed into new pressure cookers to leave the most attractive land free for speculators.

"In the urban beehives of Hong Kong Island's foreshores and Kowloon live half the people, each in less than nine square feet of space."

LIFE IN HONG KONG: SCHEMES AND DREAMS

Dreaming high over Hong Kong, staring down across the kaleidoscopic sweep of the harbour, Wong Ming — our man in the street — gazes at far-off islands misting into the horizon. Up here, on Victoria Peak, he sees the whole range of Hong Kong's lifestyles sprawling out below. Scattered sparsely across the jade green hillsides are the white mansions of the rich and super-rich: European-style country houses and a few traditional Chinese homes, the latter usually tiered with ceramic tiled roofs and curved eaves.

Below snuggles the lower executive belt, suburban Mid-Levels and its smart apartments. Farther down the city anthills into tiny alleys and the ups-and-tumble-downs of ladder streets, each connecting one main road with the next and linking mid hill with sea level. Here rise the old tenements of Western, Wanchai and Kennedy Town. The flats here are over-crowded and iron-barred, but each has a neat balcony garden — a tiny growing reminder of the farms and small land holdings of neighbouring Kwangtung (Guangdong) Province. Here, in a dense city, love of earth is reduced to the tender care of flower pots.

Even farther away, round the curve of a hill beyond Wong Ming's eyes, are the housing estates. In these dingy overcrowded hives humming with the *mahjong* clack of worker bees, labourers rest noisily on their one-day-off-a-week; windows are bedecked with a working man's flag — shirts, pants and children's socks.

Wong Ming turns to watch a Rolls Royce purring up The Peak. In the back seat a man in a dark suit sits pensively, alternately staring at the back of his chauffeur's head and reading afternoon papers. He's Chinese, of course, as are most of Hong Kong's super-rich. There are wealthy foreigners too — after all, this is not a *laissez faire* economy for nothing — but when it comes to being a straight-up out-front super-rich, only the Chinese really qualify.

Indeed, it is these people who make up the nearest equivalent that Hong Kong has to an aristocracy. Hong Kong is neither old enough, nor perhaps honourable enough, to boast a society marked by good breeding or proper lineage. Money, not genealogy, makes the man here. The great names of Hong Kong are those

Brenda Chau, left, purrs up The Peak in pink mink and pink Rolls Royce with pink chauffeur when she "feels like Jean Harlow." Meanwhile, a traditional chauffeur, right, surveys her lot.

which dominate business; Hotung, the merchant prince; Pao and Tung, the shipping magnates; Lee and Li, the banking and real estate barons; and all the mandarin rest.

Most foreigners trail far behind, both in terms of their money and certainly in terms of their significance, in the real thread of life in Hong Kong; but there are those who catch up and even overtake. The Kadoories, Baghdad Jews who made their family fortunes in Shanghai during the time of the merchant adventurers and later moved to Hong Kong,

are, as well as rich, a local byword for charitable ventures. Noel Croucher, now alas dead, was a traditionally stingy millionaire who doled out secret acts of kindness but regularly walked home to save bus fares. The Harilelas are leaders of an Indian community which is largely comprised of Sindhi merchants. Bona fide philanthropists abound, but so do the rich who become noticed through public acts of extravagance which exceed even Hong Kong's normally self-indulgent standards. Chantal Millar, a stunning South American beauty, will long be remembered as the socialite who paid a million Hong Kong dollars for a three day fund-raising social bash. She flew guests in from all over the world to party with her, then donated the proceeds to charity.

Pink Shadows and Gold Phantoms

Even more conspicuous are the Kai-bong Chaus, well known for their fancy dress costumes and his-and-hers Rolls Royces. Their three ton "works of art on wheels" are a pink Silver Shadow and a sparkling Gold Phantom. The couple, both Cambridge-educated lawyers and scions of two of Hong Kong's leading families, live in a converted garage called Villa d'Oro. Talking of their famous Rolls-Royces, they gush: "We *love* glamourous *things."* Kai-bong Chau, who describes himself as really quite shy, explains that the cars were conceived to fit two of his wife's favourite moods — the pink for "when she feels like Jean Harlow" and the gold for "Cleopatra occasions." Matching clothes (including a pink

mink) and interiors — not to mention a colour-coordinated chauffeur in pink or gold uniform — "adds to the mystique," explains Mr Chau. The paintwork was done in Hong Kong, because Rolls Royce officials in England apparently could not quite bring themselves to understand what moody wife Brenda and shy Kai-bong had in mind for their opulent beasts.

Wong Ming watches the Rolls Royce with wonder, but does not for one moment think life is unfair to him, who has so little. Instead, as he stares at the car he thinks wistfully of the day when he will *make it,* when he too will join the privileged ranks of the super-rich. Indeed, his is a dream dreamed by every poor factory worker, street hawker and construction site labourer in Hong Kong. It's a vision which feeds many local fantasies because, for many hard-working others, the dream has become real. This real dream sequence starts with a cheap watch with Russian works, a little status symbol. Then a cheap digital watch. Then a Rolex. Then a gold Rolex and/or a gold Cartier lighter. Ultimately, one wears monogrammed shirts from Italy, silk ties from France, and collects fine jade and ancient ivory. But, however fanciful a Chinese dreamer becomes, he never forgets his heritage. A rich businessman may modernize himself in a watch, suit, tie, and stiffs under a silk shirt, but the fine jade amulet is worn for more traditional reasons — to repel evil influences and bad luck.

In later dream stages, the same man will frequent auctions held now in Hong Kong by the West's great auction houses — Christie's, Sotheby's and Stanley Gibbon's. These dealers regularly come panting into acquisitive Hong Kong with their best Oriental treasures. (They know well that if a buyer in Hong Kong wants such an object, the price means nothing beside the desire to have the treasure and to take it from those others who want it too.) And if our Wong Ming *makes it* by luck, good business sense, well-applied dishonesty, or hard work, he will readily buy and carry such goods off to a house with a garden, the other sure sign of wealth. In Hong Kong only the wealthy — and farmers — have gardens. Everyone else lives in a highrise apartment.

The Queuing-Up Life

Wong Ming throws down his cigarette, sighs, and sets off for the Peak Tram with his small singing bird in a wicker cage. A breath of morning air for Wong Ming and his bird and then back to ordinary life again. Wong Ming is going home — to a bleak tiny flat in an old public housing estate, where he, his wife and their three young children live the life of Mr. and Mrs. Hong Kong Average.

The silent and rather impassive majority which plays no part in decision-making in Hong Kong, for whom life is not Rolls-Royces, pursue a lot which is a monotonous mixture of hope and ennui. From the womb to the tomb they survive great pressure.

Such people are usually born in one of the government hospitals (home delivery and midwifery are now rare) where medical treatment costs only a nominal amount but where inevitable overcrowding makes conditions uncomfortable. If they want to be born

Gold coins are preserved in plexiglass at Villa d'Oro, left. Right, dapper Hong Kong artist Gerard D. Henderson and his "Kuan Yin."

in more pleasant surroundings, their parents must pay more to go to one of the colony's government-assisted hospitals or private ones. If they later become ill, but not seriously enough to enter a hospital, they have to queue up for first-come first-serve medical aid at one of the colony's government clinics. Treatment there costs only a nominal sum, but Wong Ming often chooses to pay a more expensive private doctor. It's easier to do that than buck the sickly crowds that begin waiting at 6 a.m. for clinics to open at nine.

The kids are all at school, even the four year olds, boiling away in Hong Kong's education pressure cooker, bringing their homework back and spending weary hours every night studying for tomorrow's tests. Lots of tests here, even for the four year olds. But how else

or Australia, where they can establish a family beachhead and eventually sponsor the rest of the family over and out of claustrophobic Hong Kong. One of Hong Kong's biggest unseen exports is its young, sent away for education. Taxi drivers, factory workers, and all their family members will often club together to pay for one child's leap overseas.

Unreal Estates

Wong Ming, like more than half the population of Hong Kong, lives in a public housing estate. It was in the early Fifties that the Hong Kong government started thus to house its poor. The colony's first such estate, the now dilapidated Shek Kip Mei tenement, was built after a huge Christmas fire made 53,000 squat-

will winners be chosen? Exams determine who gets to attend the right kindergartens; then they qualify kindergarteners for the best primary and secondary schools; and, finally, they decide who gets to take university exams. After university one then begins a long lifelong climb up a fiercely competitive employment ladder.

In spite of a lack of good secondary schools, and strict Confucian ethics which often render a passive student unimaginative and uninspired, education is still the best leaping-off point for those who want to *succeed in life*. For their families too. With limited places available in Hong Kong at universities, many families scrape and save to send a son or daughter abroad, usually to the United States, Canada

ters homeless in 1953. Immigrants who had fled from hunger in China, and had erected ragged huts wherever spare patches of land could be found, were burned out of shelter in a few hours. This tragedy inspired the start of an ambitious government programme to house workers who have since become the backbone of Hong Kong's current prosperity. More recent estates are fine examples of urban renewal, but the older ones are a pathetic collection of flats where 11 people may live in a single room and share a communal kitchen, water supply and doorless toilets with the residents of an entire floor. These estates provide inexpensive housing for Hong Kong's masses, but they also have exacted a heavy toll in terms of security, social progress and hope for the future. Regularly disrupted by crimes of violence — rape, robbery and murder — many have become breeding grounds for criminals — and rats.

Illegal Chinese immigrants, many of them discontents from the communes of Kwangtung Province and the streets of Canton, only contribute to this chaos. Upon finding life here much harder than they imagined — work tedious, language difficult and money less valuable than they thought — these disillusioned dreamers have turned to crime and drugs to improve and anaesthetize their dreary lot. Some have joined the legendary "Big Circle," an association of mainland criminals said to be behind Hong Kong's many bank robberies.

Ironically, Hong Kong, despite such squalor, has become the hottest property

Old-Style Spirits In the New Territories

Farmers in the New Territories, Hong Kong's "vegetable garden," are spared most of this urban pain. These rare fortunates have been able to perpetuate a traditional and serene rural life, but legal mastery of the land has often locked even them into a demanding and thankless form of bondage.

It is in the New Territories, however, where Earth Gods still live, attended by housewives and farmers who burn joss sticks to their often shapeless clay forms. Here, water spirits still murmur in freshwater springs and ancient agricultural gods are still accorded proper seasonal respects to ensure good harvests. And traditional houses are still there: low and dark

market in the world. Rents are higher than in Tokyo; a small leasehold apartment in a "low-rent" district can cost a family more than HK$250,000. But despite such fantastic fees, flats often are sold within half an hour after going on the market (or even months before building designs have been approved or a first shovel full of dirt has been dug). These same flats may change hands six times before they are constructed, as they are passed profitably from one shrewd speculator to another. Some people here deal every day in such property futures.

A New Territories farmer waters her plants in a traditional manner, above, and boat people, right, float into an uncertain Hong Kong future.

with tiled roofs and sporting red banners which guard households from the depredations of negative spirits.

Some New Territories farmers still grow rice in terraced paddies which are fed by water channels running down through an age-old irrigation network. The fields sprawl outside old walled villages — where tiny alleys and streets frame old women in extraordinary black-eaved hats.

Such villagers — male and female alike — chug contentedly on their pipes. Some of the walled villages, like Kam Tin — a one-clan place where snarling old ladies charge visitors a dollar a photo — have, unfortunately, become aggressive "tourist traps" where edible chow dogs patrol flat rooftops and warn their masters when moneyed strangers have arrived. But alas, even in the New Territories one finds "urban" incongruities. Ancient houses now sport television aerials and the rutted pathways called streets accommodate shiny new Japanese cars. But despite such clashing modernity, some things Chinese never die. Tiny peeping windows, for example, are purposely cut small into these houses to conform to the architectural requirements of *fung shui,* a Chinese geomancy system which maintains harmony and good fortune in a dwelling according to ancient spiritual principles of *yin and yang.* These principles, however, are so mysterious and complicating that it takes a well-paid *fung shui* expert (or geomancer) to design a house properly.

Nearly all of the people here are Hakka, small leathery farming folk hardened by Hong Kong's changeable weather and tough working lives. These farmers' sons and daughters grow up here, but those who can leave for places like London and San Francisco, where they can enjoy a more comfortable and profitable urban existence. But even though they leave their family farms, once a year, at Chinese New Year, these overseas progeny and their new world money return to their villages in the New Territories and the seemingly deserted and elderly walled villages spring to traditional life once again for two festive weeks.

The Boat People, 'Floating in Jeopardy'

Distinct from Hong Kong's urban rich and poor and the easy-going New Territories farmers is another great tribe who are of Hong Kong and yet not. These are the colony's fisherfolk, they who often spend their entire lives on bobbing junks. In recent years these so-called "boat people" have come onshore to live the life of landsmen, but in Aberdeen, Yaumatei and the colony's typhoon shelters, some rarely leave their floating homes. Most of these fishing people come from two main tribes, the Tanka and the Hoklo, the great majority being Tanka.

There is not much agreement about the origin of the Tanka people. One tale says they are the descendents of a group of people who in ancient times were convicted of treason and were therefore deemed unworthy to live on land. In Canton, according to one explanation, the boat people are the descendants of a general named Lu Tsun, who lived on the island of Honan in 200 B.C. He revolted against the Emperor and was said to have ruled Canton for 30 years. After his death, his people were overwhelmed and then persecuted

by vengeful emperors. During the Tang dynasty they paid punitive taxes and during the Ming dynasty all boatmen between the ages of 18 and 45 were liable to be seized and press-ganged into the Imperial army. However, in 1730 a benevolent Emperor, Yung Ching, took pity on these people. He issued a proclamation which allowed them to live on land in villages near the water if they wished to do so. "Why should they be looked down on, simply because it is customary to do so, and forced to keep separate, passing their days floating about in constant jeopardy of their lives?" he asked.

However, despite this edict, the boat people were still despised. They were forbidden to marry landed Chinese, and they were not allowed to take Imperial civil service examina-

tions. To this day, they are still regarded by most Chinese as being inferior, and they are still victims of discrimination. Of course, there is no government discrimination against them and in recent years many have "come ashore" to take their place among regular land-dwellers. The boatlife is a tough life, and it is often for the future of their children that these people have left the sea. They know that if they remain at sea, their children may remain illiterate, having never stayed in one place long enough to receive a formal education. Besides, many of the boat people find factory work physically easier and more profitable.

Hong Kong boat people who are still seagoing — an estimated 35,000 of them — are very attached to their religious traditions. Most interesting is their ancient worship of Tin Hau, the goddess of the sea. She is one of the most popular deities venerated by the sea people, and they turn to her for comfort, solace and hope, particularly during storms. According to local tradition, Tin Hau was a good-living person who was deified after her death. One of Hong Kong's greatest festivals is Tin Hau's birthday, on the 23rd day of the third moon. It is on this day that the great fishing fleet of Hong Kong sails in all its glory — with banners flying in the wind and flags streaming out behind each vessel — to the most important of the many Tin Hau Temples in Hong Kong —

the Da Miao Temple in Joss House Bay.

Apart from such special religious occasions, it cannot be said that the life of boat people is a festive gypsy-like affair. Like most fishing people all over the world, their seagoing work is difficult and often dangerous. It is physically demanding and their on-deck lifestyle is often cramped and squalid. It is no doubt because of this — and also because of new fishing technology — that so many of the boat people have come ashore to stay.

In the past years, fish landings sold through Hong Kong's Fish Marketing Organization have jumped by one third, despite a decrease in the number of working boat people. This is explained by several developments in the industry.

Vanishing Sails

One reason is the increased use of diesel engines instead of traditional sail power. Because diesel power is more practical now, those beautiful butterfly wing sails which add such charm to Hong Kong's harbour may soon be relics of a romantic past. Picturesque though they are — indeed they are a fond symbol of Hong Kong — they limit vessels to the whims of prevailing wind and allow larger boats to work only in the winter months when the northeast monsoon provides sufficient power for them to tow their trawls successfully. Conversely, smaller sail boats — purse seiners, gill netters and long liners — are unable to risk the gusty winter monsoon and can work only during the summer southwest monsoon when winds are lighter. Today, with diesel power, all vessels and their fishermen work year round. They can also fish longer each day, and machinery cuts the amount of physical effort needed to work. The old fishing gear has gone too. Now the entire fishing fleet uses nets, lines and ropes made from synthetic fibres.

Although all this is officially considered to be for the good, the great capital investment needed these days, plus the greater degree of sophistication required to deal with newer fishing technology, has driven even more poor fishermen ashore. The industry has also become much more competitive, and this may be why a number of junk-operators in the Hong Kong fishing fleet have taken to, or perhaps continued, the colony's old tradition of China Coast smuggling. They have been known to carry consumer goods to China and to bring back gold and silver coins, musk, herbal medicines, and even, on numerous occasions, illegal immigrants who have paid their way out of China to Hong Kong. Whether the poor fishing trade is simply a justification for smuggling is debatable.

It is likely that the end of their fishing life is in sight for many of Hong Kong's "boat people." Many of them, however, are welcoming this return to land and a better life for their progeny. Though it appears to the casual observer on a tour of colourful Aberdeen that this is a free and romantically traditional life, it is really not that great. It's a very trying life, and many of the boat people are only too glad to give it up for government housing on solid land.

The wily Monkey god, left, and at right, anti litter street art.

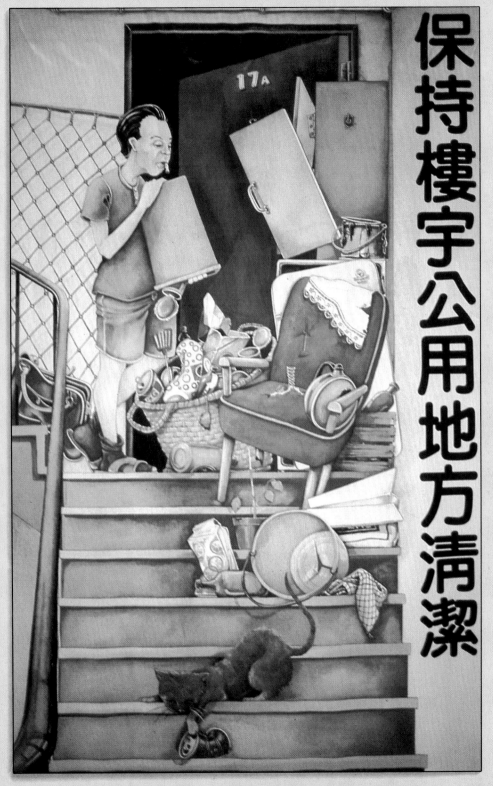

保持樓宇公用地方清潔

HONG KONG THROUGH 'INSCRUTABLE' EYES

At first glance, Hong Kong is everything described in hackneyed epithets — a cement jungle, a bustling port, a capitalist paradise, a British colony. British it still is in status, and anglicized it is on the surface. But underneath this Western facade is a very Chinese mind which stubbornly refuses to change in spite of more than 140 years of British rule.

Chinese attitudes—Chineseness, if there is such a word—remain true to their Oriental traditions, in spite of the present colonial rule and the colony's urbane, modern appearance.

The Chinese sense of superiority today does not differ much from that of centuries ago. Chinese are still of the Middle Kingdom, and everyone else is a barbarian. A mulish ethnic pride transcending nationalities has generated a unique tongue-in-cheek approach to all foreigners, including the ubiquitous British colonial.

A Chinese in Hong Kong may *kowtow* to a British lord in public (previously literally — now metaphorically), but behind a self-effacing inscrutable Oriental mask he hides a humourous contempt for all *gweilo* (foreign devils) regardless of race, colour, and nationality. Thus, the modern Hong Kong Chinese will insult the foreigner while nodding humbly, pleasing the unwitting *gweilo* and himself at the same time. Sometimes he is caught out by the handful of *gweilo* who speak his language, but this, surprisingly, is usually taken with good humour on both sides.

On Tolerating Gweilo

An abundance of nicknames for Westerners have developed over the years. The term *gweilo* originated many years ago with the birth of Chinese xenophobia. Originally it was derogatory, but since the Communist riots of 1967 it is quite openly used by both Chinese and resident foreigners. It is slang now, and more commonly used than the more polite term *saiyahn* (Western person). There are, however, other ruder terms used either vehemently or, again, humourously.

Appropriately, when a child throws a tantrum, his mother may call him a "barbarian devil," the same name she uses to deride a foreigner. And the tired Western joke that "all Chinese look alike" is turned around by Hong Kong's Chinese population, especially those not in regular contact with foreigners, to "all *gweilo* look alike."

Yet, this derision of Westerners, which in a way is a form of resistance to foreign domination, also breaks down, and its psychological opposite, the inferiority complex, surfaces. Hong Kong bus drivers, for example, are notoriously rude to foreigners, particularly Caucasians, who make up the racial majority of foreigners who visit and live here. This colonial mentality, however, is changing quickly. As Hong Kong's youthful population drags older generations into the Eighties (at times copying the West in dress or music or style, while simultaneously challenging the West) it is also demanding equality and expressing pride in being sophisticated Chinese.

God Save the Queen?

In general, the Chinese in Hong Kong look upon their British overlords as efficient and political business managers, but with comic tolerance. Theatres, for example, used to blare "God Save the Queen" as a closing finale, but the practice was dropped years ago because of a lack of patriotic reaction. A few British would stand staunchly throughout the anthem while the Chinese audience shuffled out indifferently, some not even recognizing the tune. When the Queen or some lesser royalty comes to visit, it's a heyday for funseekers and those socially inclined. Chinese school children, who scarcely know who she is, are herded to the airport and stationed along sidewalks to wave little Union Jacks and cheer for a few seconds as Her Highness's royal motorcade races by. To them, the occasion is a delightful break from class. Hong Kong's Chinese leaders and socialites briefly forget their innate Chinese smugness as they, like upwardly mobile counterparts in Britain and the rest of the Commonwealth, vie for invitations to royal functions and dream of seeing their names on the New Year's honours list announcing knighthoods and other, lesser, royal decorations.

In spite of such pretension and feigned royalism, finding a Chinese *truly loyal* (in the British sense of "Queen and Country") to the Queen is perhaps as difficult as looking for a noodle in a haystack. Even civil servants trained in the colonial education system are rarely faithful British subjects at heart. This system deliberately glosses over the history of the Opium Wars. After these wars China ceded Hong Kong to the British in a 19th Century exercise in a gunboat diplomacy as

81

indemnity for losing the battle and to stop British exports of opium into China. Hong Kong's Chinese are basically apathetic. They want simply to be left alone to make money and possibly to emigrate to the West.

Not that they do not take their jobs seriously. They do. But this is more out of an obligation to their families and themselves than to the Crown. Government jobs promise "an iron rice bowl"—a meal ticket for life. If the Sino-British agreement is to be believed, "life" will go on beyond 1997 because the new Chinese government will need administrators and managers too. British rule always appeared the benevolent lesser of other possible evils. To a refugee-minded population, most of whom have escaped Communist China in various waves since 1949, a departure of the British and a subsequent Communist takeover was not a viable alternative. Life under a Taipei government was equally unpopular. True independence was also ruled out due to China's proximity. But with the anachronistic colonial *status quo* under the British ending in 1997, the majority of the population has no other choice but to accept Hong Kong's new status, since they have nowhere to flee.

Though the Chinese in the colony feign a docile submission, sometimes to cover up a deep-seated disdain for their British superiors, the Brits are more or less accepted, even if some of Her Majesty's minions would be only lowly clerks — not managers — back home.

It is this preserved, and at times buried, Chineseness that enables a population of more than five million to survive on this miniscule dot of territory on China's southeast coast. Despite some squalid living conditions (picture a family of five or more living in one room), the concept of "getting away from it all" simply does not exist for most Hong Kong Chinese. Even escapades to the countryside or beaches are made in throngs. Radios are ubiquitous and the volume is usually turned on high so that everyone can enjoy the din, whether they want to or not.

This immunity to noise and bent for crowds is attributable partly to the gregarious nature of the Chinese character and partly to mental mutation. People born and raised in Hong Kong seem to have developed an inner barrier to cacophony. It is also one of the causes of friction between Western and Eastern mentalities. Europeans are accustomed to a quieter environment and frequently complain.

Perhaps the key to understanding the people of Hong Kong is to understand the mechanism which allows the society to function normally under such closet-like circum-

stances: they are a people living on "borrowed land" and "borrowed time" in a city constantly in the excited state of a packed stadium during a championship match. (One is always of the impression that in Hong Kong one false cry of "fire" could turn the place into bedlam.) A built-in mechanism within each individual — like an automatic valve that shuts when pressure approaches the unbearable — keeps such tension from surfacing. It enables the individual to retreat into an inner sanctuary — perhaps in the hypnotic movements of *tai chi chuan* (Chinese shadow boxing) in early morning hours among the forgetful laughter and concentration of friends; perhaps by the escape of watching a *kung fu* movie; perhaps by gorging on the teatime delights of *yum cha*. This traditional social break in a *cha* house is

accompanied by selections of teas, savouries called *dim sum,* and sometimes the chirping of pet birds being "walked" each day. Just about any form of entertainment thrives in the colony: cinemas, restaurants and food stalls, *mahjong* parlours, and fast talking street hawkers who perform to attract crowds. (It seems everything in Hong Kong is always packed, and that *a sense of place* is secured only by jostling and pushing). *I push and shove, therefore I exist ...*

Mahjong As Self-Hypnosis

Mahjong, a noisy game of tiles played by four, is the national pastime here. It fills a social void. On a Saturday night, buildings verily shake with the thunderous clatter of the tiles, and inexhaustible players become mesmerized in the game for days, numb and oblivious to other realities.

People in Hong Kong suffer the usual neuroticism, depression and mental malaise caused by big city life everywhere. But here such problems are aggravated by the public's refusal to recognize them. To the Cantonese, a psychiatrist is a Western quack who may pretend to succeed in curing "barbarian" minds, but could not hope to penetrate a Chinese brain. Here, friends and family are the individual's psychiatrist. "I'd rather talk to a friend about my problems than a stranger who calls himself a psychiatrist," a Hong Kong Chinese will say.

Thus, psychological problems remain un-

Kong's Central business district is rumoured to have come from a wealthy family which disowned her when she became insane. Daffy or not, she survives. She is always clad in colourful rags, carries a sleeping mat and maintains a regal air about her.

A Peking Puppet?

Up until the agreement settled Hong Kong's future, most people indulged in a happy-go-lucky optimism to make life tolerable. If they were poor they said it was fate; no political power meant no politics and more time for making money. Their lives were sandwiched between the two governments of Britain and China and ruled by a colonial third. They did not even consider

checked until the psychotic begins chasing people with a meat chopper. There is only one mental hospital for the more than five million people who live here. It is designed for 1,000 patients but normally houses more than 3,000. And like most "living" situations here, a person has to be highly "qualified" to be admitted. One mentally disturbed fellow who recently sought help at the hospital was turned away because the doctors did not think he was crazy enough! It was not until he smashed a television set and tried to barge into the Governor's house that the hospital accepted him.

Some of the vagabonds that roam the streets are mental patients ostracized by society. One woman who wanders day and night in Hong

rocking the colony's *status quo* because they were so well off economically. The way out of this vicious circle was by wealth, and therefore Hong Kong's population has become one of the hardest working (whether blue or white collar) on earth. If money will not get you out of the colony, it will at least make the stay (even under a Chinese government) more pleasant.

The Chinese government wants Hong Kong to remain pretty much as it is, a meeting ground for the world's communists and

Race fans at Happy Valley, Hong Kong's long popular and profitable attraction, demonstrate varying degrees of anxiety as ponies near the finish line. Are the punters winning or losing?

capitalists, a launching pad for Communist enterprises into the Western world, and vice-versa. One consequence is the 50-year (from 1997) guarantee to keep Hong Kong investments—a guarantee designed to soothe anxiety surrounding the 1997 Agreement. Ironically the conservative Peking government constantly reined in restive Hong Kong trade unions and other such untolerated dissidents.

Everyone here knows that the riots of 1967 were quelled by a directive from Peking, not by the iron hand of a British-led police force. Hong Kong Chinese count their blessings; they are better off than the Chinese in Vietnam, or communized relatives in China. They cluck their tongues at low living standards in other Southeast Asian countries. The older generation, who have undergone a lifetime of foreign and civil wars, remind their restless young that life could indeed be a lot worse. And the young have only to look back to recent anti-Chinese riots in Malaysia (in 1969) or in Indonesia (in 1965 and again in 1980) to reinforce the older generation's wisdom. Fierce travel restrictions on Hong Kong Chinese who want to visit other Asian countries are also a constant reminder. The sad truth of the matter is that Hong Kong's Chinese never have had many choices—either in the past under the strange British Crown Colony or now that the territory is to become a Special Administrative Region under the government of Peking.

Neither did the Hong Kong Chinese have any direct say as the agreement was being negotiated between the sovereign powers of Britian and China. Hong Kong's governor was on the British negotiating team but was forbidden, by protocol, to speak directly to the Chinese side. Neither was the governor nor the people of Hong Kong allowed to comment after the agreement was announced; the two negotiating governments made it clear that the agreement was an all-or-nothing affair—nothing could be changed. It made a mockery of Mrs Thatcher's promise to do nothing unless she first consulted the Hong Kong people. Referendums had been ruled out at the beginning because it was thought they might be too embarrassing. Instead, an Assessment Office was established to solicit opinions on something that could not be changed. Britain's parliamentary debate was also a farce since they too could not change anything. In fact, Hong Kong's "Hobson Choice" was between the Chinese taking over in 1997 with the safeguards in the Sino-British agreement or the Chinese taking over without any agreement.

A close-knit traditional family structure also alleviates the discomforts of living in one of the world's most densely populated areas. Generations live together in low cost, low rental government housing estates, thousands jammed vertically into high-rises. (More than 50 percent of the population is housed in this way.) However, the bigger the family, the bigger the labour force, and, of course, the greater the family income. That is why most working class families here can afford televisions, radios, stereos and other modern gadgets. For if a family consists of four employed members, each contributing HK$1,500 to household expenses, they can afford luxuries seemingly incongruous with their housing conditions. Inside the most dilapidated Hong Kong tenement, teenagers fine-tune blaring stereo sets while housewives plug in electric cookers, television sets, sewing machines and air-conditioners. Hong Kong's newly emerging and affluent middle class uses its wealth to buy things, but remains in public tenement housing because of the colony's horrific land and housing prices (the highest in the world).

Generational Differences

Tenement life, however, is not domestic bliss. Clashes among close-living family members are inevitable, especially between in-laws.

Other generational differences further complicate in-house relationships. New concepts of child rearing and nutrition have evolved, and children often become a focus of social discord. Younger Chinese parents, for example, are feeding their children more meat and milk, and infants are now nursed on formula (though breast feeding is regaining popularity). Consequently, new generations are becoming progressively bigger in build, and their modern parents are more liberal and experimental. Grandparents, however, still believe in traditional taboos concerning child rearing and diet; they prefer soybean gruel to formula, and so on. Therefore, they feel slighted when their senior opinions are not heeded; after all, they have raised five, six or seven children of their own. Tensions understandably build-up, but life goes on.

Cramped living (and working) conditions, however, make life difficult for would-be young lovers. Moments alone are rare, and the prying eyes of brothers and sisters, parents and relatives, and colleagues and workmates are not a conducive environment for composing love letters or flirting. Among the colony's few romantic retreats are lovers' lanes, but the all too real threat of being mugged in such places overshadows their appeal. Indeed, young courting couples often

band together and form ad hoc security watches. After lights are out in Victoria Park, cooing couples will occupy neighbouring benches, and if one pair runs into trouble, they shout out an "S.O.S." to twosomes nearby.

Dating and marriage are now by free choice. This, however, does not mean that parents do not have a say in marital decisions. Parental approval is usually sought, and the bride or groom-to-be is subjected to the scrutiny of everyone concerned, including close and distant relatives.

Pragmatism Versus Passion

For economic reasons, the age of marriage in Hong Kong has been delayed. Women generally marry at the age of 24 and men at 26. The pragmatism of the Chinese character often overcomes passion, and most Chinese are willing to postpone marriage until they have saved a good sum. Besides, Chinese weddings are dear. Banquets for the entertaining of clansmen can cost up to tens of thousands of dollars, and such gluttonous gatherings can be a chore for everyone: for the guests because they have to bring gifts, often in the form of cheques and gift coupons (wedding invitations often are dubbed "blackmail letters"), and, of course, to the hosts.

Concubinage (a form of polygamy) has been outlawed in Hong Kong only since 1970, but it has metamorphosed into a more familiar creature. Concubines are now called mistresses, but are still publicly displayed as concubines were, as status symbols. One Hong Kong millionaire buys cars for his five mistresses according to their rank: the first mistress has a Rolls-Royce, the second a Mercedes Benz, and so on.

The older generation of men who took concubines before the new law took effect are allowed to keep them, and their children are recognized and have legal rights to an estate, but such is not the lot of "bastard" children born to modern-day mistresses.

Counting and Discounting of II's

Hong Kong is a land of immigrants and children of immigrants. Most of the older population immigrated from China during the last few decades, but the majority of the total population is young — under 25 — and were born here. The current influx of newcomers ebbs and wanes, depending on Peking's policy whims. When China started to liberalize its immigration policy several years ago, Hong Kong, already crammed to the sky, took in 1,000 illegal immigrants a day.

Between the years of 1978 and 1980, some 500,000 illegal immigrants, II's in the vernacular of Hong Kong's officialdom (the figures are an estimate because no one really knows), swam the shark-infested tidal waters along the Sino-British border with nothing more than homemade inflatables, or paddled dilapidated boats, or climbed hills (nearly all under cover of darkness), to come to *the promised land* which is Hong Kong. Ranged against them were thousands of soldiers, sailors, airmen and police. Battalions of China's People's Liberation Army (the PLA) and Chinese coastal gunboats cooperated with British and Gurkha battalions, Royal Hong Kong Police Units, and elements of the Royal Navy and Royal Air Force, to stop the II's. But still they came in droves.

Initial government estimates indicated that

for every 10 illegal immigrants who fled from China, half were stopped by the PLA, four ran the gauntlet successfully and Hong Kong forces apprehended one. By 1980, the PLA was catching about six and Hong Kong officials estimated that only one II escaped for every one they caught. They came, of course, for a better life than that available in the communes and fishing villages of neighbouring Kwangtung (Guangdong) Province. The sparkling and tantalizing fact that the glow of Hong Kong is clearly visible for miles into Southern China, and that Hong Kong tele-

Dating and marriage are now by free choice, but parents still have a say in marital decisions.

vision transmissions are clearly received in the same area, encouraged these people.

In the beginning Hong Kong had a liberal, if puzzling, "touch base" policy, whereby an II who ran the gauntlet and arrived in urban Hong Kong — presumably to be reunited with his or her relatives — was permitted to stay. Many were aided by racketeers who serviced a lucrative "underground railway" system. In a departure from strict regulations, no questions were asked when a successful II showed up at the Immigration Department's emergency offices to apply for an identification card. This policy, which was decided upon to prevent the colony's underground and illegal population from mushrooming, was curtailed in 1980. Simultaneously, it was made a crime not to have and carry an identification card at all times, and employers were made responsible for the validity of immigrant employees. Since that law was implemented the frantic flow of II's has been reduced to a trickle.

A Rude Dreamland?

In the minds of many in the neighbouring spartan Communist society, Hong Kong's streets are paved with gold. This image has been enhanced by relatives living in the colony, who, thinking that their compatriots are starving under severe Communist rule, scrimp and save to send them money. Hong Kong residents often return to China with trunkloads of fabrics, bicycles, televisions, radios and other items that are not easily available on the mainland. And as an ego-inflation exercise, they like to brag about their great life in Hong Kong, to the wide-eyed wonderment of poor relatives in mainland villages.

But the real picture on the British side of the border may not be so rosy; and that on the Chinese side not so gloomy. One Hong Kong worker who sends a good part of his monthly salary to his brother in Canton was surprised to see his brother so plump and pink. While he sweats away more than 10 hours a day in a Hong Kong factory, his brother was enjoying daily hour-long tea breaks.

The disappointment is often bitter once a Chinese refugee sets foot on leased British soil. Their dollar-signed dreams are rudely shattered by the harshness of a highly competitive society which eliminates the economically unfit. In a desperate effort to make it in the world, some resort to crime. The HK$7 million robbery of a bank transport car in 1975, the biggest holdup in the history of Hong Kong at that time, was carried out by a band of former Red Guards from China. Well-trained in the use of firearms, they managed to pull off a clean robbery in a few minutes. Police later apprehended the gang (during the aftermath of an internecine crime syndicate squabble), but generally speaking, this sector of the population is hard to trace. Because of such official helplessness, Hong Kong is in the midst of a growing crime wave, much of it perpetrated and perpetuated by disgruntled mainlanders.

China-trained professionals such as doctors, nurses and engineers have to accept menial jobs here because their credentials are not recognized by Hong Kong authorities. A medical board examination has been set up in recent years for the qualifying of non-Commonwealth doctors, but some mainland medical graduates feel that the test discriminates against them. The English language test alone eliminates many.

China's recent liberalization policy has also flung wide open the floodgates of legal immigration. (Chinese can travel to Hong Kong on a simple internal travel document and Hong Kong must accept them due to the peculiar political situation here). Consequently, antagonism between new arrivals and local residents is mounting. This population boom also has been aggravated by inflation which has seriously affected social service projects.

There are millionaires of every variety here: some who inherited the family business, some who placed *a right bet at the right time,* and some who lifted themselves by their sandal-straps through sheer effort. Some drive different coloured Rolls-Royce to match their daily attire. Others wear the same old rags for years, and nobody would suspect that they have riches stashed away in banks.

Rags to Rolls Royce stories abound in this free enterprise entrepôt, but in this fairy tale many of the beggars-turned-prince remain outwardly humble. A successful entrepreneur may be dressed in a greasy apron, chopping away at roast goose in a restaurant, and another may be hawking noodles and fishballs at a street corner. The owner of the colony's famous Yung Kee Restaurant (his roast goose has been called one of the world's 10 best dishes) started out with such a food stall; he now presides over a multi-storeyed, mega-dollar enterprise — a high-rise golden goose, if you will.

Another industry rich with Horatio Alger Wong stories is the garment business, Hong Kong's major export industry. Many multi-million dollar garment businesses are known to have originated in family workshops employing five workers or less. By hard work, business acumen accumulated after several backruptcies, and a bit of good *joss* (luck), they *hit the big time.*

"Industrious" and "efficient" are some of the catchwords used to describe the colony's residents. Though the official work week is 44 hours, a 70-hour week is not unusual for many. Indeed, other Asian capitalists eye Hong Kong with envy. Laments one Taiwanese toy maker: "Our girls are only half as productive as workers in Hong Kong. Here people take work seriously and don't jabber at work like they do in Taiwan."

Hong Kong is also known for its resilience. One cliché often repeated is that: "despite the hardships Hong Kong faces, it is always resilient enough to bounce back." Little mention is made of the men, women and children who are responsible for such fiscal flexibility. When there is a manufacturing deadline to meet, people work non-stop for three or four days (and nights) in a row; when business is slack, they switch to other professions or survive

Yet, traditional values are changing. Industriousness and thriftiness often give way to opulence and acquisitiveness. Indeed, humble Hong Kong has broken world records in the consumption of luxury goods. Its residents are proud of being the world's highest per capita consumers of French cognac, and they love being the world's most conspicuous drivers of Rolls Royces. This profligacy has made much impact — especially on Hong Kong youth who seem to have adopted the temporal philosophy of *get it while you can*.

Several factors account for this *nouveau riche* air. One, of course, is the colony's obvious wealth. As its export business grows and industry burgeons, consumer goods loom tantalizingly within reach of a large portion of the population. All the trappings of an

through family support; and when demand exceeds supply in a certain field, the business gap is filled overnight. Thus, during the world-wide denim boom of the early 1970s, thousands of little blue jean factories sprouted in Hong Kong; and when the market became glutted with the rushed, shoddy workmanship of amateurs, these workshops folded as fast as they were born. Owners took their business elsewhere.

The root of this flexibility is a traditional Chinese pride that refuses to vegetate; and additional incentive is provided by the lack of a welfare system in Hong Kong. If laid off, people cannot wait around for government support. They have to move on to other jobs, even if at a lower status and pay, to survive.

acquisitive society emerge.

A second factor, a more subtle one, is a feeling of transience that permeates all strata of Hong Kong society. Many who *lost everything* when they fled Communist rule in China have re-established themselves in the colony, but the threat that their economic mobility may not *last forever* always hangs over their bank accounts. A speculation concerning when Hong Kong will be returned — or "liberated" — is a topic of daily conversation in corporate boardrooms and around *mahjong*

Street vendor, above, may be richer than the diamond merchant, right. There is no telling.

tables. Meanwhile, the affluent store their money in foreign banks and the middle and lower classes race desperately to *enjoy life while they can.*

Emigration is a popular way out. However, because of the massive outflow to mainly the United Kingdom, the United States, Canada and Australia in past decades, these countries have tightened immigration quotas for Hong Kong. The price of such security is costly — it means giving up a traditional lifestyle, businesses and friends, and *starting out from scratch* in an alien country. Some emigrants return to Hong Kong after establishing permanent residence in a foreign country. They shuttle back and forth annually to retain their status in both places.

Every summer, thousands of visa applicants

to university.

A number of students commit suicide each year because they failed an important examination; many more contemplate this desperate move. Thus, parents make sure that their training starts early. They hire tutors to prepare their children for kindergarten entrance examinations, an ordeal which sometimes requires two hours of testing to determine a child's Chinese, English and arithmetic skills.

Schools teach English and Chinese equally, but the language balance tilts toward English. The colonial government has adopted both as official languages (after many years of recognizing only English as the language of officialdom), but the legal language remains English. However, despite this pretence of equal treat-

flock to the U.S. Consulate and Canadian and Australian commissions. Many of these are college age students whose scores will not qualify them for admission to local universities. Such applicants have to go through a series of interrogations (sometimes humiliating) by curt visa officers who want to make sure the students will return home after graduation.

Not unlike its business community, Hong Kong's education is also highly competitive. Parents believe that their child's career is dictated by his kindergarten credentials. For if the child fails to enter a top-rate kindergarten, he cannot get into a top-rate elementary school. This eliminates any chance of going to a top-rate high school, which is a prerequisite

ment, everyone in Hong Kong knows that mastery of English is the crucial criterion for employment in major banks and corporations. Graduates of Hong Kong University, a British institution that uses mainly English, receive unofficial priority in the job market over those who complete studies at the Chinese-medium Chinese University.

Surprisingly, the average standard of English in Hong Kong is not very high. The alphabet is pounded into little heads at the age of five or less, and children sing "London Bridge" and recite "Run Rover Run," but they parrot both by rote, with little comprehension of what they are mouthing. When a Shakespearean play covered by the secondary school syllabus each year is announced, it is

often literally memorized.

Parochial schools are the most sought after educational institutions. Some parents convert to Christianity so that their children can enter these institutions. The faculty staff comprises a number of foreigners and they impose an awesome presence upon the children — with their looming frames, strangely coloured eyes and curious odour. To avoid the trouble of learning to pronounce abstruse Chinese names, they christen the students in English. In one school, a British teacher simply goes down the row and arbitrarily names her students John, Mary, Peter, etcetera. Thus, in every class she teaches, there are the same John, Mary and Peter, depending on which seat the child occupies. Some Chinese assume

sites cost tens of thousands of dollars. Therefore, the old woman prayed to Buddha in the morning and took communion from a Roman Catholic priest in the afternoon. By thus covering her beliefs she has assured herself a place in both heavens — and on the earth.

Superstition is perhaps the most appropriate name for Hong Kong's religious bent. Almost every Chinese, be he Christian, Buddhist or atheist, believes in occult forces. He believes that man can control them by arranging his furniture a certain way, by building his home in a divined location, by constructing walls to repel bad spirits, or by consulting a holy book for auspicious dates for major lifecycle events. Moreover, as gambling is a way of life for both rich and poor in this

an English name — or simply use their initials — to make their passage into the English world easier.

To many Chinese in Hong Kong, religion is a pragmatic matter. Some become baptized into Christianity for personal gains, benefits from Christian charity organizations, social status, availability of gravesites in Christian cemeteries, and other practical considerations. One old woman born and raised a Buddhist was converted to Catholicism on her deathbed because a gravesite in the Roman Catholic cemetery is much more spacious and cheaper than ordinary "pagan" plots. Land is scarce in Hong Kong, and real estate speculators regularly increase the price of every centimeter of soil, including last resting places. Some grave-

city, it makes a difference whether a person gets off his bed on the left or right side, whether he goes to the bathroom at a propitious time, or whether his wife says the right words to him. The Cantonese word for "book," for example, is poison to a gambler's ears, because that word (*shi*) sounds identical to the Cantonese word for "lose."

Conversely, superstitious people here literally raze mountains to give entombed ancestors a good view in the hope that their pleased grandparents will shower blessings on their earthly lot by guiding them to the *right lucky bet.*

Left, a jade seller and above, a traditional chinese cemetery.

HER MAJESTY'S LITTLE JOKE

Queen Victoria's consort must have offered a right royal chuckle when a messenger delivered the news that Hong Kong was to be added to their Empire.

"Albert," tut-tutted the Queen, "is so much amused by my having got the island of Hong Kong, and we think Victoria ought to be called Princess of Hong Kong in addition to Princess Royal."

Her Majesty couldn't have been criticized for lack of prescience, as Hong Kong Island has little to recommend it: the coastline is rugged, there isn't a single river, not much arable farmland, and no engineer has ever found a trace of minerals on this once desolate tropical isle.

All that Hong Kong was ever good for—according to the opium merchants who took it as booty—was 17 square miles of the best deepwater harbour in the area. Her harbour could shelter ships from any storm, be they torrential typhoons or the emotional outpourings of an obstreperous Chinese emperor.

But Hong Kong Island is only a single part of the Crown Colony. True, until the Second World War, it was the most important part, politically and economically. But like Julius Caesar's Rome, all of Hong Kong can be divided into four parts—Hong Kong Island, Kowloon, the New Territories, and the colony's numerous outlying islands.

The **"island,"** as it's popularly known, is 29 square miles of topsy-turvy real estate. The earliest British settlements were established here, so consequently Queen Victoria's little "joke" (and the place her Foreign Secretary, Lord Palmerston, called a "barren island with hardly a house upon it") is now dominated by great banks and counting houses, enormous futuristic buildings, opulent hotels, splendid residences on Victoria Peak, fine beach resorts, and the colony's oldest Chinese communities.

Across Hong Kong Harbour—a two-minute trip by the new underwater Mass Transit Railway, seven minutes by the venerable Star Ferry and four-to-10 minutes by car through the Cross-Harbour Tunnel—is the mainland town of **Kowloon**, a residential-industrial complex packed into three-and-three-quarter miles. Kowloon was ceded to the British in 1860 (under the Treaty of Peking) so the insecure Brits could better defend the harbour. Most tourists see only the tip of Kowloon, the **Tsimshatsui** district, which is Kowloon's trading venue and the site of her many hotels, bars and posh shopping centres.

This land parcel, on the southeastern tip of mainland Asia, was originally developed as the terminal for a railroad which in the old days would carry colonial passengers through China and Czarist Russia all the way to Paris, the west coast of France, and ultimately, back to London. A second purpose was for godowns to store goods being ferried to the island. The third, less savoury reason, was that Kowloon was a convenient place for prosperous British merchants to house their mistresses. The government didn't sanction either mistresses or brothels on the island, but they hardly could control the mainland.

North from Tsimshatsui along Nathan Road are the

Yaumatei and **Mongkok** districts. The latter has the dubious distinction of being listed in the *Guinness Book of Records* as the place with the densest population concentration on earth: a mere 165,000 residents per square kilometer!

East of Mongkok is **Kai Tak Airport**. To the north are numerous resettlement areas and **Boundary Street**, perhaps the most important "separation point" in the colony.

Boundary Street marks the demarcation line between Hong Kong colony, granted to the British in "perpetuity" (but which will be given up to the Chinese in 1997), and the New Territories (NT), which don't belong to the United Kingdom at all but instead were leased in 1898 by the Convention of Peking for a 99-year period (which ends in 1997).

The NT used to be called "unspoiled." A century ago, when it was known as "The Emperor's Rice Bowl" for its fine arable land, it must have had a verdant beauty. Today, though, its towns house countless factories that are hardly beautiful in an 18th Century unspoiled sense. "Progress" and population pressures have caused the government to instigate "new town" projects. "Little" market towns like **Tsuen Wan** now have populations of 700,000, and a once-tiny pirate port like **Tuen Mun** is fast expanding to house 600,000.

However, still in the NT are the colony's spacious Chinese University, some quaint walled villages and traditional rural architecture (difficult to find but worth the search). The main old towns of the NT include **Shatin** with its new racecourse and university, the northern settlements of **Tai Po** and **Fanling** (with its championship golf course). **Sheung Shui**, and, near the last train stop before China, the border town of **Lo Wu**.

Recently, the border hasn't really stopped there; Peking (government) authorities have allowed the district of **Shum Chun (Shenzhen)** to be used as a duty-free export area; consequently, many Hong Kong businessmen commute over the border on an almost daily basis, joining farmers who have done so since a border was drawn. The political and economic implications of this capitalist leasing of Communist territories have yet to be determined.

Most of the latter towns are near **Tolo Harbour**. **Tolo Channel** on the east goes up to **Mirs Bay** and China, while the harbour's northern reaches flow towards the still somewhat unspoiled district of **Sai Kung**. To the west are farms, and **Tai Mo Shan**, the highest mountain in the colony, at 3,142 feet. The westernmost sector is called **Castle Peak**. And due north is **Deep Bay**, on the China border.

Along with the New Territories, British Hong Kong has leased 234 islands which will also revert to China in 1997. (The exceptions are little **Stonecutters Island** and Hong Kong Island.) Few of these islands are inhabited, and they are probably reminiscent of what Hong Kong Island itself looked like more than a century ago.

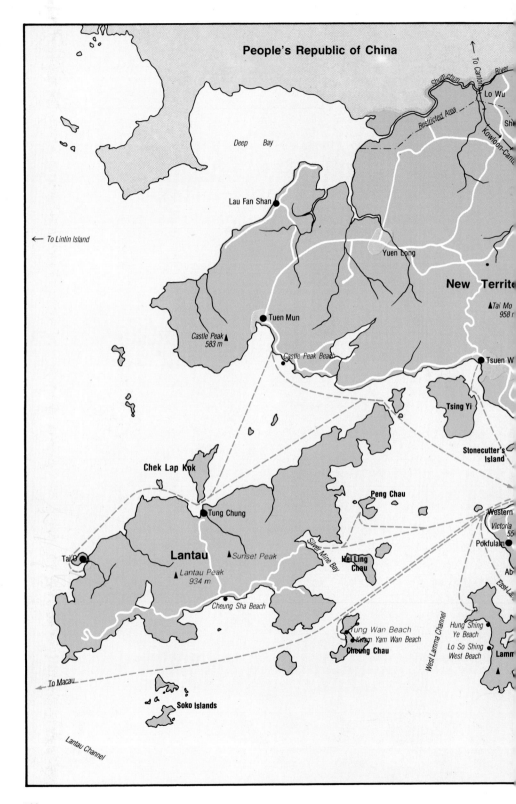

People's Republic of China

To Canton

To Lintin Island ←

Shum-chun River

Lo Wu

Kowloon-Cant

Restricted Area

Sh

Deep Bay

Lau Fan Shan

Yuen Long

New Territ

▲Tai Mo
958 r

Tuen Mun

Castle Peak ▲
583 m

Castle Peak Beach

Tsuen W

Tsing Yi

Stonecutter's
Island

Chek Lap Kok

Peng Chau

Western

Tung Chung

Victoria
55

Pokfulam

Lantau

▲Sunset Peak

Silver Mine Bay

Hei Ling
Chau

Ab

East La

Tai O

▲Lantau Peak
934 m

Cheung Sha Beach

West Lamma Channel

Hung Shing
Ye Beach

Lo So Shing
West Beach

Lamn

▲

Tung Wan Beach
Kwun Yam Wan Beach
Cheung Chau

To Macau

Soko Islands

Lantau Channel

Shataukok

Mirs   Bay

Ping Chau

ai Tan Leng
483 m

Plover Cove Reservoir

Long Harbour

Po

Tolo Harbour

Ma On Shan
703 m

Sai Kung

Kowloon Peak
603 m

Port Shelter

loon

Airport

North Point

Lei Yuemun

Clear Water Bay Beach

g Kong

Hong Kong and Environs

Area: 366 sq. miles
Total number of Islands: 235
Population: 5.5 million
Climate: Subtropical
Terrain: Mountainous
Highest Peak: Tai Mo Shan, New
  Territories (958 metres)
National Flower: Bauhinia

Deep Water
Bay Beach

se
ch Middle Bay
Beach

Beach

n Kok
ch

St. Stephen's
Beach

Turtle Cove
Beach

Hair Pin Beach

Stanley Main Beach

Stanley

Big Wave Bay
Beach

Rocky Bay Beach

Shek O Beach

Shek O

Potoi Island

Canton

Pok Lo

Waichow

Ping Shan

Kwangtung   **Province**

Siu Lam

Sun Wui

Suek K

Po On

Pearl River

Shum Chun

Lung Kong

Hong Kong

Macau
(Portuguese)

South China Sea

101

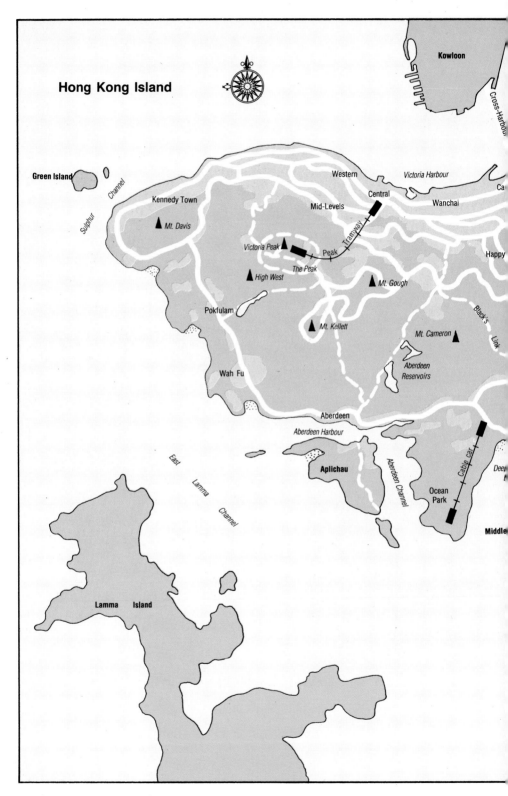

Hong Kong Island

Kowloon

Cross-Harbour

Green Island

Sulphur Channel

Kennedy Town

Mt. Davis

Western

Victoria Harbour

Central

Ca

Wanchai

Mid-Levels

Tramway

Victoria Peak

The Peak

Peak

Happy

High West

Mt. Gough

Pokfulam

Mt. Kellett

Mt. Cameron

Black's Link

Aberdeen Reservoirs

Wah Fu

Aberdeen

Aberdeen Harbour

Aberdeen Channel

East Lamma Channel

Aplichau

Cable car

Ocean Park

Deep

Middle

Lamma Island

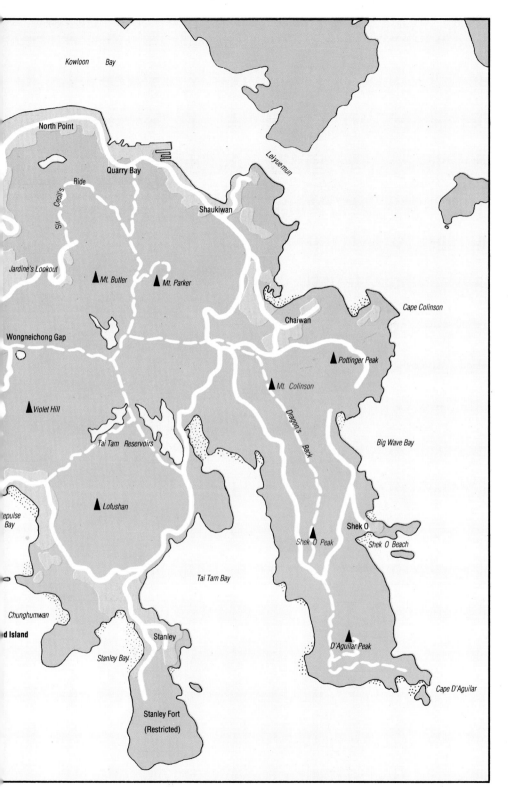

Kowloon   Bay

North Point

Quarry Bay

Str Cecil's Ride

Leiyuemun

Shaukiwan

Jardine's Lookout

▲ Mt. Butler

▲ Mt. Parker

Chaiwan

Cape Colinson

Wongneichong Gap

▲ Pottinger Peak

▲ Mt. Colinson

▲ Violet Hill

Dragon's Back

Big Wave Bay

Tai Tam   Reservoirs

▲ Lofushan

Repulse Bay

Shek O

Shek O Beach

Shek O Peak

Tai Tam Bay

Chunghumwan

d Island

Stanley

D'Aguilar Peak

Stanley Bay

Cape D'Aguilar

Stanley Fort
(Restricted)

HONG KONG, 'THE ISLAND'

Wall Street, Fifth Avenue, The Bourse

However barren it was 100 years ago, nobody standing in the middle of Hong Kong Island could ever imagine it as anything but a great metropolis and an entrepôt to the world's third largest port. Its high-rises pop up everywhere, with a futuristic look. Thirty-storey buildings are more common than 10-storey buildings. And the colony's old grey bank image is quickly being superceded by mirrored, metallic and white-slick office structures. The **Central** business district is a combination of Wall Street, Washington, Fifth Avenue, the Bourse, The City and an architectural merry-go-round.

Yet for all its urban pull, this Central vortex serves the same purpose it did nearly 150 years ago. The port, with its 7,000 visiting ships a year, was the colony's *raison d'etre*; along the old harbourfront were all her important business and banking houses, and her residents were housed in squalid and opulent suburbs around Central, where they still live today.

True, nobody realised then how much reclamation would transform the city. (Originally, Queen's Road formed the port area.) And it wasn't until relatively recently that the south side of the island was utilized extensively. Consequently, that area is still the most pleasant place in all of Hong Kong.

To see the north side of Hong Kong island (the side facing Kowloon) at its best costs not even a dollar (HK) aboard one of the ancient double-decker trams which rattle along—certainly one of the great travel bargains in the world. Incientally, Trams Tours are available as well as a special Hong Kong innovation — the private Tram Party.

Climbing the Peak

The island is dominated by **Victoria Peak** (known simply as "The Peak"). As long ago as 1860, the Governor of the colony suggested that more affluent Europeans should take up residence on the cooler Peak. This is still where the richest members of the colony live.

left, a
pper on
s beat and
low,
eonesque
entral.

CENTRAL

Mystical and Mythical Central

The centre of any great world capital is dominated by its government offices (usually of austere Roman-granite architecture), and perhaps a statue to a great past ruler in an adjoining park.

Hong Kong's **Central District** is no exception. Except that the *real* government of Hong Kong is its banks. And the *real* past rulers have been bank managers. So when one exits from the **Star Ferry** underpass, looking ahead at the great concrete vista to the south, he or she sees the spires of Hong Kong's three main banks — the new modernistic US$1 billion Hongkong and Shanghai Bank (reputedly the most expensive building in the world), the Bank of China and the Chartered Bank. (The latter two are also planning to construct new skyscraping headquaters. And the park in the foreground, once graced with a statue of Queen Victoria, today frames only a statue of **Thomas Jackson**, a chap who managed the Hongkong and Shanghai Bank for 30 years at the end of the 19th Century.

For all its hard-boned, materialistic, economic, business and capitalistic realism, there is something mystical about Central District. After all, less than a century ago nearly all of this hard ground was under water. And reclamation here has been astonishing, making up virtually all Central.

There are few truly historic buildings to give real character to Central. The blue-and-white **Hong Kong Club** was demolished in 1981 and has been replaced by a modern skyscraper. But the colonial-style **Supreme Court Building**, once evacuated in mid session because its foundations were undermined by the construction of the MTR (the underground railway) running in the area, is now repaired and houses the Legislative Council. There are no colonial buildings left.

The money of Central is mythical. So complex is the business of buying and selling land and property here, and so incestuous are the corporations which trade with each other, that at one auction in September, 1980, a record high

Central and the harbour from atop The Peak.

of HK$26,245 a square foot was the price realised to purchase land for a new office building site. Office space in Central was renting for HK$27 and up per square foot in January, 1981, and selling for an average of HK$4,500 per square foot. So all-consuming is the business of doing business here that "government" itself is shunted to the sidelines. The Governor now lives fairly isolated on the corner of Garden Road and Lower Albert Street. The **Central Government Tram** terminus behind the Hilton Hotel. And City Hall offices have been pushed to the eastern side of the Star Ferry.

So subordinate is history to the glory of this colony's fast-moving fiscal futures that virtually nothing remains even of the 1950s!

Colonial Crumbs

For those interested in nibbling at some of the few remaining crumbs of early colonial architecture, Central and its vicinity offer only a few other structural examples. In **Victoria Barracks**, at the eastern end of Central and half-way up the Peak, is **Flagstaff**

House, built in 1845. The army has moved and the whole site is scheduled for redevelopment. Flagstaff House, though, has been saved and converted into the Museum of Tea Ware. At the corner of Queensway and Cotton Tree Drive was **Murray Barracks**, once an officers mess and the place used by occupying Japanese as their Army Headquarters during World War II. This timber-stone building with deep verandahs on first and second storeys was first established in 1845. It was demolished carefully, each stone numbered, with a view to re-building it elsewhere, to make room for the new Bank of China Building, but reconstruction plans have scrapped.

Another superb old building, **St. John's Cathedral**, is near the Peak Tram terminus. This was built between 1847 and 1849 and reflects early Victorian-Gothic elegance.

But these buildings are aberrations. More to the Central style is **The Landmark** (they don't even call it a building), a structure opened in 1980 on Des Voeux Road on the site of the old Gloucester Hotel (which was demolished for the New Gloucester Building, which in turn was destroyed to make way for The Landmark). Five floors surround a vast 20,000 square-foot atrium with 100 shops. The fountain in the middle has been constructed with a cover above it to form a stage

The best place to begin one's Central tour is at the **Star Ferry Terminal**. Blinking at the right of the Hong Kong piers is the unmistakable polkadotted **Connaught Centre**, whose distinctive round windows have inspired the Chinese to nickname it the "House of a Thousand Orifices." Hong Kong's Filipino community gathers in strength here and in Statue Square at weekends. Just behind this holey wonder are the **General Post Office** and the **Government Information Service Bookshop**, which dispenses handy pamphlets from the **Hong Kong Tourist Association**. Across the street to the west from the G.P.O. and Connaught Centre are the shiney towers of Exchange Square, one of the most modern office buildings in the world and the home of the Unified Stock Exchange. Even further west is the **Outlying Ferries Pier** where Hongkongians hop a ferry, to escape to one of the more peaceful outer islands.

To the left is **City Hall**. This complex's **Low Block** houses a concert hall and theatre, a number of offices and, most important, billboards which advertise cultural programmes for the month—an obvious necessity for tourists searching for something artistic.

City Hall's **High Block** is in the same compound, just around a tiny garden. Inside this block are the **Museum of Art**, with its excellent collection of ceramics, three libraries, lecture rooms, and the **Hong Kong Marriage Registry**.

Across Connaught Road Central is an open space full of fountains and things that look like benches for bus stops. This is **Statue Square**, Central's "green" lung and gathering place for the thousands of Filipina maids on Sundays. Adjacent to the East is **Sutherland House**, easily spotted by its blue colouring, and beyond, the **Furama Hotel**.

Upon emerging from an underpass which fronts the Star Ferry Terminal, one finds one's self on Connaught Road Central. The swank **Mandarin Hotel** and **Prince's Building** are to the right, and. to one's left is **Statue Square**, with its war memorial and the aforementioned statue of Sir Thomas Jackson.

Behind this pedestrian pivot point on Des Voeux Road, the colony's great new buildings begin their grand sweep. Queen's Road was the original "Main Street," but a little footpath in front of the Queen's Road godowns and counting houses was later turned into Des Voeux. Central has spread east along Queensway with the advent of the **Admiralty Complex** and the newer **Supreme Court.**

A Chic Chandlery

Up on Queen's Road is the new site of **Lane Crawford**, the single most famous luxury department store in Asia. Founded in the mid 1850s by a sea captain who wanted to outfit visiting ships, Lane Crawford today hardly poses as a ship chandlery. But to the west, along Queen's Road, are dozens of *real* ship chandleries, on the same site where, 80 years ago, ships did dock and take on stock.

Befitting its role as the site of "original" Hong Kong, Queen's Road has other traditional crafts shops on its Western district flank. Here are shops making kitchen utensils like knives and *wok*, tea merchants, swallows' nest merchants (one of the largest is at 331

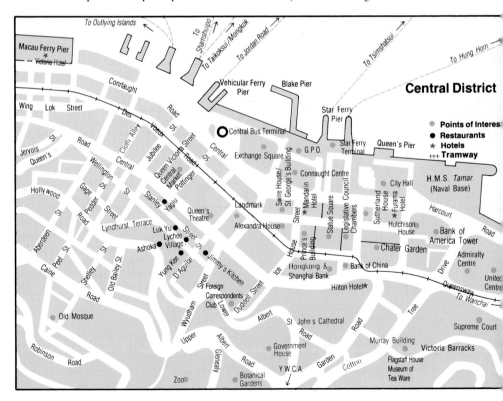

Queen's Road Central), calligraphy suppliers and silversmiths.

While in **"lower"** Central, one should also explore some of the side streets between Queen's Road and Des Voeux Road. Just west of the **Queen's Theatre** are two interesting little streets—**Li Yuen Street East** and **Li Yuen Street West**—which have stalls and shops that sell clothing, look-alike high fashion accessories and fabrics galore. Bargaining is expected here. Another popular "cloth alley" is the one closer to Western, on Wing On Street just west of the **Central Market.**

On Queen's Road looking south, one realizes why Hong Kong was considered basically worthless when first taken over. The original island, before reclamation, was simply a huge mountain. Behind Queen's Road, the old waterfront road, is a hill which rises precipitously from sea level. Climb up **Ice House** or **Wyndham** streets till they meet. That old, triangular-shaped ice storage building (circa 1911) is now the house of the **Foreign Correspondents** and the **Fringe** clubs. Wyndham is lined with shops. Another worthwhile climb is D'Aguilar Street with its fascinating boutiques.

Stanley Street, just off D'Aguilar, has some excellent restaurants, a few antique shops, camera shops, and perhaps the most famous fortune-teller in Hong Kong, Wong Kwok So, at 74 Stanley, fifth floor. Continuing up D'Aguilar, cross Wellington Street and proceed through the tiny flower market. On the right is **Wo On Lane** with its fun shops. Farther along, two lanes open off at both sides. The one on the left, **Lan Kwai Fong**, with its trendy restaurants, is Hong Kong's most modest version of London's Covent Garden.

These side streets wind up to **Hollywood Road** (see Western District), with its plethora of antique, furniture, rattan and used books shops. Along here is **Lyndhurst Terrace,** a pretty little place with shops that sell Chinese opera costumes. Lyndhurst Terrace curves down into **Wellington Street**, an avenue well-known for its *mahjong*-makers and framers.

Going up and following Hollywood Road, doing as much window-shopping as possible, one eventually reaches **Possession Street**. Possession Street marks the border between Central and the down-to-earth old Chinese section of Hong Kong called **Western District**.

The view from the famous "Asia hand" *pissoir* at the old Foreign Correspondents Club.

WESTERN

Go Chinese in Western

If one was foolish enough to try to identify the "real Hong Kong," one would think inevitably of **Western District**, which begins at Possession Street, and sprawls west to **Kennedy Town**. More practically, Western's atmosphere emerges around **Central Market**, near the fringes of busy Central.

Western was the very first district to be settled by the British. They soon moved out, however, after malaria epidemics had decimated their numbers. Its mosquitos were left to Chinese immigrants who came pouring into the colony after 1848. Today, there is virtually nothing British about this area; it is now traditional Chinese urban society at its purest: not especially pretty, perhaps, but undeniably colourful.

For one thing, Western is known as a last refuge of the Hong Kong Chinese artisan (unless you include the air-conditioned artisan "villages" in **Star House** and the **Excelsior Hotel**). Unfortuately, the world of the Chinese artisan in his natural habitat isn't seen by many visitors, but here one can marvel at *mahjong*-makers who create *mahjong* tiles that range in function and form from low-priced plastic to high-priced hand-carved ivory polished with powdered rice husks; here is the Chinese herbalist, with his fabulous aromas of snake musk, herbs, ginseng and powdered lizards. All are part of intriguing pharmacopoeia potions that date back 4,000 years.

Surprises on Every Corner

In Western, too, are the chop-makers who carve name stamps along **Man Wa Lane**. This is a great Chinese art. Perhaps only the Arabs have as much respect for calligraphy as the Chinese. And watching a Man Wa chop-carver sculpt a man's name out of stone, ivory, jade or wood is a fascinating experience. (Remember that there are male and female calligraphic styles: when background material is carved out, the chop is male; when the characters are gouged out, it's female. Freudians can

Western ice shop merchant.

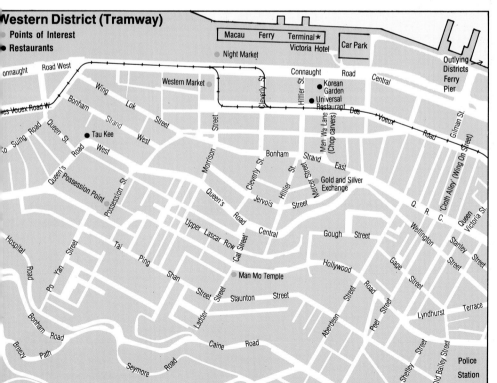

Western District (Tramway)

● Points of Interest
● Restaurants

conclude as they wish.)

Western is also a home to jade-carvers, opera costumers, fan-makers, pottery-shapers and eggroll-bakers. There are Chinese surprises on every corner.

A good place to begin pottering around Western is at the **Chinese Merchandise Emporium**, opposite Central Market. Four floors of goods from China are sold here more cheaply than in China's own **Friendship Stores**. These stores import their merchandise from the mainland, but are owned by Peking's Hong Kong representatives.

The best time to visit Central Market is at 6 a.m. when all meats, seafood, poultry, fish and vegetables are unloaded.

A Poor Man's Nightclub

At the harbour are the silver towers of the Shun Tak Centre and the Victoria Hotel, which house, underneath the main piers for vessels plying the waters to Macau. The old jet-foil pier is now a "temporary" pier for ferries heading to China. (Temporary is an interesting word since it was the "temporary" Macau Pier for more than two decades.) At night, the parking lot in front of the "temporary" pier is converted into a popular **"Poor Man's Nightclub,"** where outdoor stalls sell Chinese food, shirts, watches, pirate cassette tapes, and virtually anything else made of plastic, imitation gold, silver, leather and ivory et al.

A little lane leading to the ferry pier's right side between Queen's Road and Connaught Road is Man Wa Lane, the aforementioned street where chop-makers make and ply calligraphic stamps. At right angles to this, between the continuation of Queen's Road (Bonham Strand) and Des Voeux Road is colourful **Wing Lok Street** with its shops selling herbs, odd medicines, perserved seafoods and tea.

One will now reach **Possession Street**, which should have great patriotic significance for the colony. It was around here that the British formally annexed Hong Kong in 1841. At that time the island extended only as far as Queen's Road. However, land here has been vastly reclaimed over the years, so no monument marks the exact annexation rites site. The only memento to the HMS *Sulphur*, whose crew was the first

to step ashore officially, is **Belcher Street**, west of here, which was named after the *Sulphur's* captain. As for atmosphere, Possession Street looks like a reversion to the 19th Century, as no vehicular traffic is allowed. Rather, sounds and ambience here are generated only by people. Here, too, are fortune-tellers, and on **Fat Hing Street** is a line of shops which specialize only in traditional baby goods.

Just one block above Bonham Strand is **Jervois Street**, another "speciality" street, this one devoted entirely to snake restaurants and Chinese wineshops.

As one probes deeper into Western, it's easy to forget "colonial" Hong Kong. The district past **Bonham Strand** (a marvellous street for printing shops) looks more like a movie set for an old Fu Manchu picture. City planners have classified this area as a slum, but architecturally this district—with its old four-storey buildings with ornate balconies and carved balustrades—is more colourful and convenient than the colony's more modern housing estates. And every little street has its own "exotic" specialities: ginseng and birdnests, sharkfin and jade, funeral wreaths and

Butcher, Central Market.

snake wine, fortune-tellers and calligraphers, ivory and stone carvers.

Western District is a district for walking, for poking into little alleys and getting lost on improbable side streets. Try, however, to avoid the early morning hustle and bustle of the harbour unloading.

On Walking One's Bird

Hang Wen, at 119 Queen's Road Central, is a "bird restaurant," where early morning tea-drinkers bring their ornately-caged pet birds together for a group sing. On the corner of Bonham Strand and Cleverly Street is another such birdshop. And only a few blocks over, rice merchants meticulously blend a dozen varieties of rice.

Look for the key-cutters, tinkers, carpenters, cobblers and barbers in any alley. Their miniature factories operate in about 20 square feet of space. Booths may be simple upended crates, and the materials of their trade are stacked outside. Bow-drills are of ancient design and timeless utility, as are other tools. Rope-laying factories, alive with another old Chinese craft, go about their business in the open air. Here you'll discover a veritable carnival of teashops, handicrafts factories and restaurants where tourists rarely go.

Minibuses and trams clank along the main streets, but walk as much as possible, all the way to Western's end, at **Kennedy Town**, where you'll find one of the colony's oldest Chinese settlements. Still very crowded, it has a Portuguese-style *praia*, a road which curves along original footpaths bordering **Belcher Bay**. Past this are some uninteresting slaughter-houses and squatter shacks— but an unparalleled view of the waters leading to Macau. Looming in the foreground is **Green Island**. This is **"lower" Western district**.

Portuguese Architecture

The hilly upper region of Western (which is actually part of Mid-Levels) is totally different; here the architecture is less Chinese than Portuguese—with tiled pitch roofs, stucco walls and projecting balconies. Here also are a few fine houses, the **University of Hong Kong**, and—as usual—splendid views of the harbour.

Herbalist,
Wing Lok
Street.

If one decides not to go all the way to Kennedy Town, be advised that it's easier to reach Western and Mid-Levels via Western Street off Queen's Road. Otherwise, when in Kennedy Town, travel up Smithfield Road to Pokfield Road, then backtrack toward the University. Pokfield turns into Pokfulam Road, then passes by Belcher Gardens into the University of Hong Kong (which opened in 1911, though some buildings there date to 1886). Some of the architecture is interesting here. The **Anatomy Building**, the **Government Bacteriological Building** and the **Vice-Chancellor's Lodge** were all built before World War II.

Antiquities, Real and Fake

For tourists, the most interesting place may be the **campus museum** which houses a good collection of pottery and porcelain. Nothing especially rare, but well preserved pieces. The **University Press** has a number of very interesting titles for scholars who appreciate such things.

Coming back to Central district via **Bonham Road** can be an exhilarating experience. There is nothing of distinctive tourist interest en route, but the occasional views are grand (especially the numerous peeks at lower Western District). The old but fast-disappearing architecture of schools and mansions en route is also a fascinating glimpse into Hong Kong's colonial past.

Past Bonham Road and Caine Road, you might want to detour north a block to **Robinson Road** to see the austere **Ohel Leah Synagogue**. Jews have been in Hong Kong since its founding, but this building wasn't opened until 1901. It was financed by Hong Kong's prominent Sassoon family. The building is in Spanish style, with two towers, an imposing porch and elaborate interior carvings. The outside landscape is quite pleasant. Nearby is a **Jewish Recreation Club**.

While returning to Central, don't miss a cruise down one of the most fascinating of all local shopping areas: **Ladder Street**. This road zig-zags down steep inclines from Caine Road down to Hollywood Road and Queen's Road Central. Nobody knows when its broad stone steps were constructed, but old records say that this 65-meter "street"

Cobbler, Western.

was built so sedan chair bearers could more easily carry their human cargo from Hollywood Road to residential Caine Road. On Ladder Street (not to be confused with the "ladder streets" further over in Central) are some of Hong Kong's earliest houses, including old shuttered buildings with wooden balconies and elaborate carvings. Where Ladder Street meets Hollywood Road is the area's so-called **"Thieves Market"** (also known as "Cat Street," perhaps because it was once the middle of a red light district). The lanes here are filled with incredible bric-a-brac, fake and real antiques, and more stalls than one can ever browse through. Bargaining is the rule here — whether for a safety pin, shoelace or (if you should be so lucky) a Tang dynasty horse.

One can continue down to Queen's Road, or continue to explore the latter-day wonders of **Hollywood Road**. Here are dozens of antique shops, furniture shops, rattan shops, and places selling blackwood chests, snuff bottles, porcelains and ad antiquem. Don't look in the windows, but go in and explore here . . . look especially in the dark corners, where owners sometimes hide their best pieces.

raditional erb tea auldrons.

While on one of these zig-zagging ladder streets, pause a moment and consider the following impressions of this area penned by the lady traveller Isabella Bird Bishop who was here during the great Hong Kong fire of 1878:

Escaping from an indescribable hubbub, I got into a bamboo chair (and was borne up) streets choked with household goods and the costly contents of shops . . . Chinamen dragging their possessions to the hills; Chinawomen carrying children . . . making a scene of intense exictement.

God of Civil Servants

At the corner of Hollywood Road and Ladder Street is **Man Mo Temple**, built around 1842 on what must have been a little dirt track leading up from Central. Tourists regularly throng through Man Mo—but this doesn't inhibit its regular worshippers who animatedly create thick and redolent clouds with their burning joss offerings.

Man is the God of Civil Servants and of Literature. (Within Mandarin society, civil servants were, by definition, the most well-educated and sophisticated.) Mo is the God of Martial Arts or War, more popularly known by his worshippers as Kuan Ti or Kuan Kung. Guarding their temple are the Eight Immortals. Inside are two solid brass deer (which represent long-life), and a colourful wooden carving. And near the altar are three sedan chairs protected in glass cases. Years ago, when Man and Mo's icons were paraded through Western on festival days, these were the chairs on which they were transported.

If the atmosphere looks vaguely familiar, this is because this area was used as a set in *The World Of Suzie Wong*, the popular Hong Kong-based film that starred Nancy Kwan and William Holden. Apparently, this corner of Central and Western was more "Wanchai-looking" than the Wanchai District where the film supposedly took place.

After this bit of cinematic and spiritual pause, one can either walk back to Central or take a taxi to the Peak Tramway. We will now leave this very crowded, colourful and chaotic part of Hong Kong for a place of solitude, snobbishness and sophistication.

THE PEAK

Victoria Peak—*The* Peak to those who have made it to society's top—wasn't always regarded with such awe. "Although beautiful in the distance," wrote an early travel writer, "it is sterile and unpromising upon more close examination." Indeed, for the first six years of the colony, hardly anybody travelled to those inhospitable heights.

In 1847, the Colonial Surgeon, William Morrison, recommended The Peak for reasons of salubrity. And in 1860, the Governor, Sir Hercules Robinson, recommended that Europeans go to The Peak to get away from the unhealthy malarial climate in the lower regions. But it wasn't until 1888, when the **Peak Tramway** (actually a funicular railway) was opened, that The Peak became *the* Peak. Everybody who was (and is) anybody longs to live on The Peak. Before the tramway, sedan chairs transported lucky colonials to the top. Such coolie-powered ostentation died long ago, but palanquins are still used during charity races staged to benefit Matilda Hospital once a year.

The Peak is as beautiful now as its always been. And it's a cooling refuge even in the hottest season. The Peak still has fine old houses with large bay windows, Chinese blackwood furniture, jade cabinets, and some of the world's finest silver cutlery and porcelain.

The most affluent residents up there compete for the best chefs and stage the colony's most sparkling dinner parties. Its best flats and houses are rented out by the government—as Peak perks, if you will—to the colony's senior civil servants; or earmarked by the *hong* (Hong Kong's massive trading conglomerates) for their top executives. Swimming pools have been installed in lieu of verandahs, and bungalows now dot the area's greenswards, but the area's wilderness beauty adjacent to stately homes graciously survives.

Walks around The Peak abound for the nature-lover. On a clear day, one can wander through forests of bamboo and fern, stunted Chinese pines, hibiscus, and vines of wonderfully writhing beauty. Ornithologists still go up there to log sightings of blue magpies, sparrow hawks and kites.

The best way to see The Peak in all its bucolic glory is by walking around **Lugard Road**, which begins just opposite the Peak Tram's upper terminus at 1,305 feet above sea level. Just to the right is the **Peak Tower Restaurant**, which offers magnificent views, if clouds haven't smothered them.

Clouds on The Peak *can* be a nuisance; some residents have to telephone lowlier friends on the plains to find out what the day's weather is like below cloud-level.

Walking to the right of this mini-shopping centre, one can marvel at some of the world's finest vistas—scapes which sprawl all the way to China and Macau. Going around Lugard Road to where it intersects with **Harlech Road**, one sees first the harbour, then **Green Island** and **Peng Chau** to the north, **Lantau** and **Macau** to the west, **Cheung Chau** further west, **Lamma Island** to the southwest, and finally the great masses of junks and sampans at **Aberdeen** to the south. This hike takes about two hours from the Peak Tramway and back again.

For the really energetic, **Mount Austin Road** leads one to the gardens of a

Preceding pages, a Peak scape

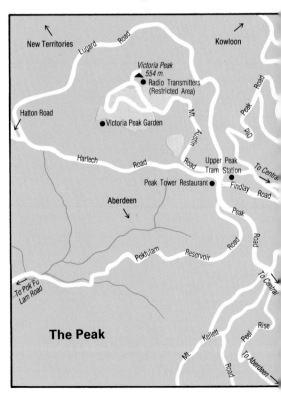

The Peak

building which was once the summer residence of the Governor. This building was destroyed during World War II by the Japanese, but the walk about its former grounds is still stupendous. Strolling out to the edge of Mount Austin Road on The Peak's barren hillsides at sunset, one is again treated to astonishing views of the colony. And up here — at The Peak's very peak — you will be 1,805 feet above sea level.

Coming down by the steep Peak Tram, one realizes that the Tram is not just a "tourist attraction," no matter how many tourists crowd it. No, this is as much a local commuter vehicle as New York's IRT or London's Tube.

The Tram runs from 7 a.m. (rush hour; not a tourist in sight) to 11 p.m. and hasn't had a single accident since its opening in 1888. As at the beginning, it still has two cars which carry 72 passengers and one driver, and is pulled up and lowered by 5,000-foot steel cables wound on drums.

While descending on the tram, one can stop at **Barker Road** and indulge in some of the finer views and footpaths through the Peak forest. This road leads to exclusive **Plantation Road**. The next

stop is **May Road**, where the Tram negotiates one of the steepest passenger vehicle gradients in the world.

The stop on **Bowen Road** has one of the better views of **Wanchai**. Joggers run here day and night, and it's said that wild monkeys can sometimes be seen in the trees.

The following two stops, **Macdonnell Road** and **Kennedy Road**, each lead to the entrance of the colony's **Botanical Gardens** and **Zoological Gardens**, which house good collections of flora and fauna. An aviary here has about 700 birds of 300 species. The best time to visit is dawn, when locals are engrossed in *tai chi chuan* exercises. This rather curious exercise, which looks like a slow-motion ballet is a shadow-boxing exercise which dates to the time of Confucius, utilizing movements and breathing inspired by Buddhist meditation forms. Coordination and s-l-o-w movements typify good *tai chi* style. As noted above, contemporary joggers are equally in abundance here.

The tram's lower terminus is just up from the Hilton Hotel on Garden Road—far below the upper echelons of Hong Kong society.

The Peak's upper terminus.

WANCHAI

In the celluloid version of *The World of Suzie Wong*, the *very* snobbish Sylvia Sims, at one of her Peak dinner parties, embarrassed the late William Holden to no end by speaking about the unfortunate denizens of **Wanchai**.

At that time, in the mid 1950's, the contrast must have been juicy. Of course, plenty of Peak-dwellers went slumming in Wanchai, much as 1920s flappers would go to Harlem for flippant fun. But Wanchai nightlife was not meant for the Peak's *taipan*. As far back as the late 1940s, it was a hangout for sailors. Writer Harold Stephens recalls that in 1949, when he first prowled here, there weren't more than four bars in the area, but they were crowded with visitors out for a good time. During the 1960s, Wanchai helped give rest, recreation and succor to thousands of American, Australian and New Zealand soldiers and sailors on R & R from Vietnam, as well as hundreds of thousands of merchant marines from hundreds of countries. Then, as now, Hong Kong was a popular port-of-call.

Not the Same Old Wench

Today, Wanchai lives on its reputation. Like an old prostitute, aged to the point where she's now the madam of a brothel, Wanchai now slouches more than she slinks. But she's a bit shabby these days. She's seen it all, and has good stories to tell, but it takes extra energy to put life into the old girl.

As for the Wanchai girls, they still stand around bar-doors and give a perfunctory "pssst" to potential customers. But these days they're sadly overwhelmed by newer and more palatable and exotic nocturnal delights.

Wanchai's "red light district" now plays second fiddle to more liberated nightlife venues: gaudy big hostess clubs (ornate and expensive, with huge bands and pushy women who sit at your table for a dollar a minute); dozens of topless bars (if nipples could yawn, those here would); discos (which have all the electronic, stroboscopic and psychedelic audio-visual gadgetry that Hong Kong money can buy); and raucous English-

ft and low, Hong ng by ght and y.

121

style pubs (where the dartboards usually get more action than the women across the street).

There are also peculiarly Eastern forms of entertainment. Like Chinese ballrooms, which rarely see foreigners. Good reason for that, too, as the places are dingy, alcohol is almost never served, and all that one can do is sit in semi-darkness and wait for a hostess to make pleasant conversation in Cantonese or Chiu Chow.

Wanchai is also the place for neon-light garish "sign-collectors": "Lee Kee Boots" and "Lee Kee Motors" and "Shanghai Food Chinese Style" verily explode in their electronic and gas-charged brilliance.

The "Wanch" is *the* place for the night people (some bars never close) and night-strolling. Here are brightly-lit fruit markets, souvenir shops, second-hand bookshops, and tailors open until midnight. (Warning: tailors here vary from tacky to svelte—and a suit made in 24 hours can unravel just as quickly.)

The Wanchai area is also host to some superb restaurants: **Rigoletto** has some of the best Italian food; a seat by the window of the **Fenwick Street** restaurant is *the* place for Wanchai people-watching: **Perfume River**, next to the **Singapore Hotel** and the **Saigon** on Lockhart Road have minty fresh Vietnamese food; **SMI** reeks of marvellous curries reminiscent of the Straits down south. As for Chinese restaurants, Wanchai has literally thousands, as well as endless outdoor noodle stands. On Lockhart Road, Wanchai's "Main Street", are bars for old-time Hong-kongians—the **Old China Hand** and **Horse And Groom**—which perpetuate a dartboard atmosphere favoured by U.K. blokes in addition to the expected plethora of girlie bars.

Cultural Wanchai

Nobody thinks about Wanchai for culture, but it does harbour the **Hong Kong Arts Centre** on its Harbour Road. Opened in 1977 with contributions from the public, the Arts Centre has 15 floors of auditoria, rehearsal rooms, theatre workshops, restaurants, and the offices of numerous cultural organizations. On any given night, the Centre may be presenting a Shakepearian play, a Japanese Kabuki ensemble or a Humphrey Bogart and Marlene Dietrich film.

Across the street is the **Academy for Performing Arts**, the territory's newest cultural additon.

Larger ensembles are featured at the other end of Wanchai, in the **Queen Elizabeth Sports Stadium**, on Oi Kwan Road. Opened in 1978, at a cost of HK$50 million, it has a seating capacity of 3,500 and hosts anything from Saddler's Wells Ballet to basketball games. There are facilities for volleyball, badminton, boxing, fencing, judo, and even kung fu. Nearby, on Gloucester Road, is the **Government Sports Stadium**, the scene of regular football matches.

The name Wanchai is equivalent to nighttime shennanigans. "Nighttown" glows along the main east-west artery of **Lockhart Road**. But by day, The Wanch's atmosphere is totally different. Due to the high rents in neighbouring Central, many businesses have spilled into Wanchai, creating a ready clientele for better restaurants and shops. The Wanchai Reclamation, between Gloucester Road and the harbour is now alive with office blocks (Sun Hung Kai and China Resources buildings, the Causeway, Great Eagle and Harbour centres) and an exhibition centre.

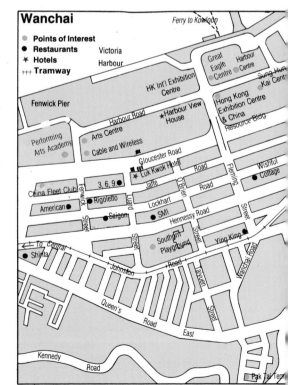

Lucky Mirrors

Two blocks to the south of Hennessy Road is a far more "Chinese" section of town, **Queen's Road East**, which formed the harbour area before land reclamation Here one finds famous Chinese furniture-makers working right out on the street, where they fashion camphorwood chests and hardwood tables and chairs. Little lanes which wend further south from Queen's Road East may be devoted entirely to the selling of pets or lightbulbs, bathtubs or flowers.

Here also are two well-known Chinese temples. On **Stone Nullah Lane**, to the right off Queen's Road East, is **Pak Tai Temple**, built only a century ago but home to a 10-foot copper image dating to 1604. Closer to Central is Tik Loong Lane, which leads pilgrims to **Chai Kung Woot Fat Temple, the Temple of the Living Buddha.** At this extraordinary place, people who have overcome illnesses leave offerings in the form of mirrors with lucky inscriptions. Thus, the temple interior is dazzling!

Between Queen's Road East and Hennessy is Johnston Road, bisected by **Southorn Playground**, a place where Chinese opera is often presented at night (as are go-karting events). Parallel to Hennessy to its north is Lockhart Road, Gloucester Road and finally Harbour Road. Little of touristic interest here, unless one is interested in 1960s office buildings.

On Gloucester Road, however, is a place which will induce tears of nostalgia in the starstruck eyes of world of Suzie Wong-lovers. This is the **Luk Kwok Hotel**, the infamous "short-time" hotel where the fictional Suzie lived, loved and worked. The movie was not really made here (it was shot mostly in Western), and today, the Luk Kwok is rather posh and no longer the quaint little place—with a big dance floor and a wonderful series of balconies and shaky staircases—you saw in the film. The Luk Kwok is now a family hotel but should you look behind her, avoiding the bright lights of discos, you may still catch a few glimpses of old Wanchai in the alleys — though they shall soon pass to dust under jackhammers and cranes.

Wanchai
electro
commerce.

HAPPY VALLEY

Western District was the first Hong Kong suburb occupied by Europeans, but they soon deserted it and moved to a spot which seemed healthier. They optimistically named this second living area **Happy Valley**. Happy Valley was relatively distant from the sea, was somewhat deserted and, most important, didn't have "unhealthy" and malaria-ridden rice farms in its vicinity. (By the late 1840s anti malaria laws had been passed which banned farming on the island.)

Playing the Ponies

In 1841, shortly after Happy Valley was settled, the colony's happy-go-lucky residents created the greensward and edifice which has made Happy Valley world famous. This is the Royal Hong Kong Jockey Club's **Happy Valley Racecourse**. Until a few years ago, this horse-racing oval was the only one in the colony. It's less than one mile long,

but during the October-to-May racing season, it attracts thousands of race-goers (about 35,000 a running). Night-racing here is very impressive, and if you'd like to experience this, visitors' badges and information can be obtained from the Hong Kong Tourist Association. (Racing tips are published in all the English-language newspapers, and are broadcast on television for the benefit of serious pony-players.) There isn't a spot anywhere in Happy Valley which doesn't give visitors at least a partial view of the race track. And indeed, the name of the district has become synonymous with the sport. Curiously, Happy Valley is also a favourite shopping zone.

Geographically, Happy Valley's would-be happiness begins on Queen's Road East, at the corner of long winding **Stubbs Road**. To savour her best views, though, one should zigzag to the top of Stubbs Road, to Peak Road. Here squats a beautiful four-storey house built by a Chinese merchant in traditional Chinese chauvinist style (with a different storey for each wife). A few blocks down is another Chinese-style house, this one with a green roof (green signifying that the owner was

Happy Valley.

wealthy and wanted to flaunt the fact). Film buffs might be interested to know that this was the movie home of Clark Gable and Susan Hayward in *Soldier of Fortune*, one of Gable's last film roles before he died.

Just above the intersection of Tai Hang Road with Stubbs Road is an official **rest garden** and **lookout point** which frame an unimpeded view of the harbour, the Kowloon promontory and, of course, the race track.

Nearer Stubbs Road's bottom, at the corner of Queen's Road East and Stubbs Road, is a fine **Sikh temple**, dating to the last century. Opposite that is a **Tuberculosis Sanitorium**.

Celestial Kitsch

Travelling east on Queen's Road one will find five segregated cemeteries.

First is the **Muslim Cemetery** near a mosque (which is dotted with curious Chinese language headstones). Next to that lies a **Catholic Cemetery**, established in 1847. The largest final resting place here is the **Colonial Cemetery**, first occupied in 1845. Lovers of epitaphs won't find this historical place as

interesting as Macau's literate Protestant Cemetery, but it does have many interesting old headstones which were placed over the remains of early missionaries, soldiers and sailors. Its most famous inhabitant is Lord Napier, who opened up trade with China and died at Macau in 1834.

Beyond these three cemeteries is the **Parsee Cemetery**, circa 1852. And on nearby Shan Kwong Road is the **Jewish Cemetery**, consecrated in 1855; its oldest surviving tomb is dated 1859.

Like Stubbs Road, nearby **Wongneichong Gap Road** also offers superb views of the city. (One mustn't confuse Wongneichong Gap with Wongneichong Road, which is adjacent to the race-course.) Also on this road, which leads to Repulse Bay Beach, are **tennis courts** and the venerable (founded, 1851) **Hong Kong Cricket Club** which moved here from Central in 1975.

A Chinese Disneyland

Outside of its race-course, Happy Valley's second most well-known attraction is a place which looks like a hallucinogenic vision of a Chinese Disneyland. This is the Aw Boon Haw (formerly Tiger Balm) Gardens on Tai Hang Road. The 150,000 square-foot amusement park stands in celestialy kitchy splendour — as a garish Chinese "Disneyland." This zany site has terraced grottos which are profligate with bizzarre stone sculptures and garish reliefs from the most awesome and awful tales of Chinese mythology. Garish is not *exactly* the right word... ostentatious, gaudy, psychedelic, call it what you will. It says something about the Chinese mind, but we leave the visitor to deduce what that might be.

However, there will be no questioning of good taste after one visits the mansion at Aw Boon Haw Gardens. This estate houses one of the finest jade collections in the colony. Permission must be granted for entering it, but the Hong Kong Tourist Association can assist with such arrangements.

While on Tai Hang Road, you can see on nearby hillsides hundreds of little shacks; these are the temporary homes of squatter refugees who are awaiting resettlement by the government. Further up and due right can be seen one of the larger resettlement estates, **Lai Tai**.

Athlete.

CAUSEWAY BAY

Cruising down from Tai Hang Road to King's Road, opposite **Victoria Park**, you enter a fascinating modern sector of the island: **Causeway Bay**. (The area can also be reached more directly by tram, bus or a taxi from Central.)

Causeway Bay is bounded on the east by Victoria Park, on the west by Canal Road, on the south by **Caroline Hill** and Leighton Road, and on the north by the harbour. Causeway Bay really was a bay until the 1950s when the bay disappeared into a great land reclamation project. (What was then Causeway Bay is today Paterson Street.)

Sunset by Sampan

The present-day "bay" is occupied by the **Royal Hong Kong Yacht Club** on **Kellett Island** (which also was once a "real" island), and the **Typhoon Shelter**. To get there, cross Victoria Park Road in front of the **Excelsior Hotel**. At sunset hour, you will immediately be besieged by a gaggle of women. Don't get the wrong idea. All they are offering is a chaste ride in one of their "floating restaurant" sampans. No hanky-panky is ever suggested. Besides, there is no room for hanky-panky, because the deck is filled beam to boom with tables and chairs. Bargain for the sampan (before you get on, obviously). The price should come to about HK$60 to $100, depending on the sampan's size.

Your sampan will weave its way through the crowded sea lanes of the typhoon basin by paddle power, a-bobbing while dodging other restaurant sampans, fishing junks, pleasure yachts, and large passenger ferries. The place is alive with water traffic. Bring your own wine, if you wish, because the bar sampans (which buzz your craft moments after it clears land) add offshore mark-ups to the price of their booze. Cold beer, however, is reasonably priced.

Kitchen sampans pull up next, vying for orders and showing off their fresh prawns, crabs and fish. Seafood, noodles, congee, omelettes — just about anything edible—can be prepared before you in these precarious floating kitchens.

Music is provided by a live band-sampan. A song list is passed over for your consideration, but be warned that by popular colonial opinion, this floating combo is considered to be the worst, most out-of-tune band in Hong Kong, or perhaps the world. The "song menu" usually includes two selections. No other music is played, and the band's favourite and standard tune is—would you believe—"The Yellow Rose of Texas." This floating musical repertoire has not changed in a decade. Cost: HK$25 per tune.

Though they hardly serve Chinese haute cuisine, restaurant sampans are a fun experience, and the food is fresh, tasty and filling.

Going to the loo on these little restaurant sampan is also an experience not to be missed, especially by the ladies. A tiny cubicle in the stern is curtained off when you make appropriate anxious gestures. Some actually have a pot (which empties directly into the bay) and others just an open hole you squat over. If such appointments are unacceptable, or if her ladyship is not an able contortionist, don't give up. Make even more proper and disgusted

Preceding pages, The Royal Hong Kong Yacht Club on Kellet Island

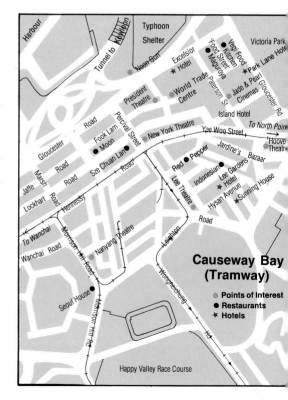

Causeway Bay (Tramway)

● Points of Interest
● Restaurants
★ Hotels

gestures, and your sampan lady will scull over to a luxury yacht where, for a modest tip to the boat boy, you may relieve yourself in grander and more civilized comfort.

This part of Hong Kong's waterfront also features a unique genuflection to the musical genius of Noel Coward: the **Noon-Day Gun**.

Nobody is absolutely certain why the gun is fired at noon everyday, but according to a century-old legend this ritual, now a Hong Kong tradition, began one day in the mid 1800s when one of the Jardine's opium boats sailed into the harbour and a willing minion gave the boat a 21-gun salute. Hong Kong's Governor was incensed that a mere purveyor of "foreign mud" should receive the same greeting as an official figure, so—as penance—he ordered that the gun be fired at noon everyday in perpetuity.

Ergo, Coward's lyric: "In Hong Kong, they strike a gong and fire a noon-day gun, to reprimand each inmate who's in late."

The legend may not be true—the penance sounds too Greek, almost Pro-methean. The real truth is probably that the Jardine's managing director got a reprimand in the Royal Hong Kong Jockey Club ("These things just aren't *done*, dear boy."). Whatever the rascal reason, Jardine's doesn't regret the story. Every New Year's Eve, Jardines executives, in their fanciest bib 'n tucker stand by the gun and ceremoniously fire it at midnight to the discreet applause of a small colonial gathering.

"Modern" Causeway Bay

Causeway Bay's "modern" history began in 1973 when the Cross-Harbour Tunnel was opened. This underwater freeway is one of the largest tunnels in Asia. Its four lanes cross two kilometers of harbour water between Hong Kong and Kowloon.

With this tunnel came the inevitable: Causeway Bay was transformed into a thriving little city. Three deluxe hotels opened—the **Park Lane**, and **Lee Gardens** and the **Excelsior**. Next door to the Excelsior is the **World Trade Centre**, a 42-storey complex chock-a-block with plush offices, restaurants and night clubs. In the same building is the **Palace**

Street life, Causeway Bay.

Theatre, which was transformed from a supper club to a posh cinema.

Street blocks behind the Excelsior have shopping outlets which sell goods at prices cheaper than similar stores located in Central or Kowloon. Fine big department stores (**Daimaru, Matsuzakaya, Sogo,** all Japanese, and branches of **China Products** and **Lane Crawford's**), movie theatres and literally hundreds of little hi-fi and camera shops crowd over into Hennessy Road and continue west down to Canal Road. Most are open until 10 p.m. each night.

One block to the east of Paterson Street, at right angles to the Plaza Hotel and Victoria Park, is **Food Street**. In Food Street's two blocks and 80,000 square feet of space are 28 diverse dining places, more than 200 chefs and menus listing some 2,000 dishes. More than 100,000 people gorge themselves here each week on Peking duck, Punjabi *dahl*, American beefsteak, Cantonese congee, Japanese *teppanyaki*, and garlicky Szechuan eggplant— among innumberable other dishes. The quality varies, but Food Street is good fun; its fountained and canopied lanes are worth a good half hour of nighttime.

Due east two blocks is the aforementioned Victoria Park, which is busy about 20 hours a day. Around 4 a.m. *tai chi chuan* and jogging exercises begin. Later, tennis players on 14 different courts begin playing. And by mid-morning, football players, kite-fliers and swimmers are exercising. Each December, the park plays host to a **Hong Kong International Karting Prix.** And during the Chinese New Year and the colony's Autumn Lantern Festival, the park is aglow with flower displays— of peach, orange and narcissus blossoms—and hundreds of candlelit lanterns; it's one of the colony's most beautiful annual sights.

Across from Victoria Park is **Tin Hau Temple Road**, whose temple dates back to 1747. On nearby Tunglowan Road, near the **Park Theatre**, is **Queen's College**, the oldest Anglo-Chinese school, founded in 1862. And on the northern side of this street is the **Causeway Bay Magistracy**. Daily courtroom sessions, conducted in English, are open to the public.

So much for "modern" Causeway Bay. "Old" Causeway Bay has existed since the beginning of Hong Kong. The first Jardines godowns were on **Yee Woo Street** (*Yee Woo* is Jardines' name in Shanghainese) which is a short continuation of Hennessy Road. In this sector is **Jardine's Bazaar**, a marketplace which also dates back to those "foreign mud" and buccaneering days. Today, Jardines Bazaar and nearby **Jardine's Crescent** are equally fascinating.

Indeed, each street in this area has special shopping wonders. **Pennington Street** is known for its shops making paper effigies for funerals, Chinese medicine shops and old-style pawn shops (where the chief pawn-broker sits high up in a judgement seat like the Lord of Justice himself). At an herbalist teahouse, for only HK$1 a bowl, you can enjoy "24-flavoured Tea," a brew prepared with different seeds, lichen, grasses, roots, stems and fungi.

On nearby **Irving Street** are soya sauce and wine shops. And on **Fuk Hing Lane**, 100-year eggs and eartnenware pottery venue, you can pick up fine *wok*, Chinese all-purpose cooking pans.

This maze opens up to Hysan Avenue, where sits the **Lee Gardens Hotel** and **Lee Theatre**—a theatre which usually features Western artists. There are many boutiques here — and also along blocks bordering the Lee Gardens Hotel are more "ethnic" restaurants than anywhere else in the colony. A five minute walk and you will discover Vietnamese, Indonesian, Russian, Cantonese, Shanghainese, Malaysian, Indian, Korean, Chiu Chow, Italian, Japanese, and good old European and coffee shop food, all at very reasonable prices.

Turing to the east, head up Leighton Road to Caroline Hill. Here is the colony's largest girls orphanage, **Po Leung Kuk**, founded in 1880 to aid girls who in years past had been kidnapped into slavery. The nearby **Morrison Hill Sports Club** hosts numerous sporting activities.

On the way to Causeway Bay's main artery, Hennessy Road (due west) is Canal Road. It is here where Causeway Bay meets Wanchai. Facing west and across the street to the left is a row of traditional Chinese butcher shops with warm (meaning fresh) meat. Butchers with huge cleavers argue with housewives over prices.

NORTH POINT, QUARRY BAY, SHAUKIWAN AND CHAIWAN

East of Victoria Park, Hong Kong becomes a shabby industrial area, where more and more highrises sprout with every new joint venture.

However, the best way to explore the four major sections of eastern Hong Kong—**North Point, Quarry Bay, Shaukiwan** and **Chaiwan**—is by tram. Sitting on a tram's upper deck, you can say bye-bye to Victoria Park, and cruise and relax for 45 minutes.

Red Stars at the Sunbeam

The first eastern Hong Kong district is **North Point**, which has a few movie theatres, a couple of good department stores, and a ferry service to **Kwun Tong** on the Kowloon side. The most interesting theatre here is the **Sunbeam**, at 423 King's Road. Because it's owned by impressarios with Peking cultural connections, this theatre features live performances by renowned Communist Chinese entertainers. Unfortunately, the Sunbeam's Red stars are never promoted in Hong Kong's English language press.

Continuing due east, one's tram lurches past the **Hong Kong Funeral Home**, the largest mortuary on the island. Opposite are dozens of convenient wreathmakers. You are now in **Quarry Bay**. To your left is the harbour, and to the right are bare green hills. Continuing along **King's Road**, you come to **Taikoo Shing** on the left, one of the new vertical cities that have sprung up. The main interest for visitors is **Cityplaza**, the shopping and entertainment complex. Located here are hundreds of shops, ice and roller skating rinks, bowling alleys, cinemas, **Tivoli Terrace** — an excellent sidewalk cafe run by Jimmy's Kitchen (one of the colony's most venerable eating establishments) — and the Italian delicatessen, **Vini & Salumi.**

A bit past the main part of Shaukiwan town, just off the main road, is the interesting **Tam Kung Temple** on A Kung Ngam Road. Tam Kung isn't a character usually found in Chinese mythology text, because he made his late spiritual debut during pre-British Hong Kong years. He is a boy-god who predicts the weather and is thus a favourite patron of fishermen. On Tam Kung's birthday, on the eighth day of the fourth moon (around May), fishermen sail here from other parts of the colony to pay their respects with dragon-dancing, spirit medium rituals, incense burning and colourful processions through Shaukiwan's busy streets.

To continue on to the far eastern end of the island, board a local mini-bus.

The next settlement in this direction is **Chaiwan**, which squats around **Leiyuemun Bay**. Chaiwan has a few parks, housing estates, a huge Chinese cemetery, and an old English fort.

The road that forks to the right leads to Shek-O Beach on the south side of the island.

There isn't much to do in Chaiwan. During the windy season, some photographers like to go out to a nearby hillock and photograph the sprawling Chinese cemetery. Following such breezy weather the cemetery is blanketed by colourful kites which have escaped from their owners.

Tram stop, Hennessey Road.

SOUTHSIDE:
SHEK O, STANLEY,
REPULSE BAY,
AND OCEAN PARK

"Unofficial" visitors cannot continue due east from Chaiwan town because this road leads to the sensitive military intelligence base of **Little Sai Wan**. But by backtracking a bit, and turning right down **Shek O Road**, one travels directly to the south side of Hong Kong Island—and a totally different world.

Southside Hong Kong is a region of rocky coasts and smooth white beaches; of little fishing villages and unhurried markets. Neither an office building nor factory is anywhere in sight. But on summer weekends, every office, factory and farm worker in the colony seems to descend on the southside's shores.

Of Hong Kong's 36 gazetted beaches, the southside of the island has 14. A few, like **Rocky Bay** on the road to Shek O, have virtually no facilities, save an unparalleled view and an uncrowded beach. Others, like Repulse Bay, feature busloads of tourists, a McDonald's hamburger stand, and about as much peace and quiet as a carnival.

Shek O and Big Wave Bay

Shek O Beach is somewhere at middle ground. The road from Chaiwan skirts **Mount Collinson** on the left, and **Tai Tam Harbour** to the right. At a fork in the road, one can go left about four miles to **Big Wave Bay** (a pretty beach, but with absolutely no public transportation to the beach). The Shek O beach and village, about the same distance from the fork, can be reached by public bus and Big Wave Bay's beach is is a 30-minute walk from Shek O.

The marketplace at Shek O Village caters almost entirely to bathers. Soft drinks and a few snacks are available. What the market and beach hide, though, is the site of some truly luxurious homes. Following paths at right angles to the beach, one can wander through lane after lane of high-walled mansions owned by some of Hong Kong's most affluent citizens.

Past the village, one can stroll out to **Shek O Headland**, facing the islands of **Tai Tau Chau** and **Ng Fan Chau**. To the right is the southernmost point of the island, **Cape D'Aguilar**. It was from Shek O Headland and this peninsula that almost nightly appearance of Vietnamese refugee boats could be seen in recent years as they drifted listlessly, looking for a safe harbour and freedom. They are rarer now, but still appear on the horizon from time to time.

A good 18-hole golf course is on the road just before the beach, but one must belong to the **Shek O Country Club** to dig divots there.

Trekking at Tai Tam

After the first turn-off to Shek O, the road from Chaiwan continues in a curve to one of the most well-trodden hiking spots on the island: **Tai Tam Reservoir**. This was the first reservoir erected in Hong Kong, its earliest section completed in 1899. The two-hour walk in lovely areas surrounded by mountains, begins on **Tai Tam Road**, skirts around the different reservoirs, and ends at **Wongneichong Gap Road** near the **Hong Kong Cricket Club**. Boaters can also enjoy the scenery by renting boats out on the water run-off areas below **Tai Tam Bridge**.

The most strenuous walk of all trails not only around the reservoir but continues on a little catchwater path to the top of a hill, along the whole southern coast and on past **Deepwater Bay** and **Stanley Village**. There is nothing difficult about this path (which runs alongside a culvert atop the hill), but hiking down to the lowlands requires extra effort. Once one sights **Repulse Bay**, the gradient steepens and, indeed, unwary climbers have experienced serious accidents by trying to take a shortcut to the road. The best plan is, ironically, to reach the gully by literally breaking into a prison. After Deepwater Bay and Repulse Bay, the hill curves down into Stanley Village. But the path here leads directly into **Stanley Prison**, one of the colony's security establishments for malefactors. To the surprised looks of guards, you'll be descending *into* the prison. Simply shrug your shoulders and walk on an outside path to the exit.

Stanley: Pirates and Markets

That's the most unusual way to get to Stanley Beach. More usual from Tai

Tam is to take public transportation or a car past Tai Tam Reservoir along the coast to **Turtle Cove** to Stanley Village Road and the village itself.

Despite Stanley's veddy English-sounding name (it was named after Lord Stanley, the 19th Century Secretary of State for the Colonies), Stanley was a thriving Chinese capital long before the British set foot here. In fact, a **Tin Hau Temple** here documents that the town was founded in 1770 by a pirate, Chang Po Chai, who captured the island.

Once one of the colony's best-kept shopping secrets, today **Stanley Market** attracts thousands of visitors on weekends, though it's open every day. Here, down a few steps from New Street, is a large area with shops selling fashionable clothes (usually over-runs or seconds), rattan, fresh food, ceramic jugs, budget art, hardware, brass objects, Chinese products, vases, jeans, sweaters—practically everything.

Eating used to be a second-rate experience in Stanley. But in 1979, **Stanley's Restaurant** opened along the main street facing the harbour and proceeded to serve French food at fair prices.

There are a few more institutions of some interest here. The **Hong Kong Sea School**, for example, is a unique institution. It accepts only boys from underprivileged environments, about 550 a year. Each pay HK$80 a year (if they can afford it), and they then are trained to join the ranks of Hong Kong's most advanced seamen. Modelled on the United Kingdom's National School of Seamanship, it imposes a spartan regimen on the boys, but also trains them in all the basic and advanced techniques of seamanship.

Down the road is Stanley Prison, and to the right of this is the **Stanley Military Cemetery**, a quiet and fitting reminder of the part which Stanley played in the Second World War. It was in Stanley—at both the prison and at nearby **St. Stephen's College**—that the Japanese kept British prisoners-of-war interned. Near the cemetery is **St. Stephen's Beach**, a cleaner and more pleasant place than Stanley's main beach.

Repulse Bay: Crowds and Chic

From Stanley, one may travel to the "capital" of the south side, **Repulse**

Stanley Village and Beach.

Bay, directly on Repulse Bay Road. The 15-minute trip (which doubles in time on jammed summer weekends) leads to **South Bay** and **Middle Bay** beaches, which are usually less crowded by far than the madness which is Repulse Bay Beach on weekends.

Repulse Bay Beach has everything, except peace and quiet. It had one of the finest resort hotels in the East — **The Repulse Bay Hotel**. It also has hamburger and noodle stands, thousands of blaring transistor radios, luxurious high-rises, and a beach which gets filthy on weekends (due to an invasion of some 25,000 bathers).

Unfortunately, the hills remind one of a very sad story. It was over those same hills that invading Japanese came pouring at the end of 1941, determined to make the grand Repulse Bay Hotel just another building in "The Captured Territory of Hong Kong." The hotel at that time was a military target, because British and Canadian troops used it as a headquarters (to keep open the road between Stanley and Aberdeen). After three days of fighting, the hotel was taken, and Commonwealth prisoners were marched to **Eucliffe Mansion**, to the right of the hotel and about one-quarter of a mile away. Here, most of the prisoners were executed, and survivors were put into the **Stanley Internment Camp**.

Two questions are always asked about Repulse Bay:

(1) What is "repulse-ive" about the bay? Except for the Monday morning garbage cleanup, nothing. It was named after the battleship HMS *Repulse*, which took an active part in the thwarting of pirates who plundered here in the early days.

(2) What is that huge statue just to the right of McDonald's and fronting the life-saving club? Elementary. She's the most popular of all goddesses in Hong Kong, **Tin Hau**. She is the Queen of Heaven, but—most important—she is the protector of fishermen and anybody engaged in seafaring activities.

Southside Attractions:
Deep Water Bay and Ocean Park

From Repulse Bay, the coast road curves westward over some of the colony's most beautiful scenery—to Deep

Water Bay, Ocean Park and Aberdeen. (If going by bus, one must surely sit on the top deck to soak in this ride's magnificent vistas.)

Deep Water Bay has some very beautiful mansions (including the house where *Love Is a Many-Splendoured Thing* was filmed). It also has a good 9-hole golf course managed by the **Royal Hong Kong Golf Club** (open on weekdays to tourists). Further along is the more exclusive **Hong Kong Country Club**.

Nearby is a street which leads to the **Police Training School** and one of Hong Kong's biggest tourist attractions: **Ocean Park** and the adjacent Water World (May to October only),

Opened in 1977, Ocean Park cost HK$150 million. It is owned and subsidised by the Royal Hong Kong Jockey Club. Located on 170 acres of land, it is the world's largest oceanarium.

The Park actually consists of two sections: a **Lowland** site with 40 acres, and a **Headland** site of 130 acres. The two sectors are linked by a 1.4 kilometer **cable car** bridge.

On the Lowland are a number of gardens, parks, a children's zoo (which includes a remarkable trained-bird show) and sometimes other attractions. But it's the Headland, at the end of a spectacular cable car ride which overlooks the South China Sea, which has the most interesting exhibits. The **Ocean Theatre** there is the largest marine mammal theatre in the world, with a seating capacity of 4,000 and a pool fit for dolphins, killer whales, and sometimes visiting diving shows. **Wave Cove**, nearby, simulates a rocky coastline, with a special machine that generates waves up to one metre high. At two different levels, sea lions, seals, dolphins, penguins and sea birds may be seen diving or skimming along the cove's surface. Finally, there is an **Atoll Reef** with more than 300 different fish species and about 30,000 swimming specimens. It is the largest aquarium in the world, containing two-million litres of seawater. One can view this aquarium from three different levels.

In 1984, the park opened **Water World** and an amusement park section, which includes The Dragon, one of the world's longest (840-meter) roller coaster. Call 5-532-3244 for opening hours, show times and admission prices.

On the headland is also the amuse-ment park section with various rides including The Dragon, one of the world's longest rollercoasters (840 metres), which seems to whip out over the beautiful South China Sea at each pass. Tickets cost HK$70 for adults, HK$35 for children. Add HK$7 and HK$3 per adult and child, if you take the convenient special bus (round trip) from Central District. Call 5-550947 for information.

In 1984, the adjacent Water World section was opened. This is a water play park with dozen different activities including water slides and a lovely beach. It is only open from May through October. The cost is HK$40 for adults, HK$20 for kids, with special low evening prices. (Again, add HK$7 and HK$3, per adult and child, if you take the special bus from Central. Call 5-556055 for information.

The main road, **Wong Chuk Hang**, proceeds left towards Aberdeen and soon passes by the **Grantham Hospital** (on the right) which treats heart diseases exclusively. Also near here is the **Aberdeen Trade School**, run by the Catholic Church to educate the children of Aberdeen's boat people.

Below, Marina life in Ocean Park. Right, cable cars on their way to Ocean Park

ABERDEEN

Aberdeen has a character unlike any other town in the colony. Its charm, though, is questionable because this naturally ideal typhoon anchorage is home to about 20,000 of Hong Kong's 70,000 "boat people" and their 3,000-odd junks and sampans.

The 'Egg People'

The term "boat people" has two meanings: one refers to Vietnamese refugees who came pouring into Hong Kong during the late 1970s, causing a momentary population-plus panic. (The panic was soon allayed when manufacturers realized that the Vietnamese were an ideal source of cheap labour.) The more traditional boat people are those who have been living on local waters for thousands of years.

The latter group of these boat people consists of two main tribes; the Tanka (literally the "egg people," because they used to pay taxes in eggs rather.

than cash) and the Hoklo. Other Chinese have never accepted them (pre-Communist China wouldn't even permit them to settle on land), but Hong Kong is encouraging them to leave their boats. Schools for their children are opening up, housing estates are being constructed for them, and as land is gradually reclaimed from the harbour, the fishing people are being lured to work in factories.

Romantics might bemoan this loss of "traditional life," but these hot metal-roofed boats are really a "floating slum" and an obviously inconvenient lifestyle. Nobody, however, is forcing the boat people to leave their life-styles: they make their own choice.

'Little Hong Kong'

At any rate, tourists are still seduced by the colourful 30-minute ride through Aberdeen Harbour (for about HK$50). They still enjoy the chaotic atmosphere, the incredible collection of sea life and the dynamism of this city upon the water. They also enjoy the opulent Chinese **floating restaurants** (one must take a sampan to dine there), which are

Preceding pages and below, the junk fleet; right, Aberdeen boat boys.

not in Aberdeen Harbour proper anymore, but in the "yacht basin" of Shumwan, across from the Aberdeen Boat Club and the Aberdeen Marina.

What, though, does the southern Hong Kong town of Aberdeen have to do with that Scottish town of the same name? Only that the village wasn't named after the Scottish city, but for the Earl of Aberdeen, the 1848 Secretary of State for the Colonies. To the Chinese, Aberdeen is still called *Heung Keung Tsai*: **Little Hong Kong**.

And like "big" Hong Kong, Aberdeen hardly lacks for wealth. Perhaps most of the wealth has come through smuggling instead of legitimate enterprises, but **Main Street** here has quite a few banks, countless jewellery shops and a feeling of financial movement.

To see this area best, begin with the town's **Tin Hau Temple** built here in 1851. The temple is rather shabby most of the year, but during April's Tin Hau Festival, it is alive with ceremony and thousands of gaily-decorated boats converge on Aberdeen's shores. It's an event not to be missed. Along Aberdeen's Main Street is a good **China Products Emporium** and an interesting **Fisherman's Hall** where wedding receptions and elections are held.

The four side streets between Aberdeen's Main Road and Chengdu Road all have their own character. Northernmost **Lok Yeung Road** has a little shop selling pet food—not only for fish and birds, but also for caterpillars! And street barbers still cut a mean head of hair here.

Traditional Boat-Builders

At **Wu Pak Street** there are a few good general markets, plus a papermaking shop for funerals. Finally, at **Wu Nam Street**, one can take a little ferry four times a day to **Sok Kwu Wan**, a tiny settlement on **Lamma Island**, to sample that isle's good seafood. Why so good? Because the ferry is managed by the progressive Sok Kwu Wan Fishermen's Society. They should know!

Another good ferry ride—optional, because a bridge now links the mainland to that destination—is the one to **Apleichau Island**. This island, just two minutes away from Aberdeen, houses the colony's great boat-builders. They make ferries, sloops, cruisers, speedboats, yachts and steel lighters, as well

as traditional sampans and junks. For the latter, it takes only three months to make an 80-foot junk from teak logs, a traditional task they complete using no blueprints. An innate sense of knowing what's right takes the place of formal plans. Usually somebody in the yards speaks English.

Near the island's landing is a shrine to its local god, Hung Shing, a legendary weather forecaster. Few people pay homage at this **Hung Shing Shrine**, because Tin Hau is more popular.

On the outskirts of Aberdeen is the **Holy Spirit Seminary**, which overlooks the town. This seminary, built in 1931 to resemble an old Chinese fort, welcomes visitors.

Jade Palace Restaurant is at 2 Wah Fu Road. This restaurant's five floors house an extraordinary collection of eating places: French, Cantonese, Shanghainese, Pekinese, Hong Kong's only Hunanese restaurant and a proper nightclub.

Up the hill towards Pokfulam is **Chi Fu Fa Yuen**, another huge housing development with its own shopping centre which includes the Chi Fu village, a "traditional" Chinese village.

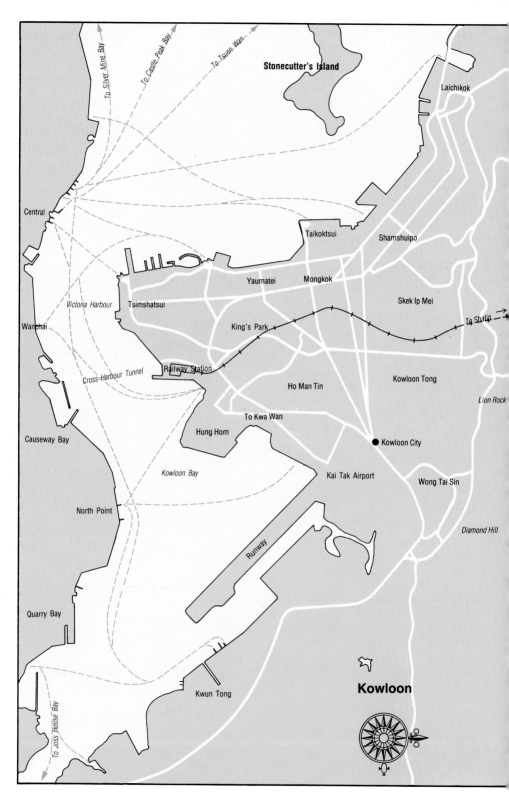

Stonecutter's Island

Laichikok

To Silver Mine Bay

To Castle Peak Bay

To Tsuen Wan

Central

Taikoktsui

Shamshuipo

Yaumatei

Mongkok

Skek Ip Mei

Victoria Harbour

Tsimshatsui

King's Park

To Shatin

Wanchai

Cross-Harbour Tunnel

Railway Station

Ho Man Tin

Kowloon Tong

Lion Rock

To Kwa Wan

Causeway Bay

Hung Hom

● Kowloon City

Kowloon Bay

Kai Tak Airport

Wong Tai Sin

North Point

Diamond Hill

Runway

Quarry Bay

To Joss House Bay

Kwun Tong

Kowloon

KOWLOON, 'NINE DRAGONS'

Kowloon, though geographically a part of the Chinese mainland, is politically British soil, having been ceded to Britain in 1860 under a Treaty of Peking which was negotiated as a Chinese concession at the time of the so-called Opium Wars. This was the second of three treaties that created the present Royal Crown Colony of Hong Kong.

The name Kowloon is made up of two Chinese words, *gau*, meaning nine, and *lung*, meaning dragon. Tradition says that a boy Emperor who once lived here noticed there were eight hills so he called them the "Eight Dragons." A servant pointed out that an emperor is considered to be a dragon also; therefore, with the eight hills plus the boy Emperor there were really nine dragons—*gaulung*. This was transliterated to English as *Kowloon*.

Since the government's answer to the colony's shortage of usable land is to grind down mountains and push this earth into the sea, a visitor can no long-

er count eight dragons, let alone nine. However, there is a little park near Kai Tak Airport where the boy Emperor, Ping, and his Chief Minister died. They had been driven by Mongol invaders to the edge of the land and, to avoid their being captured, the Chief Minister took the young Emperor into his arms and jumped into the sea, thereby ending the Sung dynasty. Ping was the first and last Chinese emperor ever to live in what is now Hong Kong. In that park is a rock inscribed *Sung Wong Toi* which means the "*Sung Emperor's Terrace.*"

Shopper's 'Paradise'

In area, Kowloon is a mere three and one quarter square miles, but it is this small area that most people remember after a visit to Hong Kong. Kowloon is *the* "shoppers' paradise" most visitors aim for, and also the site of most of the colony's big hotels that cater to tourists and businessmen.

eceding
ages, in the
ross-
arbour
unnel and
dockside
owloon.
elow, old
owloon,

At the tip of the peninsula, **Tsimshatsui**, is the **Star Ferry concourse**, and the **Ocean Terminal/Ocean Centre Harbour City complex**. Then comes *the* "**Golden Mile**" with its myriad shops and Kowloon's answer to the Suzie Wong style of night-life. Next to Tsimshatsui is the Yaumatei district where people live aboard junks and barges. The **new railway station** that has replaced the old **Kowloon-Canton Railway Terminal**, where people used to board steam-powered trains for travel all the way to Europe, is in **Hung Hom** on the other side of the "tip." In Hung Hom next to the railway station, is the Hong Kong Coliseum, a massive indoor stadium which seats more than 12,000.

Just beyond is **Kai Tak Airport**, actually a legal part of the New Territories, but looked upon as being in Kowloon. Flights land and lift off from Kai Tak on an average of one every $2\frac{1}{2}$ minutes during peak arrival and departure hours.

Nearby is the famous (in Hong Kong) **Kowloon City Market**, an incredible concentration of outdoor and indoor stalls centred on **Lion Rock Road**. A few hundred yards away is the infamous

Walled City. Although little remains of its original walls, there is an invisible barrier that is totally real. Read on for details.

Further east, in the middle of a huge housing estate, is the **Lei Cheng Uk Tomb**, discovered in 1955 during excavations for a housing estate. "The tomb was built during the Han dynasty, when Kowloon was under the administrative district of Tung Kun, in the Wu Kingdom which took control of south China (including present-day Hong Kong) in the period immediately following the collapse of the Han empire," according to J.C.Y. Watt of Hong Kong's City Museum. It dates back to between 100 and 200 A.D. and comprises three rooms where you can still see shards of crockery and other relics from those ancient days.

On the border of the New Territories is the largest privately-financed housing project in the city, **Mei Foo Sun Chuen**, and nearby is the **Laichikok Amusement Park**. The park has rides and games, a house of horrors and a rink for ice-skating. There is also something new there, a **Sung Dynasty Village**.

Harbour-sid in the opule Regent of Hong Kong.

TSIMSHATSUI, 'THE PENINSULA'

When exploring Tsimshatsui, start at the **Star Ferry**. It's no longer the only starting point, because you can now drive through the **Cross-Harbour Tunnel** from Hong Kong Island, or whiz under the harbour on the **Mass Transit Railway**. But for a century, the only way from the island was the faithful Star Ferry, and the reason for going there was to catch the train to Europe. Where the old clock tower stands was "this end" of The Orient Express, the Far East terminus of the rail journey to and from London. Nearby is the **Peninsula Hotel**, where people stayed before boarding the train.

At the **Star Ferry concourse** are some small shops, news vendors, who hawk many overseas newspapers, and a wharf for the harbour's tourboats.

Next to the Star Ferry wharves is **Star House**, which contains the first of the shopping arcades. There is the large **Chinese Arts and Crafts** store, where everything from garments to expensive porcelain may be purchased.

Adjoining the **Star House/Hong Kong Hotel complex** is the **Ocean Terminal/Ocean Centre/Harbour City complex**, the largest air-conditioned and interconnected shopping centre in the whole of Asia. Across the street (Canton Road) is Silvercord, another huge shopping centre which houses the Asia Computer Plaza.

A short walk from the Star Ferry takes you past the old **YMCA** (with modern additions, including a swimming pool) and the venerable (1928) Peninsula Hotel. Across the street is the new egg-shaped **Space Museum, Planetarium** and **Space Theatre**.

Across Nathan Road

Across **Nathan Road** —the start of Hong Kong's famous Golden Mile tourist belt—is the **Sheraton Hotel**, new compared to **The Pen** but now a part of the scene. Across Chatham Road from the Sheraton is **Regent Hotel**, a relative newcomer (opened in 1980) but already famous for its 40-foot high, glassed-in

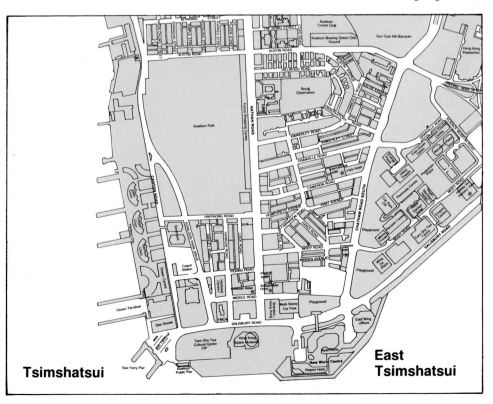

Tsimshatsui

East Tsimshatsui

lobby. Built on the reclamation, it looks across the harbour to Hong Kong Island and lofty Victoria Peak.

Here, at the bottom of Nathan Road, one's overall impression of Tsimshatsui is tall buildings and advertising signs and shop shingles stacked one atop another as far the eye can see. For a grand commercial impression, stand at this same spot after dark and enjoy the dazzling brilliance of neon-upon-neon.

Nathan Road was named after Sir Matthew Nathan, a major in the Royal Engineers who built the road and later became Hong Kong's Governor (in 1904). During Nathan's time this road was a meandering track lined with banyan trees (some of which can still be seen near the **Miramar Hotel**). Citizens used it to drive out to the countryside in horse-drawn buggies for Sunday picnics. Nathan's futuristic notion that Nathan Road would one day be part of a big commercial centre seemed so laughable then that his road was called "Nathan's Folly."

Today there are glittering jewellery shops, camera stores and hi-fi outlets, thousands of them, crammed to the sky. Indeed, those technological playpens and numerous Oriental crafts shops which crowd Nathan Road and its cross-streets are what most visitors to Hong Kong remember when they return home. Gold, diamonds, jade, pewter, ivory, watches, cameras, rugs, carpets, carvings, candelabras — specialty and sundry shops here stretch on and on. There are linens, silks, cottons, tables, chairs, cupboards, cots, cribs, pots, vases, paintings, etchings, and just about anything else you can imagine.

Looking for food? Restaurants also exist all along Nathan Road and its sidestreets. Formal dining rooms and coffeeshops are easily spotted in the major hotels, and there are innumerable others outside. At least five types of Chinese cuisine—Chiu Chow, Pekinese, Shanghainese, Cantonese and Szechuan—are available in addition to Korean, German, Hungarian, French, Malay, Indonesian, Italian, New York kosher, and many others.

Kowloon's Tsimshatsui is also the heart of Hong Kong nightlife. In addition to Chinese opera and traditional theatre, there are glittering international chorus line-cabaret acts in the major hotels. And for gentlemen with hours and dollars to kill, acts of even more

universal appeal are performed in the numerous topless bars situated on sidestreets off Nathan Road. You can still find girlie-bars that retain the flavour of halcyon R&R days of the Sixties and Seventies. One of the oldest haunts is the **Red Lips Bar** on Lock Road.

'Bar City'

Most of the vintage servicemen's bars have been peacefully overshadowed by the more recent "topless bars," the most famous being the **Bottom's Up** on Hankow Road.

Discos are also losing ground as the audio emphasis shifts from canned music to live bands. Kowloon even has some old-fashioned piano bars that offer a quiet ivory-tickling interlude.

Because the colony is always at the forefront of modern efficiency, Hong Kong also offers packaged joy in the form of frenetic tours of **Bar City** in the **New World Centre**. Here are three bars in one venue—including cowboy-style hooting at Country 'n Western watering holes and acrobatics at a Japanese disco.

Below; celestial projector inside the new Space Theatre in Tsimshatsu Right; making change, Kowloon.

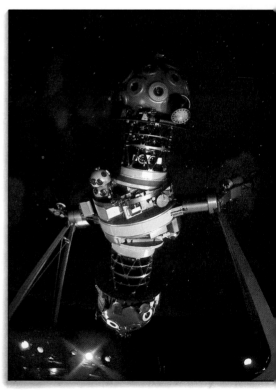

YAUMATEI

Heading north on Kowloon's Canton or Jordan roads, you will surge with the peninsula's traffic into the **Yaumatei District**, an area known for its large typhoon shelter where Hong Kong's famous boat people anchor their floating homes.

Bobbing Brothels

It has been said that some citizens of Yaumatei's boat city live a lifetime without setting foot on shore. This is probably not true, but there are men in this floating community who rarely need to step onto dry land. They go out to sea for fish, return to unload their catch onto other boats, then use the money earned to buy domestic necessities from passing boat-stores. Inhabitants can have a haircut, medical aid or attend a church service—all without going ashore. And some of their children can attend floating schools.

Yaumatei typhoon shelter is also famous for its infamous floating brothels — one-girl sampans that don't guarantee privacy. A passionate customer may find that while rocking in his little love-boat he's creating waves and disturbing neighbours who are playing *mahjong* or watching loud television to port and starboard of his buoy aft. This is grand watersport, but would-be love-boaters should be warned not to sampan-hop alone in this area at night.

Just inland from the teeming waterfront is **Shanghai Street**, a matrimonial avenue well-known for its traditional shops selling old-fashioned gold ornaments and other such items for a Chinese bride's trousseau.

At the junction of Kansu and Reclamation streets is the colony's famous *jade market*. The closest MTR station is Jordan Road, where dealers offer jade in every sculptable form — from large blocks of the raw material to tiny, ornately-carved chips. Some jade pieces here are priceless; others are almost worthless: It's open from 10 a.m. to 4 p.m., and most of its customers are Chinese, so you know it's not a typical tourist trap.

In the **multi-storey carpark** at Yaumatei you'll find practitioners of an age-old Chinese craft, professional let-ter-writing. Here a calligrapher will transcribe a letter in pen (or brush) and ink, or he'll bash it out on a typewriter, whichever you prefer. They handle love letters and business correspondence with equal ease.

Yaumatei's **Temple Street**, originally famous for its temples, is now renowned for its **night market** that lights up after the sun goes down. Here, between Jordan Road and Kansiu Street you'll find a riot of colour and activity, with an endless array of market goods.

In the Temple Street area are four temples, grouped together in **Public Square Street**. The colony's main **Tin Hau Temple** was built on these shores more than 100 years ago. Land reclamation has forced it to move inland, but Yaumatei's boat people hike to it regularly to worship sea gods, particularly Tin Hau, the protector of fisherfolk (see pg. 251). Also in this district are fabulous temples built to honour **Shing Wong**, a spiritual magistrate, and temples dedicated to **Tei** and **Kuan Yin**, the Chinese gods of earth and mercy. (See the feature section article on temples and deities for details.)

Preceding page, Tsimshatsu in neon; dockside nightlife, Yaumatei Typhoon Shelter, right.

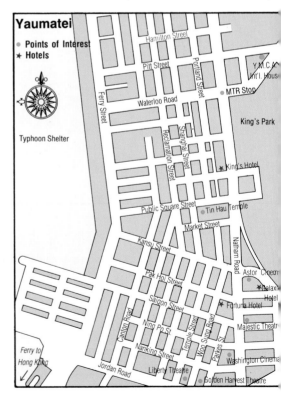

MONGKOK, SANPOKONG, AND KWUN TONG

Hong Kong is well-known as the most densely populated place on earth. And within Kowloon is a district which is the most densely-populated part of Hong Kong. It's called **Mongkok**, and here live an estimated 165,000 people per square kilometer.

Wrong Corner

Many stories are told about how Mongkok got it's name. In the first place, the word or name does not exist in any Chinese dialect. The "kok" part of it means "corner" in Cantonese, and one popular hypothesis notes that the name was supposed to be Wong-kok, meaning "Wong's Corner," but a sign painter inadvertently stenciled the "W" upside down, thus making it Mong-kok instead.

One Mongkok point of interest is the **Juno Restaurant**, one of the earliest examples in Asia of a revolving restaurant. Also, shops along this stretch of Nathan Road have many bargains not found on the lower and pricier end of the "Golden Mile."

Sanpokong, one of Kowloon's first manufacturing areas, is located just opposite Kai Tak Airport in a crowded and dirty jumble of streets bordered on one side by Choi Hung Road and on the other side by Prince Edward Road. Businessmen who visit the colony's factories know the place well. For tourists, the only reason to go there would be to browse through **factory outlet stores** on Tai Yau Street and on sidestreets such as Ng Fong, Luk Hop, Pat Tat and Sheung Hei. Pay attention to the barrow men who may also be wheeling and dealing.

Kwun Tong is considered part of Kowloon administratively but is actually part of the New Territories. It houses numerous industrial facilities and therefore is one of the colony's newer centres for manufacturing, industry and housing estates. It is important enough to be serviced by new four-lane highways (rare in Hong Kong) and ferries from Central, plus it is the final stop on the Mass Transit Railway.

Kwai Chun container terminal.

156

Again, there is not much of interest to tourists except a few factory outlet shops and a fascinating **Temple of the Monkey God**, located in the **Saumauping housing estate**.

A Celestial Rascal

The Monkey God in Chinese religion is known and loved by children. He is a kind of Oriental Santa Claus, Charlie Chaplin and Mickey Mouse reincarnated into one. Chinese children are raised on stories of the Monkey God, a rascal who raised so much hell on Earth he was sent to Hell.

It is a well-known but difficult-to-find temple (the only way is to ask area residents or a local taxi driver). However, you will soon find a fine shrine dedicated to the Monkey God in his most-exalted form as *Chai Tin Dai Sing*, or the "Great Sage Equal to Heaven." According to some of the stories about him, he was more than equal to Heaven, which is why he was banished.

Worshippers at this temple seek health, peace and happiness. There is a medium here who speaks for the Monkey God, and an interpreter relays his messages to the faithful because the medium uses a language unknown to anyone except himself, the interpreter and, of course, the Monkey God.

If you happen to visit in the last week of September you can experience a show here that can only be described as a "happening." It's the annual birthday celebration for the Monkey God, and worshippers produce a show worthy of Barnum and Bailey at their most bizarre. The medium first prays until the Monkey God takes over his body and proceeds to use the medium's body to prove his supernatural powers. For openers, the medium will plunge his hands into boiling oil without any burns or discomfort being inflicted upon himself. Thus, the demonstration continues eventually ending with a grand feast.

The Mass Transit Railway (MTR) makes access to Kwun Tong easy these days. From that stop it's just a short taxi ride to the village of **Leiyuemun**, a tiny fishing village at the eastern entrance of the harbour called **Leiyuemun Pass**. Here you can buy a "jumping" (live) fish and take it to a nearby restaurant for immediate cooking.

Tenement, Mongkok.

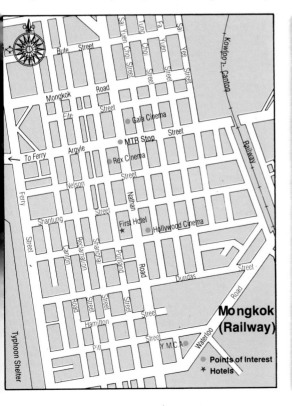

KOWLOON CITY

Nearby the sleazy Walled City is the **Kowloon City Market**, centred on **Lion Rock Road**. This marketplace will keep you busy for a couple of hours at least. Its byways are a good strolling experience. Here you'll find everything from bananas to barbecues, shoes to swine, cheongsam and entire sets of porcelain dinnerware—at prices far less than in the regular "tourist-oriented" districts.

Not far from the Walled City is the **Wong Tai Sin Temple**, which sits a few yards from the MTR station of the same name (see pg. 252). It is situated on **Lung Chung Road** in the midst of modern towering skyscrapers.

Like many Chinese temples, this one is not merely a place of worship, but also a centre for community affairs.

From a distance your eye is attracted to Wong Tai Sin's bright yellow roofing tiles, which were brought from Kwangtung Province across the border. Much of the temple's stonework was likewise imported from many of the same Chinese quarries that have supplied temple builders in China during the past centuries.

Lucrative Fortunes

One of the most important icons at Wong Tai Sin was brought to Hong Kong by a family in 1915. It was a painting they had worshipped in a temple in China called Sik Sik Yuen. It was first placed in a small temple in Wanchai, but later moved to this new Kowloon site. Backed by the powerful Lion Rock, and fronting the sea, geomancers agreed that this new site had good *fung shui*. The temple was completed in 1921 and served for 50 years, before it was again rebuilt.

For its first 35 years, until 1956, the temple was completely private, but then it was opened to the public at an admission fee of HK$0.10. Proceeds went to charity, and so far about HK$4 million dollars have been raised this way.

Devotees, Wong Tai Sin Temple.

158

In addition to admission, the temple's donation boxes raised so much money that the old temple was pulled down and a new one constructed. The HK$4 million edifice you see now was opened in 1973. More fund-raising is evident as you approach the temple. Here are a series of little fortune-tellers' booths. Each fortune teller pays a monthly rental for his stand. The temple's current earnings, about HK$250,000 a year, go to hospitals and schools.

As you approach Wong Tai Sin you may hear the shaking of a *chim*, a wooden cup full of prayer sticks. The *chim* is shaken until a stick falls out. The number of the stick is then carefully noted, and later, a worshipper will have his stick-fortune interpreted by a seer at one of the rented stalls.

If you see somebody shaking out another stick, and then another, it doesn't mean he's increasing his odds of getting a good fortune told. Rather, he's shaking a stick for each of a number of relatives or friends. He'll collect a message for each of them and report their fortunes when he gets home.

The rear of the temple's main altar is carved to show, pictorially and in calligraphy, the story of the great god Wong Tai Sin. Originally he was a shepherd boy. However, Wong Tai Sin was blessed by an immortal who showed him how to refine cinnabar (vermillion, a red mercuric sulfide, HgS) into an immortal drug.

After doing this, he secluded himself for 40 years and remained alone until his brother found him. The brother (ever practical) asked him what he'd done with the sheep he was supposed to be guarding. The immortal Wong Tai Sin took him to a spot where there were many white boulders, and instantly turned them into sheep.

Kowloon's answer to the "short-time" hotels of Wanchai and Causeway Bay is found in **Kowloon Tong** where they are known locally as **blue motels**. They are an economic anomaly in today's Hong Kong, having somehow escaped the so-called Rent Spiral. In a city where apartments are advertised for sale at HK$5 million (that's US$1 million!), and where a flat can cost HK$20,000 a month to rent, it seems strange that a trysting couple can have one of these little rooms for only HK$50 an hour.

THE WALLED CITY

A 'No Man's Land'

Not far from Kai Tak Airport is Kowloon's infamous **Walled City**, a historical and geographical embarrassment. Way back, when the Hong Kong government asked for a lease on the New Territories, the lease had an "uncertain" clause in it. The Chinese said that Britain could have jurisdiction over all of the New Territories except **Kowloon City**. The lease was signed despite this clause and official Hong Kong objections to having a "Chinese presence" smack in the middle of the British colony. It didn't seem right somehow, and it wasn't.

Another Walled City theory notes that each government made its own map of the New Territories to be leased, and the boundaries did not match, therefore leaving this "no-man's-land" as a part of China, and not subject to the terms of the New Territories lease.

Whatever the legal case, the Hong Kong government soon found a suitable reason for throwing a Chinese garrison out of Kowloon City, but they never made any attempt to develop the area, because they did not want to upset the Peking government. Thus, squatters could move in from China and set up safe housekeeping inside the Walled City. They did so but had to make do without the public facilities maintained in other parts of the colony. The only real privilege these squatters had was that they could commit a crime in Kowloon and "escape" into the Walled City. The Hong Kong police hesitated to arrest anyone, even if they could find them, in what Peking considered part of Mainland China. Often, Walled City thieves and thugs were deported rather than convicted.

World War II changed things. Japanese occupation forces ordered the population to depart, so the Walled City became a walled ghost town. Its walls were torn down and the stone used to extend Kai Tak Airport's runway. After the war people returned, in even greater numbers, and squatters reoccupied this now un-walled city. As the rest of colony was rapidly modernized—with running water, electricity and social services—the old Walled City district became a disorganized tangle of dilapidated housing, open sewers and illegal power and telephone lines.

Indeed, the only thing well-organized here was crime. As before, it was *the place* for crooks or drug peddlers to hide. Police were again hesitant to enter this refuge, and those who did could not apprehend a miscreant in the crooked and narrow (many less than four feet wide) streets.

A Cesspool of Crime

By the mid Sixties the Walled City was a cesspool of crime and filth. A massive crackdown on drug syndicates has reduced some of the area's misery, but it still remains an embarrassment to the Hong Kong government and a strange point of territorial honour to the Communist Chinese.

The Hong Kong government realized that the Peking government does not recognize the validity of the New Territories lease negotiated long ago by China's Imperial Government. Therefore, the British did not want to do anything that might incur the wrath of their fickle Chinese landlord. Consequently, Kowloon's "Walled" City was generally left alone. The Sino-British agreement returning all of Hong Kong to China solved the problem, and improvements can probably be expected.

Visitors are advised to stay out of the Walled City. They might risk a stroll along **Tung Tau Tsuen Street**, which is on the Walled City's perimeter, and where there are rows of **illegal dentists' shops** operated by dentists from China who can't qualify for government licenses; but otherwise, stay out! Between shops you'll see dark stairways which lead down into the gloom; these are narrow, filthy "streets," much like byways in a human-sized rabbit warren, or a confusing obstacle course in a circus' house of horrors. There is an invisible boundary here. One step from a sunlit street in the colony and you'll be within a mad maze from which there is a good chance you may never return. For the visitor—and for most Hong Kong residents—a casual stroll *past* the Walled City is adventure enough.

Gangster, Shaw Brothers celluloid epic.

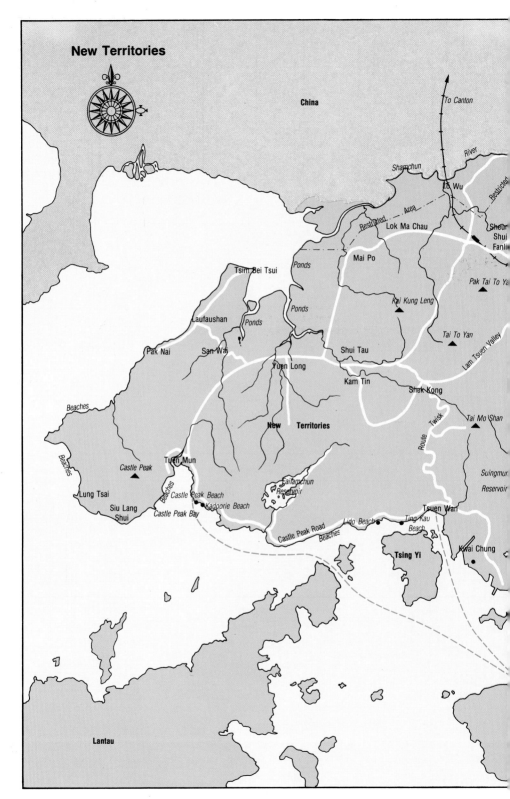

New Territories

China

To Canton

Shamchun

River

Lo Wu

Restricted

Restricted   Area

Sheung
Shui
Fanli

Lok Ma Chau

Mai Po

Tsim Bei Tsui

Ponds

Pak Tai To Ya

Kai Kung Leng

Ponds

Laufaushan

Ponds

Shui Tau

Tai To Yan

Pak Nai

San Wai

Yuen Long

Kam Tin

Lam Tsuen Valley

Shek Kong

Beaches

New   Territories

Tai Mo Shan

Route Twisk

Beaches

Castle Peak

Tuen Mun

Suingmur

Reservoir

Lung Tsai

Beaches

Castle Peak Beach

Sailamchun
Reservoir

Siu Lang
Shui

Castle Peak Bay

Kadoorie Beach

Lido Beach

Ting Kau
Beach

Tsuen Wan

Castle Peak Road

Beaches

Tsing Yi

Kwai Chung

Lantau

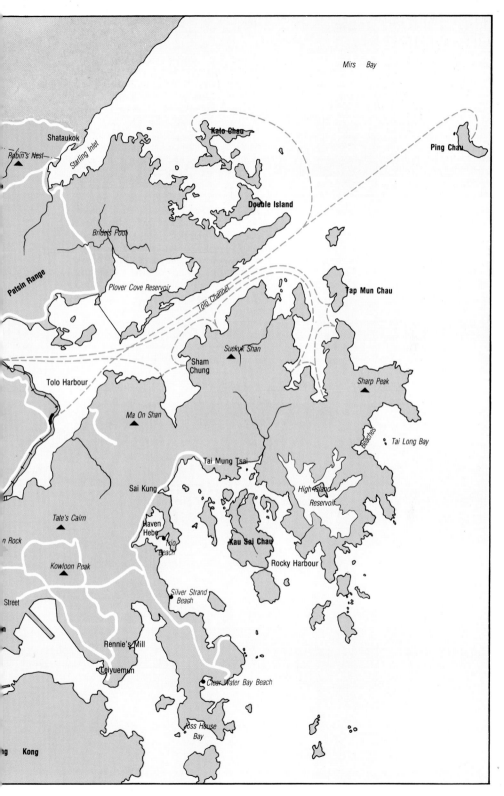

Mirs   Bay

Shataukok

Robin's Nest

Starting Inlet

Kato Chau

Ping Chau

Double Island

Patsin Range

Bride's Pool

Plover Cove Reservoir

Tolo Channel

Tap Mun Chau

Sham
Chung

Suekuk Shan

Sharp Peak

Tolo Harbour

Ma On Shan

Beaches

Tai Long Bay

Tai Mung Tsai

Sai Kung

High Island
Reservoir

Tate's Cairn

Haven
Hebe

Kau Sai Chau

n Rock

Kio
Beach

Kowloon Peak

Rocky Harbour

Street

Silver Strand
Beach

Rennie's Mill

Leiyuemun

Clear Water Bay Beach

Joss House
Bay

ng   Kong

THE FAST-CHANGING NEW TERRITORIES

Many visitors to Hong Kong see only a small fraction of this unique British colony. Most concentrate on bargain-hunting in Central and Tsimshatsui, sometimes interrupting their shopping sprees with a water tour of Aberdeen or an obligatory bus trip to the top of The Peak. Other more adventurous folks book a ferryboat trip to either Lantau, Cheung Chau or Lamma Island, where they see an easier-going part of Hong Kong.

All of these usual excursions are good fun, but even if you take in some of the outer islands, you've still missed out on more than 350 of Hong Kong's 400 square miles. Indeed, a Hong Kong visitor is short-changing himself if he doesn't spend at least one full day exploring the colony's **New Territories**.

The New Territories include the area right down to Boundary Street in Kowloon, but most people here say you're not really in the New Territories until you've travelled beyond Lion Rock Tunnel, Kowloon's Walled City and Laichikok. Actually, the Li Cheng Uk Tomb, the Walled City, Kwun Tong, and Kai Tai Airport are all part of the New Territories lease, but they are popularly considered to be in Kowloon, or "New Kowloon." The **Kwai Chung Container Terminal** and most factories are also in the New Territories.

You can start your New Territories tour by heading out toward **Castle Peak** (see map) or towards Shatin and Taipo. Alternatively, you can travel on Clearwater Bay Road which leads to the **Sai Kung Peninsula**.

On the Castle Peak side of the Kowloon peninsula is **Laichikok Amusement Park** which has been entertaining people for decades and is one of the world's few places where you can enjoy Chinese opera and ice skating in the same compound. Something new has been added, a **Sung Dynasty Village**. It's a recreation of a part of a village that existed in China 1,000 years ago. Everything in the place has been made exactly as it was in olden times, from the wineshop to the "bank" (the same kind in which the first paper money in the world was used). The village's im-

Wedding at the Sung Dynasty Village.

pressarios stage special performances for visitors that include a traditional wedding ceremony and kung-fu demonstrations.

Just around the corner from Laichikok is **Kwai Chung**, the aforementioned complex of five container terminals, and the industrial community of **Tsuen Wan**, a good example of Hong Kong's "New Town" developments. It is the end of one **MTR** line and when you look at the skyline of this city with a projected population of a million people, it is difficult to imagine its romantic, often violent, and essentially rural past.

The Tsuen Wan area has been inhabited since time immemorial, but the recent Chinese presence seems to have begun about the 2nd Century A.D. In the 13th Century the Chinese empire stretched to this area simply because the Chinese Emperor was being driven south by invading Mongols. In 1277 he and his entourage arrived in Tsuen Wan. Later, between 1662 and 1669, when the Formosan pirate Koxinga was building his empire, the Manchu government ordered a mass evacuation of coastal areas to save the populace from that marauder. Koxinga's forces demolished the vacated settlement of Tsuen Wan and it was not repopulated until the late 17th Century.

In the Country

In 1898, at the time the New Territories were leased to Hong Kong's colonial government, the total industry of the Tsuen Wan area consisted of 24 factories. These factories produced incense powder, and were powered by waterwheels turned by streams running down the mountainside. The population then was about 3,000. The year 1919 saw completion of **Castle Peak Road**, and by 1961 there were 250 industrial enterprises employing about 24,000 of the New Territories' residents.

The container terminals you now see were built entirely on reclaimed land. Leases have been granted on **Tsing Yi Island** to industrial enterprises such as tank farms, power stations and other ventures that require only initial access by water. When land access was needed, the government contributed to the cost of the bridge you now see spanning **Rambler Channel**.

From Tsuen Wan, heading out to-

ew Wax
useum
gures, Sung
ynasty
llage.

ward Castle Peak, you suddenly, surprisingly, find yourself in the country! If you take the **Tuen Mun Highway**, you will race along a modern motorway with few views of the countryside, except for brief glimpses of gardens sliced by modern clover-leaf interchanges and flyovers. If you keep to the old Castle Peak Road, there is a completely different view. The old road takes you slowly round many a winding turn along the coastline. If it's summertime you can stop at any of the many beautiful beaches for a swim. Recommended is **Kadoorie Beach**.

From this road you'll see more of the New Territories' agriculture, mostly terraces where produce is grown for the urban market—much of the produce being lettuce, cabbage, carrots, and other items familiar to Western visitors. There is still plenty of evidence of traditional Chinese farming; people plant rice by hand, and till their fields with plows pulled by water buffaloes.

Worth at least a quick look is the **Pearl Island Hotel**, situated on an island that looks out across the channel to Lantau Island.

Indeed, while on this road one begins to understand why the oldest of the New Territories' walled villages, Kam Tin, was given a name which in literal translation means Embroidered Fields.

Gurkhas, Gardens and Immortals

A little farther on is the headquarters of the colony's **Gurkha Regiment**, those world-famous Nepalese fighters who have for so many years supported the armed forces of the British Commonwealth. You can visit the Gurkha camp, but only by special arrangement through the British Forces Public Relations Office (Tel: 5-2893-3111).

At the $13\frac{1}{2}$ milestone on Castle Peak Road is **Dragon Garden**, where occasionally, by special arrangement, group tours are accepted at a small fee per person. This is a traditional Chinese garden, built by a wealthy Hong Kong businessman, and comprises grottoes, ponds, **a neo-imperial mausoleum** and a 50-foot sculpture of a dragon lying half submerged in a pond. Many of the plants in this garden were imported from China.

Near Castle Peak itself is a huge tem-

Bullock farmer near the Kadoor farm.

ple called **Ching Chuen Koong**, and it is unusual in several ways. For one thing, it is home for aged people who have no relatives or means of support. Secondly, it is a repository for many Chinese art treasures, including lanterns more than 200 years old and a jade seal more than 1,000 years old. There is a library of nearly 4,000 books, which document the history of the Taoist religion.

The interior of the main room is as ornate as in ancient temples, with red and green rafters under a roof and beams painted in a green and yellow pattern. The roof is raised above the tops of the walls, and spaces between the roof and walls are filled in with lattices of red and yellow carved wood.

This temple is dedicated to Lui Tung Bun, one of the so-called Taoist Immortals. He was born in 789 A.D. and became a Taoist missionary after he was inspired by a dream known in mythology as the Rice Wine Dream. Whatever caused his inspiration, it set him on the path of good works and he spread the works of the Taoist faith rapidly, ridding the earth of many evils.

He also had the help of magic weapons, such as a **devil-slaying sword** and **magic fly-switch** that you'll see displayed alongside his statue in the temple. At the front of the altar is a **thousand-year-old jade seal** kept in a glass case. The altar is protected by two statues that were carved from white stone about 300 years ago for a temple in Peking. Each statue is estimated to be worth about HK$75,000.

Inside the temple you'll see room after room of small photographs of people who have died. Their relatives pay the temple's keepers to have these pictures placed in special numbered slots, and forever after living progeny can visit to pray for their departed ancestors.

Tuen Mun is another of Hong Kong's industrial "new towns," or small cities created to accommodate the spillover of population.

'Cup Fairy Hill'

Near Tuen Mun, on the slopes of **Castle Peak**, is a much smaller temple, but one just as interesting as the one mentioned earlier. Though it is fairly high up the slope, there is a paved road that runs almost to its entrance. Despite a lone light bulb, there is a feeling of

Oyster
fishermen,
Yuen Long.

antiquity about this shrine.

This small **Pei Tu Temple** is dedicated to a character of Chinese mythology who was really quite a character! It seems he was a monk, but not a totally honest one, and was forever getting into trouble. One night he stayed with a family and in the morning took off with a prized golden statue. His perturbed host and friends pursued him on horseback, but they couldn't catch him. At last they spotted him and chased him to a bend in the river, where he seemed to be cornered. He called upon one of his magic skills. He took out his wooden bowl, stepped into it, then pushed off across the stream. All the horsemen could do was watch. They couldn't risk their horses or lives in the deep, fast river. From that time on the rascal monk was known as the "Cup Ferry," which in Chinese is *Pei Tu*. When he was finally driven south as far as Castle Peak, then called "**Green Mountain**," he stopped running and established his monastery on this hillside. Hence it is called *Pei Tu Shan*, which means "**Cup Ferry Hill**."

On one side of the gateway of the Pei Tu Temple is an inscription stating:

"There is no gate in this gateway because we do not want to keep people out." It's a refreshing message in an ever more security-conscious world. On the other side of the gateway is another message saying that the temple is always clean because no one ever leaves any trash lying around—a gentle hint for visitors and worshippers.

Lau Fau Shan Fishmarket And Mai Po's Fairview Park

A must on any trip around the New Territories is **Lau Fau Shan**, a huge fishmarket near **Yuen Long**. Here you'll find a restaurant with an entryway and walls decorated with thousands of oyster shells, each about five or six inches long. A "street" much too narrow for an automobile passes by dozens of restaurants, both small, open-air affairs and smart, air conditioned places. Here are sellers of dried fish and salt-fish, and many places hawking live shrimp, prawns and larger fishes. Look at the fishes swimming around in the tanks, pick one out, pay for it, then take it to one of the nearby restaurants and have it cooked. However, don't eat the

Dried fish merchant, Yuen Long.

sometimes contaminated raw oysters.

At the end of the street is a **fishmarket** where boats unload the previous night's catch and where the day's weighing and bidding activity cause a deafening hullabaloo. There are mountains of empty oyster shells and live oysters up to four and five inches in size. Out on the dock you can see China just two miles away. Many illegal immigrants have swum across the bay here to escape from China.

Yuen Long is another redevelopment project. It was a traditional market town set in the middle of the largest flood plain in the New Territories. Its population, before redevelopment, was 40,000, and that is expected to grow to one million when all the residential and commercial land in this area has been developed as planned. Formerly a centre for privately-run marketing, the town is rapdily taking on a labour-intensive, light industrial role which is expected to absorb up to 20 percent of this area's work force.

North of Yuen Long is a new housing development, set in the **Mai Po marshes**, that is a marvel for all visitors from North America. **Fairview Park**, when the first stage of its housing was completed, gave North American visitors the eerie feeling that they had somehow slipped through a time and location warp into a small town or suburb in the American Midwest of the late 1940s or 1950s. Here are perfectly straight streets, prim two-storey houses of only three varying designs, white-picket fences, little gates, and a pair of young trees planted in each home's green lawn.

Walled Villages

Fairview Park, which is populated almost exclusively by Chinese families, is a true meeting place of East and West. Happy throngs of mostly young people enjoy modern, light, airy homes with little of the noise and industrial pollution of other parts of Hong Kong. Here there is sunshine and fresh air, and soon there will be industry nearby and on-site facilities for recreation and entertainment. At the back of the estate is a sort of "environment wall." On the other side are the Mai Po marshes as they always were, supporting wildlife. It's a great spot for bird-watchers.

lassical
noments in
10-year
onfucian
eremony,
am Tin.

Also near Yuen Long are the **walled villages** of **Kam Tin**. The most popular for visitors is the **Kat Hing Wai village** (which is often mistakenly referred to as the Kam Tin Walled Village).

There are 400 people living at Kat Hing Wai, all with the same surname, Tang. Built in the 1600s, it is a fortified village with walls 18 feet thick, guardhouses on its four corners, arrow slits for fighting off attackers, and a moat. The "authenticity" may seem spoiled by some of the modern buildings inside, complete with television aerials peeping over the old-time fortifications, but there is still only one entrance, guarded by a heavy wrought iron gate. You can enter the village for a nominal admission fee, but in ancient times, that gate was used to keep out undesirables. Something else that's only allowed by permission, and payment, is the taking of pictures of the elderly folk sitting around the gateway. Only after coughing up a couple of dollars can you snap away. The commercialism continues inside, where at least one street is lined with vendors.

Kam Tin also has a small "Suzie Wong" bar scene, well known to British soldiers stationed in the NT, but virtually unknown to most residents and visitors alike.

An exciting next stop is near the **Lok Ma Chau Police Station**. There, you can stand on a hilltop and gaze at a lot of flat land parted by a meandering river. That river is the **Shum Chun**, and it marks the **Chinese border**. Unless you plan to take a China tour, this is as close as you'll ever get. That can be quite a thrill, even though China has opened its doors to visitors. Before 1978, this was as close as most people could get to the Celestial Kingdom.

If the visitor happens to be a business person, he or she will enjoy an added thrill here, because there is something new just over the border, something to gladden the heart of any entrepreneur who deals in light manufacturing or assembly of products. In keeping with the many other changes of attitude on the part of the now-progressive Peking government, China has opened a section of land just across the border in **Shum Chun** for industrial purposes— to encourage joint ventures between overseas investors and Chinese communes. There are already more than

Hakka couple from the New Territories.

1,000 such ventures operating in this **Special Export Zone.**

Patience may be required for some of the intricacies of the negotiations, but the bottom line results in many cases have been deeply satisfying, particularly for manufacturers who crave low operating costs and unskilled labour. One factory owner faced with a rapidly-increasing wage bill at his factory in Hong Kong began by suggesting to Chinese authorities that he hoped to pay commune workers 20 percent less than he had paid in Hong Kong. The Chinese negotiator said he thought commune labourers would be pleased with 50 percent less. As it turned out the workers were more than pleased to sit all day in an air-conditioned building and assemble gadgets than to labour for a pittance in nearby paddy fields. For many mainland Chinese it is an unexpected introduction to the Modern World. Otherwise, they would have to undergo the inconvenience of swimming shark-infested waters to escape from China.

In spite of the so-called "new towns," and the modernization of China across the border, it is in the New Territories,

in the vicinity of Yuen Long, that you see aspects of traditional Chinese life that do not exist even inside China itself.

Waiting for a Good View

You'll see clusters of what appear to be huge pickle jars, with wooden lids, sometimes six or eight parked on a hillside. These pots contain the bones of Chinese dead. The people have died and been buried long ago, but after a number of years their bones are exhumed and placed in jars here to await consignment to their final resting place. This process takes a long time, because the exact arrangement of a grave is tremendously important and may take a long time to ascertain.

The graves, shaped like concrete armchairs, are sometimes huge. You can see them on hillsides, and if you stand by one you can usually view the sea or a pleasant valley. The *fung shui* (wind and water) placement of a grave is important. The departed relative is going to be stuck on that hillside forever, so to keep him happy his descendants bury him where he can enjoy a new view and favourable breezes—conditions which are increasingly difficult to find even in living Hong Kong. The other reason for the long wait before a proper burial is that these graves cost a comparative fortune, and it may take a hardworking family many years to save up enough money to purchase a well-appointed tombsite.

Twisting and Turning On Route Twisk

And speaking of construction, there's plenty of it going on in the New Territories. You will see women working along with men here. Here are hardworking **Hakka women** dressed in black pajama-like suits, *samfoo*, their faces framed by black curtains around the brims of their wide coolie hats. They come from a mysterious and very traditional matriarchal society and think nothing of labouring at jobs that Westerners consider to be for-men-only. Proceed with caution if you are tempted to photograph these women. They dislike photographers, and will literally chase a shutterbug across a field. So, use a super-long lens, or be prepared to shoot and run.

akka caddy,
anling

From Yuen Long and Kam Tin you have a choice of two return routes to the city.

One is via **Shek Kong**, which is the big **British military garrison** and **airfield**. From Shek Kong village **Route Twisk** begins, and takes you on one of the best scenic drives in Hong Kong. Within minutes you are high in forested mountains, apparently far from all human habitation. Route Twisk twists and turns for miles and then suddenly plunges you right back into the techno-industrial age of modern **Tsuen Wan**.

Before turning into Route Twisk, you can continue on Lam Kam Road to **Paak Ngau Shek** in the **Lam Tsuen Valley**, where the **Kadoorie Experimental and Extension Farm** is located. Aside from the farming, this area is much like a manicured garden in a rural setting.

Another scenic rural route takes you from **Shek Kong** to **Fanling**, where there are three fine **golf courses**. If you want to use them, phone 0-901-211 for details. You can arrive anytime after 7 a.m., go to the reception desk, pay green fees of HK$400 per day, and tee off. Clubs can be hired.

Also nearby is **Luen Wo Market**, the region's traditional marketplace.

Fanling and nearby **Sheung Shui** are undergoing a redevelopment plan to make another "new town" that will accommodate 170,000 people, the bulk to be housed in Sheung Shui. The area near the **Fanling Railway Station** will be a public housing development for 20,000 people plus a residential and commercial development for another 4,000 people, to be privately developed.

Meanwhile, a tasteful reminder of old "colonial" days is the **Better 'Ole Bar and Restaurant**, near the golf course and just a few steps from the Fanling Railway Station. It started out as a pub but now is a pub and restaurant, with a full menu of European and Chinese food, and a cozy old-fashioned oak paneled bar from the original pub. It is still patronized by British public servants, especially police and military personnel. At night there's a band belting out dance music.

Tai Po: 'Buying Place'

Just around the corner from the Better 'Ole, but by no means easy to find, is one of the New Territories' least visited temples. It is called **Fung Ying Sin Koon**, a name meaning "paradise." There is an intricate system of pathways and steps leading to the altar and its grounds include many waterfalls and shady benches suitable for meditating.

Tai Po is a place name meaning "buying place," and the town certainly lives up to its name, serving as it has for many years as a place for farmers and fishermen to meet and exchange goods. The old town lies at the northeastern end of **Tolo Harbour** where the highway crosses the **Lower Lam Tsuen River**. On the northeast side of the river is the famous **Tai Po Market** which includes a huge fish market and dozens of vegetable stalls. **Fu Shing Street** will give the visitor a good idea of market town life in the New Territories; it is packed with shops selling everything from rattan furniture to thousand-year-old eggs.

Not far away, but with its own railway station, is **Tai Po Kau**. From here, or from the train, you can see the departure and return of the fishing fleet. And the wharf—where you can catch a ferry to and through Tolo Harbour—is just a short walk away. (The wharf for ferries to **Ping Chau Island** and **Mirs Bay** is in Tai Po itself.)

Gilded Yuet Kai, Temple of Man Fat, Shatin, and at right, Scarlet Buddha at the Temple of Ten Thousand Buddhas.

Like all the "new towns," Taipo is undergoing the transition from an old market town to a modern city; its former population of 30,000 is expected to rise to 220,000!

Mirs Bay is largely undeveloped. Because it's well off the beaten track, its population of islanders cling to traditional employment forms such as fishing and vegetable-growing. In recent years the bay has achieved dubious fame as a watery escape route for illegal immigrants swimming for Hong Kong. Reports of illegal immigrants being apprehended—and the sighting of the bodies of numerous persons who have drowned in the attempt—are everyday news. Slightly more interesting in early 1980 were reports of marine police beefing up their forces to stop vicious racketeering in illegals. Opportunists were going so far as to buy a high powered speedboat on a time payment basis, then make just one overnight run to pick up illegals off Mirs Bay's China shores and run them back to the urban part of Hong Kong. The fees paid by even a half dozen grateful illegals more than covered the cost of the down payment on the boat.

Just to the east of Tai Po on Ting Kok Road is the famous **Tai Ping Carpet Factory**, a must on most visitor tours, where you can see all phases of Chinese carpet-making. Call 0-656-5161.

South of Tai Po, about halfway to Shatin, is the **Chinese University**. For further information and a tour of the campus, phone 0-635-2111. Across from the University is the lovely **Yucca da lac,** an outdoor restaurant with superb views, if you want a break.

Whether you enter **Shatin** by road or rail, there's no doubt you'll be amazed to find a bustling metropolis in the middle of the agricultural New Territories. Massive housing projects occupy fields where just a few years ago the greatest activity was water buffaloes pulling plows in rice paddies. The New Town Plaza is a massive shopping and entertainment complex, while Riverside Plaza Hotel along the banks of the Shing Mun River is another modern addition.

Shatin's 12,800 Buddhas

The **Shatin Valley** has several places of worship, of which three are worthy of note:

First is the **Temple of Ten Thousand Buddhas**, which can be reached by climbing 431 steps up the hillside above the **Shatin Railway Station**. There you will find a main altar room with 12,800 small Buddha statues on its walls. The temple is guarded by huge, fierce looking statues of various gods, and by just as fierce watchdogs which are chained up in the daytime. Also in the complex is a **nine-storey pagoda** of Indian architectural design, commemorating a Buddha who was believed to be the ninth reincarnation of Prince Viṣhnu.

A further 69 steps up the hill is the **Temple of Man Fat**, where you can meet the man who created this temple and pagoda complex—even though he died years ago. His name was **Yuet Kai** and he was a monk who spent a lifetime studying Buddhism and living a meditative life. His greatest concern was immortality. When he died he was buried, but, according to Chinese custom, his body was later dug up to be reburied in its final resting place. However, the body was found to be prefectly preserved and radiating a ghostly yellow glow. Since there was obviously something "supernatural" about Yuet Kai, it was decided to preserve his body in gold

An interior set at the Shaw Brothers Movie Town.

leaf for posterity.

From the Ten Thousand Buddhas Temple you can see, across the valley, the famous **Amah Rock**, which looks like a woman standing with a baby on her back. Legend has it that a local fisherman once went to sea and did not return with the fleet. His wife waited patiently for his return, day after day, but he did not appear. After a year the gods took pity on her and turned her into stone. These days the rock is a place of worship for faithful Chinese women.

From either of these two places of worship you can look down on a third place of worship, one much more in tune with the present day spirit of Hong Kong. This shrine is dedicated to Instant Wealth, or The Fast Buck, and is called **Shatin Racecourse**. Thousands of punters (the grandstands hold 75,000) go there every October through May horseracing season to bet money on the ponies and then pray for good fortune. There is really only one winner in every race, however, and that is The Royal Hong Kong Jockey Club. After every race hundreds of thousands of crips Hong Kong dollars flutter into the Jockey Club's coffers. Fortunately for Hong Kong, the winnings from these races, as with those earned at Happy Valley racecourse, are spent on charitable projects.

Another place of interest is the **Tsang Tai Uk**, which means Mr. Tsang's Big House. It's a **walled village** built in the mid 19th Century by a wealthy quarrymaster as a retreat for his large family. As you emerge from the **Lion Rock Tunnel**, the village is on your right, just a stone's throw from the motorway. Actually, most of Tsang's progeny have moved elsewhere, and the fortress is now rented out to more distant relatives of his family. However, this remnant of the colony's opulent early days will be preserved in spite of the usual pile-driving march of high-rise development. This village is rarely visited by tourists (because of difficult access) but the people here are pleasant and the village less commercial than the more frequently visited Kam Tin walled village.

A tour of Hong Kong's New Territories provides the visitor with a good look at Chinese traditional life, but at the same time there is evidence everywhere of the urgency of modern development. A great relief from this mad rush into the use-of-space age is afforded by a separate trip to another part of the New Territories called the **Sai Kung Peninsula**.

Beyond Kai Tak Airport follow Clearwater Bay Road past some new developments, then turn off onto **Hiram's Highway** which takes you to **Sai Kung Village** (slated for redevelopment, but not yet touched by it) and you'll be in an area preserved as a **country park**. It is not even open to private motor vehicles. This is a part of Hong Kong where you can don hiking boots and backpack and go into the woods for several days.

If you stayed on Clearwater Bay Road, you would find a different scene: luxurious villas set among lush hills, and Hong Kong's answer to the Hollywood of the Forties and Fifties. This is the **Shaw Brothers Movie Town.** Here, many a mini-epic has been committed to celluloid, and all the stars are Celestials. The only Occidentals present are language-dubbers, so don't be surprised if you see a Mandarin film and the mighty warriors have Pittsburgh accents or a trace of Strine. To visit Shaw's, phone their office at 3-291-511.

Beyond Shaw's the drive is scenic with almost a Mediterranean flavour. There is the posh **Clearwater Bay** country and villas that look down on beautiful beaches and at impossibly green islands which cluster like jade in the expanse of deep blue water.

An extra indentation in the shoreline of Clearwater Bay is **Joss House Bay** which really comes alive once a year on the birthday of the sea goddess Tin Hau. Hundreds of junks and sampans head for the **Tin Hau Temple** here to pay their respects to the Queen of Heaven, who is also commonly known as the Goddess of the Sea.

This temple was built by two 11th Century brothers who allegedly were saved by Tin Hau after their junk was destroyed by a typhoon. While they were lost at sea, the brothers held onto a statue of Tin Hau, prayed for her help, and eventually they reached **Tung Lung Island** alive. Later, after they had gone into business and become wealthy, they built a temple on the island and dedicated it to Tin Hau. That was in the year 1012. Another later typhoon wrecked the temple, but descendants of the two brothers built its replacement in 1266 at this site.

HONG KONG'S OUTLYING ISLANDS

It is something of a minor tragedy that so few visitors make time to go to the outlying islands, for it is here that the real magic of Hong Kong is uncovered, an inheritance which brings Hong Kong in line with its apparently more traditional neighbours. On the islands are ancient villages, little fishing communities, monasteries where for centuries man has contemplated the foolishness of worldly concerns, and natural amenities central Hong Kong seems short of: grass and trees and quiet moments and long empty beaches. Fortunately most of these places are only an easy ferry ride away from the Hong Kong most people know.

Although the British Crown Colony of Hong Kong is just short of 150 years old, archaeologists have ascertained that man has been living around this area for close to 6,000 years.

Whether Hong Kong's original inhabitants were the forerunners of those who are here today, no one really knows. The ancient tribes who left their marks on Hong Kong—in the form of rock carvings found on Lantau, Po Toi, Tung Lung, Cheung Chau, and Kau Sai Chau islands—have probably long since travelled further. One scholar, William Meecham, in his book *Rock Carvings of Hong Kong*, has related these early residents to the Yueh tribes, whose closest living descendants are probably the Vietnamese people.

Apart from these ancient stone-carving residents of Hong Kong and its islands, in the last thousand years those who have made their homes on the islands have mainly been the area's traditional fisherfolk and farmers—the Hoklo, the Tanka, and the Hakka. Older descendants of these agrarian tribes have managed to maintain their traditional life-style, but their children are now among the great number of contemporary Chinese who have gone overseas to live and work. In some families every member of the "younger generation" has gone to work in London's Soho district or San Francisco's Chinese restaurants (from where they send money back to their parents to enable them to maintain their satisfying but fast-dying life-style). And, as the old people die, so too are some of the islands dying, leaving only ghostly villages behind.

"Progress" is bringing to an end 10 centuries of pastoral life here as roads are paved and telephone and electricity services are installed. The future on Lantau, for example, may include an airport and a container port. A large power station is already being built there, two live-in resorts (one with a deluxe resort hotel) are in the offing.

Soaring property values have also brought land developers to the islands—those who want to build big luxury housing developments, and those who have a stake in the visitor industry. They understandably want to get tourists out of the shopping districts so they will spend more time—and money—in the colony. As in any resort area, there are two sides to this kind of development: on the one hand, it brings a share of prosperity to those who would otherwise miss out and it shows off some of Hong Kong's more charming areas. Conversely, the coming of money and a "modern age" signals the ruin of traditional life-styles.

Left, Bun Festival participant and below, beach on Lantau Island.

MISTY LANTAU, 'BROKEN HEAD'

Of all the outlying islands, the greatest in size, and perhaps in atmosphere, is **Lantau**, which has a land area twice that of Hong Kong Island. In some ways, it is still not too late on Lantau to experience rural village life-styles which have endured unchanged (except perhaps for television sets) since the fall of emperors, colonization and the decay of kingdoms and colonial empires.

In Cantonese *Lantau* means "Broken Head," perhaps because its rugged dignity is dominated by the ragged and two-part **Lantau Peak** that rises 935 metres high at the heart of lizard-shaped Lantau.

Follow the Wind

The island is cobwebbed with little wandering pathways and dusty trails which spiral up, down and around her scenic mountains. A firm reminder to walkers: nature and the elements rule here. Therefore, there are few roads but many fine walks through areas that have been specifically set aside as nature reserves.

A particularly good opening trail circles the blue **Shek Pik Reservoir**, on the west slopes of Lantau Peak. This 5,500 million gallon reservoir gathers most of the freshwater carried from Lantau's heights by rushing streams and rivulets.

Because Lantau is twice the size of Hong Kong Island, but supports a population of only about 15,000 inhabitants, the sense of space and peace here is the opposite of that on the more populated island (provided, of course, that you avoid busy weekends when many of the colony's more urbane residents flock here for a respite from their workaday freneticism). It is because of this peace and the sheltering serenity of the island that there are so many monasteries here, both Christian and Buddhist.

For those who land at **Silver Mine Bay**, Lantau's main visitor point, regular buses travel from there along Lantau's southern resort coast to the brightly painted red and gold **Po Lin Monastery**. This popular monastery is set on a steep hill due north of the Shek Pik Reservoir.

Here, in a large visitors' dining house, you can enjoy a good vegetarian lunch served by Po Lin's resident monks. It is also possible to stay here overnight in small guest bungalows.

Also, west of Po Lin, in the direction of **Tung Chung** on Lantau's north coast, is an excellent walking path that skirts mountain ridges and drops through small canyons and over rushing streams en route to Lantau's **Yin Hing Monastery**, a haven rich with traditional Buddhist paintings and statues. This monastery sits on a slope and commands a fine view of the surrounding mountains, farming country and the blue South China Sea.

For those who would like to break up their Po Lin area tour with a local-style high tea hour, there is a proper tea plantation and teahouse called the **Lantau Tea Gardens** just a short walk away from the Po Lin Monastery compound. The Gardens has rooms for rent, barbecue facilities and a free camping area. Its proprietors also rent mountain ponies for visitors who would rather ride than hike along local trails. And yes, the tea is delicious.

On Lantau's northeast coast, meanwhile, is a meditative spot with a decidedly different aura. This is the **Trappist Haven of Our Lady of Liese (Joy)** at **Tai Shui Hang** which is maintained by a closed Christian order sworn to silence.

Because the Trappist monks are protective of their privacy, they do not welcome casual visitors to their inner sanctums, but they do allow people to stroll through their grounds and admire the plump dairy cows they raise. This **Trappist dairy** is one of the chief suppliers of fresh milk for Hong Kong's quality-conscious hotels.

The Trappists also serve a simple fare to hungry travellers; and it is possible to spend an evening in their simple dormitory or a two-room guest house. The best way to reach the monastery, besides hiking there overland, is to catch a ferry to nearby **Peng Chau Island**, then hire a sampan to take you across the narrow channel between Peng Chau and Tai Shui Hang on Lantau.

Lantau is also a fine place to observe the "living" traditional lives of the colony's fast-disappearing "boat people." In the popular arrival point and small fishing village of Silver Mine Bay (or **Mui Wo**), boat people will be seen crowded aboard numerous junks and sampans in that protected waterway.

Anyone who has seen a junk close up has to marvel at the fact that such a thrown together rough and tumble collection of timber, barrels, poles and rough-hewn planks can cope with Hong Kong's typhoon-ridden seas. But they do—and when a nasty storm hits the colony, the biggest of these junks go out to sea to do battle there with nature, rather than risk being battered into splinters near shore.

Semi-Land Dwellers

In Lantau's principle town, **Tai O**, on the west coast, the island's Tanka boat people have turned semi-land dwellers. Some of their larger junks have been turned into three-storey "permanent" living structures that have been gathered together into a seaborne slum. Further up a Tai O creek, they have also built rickety homes on stilts over parts of the creek where waters rise during tide changes. It's as if they cannot quite bring themselves to totally become land-dwellers, even though their stilt homes cannot possibly sail away.

Another fine place to study these sturdy old seagoing horsecarts is at **Penny's Bay** on Lantau's north coast. One of Hong Kong's best-known shipmakers is based there. His shipbuilders make not only traditional junks, but also modern cruising craft.

While on the northern side of Lantau, try to visit **Tung Chung**, an old fortress and bay that curves around the pointed southern tip of little **Chek Lap Kok Island**. On a hill overlooking this little harbour you'll spot an **old fort** which was built in 1817. This fort's thick ramparts still stand, as do six old cannons, much as they did during the last century when they guarded this town and bay from smugglers, pirates and unexpected "Outer Barbarians." It's a peaceful little redoubt, reminiscent of old buccaneering days along this historic Chinese coast.

Another hideaway which beckons persons interested in peace and quiet is the **Lantau Mountain Camp** at about the 769 meters elevation of **Sunset Peak** (869 meters). This camp consists of 20 small stone houses which were built

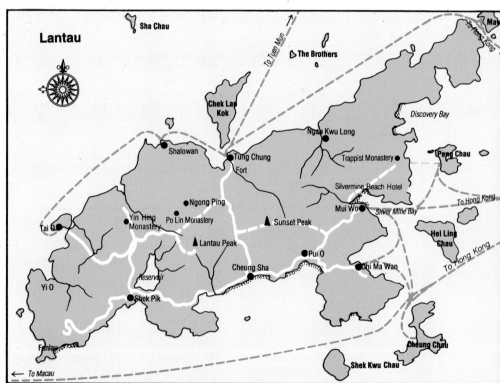

before World War II as a rest haven for the colony's Christians and Christian missionaries on leave from China. They can also be rented by laymen who make reservations in advance.

Expansive Lantau is also understandably famed for its many long, smooth and often empty beaches. The finest sandy sweeps are on the southeast coastline that arcs from **Cheung Sha** south of Silver Mine Bay to **Tong Fuk**. The most popular and crowded beach (probably because it is the easiest one to reach) is **Silver Mine Bay Beach** and a resort of the same name near the Silver Mine Bay ferry landing. From Silver Mine Bay you can travel by good road to the aforementioned Tai O village. It is an old, somewhat grubby place, but truly ethnic in the complete Chinese sense.

This bus route from Silver Mine Bay to Tai O passes through **Pui O Village**, a nondescript seaside village whose main claim to fame (for visitors) is the **Tong Fuk Provisions Store**. This out-of-the-way store not only stocks ample provisions of cold wine and beer, but is also a restaurant serving both Chinese and Western food. It is nicknamed "The Lantau Hilton" because the owner is a retired chef from the Hong Kong Hilton Hotel.

Off-the-beaten-track Tai O can also be reached by ferry from Central. En route to Tai O the **Central-Tai O Ferry** puts in at Tung Chung, the northern shore fortress village, so by planning your day in advance you can enjoy both Tai O, Tung Chung and a fine cruise.

Traditional diversions abound on this island, but the hand of progress hovers ominously over her mist-shrouded peaks:

A major development on Lantau is **Discovery Bay** and when finished, it will sprawl over a 1,500-acre site. At the moment, it is one of the most pleasant places to live in Hong Kong, right by the beach in a well-planned, uncrowded community.

The **Sea Ranch Development** on the southernmost tip of **Chi Ma Wan Peninsula** is another project. It too has apartments in a lovely environment.

Both locations are served by hover-ferries, which run from Blake Pier in Central. And notwithstanding, Lantau remains a good place to escape from the hustle and beep of urban Hong Kong.

Preceding page, a Lantau monk and below, the Po Lin Monastery.

LOVELY LAMMA, 'STONE AGE ISLE'

The third largest of the outlying islands, and somehow less well-known both to visitors and to local people, is **Lamma Island**. It is nicknamed "Stone Age Island" because of its archaeological association with some of the earliest settlements in Hong Kong; and perhaps also because it is, *as yet*, quite free of high-rise buildings, cars, factories, and a planned power station.

Though it is only just over five square miles in area, Lamma is rich in green hills and beautiful bays. And—because it's mountainous—there is a very small area of cultivation. Eroded mountain tops dominate the island's grassy lower slopes.

Lamma is an island totally devoted to fishing and has a small population, less than 6,000 people (which includes a surprising number of Europeans who want to "get away from it all" and commute to urban Hong Kong daily for work). These residents are spread out between Lamma's two coastal villages and scattered homesites. Although Lamma has a regular ferry service it has remained relatively undiscovered — much to the joy of those who moved out to its peaceful ambience.

'Weekend Admirals'

The nearest Lamma village to Aberdeen—from where a round trip by privately-chartered sampan will cost about HK$25 — is **Sok Kwu Wan,** which lies on the eastern shore of a long fjord-like inlet known as **Picnic Bay** and is the haunt of Hong Kong's "Weekend Admirals" or "Saturday Sailors," the nautical names given to the colony's pleasure-junk captains.

Its quay is lined with excellent fresh seafood restaurants—**the Lamma Hilton** (no relation), **Peach Garden, Fu Kee** and **Chow Kee** seem to share most of the business—so treat yourself to a bargain repast while you are here.

It is possible to walk the entire length of the island to Sok Kwu Wan's sister town of **Yung Shue Wan** at the north end of Lamma. This trek follows a gentle hilly track up and down dividing valleys and treats hikers to a spectacular view across the sea to the Chinese **Lemas Islands**. The entire journey can be negotiated in a couple of hours, thereby leaving time for a fine Lamma seafood meal.

Both towns here offer the best of many Chinese worlds to the curious onlooker. Not isolated, yet underdeveloped, Yung Shue Wan has an excellent street market and the air is pungent with the smell of drying fish. Vegetable farms stretch up behind the village. At Sok Kwu Wan, visit the lovely **Tin Hau Temple**. The road which connects these two towns leads a walker first through neat patches of paddy and an occasional cluster of brightly-painted houses, then along **Hung Shing Ye Beach**, a long, clean and sandy beach that is usually almost deserted. Further along, the road gives way to narrow dusty track and all signs of cultivation are left behind, leaving only wild and rugged hills. A gentle climb along the sides of the hills reveals breathtaking scenery below and, eventually, an aerial view of Sok Kwu Wan, distant Hong Kong, Cheung Chau, and Lantau.

Village woman.

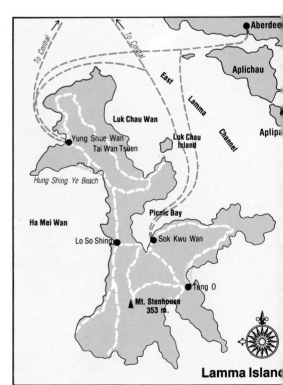

Lamma Island

184

CHEUNG CHAU, 'OLD CHINA' ISLE

Cheung Chau is different. It is much smaller than Lantau, for one thing, and it is urbanized in a rather charming "Old China" way.

Pastels and Pines

Indeed, if it weren't for the distinctly Chinese junks and sampans which crowd Cheung Chau's curving little harbour, one's first sight of Cheung Chau would deceive the eye into believing that this is an Old World Mediterranean port—a neat little place with pastel homes set into pine-studded hills.

This dumbbell-shaped isle—with hills at its either end and a village nestled in a connecting rod of land—is narrow enough that you can walk from **Cheung Chau Harbour** on its west side to **Tung Wan Harbour** on the east in a few minutes.

Cheung Chau is a fishing island, with a few farms in its more distant reaches, and her main town is a tangle of alley-ways which thread one into another. There is no vehicular traffic, a Hong Kong phenomenon which gives the island an automatic serenity.

People here live open to the streets—cutting vegetables on their doorsteps—all the better to talk to their neighbours—and playing *mahjong* outside in the garden—all the better to communicate their enjoyment of this noisy game.

Cheung Chau's sense of community is strong, but it does not exclude the visiting stranger. People here are friendlier than the hurried city dwellers in Hong Kong's Central District. Many Europeans have moved here "to get away" from bustling Hong Kong.

The Infamous Cheung Po Chai

The island was once the haunt of pirates, piracy having been one of the less honourable but most popular professions in these ancient Chinese waters. One of the greatest pirates of all, **Cheung Po Chai**, used to hide out on this island (with his English mistress) when he was in danger. His tiny **cave retreat** can still be explored, and the children on Cheung Chau will happily

The harbou at Cheung Chau, belov and at right devotee at The Temple of the Jade Vacuity.

show you the way to this famous lair. Legend says there is treasure there too, but no one has yet found it. Ah, but those were the old days; today, folk of Cheung Chau are largely preoccupied with fishing, junk-building and, perhaps, a bit of smuggling on the side.

Once a year the whole island community comes together for a big **Bun Festival**, a celebration held to exorcise wandering and malicious ghosts who have been unable to find rest in this world.

The festival, known as **Ching Chiu** in Cantonese, originated many years ago after the discovery here of a nest of skeletons, probably the remains of people killed by pirates. After this discovery the island was plagued by a series of misfortunes, and the islanders eventually called in a Taoist priest to ask for his help. He recommended that they should placate the restless spirits of the murdered people by making offerings to them once a year. Ever since then the island has held an annual four-day Ching Chiu Festival between the last 10 days of the third moon and the first 10 days of the fourth moon (usually in late April or Early May). During this time no one on the island is supposed to eat meat and no fishing boats put to sea. Instead of normal work there are Cantonese operas in roughly constructed shelters, street entertainment and finally a great festival day on which bamboo towers covered with edible buns are dismantled.

These specially inscribed buns are given to the thousands who stand around, to bring them good fortune throughout the coming year. People used to scramble wildly up these bun-towers—because the highest buns are the luckiest—and consequently fights would break out. The scramble is now forbidden, but it may be allowed again. The principle bun festival rites are held in the waterfront **Temple of the Jade Vacuity**, Cheung Chau's oldest temple.

There are excellent beaches to be found on Cheung Chau. They can be reached either by walking on the peak road across the island through the little homesteads where vegetables are grown and chickens raised, or by hiring a small sampan for a very modest fee.

The main beach, but not the nicest, is just across from Cheung Chau harbour on the other side of the narrow isthmus.

Interior and exterior Bun Festival devotees.

'OTHER ISLANDS'

Some of the more distant outlying islands have even more elusive charms, though occasionally the charm is slightly melancholy because these islands are more or less deserted.

Ping Chau: A 'Ghost Island'

Out at Mirs Bay northeast of Kowloon, is **Ping Chau**, one of the colony's most remote "inhabited" isles.

Ten years ago this almost enchanted island had a population of 3,000. Now it is down to three, including the island's caretaker. The cattle which the islanders used to raise are left to run wild now that farmers have gone—most of them to live at Tai Po in the New Territories. Most of Ping Chau's native sons and daughters are in London, working in Chinese restaurants.

This exodus began in 1969. The islanders emigrated and left behind their charming stone-built houses, some of them like traditional homes seen in Kwangtung (Guangdong) Province. Their many courtyards and winding passages have been left behind to howl empty in Mirs Bay's wind and rain.

'10,000 Layer Cake Rock'

Just beyond Ping Chau are the misty hills of China's **Po On District**, an intriguing sight that inspires one to head straight for China instead of returning back to Ping Chau's docking place at Emperor Point.

On Ping Chau there are long white beaches of smooth sand scattered with seashells, starfish and spiked sea urchins. Coloured rock which forms the base of the island and descends into Mirs Bay waters is called "**10,000 Layer Cake Rock**" by the Cantonese, after a cake of the same name found in most local bakery shops. Other delightful names are the "**Seashell Cave**," so-called because the sea has honed its wall to a finish as smooth as glass. Also fascinating are "**Dragon Fall Hill**," "**Breast Cave**" and "**Hard-to-Get-Over-Water**".

Passing through Ping Chau's virtually deserted village—only an old careta-

Outer
harbour
maritime li

190

ker, his daughter and an elderly widow remain to run a shop for occasional visitors—the visitor will see how the villagers have used shale, stone and shingle to roof their cottages.

Because this "ghost island" is so close to China, in recent years it was a favourite target for "freedom swimmers" who swam across these waters in attempts to escape from their Communist motherland. Nowadays Ping Chau is little more than a picnic place for those who take the ferry from Tai Po Kau. But it's a fine picnic place, with charms which exceed those of many other islands. Quiet beauty and the slight melancholy of her deserted village add an extra dimension to a holiday here.

Probably the best Ping Chau beach for a picnic is **Lai Tau Wan** with its attractive white sand and clean sea—amenities which are becoming increasingly rare in Hong Kong. The entire island is only about half a square mile in area, so it is easily travelled.

Also in Mirs Bay is **Tap Mun Island** with its thriving fishing community. The only access to Tap Mun is by ferry through the **Tolo Channel** from **Tai Po Kau** at the New Territories.

Tap Mun: Fisherfolk Haven

The island is well worth visiting, because it is an important base for Hong Kong's fishing folk. It has, in common with most of the other outlying islands, a **Tin Hau Temple** dedicated to the goddess of the sea. This temple is frequented by fishermen, even those from Shatin and Tai Po, because it's the last Tin Hau temple en route before junks and sampans head for open sea. Therefore, fishermen make a special point of visiting the temple to make offerings and pray for a safe return from their voyages.

The Tin Hau Temple is more than 100 years old and it and the one village on Tap Mun have risen around an inlet which forms a natural harbour for fishing boats. It is usually busy with fishing and work boats, and along the edge of the inlet is a line of cheek-to-cheek old cottages. It is a central exchange point for fisherfolk from all over this watery region.

There is one odd thing about this particular Tin Hau temple. When East winds roar, their sounds can be heard in a crevice under the altar. This eerie

howling is interpreted by fisherman as a warning of storms to come.

On the other side of the island, the eastern side, is the **Tap Mun Cave** where the sound of temple drums and gongs being beat inside the distant Tin Hau Temple can be heard. Local people believe that this cave runs underground the island from one side to the other. This picturesque island is a favourite with the colony's more adventurous picnickers; and there are shops and restaurants on it to cater to visitors who do not bring along picnic lunches.

Kat O Chau; Ancient Ambience

A lovely Tap Mun neighbour is **Kat O Chau**, or "**Crooked Island**," a richly green island thick with butterflies, wild flowers and a continuous chorus of frogs and cicadas.

Kat O is larger, but it's a rather sleepy island with an atmosphere reminiscent of ancient China. On this timeless Chinese isle the houses are built of traditional brickwork and tiles topped with ceramic tile eaves. The inevitable Tin Hau Temple here is decorated with perfectly preserved blue and green glazed ceramic friezes.

Kat O's people number about 2,000 Hoklo fishermen, who usually are dressed in the traditional black costumes of the Hoklo tribe. They spend their days catching, drying, selling and eating fish. The island is renowned for its abalone, squid and mussels, so it would be a good idea to make plans to eat these before catching a ferry back to Hong Kong.

There are many other islands that are not accessible by public transport, but they can be visited if you have access to a private boat. Others which are well worth a visit and are accessible by ferry are **Ap Chau**, **Po Toi** and **Ma Wan**.

Ap Chau's True Believers

Ap Chau is another fishing island with one unusual feature about it: the 500 fishermen and their families are all members of the True Jesus Church, which is headquartered in Taiwan. In 1965, the whole island clubbed together to build a **True Jesus Church** and they have regular meetings where the 80 families communicate in strange tongues and shake in ecstasy during their ser-

Outlying island beachlife.

vices. The only other notable characteristic about zealous Ap Chau is that it has no electricity.

Po Toi is a tiny island inhabited by some 200 people. It has a **haunted house** and some curious **rock carvings** which might possibly be the epitaph of an emperor who is rumoured to have died on or near Po Toi.

An even smaller island, 215 acre **Ma Wan**, is notable only because it was once the site of a Ching dynasty **custom station**.

The Soko Group

The **Soko Islands** are a group of sparsely populated islands off the southwest tip of Lantau. Most of Soko's inhabitants are on **Tai A Chau**, the largest island in the group. There are nearly 200 people there, and indications are that they have been there for at least 150 years. This is documented on a large ritual bronze bell which hangs in Tai A Chau's **Tin Hau Temple**. The Soko islanders have traditionally been fishermen, but they have now branched out into other commodities. They raise pigs, using stock bred specially at the Kadoorie Experimental Farm in the New Territories, and in the early 1960s the islanders started growing and selling pineapples. Soko families also share a large **man-made fishpond** from which they take fish for their own domestic needs.

Sek Kwu Chau

As a curious footnote to this section, it is worth mentioning **Sek Kwu Chau**, a small island near Cheung Chau. It is not possible for the casual visitor to gain access to Sek Kwu Chau as it is now given over to the residential treatment of drug addicts. It is run by a private body, **SARDA**, for the rehabilitation of heroin addicts. Heroin addiction is a major problem in Hong Kong and most forms of treatment are fairly ineffective in that they may remove the physical addiction, but replace the life-style of the addict with nothing more fulfilling. Therefore, the rate of re-addiction is heavy. On Sek Kwu Chau, however, the addicts come voluntarily but must agree to stay for at least six months. They, in fact, stay for an average of a year and many for up to 18 months.

THE 'LATIN ORIENT'

Macau has also been hit by the speculation about its future as its neighbour Hong Kong, but as its governor Rear Admiral Vasco Almeida de Costa explained: "Macau is not a colony." Portugal's constitution defines Macau as a "Chinese territory under Portuguese administration. The present status... serves the interests of Portugal, China and the population of Macau." Nevertheless, Beijing began negotiations with Macau in 1985 with a view to sorting out that territory; probably by Hong Kong's 1997 deadline.

With the lure of her casinos and hotels, Macau now has a large infrastructure which has converted the sleepy "Latin Orient" image into a high-rolling "Las Vegas (or Monaco) of the East" life-style, while keeping a bit of the Iberian charm.

As befits the oldest European settlement on the South China coast, Macau's antiquity is there to be seen. Unfortunately, most Macau tourists see only a tiny part of this 6.1 square mile territory (without its neighbouring islands of Taipa and Coloane, Macau is only 2.1 square miles). And most of what they "see" races by the windows of an air-conditioned bus.

Forgetting "official tours" for the moment, one of the best (and quickest) ways to see Macau is by car. Guides accost visitors as soon as they clear immigration at Macau's **hydroil-jetfoil pier.** Generally, the hiring of a knowledgeable guide is a matter of luck, but some of the local drivers are quite good. They've collected most of the free visitor pamphlets published by the Department of Tourism and are suprisingly knowledgeable. Officially, the cost of a tour is Ptc. 62 per person for about 60 to 90 minutes; unless you want to lounge about, this is about all the time you'll need to cruise the greater Macau area.

Macau

- ● Points of Interest
- ● Restaurants
- ✱ Hotels
- ● Town

Macau

Area: 2.1 sq. miles (including Taipa and
  Coloane, 6.1 sq miles)
Population: 500,000
Climate: Subtropical

China

Barrier Gate

Ilha Verde

Lin Fong Miu

Canidrome

Lacenda

Mong-ha Fort
and Hotel
& Tourism School

Avenida de Venceslau de Morais

Admiralte do

Avenida

Kun Iam Temple

Avenida de Demetrio Cinati

Luis De Camões
Museum & Garden

Lou Lim Ioc Garden

Sun Yat-sen House

Rua dos Pescadores

Inner Harbour

Old Protestant Cemetery

Reservoir

St. Paul's Basilica

Monte Fortress

Hotel Estoril

Jai Alai
Stadium

Guia Fortress

Jet to
Hydrof
Pie

Floating Casino

Rua das Lorchas

Fat Siu Lau

St. Dominic's Church

Hotel Royal

Start/Finish
Macau Grand
Prix

Hotel Matsuya

Ferry
Pier

Cathedral

Restaurante Portuguese

Macau Forum

Leal Senado

Grande

Hotel
Oriental

St. Augustine's Church
St. Joseph's Church
Dom Pedro Theatre

Rua da Praia

Hotel Sintra

Presidente Hotel

Guia (Grand Prix) Circuit

St. Lawrence's Church

Avenida

Hotel Lisboa

Amizade

Outer Harbour

Government
House

do

Bridge to Taipa

People's Republic of China

Penha Hill

Ma Kok Miu

Hotel Bela Vista
Henri's Galley

Wan Tzu

Macau

La-Pa

Taipa

Governor's Residence

Island

Hyatt
Regency
Hotel

Pinnochio

Pousada de Santiago
Barra Fort

Coloane

Pousada de Coloane

Trotting Track

On preceding pages, a Chinese funeral service, foreground, and beyond, a view of old Macau in 1839 (painted
by the French artist Auguste Borget).

HISTORIC MACAU

The first stop is usually **Penha Hill**, atop which stands the magnificent **Bishop's Palace**, unoccuppied for many years now. From one vantage point there, you can see across the **Old City** to Macau's **Inner Harbour**, and less than a mile farther, China. From another point, you can see **Outer Harbour** approaches and the island of **Taipa** which is connected to the peninsula by a bridge. In case you are wondering why tiny Macau has such a huge Bishop's Palace—larger than anything in this area outside the Philippines—the answer is that at one stage in early Eurasian history Macau was *the* Asian seat of Roman Catholicism. Bishops here controlled all of the church's missions from Goa to the Moluccas and Nagasaki.

Macau was also the training and publishing centre for all Roman Catholic missionary efforts in this part of the world.

The Bishop's Palace complex also houses **Penha Church**. Though the present building dates only from 1935, the first chapel here was dedicated in 1622. It has been said that peninsular Macau has more churches per square mile than Vatican City, and if you try to visit just the ones mentioned here, you will probably agree.

Perhaps the most striking Macau church is the towering facade of **St. Paul's** with its impressive grand staircase. Historians call it the finest monument to Christianity in the Far East.

Unfortunately, the site must have had bad *fung shui* (if we may be allowed to mix Chinese Taoism with Portuguese Christianity). The first church at this site was destroyed by fire in 1601 and construction of a new one was begun the following year. The classical facade you now see was added before 1630. In 1835 another fire (in the church's kitchen) spread and eventually destroyed St. Paul's adjacent **college**, a **library** reputed to be the best east of Africa, and, again, the church. In 1904 efforts were made to rebuild the church, but, as you will note, little was done. Today the grand facade of St. Paul's remains as Macau's most enduring visitor symbol.

Macau pedicab transport.

If you are touring by taxi, the driver usually races on to one of the colony's Chinese temples, but ask him instead to take you to **Monte Fort (St. Paul's Fortress)** which overlooks the facade (look to the right as you face the facade and you will see the fort's massive stone walls above). This fortification was built in the early 1620s. When Dutch ships attacked and invaded Macau in 1622, the then half completed fortress was defended by 150 clerics and negro slaves. A lucky cannon shot by an Italian Jesuit, Jeronimo Rhu hit a powder keg being carried by the invaders and the badly injured Dutch were defeated.

A-Ma, Ma Kok Miu, Macau

Tours here always include the Chinese temples of **A-Ma**, for which Macau is named, the **Kun Iam Temple**, famous for its table on which the first Sino-American treaty was signed in 1844, and the **Lin Fong (Lotus) Temple**.

The Temple of the Goddess A-Ma squats beneath **Barra Hill**, at the entrance to Macau's Inner Harbour. It is the oldest temple in this Portuguese Territory, said to date back 600 years to the Ming dynasty. It certainly was there in 1557 when Macau was ceded to Portugal. The original temple was said to have been erected by Fukinese fishermen and dedicated to Tin Hau, the patron goddess of fishermen. It was then called Ma Kok Miu (Ma Point—or peninsula—Temple). The Chinese named the area A-Ma-Gao or the Bay of A-Ma and the arriving Portuguese picked up on the name. The oldest surviving part of this temple is a lower pavilion to the right of its entrance. There is a multicoloured, bas relief stone carving here said to be a rendering of a Chinese junk which carried A-Ma (who is Tin Hau in Hong Kong) from Fukien Province through typhoon-ravaged seas to Macau, where she walked to the top of Barra Hill and ascended to heaven.

The second temple complex of Kun Iam (which in Cantonese is pronounced Kuan Yin) is dedicated to Buddhism's Goddess of Mercy. Some sub-temples in this complex are dedicated to A-Ma. The present temple dates back to 1627 and was built on the site of an earlier 14th Century temple. Foreign visitors, particularly Americans, will be pleased to know that at a **stone table** in this temple's courtyard, the first Sino-American Treaty was signed on July 3rd, 1844, by Ki Ying, China's Viceroy in Canton, and Caleb Cushing, a lawyer and former congressman from Massachusetts who was U.S. President John Tyler's "Commissioner and Envoy Extraordinary and Minister Plenipotentiary" to China.

The third temple, the Lin Fong (Lotus) Temple, built in 1592, is quite near Macau's 19th Century **Portas do Cerco** ("Border Gate"). In the old days it served as a guest house for mandarins travelling between Macau and Canton. Its most recent restoration took place in 1980, but it is still an excellent example of classical Buddhist architecture. Clay friezes over its entrances are some of the best examples of Buddhist art in this region. An image of the sea goddess Tin Hau stands tall over the main altar, beautifully garbed in silk robes and an opulent headdress.

The nearby Portas do Cerco, Macau's main border gate, was built in 1870. Just a few years ago the gate was closed to foreigners (though Chinese passed through it in each direction daily) and visitors were forbidden to photograph

acade of St.
aul's, left
d below,
St.
ichael's
atholic
metary.

it. Today the gate is open from 7 a.m. to 9 p.m. to accommodate those going into China to resorts across the border. And you can now snap away here to your camera's content.

'The Father of Modern China'

Most tours make a quick visit to the **Dr. Sun Yat-sen Memorial House**. Dr. Sun—the "Father of Modern China" who is revered in both Peking and Taipei—lived here when he practiced medicine at nearby **Kiang Vu Hospital**. (He was one of the first Western-trained Chinese doctors in this area.) His birthplace is across the border in China's **Cuiheng Village**. If you are wondering why the memorial is not as old as you'd expect, this is because in the 1930s it was used as an explosives depot and accidentally blew up one day. What you are looking at is a new structure built near the original monument site.

Another "classic" worth a visit is the **Leal Senado** ("Loyal Senate") building on Macau's main square. This building was dedicated in 1784 and its facade was completed in 1876. It was restored in 1939 and more internal restoration was recently completed. The title "Loyal" was bestowed on the Senate on May 13, 1809 by Portuguese King John VI (who was Prince Regent at the time) as a reward for continuing to fly the Portuguese flag when the Spanish monarchy took over the Portuguese throne.

An inscribed tablet here grants Macau its sacred title: "City of the Name of God, There is None More Loyal." The original tablet dates from 1654, and was placed here by Macau's Governor and Captain-General then, Joao de Souza Pereira. Half the offices on ground floor have been converted into a beautiful gallery for special exhibitions.

Head up the Senate's staircase to the fine wrought iron doors and beyond. Admire the beautiful Portuguese tiles on the walls, absorb the scene of the beautiful garden below, and run your fingers over the Senate's belltower. The **library** and **council chamber** here include beautiful examples of Old World woodwork.

Kwangtung Pottery

Two other areas often missed by quickie tours—but very accessible by walking or taxi—are the **Camões Gardens and Museum** and the **Dom Pedro V Theatre**. The museum—named after Portugal's most famous poet, Luis de Camões (1524-1580)—is now completely renovated and houses an excellent collection of **European prints** and **Kwangtung pottery**. This 18th Century building was once the residence of the president of the select committee of the East India Company, the all powerful firm which for centuries "ruled" the area from India to the South China Sea. The completely-restored theatre is tiny—about 350 seats—but charming.

An interesting and contrasting, episode in Dom Pedro V's long history euded in 1985 when the Crazy Paris Show, stititlating French strip extravagana moved to larger premises in the Lis boa Hotel after half a decade of bounding that ancient stage with sexy routines.

Don't miss seeing many of Macau's old churches; you shouldn't, because most of the intrigue and history of this colony's past 400-plus years took place behind their sanctified walls.

Below the tombstone tale in the Old Protestant Cemetry. At right, St. Francis's humerus and other relics of the Japanese martyrs once housed in St. Joseph's Cemetery.

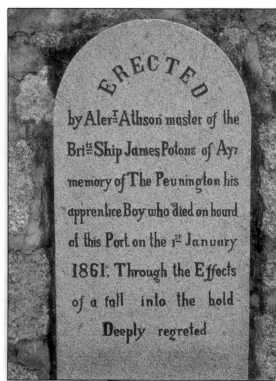

At St. Dominic's:
Christian-Oriental Motifs

The church of **St. Dominic** is one of the oldest and most famous, dating from the 17th Century. (Spanish Dominicans had a chapel and convent on this site as early as 1588.) To gain entry, ring a bell to the right of the facade. When you get inside, you will note that many of the Christian motifs are of an Oriental style.

The baroque-style church of **St. Augustine** is the largest in the region. The present structure dates from 1814, and its ornate facade from 1875, but Spanish Augustinians founded a first church there in 1586.

Just near the Dom Pedro V Theatre is **St. Lawrence's**, another church which dates from the 16th Century, but which was rebuilt in 1803, 1846 and 1892. It is one of the most elegant of Macau's religious edifices. Its double staircase, iron gates, towers, and crystal chandeliers are European, but the roof is made of Chinese tiles. It overlooks the pastel pink government administration building.

Perhaps the starkest proof of the recent deterioration of both Macau and her once mighty Roman Cahtolic presence is the **church and seminary of St. Joseph**. This Jesuit seminary was dedicated in 1728 and its sole purpose was to establish religious missions in China, a task it performed admirably. Today its vast halls, classrooms and living quarters are empty, but badly needed renovation is in progress. It is the home of Msgr. Manvel Texieira SJ, Macau's oldest Portuguese (arrived in 1924) and foremost historian. Even he has not managed to salvage all the valuable books, maps and drawings in random storage here.

The church of St. Joseph's (circa 1746) is reached through the seminare or through the street, if the front door is open. The church is now used only once a year on New Year's Eve to celebrate a special Mass. Though the sacred relic— a six inch piece of bone from the left arm of St. Francis (ardent Macanese and Portuguese Catholics believe the relic protects the city from natural disasters)—has long been moved to the Chapel of St. Francis on Coloane Island, the statues in the lovely chapel were salvaged from St. Paul's in 1835.

There are a couple of other places

Below left; Roman Catholic and below right, a traditional firecracker maker.

nearby not on the usual tourist route. One is the **Barra Fortress** which has been turned into the deluxe **Pousada de Sao Tiago,** a new hostelry developed within the walls of this 17th Century fort.

The Oldest Lighthouse

The **Guia Fortress and Lighthouse** (there is also a chapel) is the first thing you see when you approach Macau by sea. This 17th Century landmark stands atop **Guia Hill** guarding coastal approaches. This Western-style lighthouse is the oldest on the China coast. Interesting tunnels underneath this beacon are not open to the public.

Protecting the other approach to the city is the 19th Century fortress of **Mong-Ha**, built to provide a defense vantage to guard the Portas do Cerco. It too is now a small government inn. Other buildings (new and old) house the Macau Hotel and Tourism School.

'Las Vegas of the East'

Sleepy Macau is also vicariously known as the "Las Vegas of the East," or, if you are a European, the "Monaco of the East." Indeed, gambling is the main reason over four million visitors each year—83 percent of them Hong Kong Chinese—make the 40 mile sea cruise across the Pearl River Estuary to this Portuguese territory.

Lady Luck—who lurks in five casinos, dog-racing and trotting tracks, and in a jai alai *fronton* here—theives on gambling mad Chinese.

Macau's four casinos, each one virtually packed every day, feature Western and Chinese games of chance. If you tire of conventional craps, roulette, baccarat (*chemin de fer*) or blackjack, you can try your hand at Chinese *fantan*, *sik-po* and *pai-kao*. Also popular are Keno and slot machines.

Four of the casinos are classified as "international" casinos. These are located in the Lisboa and Oriental Hotels, the Jai Alai Palace and on a permanently moored floating barge in the Inner Harbour called the Casino de Macau (or the "Floating Casino"). The fourth casino, the Kam Pek on Travessa A. Novo (just off Avenida Almeida Ribeiro), is a smaller casino which specializes in Chinese gambling games.

Sleepy Macau.

For those unfamiliar with Chinese games of chance:

Fan-tan is played with buttons. An unknown number of buttons are put under an inverted cup and then counted out in groups of four. You bet on how many buttons will be left in the last group counted out—one to four.

Sik-po is a dice game in which three dice are shaken and their numerical value tallied. Bets are on Small (*siu*), four to 10, or Big (*Dai*), 11 to 17, rolls. You can also bet on specific numbers — singly or in combinations.

Pai-kao is Chinese dominoes.

There is no such thing as a miracle book that will help you win at any gambling game, but there are two books available here which will explain Macau gambling games in detail and, hopefully, lead you in an auspicious direction. These are the *Gambler's Guide to Macau* by Bert Okuley and F. King-Poole (HK$20) and *The A-O-A Macau Gambling Handbook* (HK$7).

'Mr. Bigs' and Taipa Trotters

Despite—or perhaps because of—numerous rumours of trackside fixing and other foul play, greyhound racing seems to attract the Pearl River's hardest core gambling crowd. "Mr. Bigs" abound in Macau's dog-racing venue, the Canidrome on Avenida General Castelo Branco.

On good nights the Canidrome roars with money madness of the purest sort. Even in jaded Macau, this place is quite a scene. Ironically, this high-energy gambling place is situated only three quarters of a kilometer away from the straight-laced People's Republic of China.

The Canidrome's regular 14-race cards begin at 8 p.m. on weekends and on public holidays. Admission is Ptc. 2 to public seats, Ptc. 5 member's stand and Ptc. 80 for six-person boxes.

The latest running attraction in Macau's varied gambling world is Asia's only trotting track, the Macau Trotting Club's Raceway on Taipa Island. Australian trotters have been imported to run the sulkies around this track.

Trotting races take place every weekend and sometimes during the week, but dates are not fixed. A usual 10-race card starts at 2 p.m. on weekends and 7:30 for evening races. Public stand tickets are Ptc. 3 and

Highrollers' neon beacon above the Casino Lisboa.

206

are sold in **Lori Jewellery** in the Lisboa Hotel.

Jai Alai

Though suspiciously foreign to most local gamblers, the sleek new **Palacia de Pelota Basca** (Jai-Alai Palace) is Macau's biggest and best-appointed locus for profitable sport. Filling a gap left in Iberian pride when bullfights were ended in the late 1960s, the 4,500-seat *fronton* (near the Outer Harbour, opposite the ferry piers) offers a daily slate of contests among an agile squad of wicker-armed and plastic-helmeted professionals. Wagering follows a simple, racetrack-style parimutuel system (bets from Ptc. 2 to Ptc. 250). with a small handbook available free to assist the uniformed.

The nightly matches during the week begin at 7:30 p.m. and at 2 p.m. on weekends and public holidays. For those needing further stimulation, the Jai Alai Palace also houses a casino.

Just near the Ferry Terminal and the Jai Alai Stadium is the Macau Forum, a three-storey convention centre with four conference halls.

The Macau Grand Prix

Asia's Monaco wouldn't be complete without an annual motor-car race. So, like its glittering Mediterranean sister, Macau each year (on the second or third weekend in November) cordons off a twisting, through-the-streets grand prix race course that starts and finishes on Avenida da Amizade near the ferry piers. Racing drivers from around the world race Formula III cars for 32 laps around this 3.8 mile Guia Circuit.

The Macau Grand Prix begins at 2 p.m. on race Sunday. When this race was first run in 1954, the winner took 4 hours, 31 minutes and 19.1 seconds to complete 51 laps. He posted an average lap speed of 49 mph in his Triumph TR2. Today, average lap speeds are over 90 mph, with cars sometimes hitting 140 mph on the waterfront straightaway. The official lap record is 2:20.64 (for a lap speed of 97 mph) set in the 29th Grand Prix in 1982 by the winner Brazilian Roberto Moreno. (Masahiro Hasemi clocked 2:20.48 in practice but it does not count.)

This racing weekend also features

another international grand prix, a secondary race for motorcycles that has been run since 1967. Also held during this fast moving grand prix week are production car and endurance races.

Screeching tires, sunshine and gaming tables draw a well-heeled, thoroughly hedonistic crowd to Macau's Grand Prix Week. Macau is inundated with some 50,000 racing aficionados, and this otherwise quiet territory swings with pre and post-race parties.

If you don't make hotel reservations well in advance it is next to possible to find a room in Macau at this time.

The "Other Macau"

The "Other Macau" is not on the peninsula that is generally regarded as Macau, but consists of the two islands of **Taipa** and **Coloane**. Previously, access to these islands was by small ferry boats which, in the case of Coloane, could only be approached at high tide. Today, Taipa is connected to the mainland by a beautiful arching bridge. Access these days is as simple as getting into a taxi or climbing aboard a local double-decker bus.

Taipa and Coloane's cobble-stoned villages have grown a bit, but they are still tiny, rural and charming—a cross between out-of-the-way Iberian villages built around a central plaza and surrounded by typical old Chinese farming communities.

Taipa was also at one period in its history (1717-1723), the busy centre for Western trade with China when an Imperial edict banned English and French ships at Canton and insisted they moor at Taipa instead. The major industries on Taipa in the old days were junk-building and the manufacture of fire-crackers. A Macau **trotting track** project was initiated here in 1980, and the **University of East Asia** opened in 1981.

Taipa's "Latin Orient" ambience, however, still lives. Indeed, the small *praia* just below Largoda Carma rivals its larger and more famous predecessor on the Macau peninsula for beauty, elegance and romance. To preserve this 19th century ambiance, a **Casa Museu** (house museum) has been created (completed with period furniture) out of one of the five old houses, the first step in what will be a cultural complex.

Coloane, too, seems to have been forgotten for many years, but is now bursting back into prominence because of its superb **beaches**. Coloane is almost twice as big as Taipa (2.6 square miles in area compared with Taipa's 1.4 square miles), large enough to have **pine tree plantations** (which give a lovely and improbable pine scent to this tropical isle).

Coloane is so close to China you can see quite clearly and easily a Chinese fishing village that sits only a quarter mile beyond a strip of water. And with a strong pair of binoculars, you can see the villagers meandering about, doing their Communist things.

One of Coloane's beaches, **Kao Ho**, situated on the northern end of the island, was a traditional haven for South China Sea pirates. Most of the islanders patronized piracy, which apparently was their main source of livelihood. But the pirates overstepped their watery bounds. After a mass kidnapping of Chinese children from Canton, and a subsequent refusal of outrageous ransom demands by Coloane's buccaneers, Portuguese authorities went after the pirates and defeated them in a two-day battle in July, 1910—only 70 odd years ago. A memorial to this incident is set into a tiny square in front of the Portuguese **Chapel of St. Francis Xavier.**

This tiny chapel houses a relic, a six inch piece of bone from the left arm of St. Francis plus the revered bones of Vietnamese and Japanese martyrs who were slaughtered because of their religion in centuries past.

Except for race fans who frequent Taipa's trotting-track. Coloane is probably the more popular of these two Macau Islands, usually because of the **Pousada de Coloane on Cheoc Van Beach** and the **Hac Sa Beach** area. Coloane is connected to Taipa by a causeway. At Hac Sa Beach, there is a park of the same name with a swimming pool and sports-facilities. Cheoc Van Park, on the beach of the same name, also has pool facilities. Coloane Park is a combination walk-in aviary and gardens with barbecues, restaurants and walks.

Right, "A Family Group in Macau" by George Chinnery.

209

THE STAR FERRY

Hong Kong, which in Cantonese means "Fragrant Harbour," provides a spectacular venue for the double-ended double-decker green and white Star Ferries which ply an eight-tenths of a nautical mile route every few minutes (an average of 455 crossings daily) between Hong Kong Island's Central and Kowloon's Tsimshatsui. They run so frequently that one of the Star's senior coxswains has reportedly logged a million miles on the cross-harbour route.

Residents and tourists can be easily differentiated. The tourists are normally toting cameras and are understandably agog at the harbour's charming panorama of junks-lighters-sampans - freighters - tankers - motor-boats-ferries-and-warships which are constantly manoeuvering through this confined waterway. The colony's jaded residents, meanwhile, are tucked into a newspaper or, if it's racing season, a scratch sheet giving tips and odds on the day's nags.

Indeed, the Star Ferry is so vital a part of life in the colony that a late 1950s fare increase of 5 Hong Kong cents was enough to spark a riot.

The Star Ferry Company traces its origin to 1870 (only three decades after the founding of the colony) when a chap named Grant Smith initiated a first cross-harbour ferry service with a twin-screw launch. Eighteen years later, an Indian resident, Dorabjee Nowrojee, introduced the colony's first steamboat ferry service, a system which ran between Pedder Wharf and Tsimshatsui every 40 to 60 minutes except on Mondays and Fridays when the "vessels were withdrawn for coaling."

In 1898, Nowrojee was bought out by the Star Ferry Company which a year later replaced his older boats with two coal-burning double-decker ferries, the *Morning Star* and the *Guiding Star*.

Ten Hong Kong cents at the turn of the century entitled you to a first class one-way trip. And Chinese peasants who used the lower deck paid only 1 Hong Kong cent per crossing. In those first years, the average annual passenger traffic was about 600,000.

By 1904 three more vessels had been added to the Star Ferry's fleet and fares were increased to 15 and 10 Hong Kong cents for first and economy classes.

At the turn of this century, piracy was still rampant here, and the Royal Navy was quite busy keeping local waters free of pirates. Thanks to their lucky stars, a Star Ferry was never pirated.

The only serious peacetime accident happened in April 1937, when the *Meridian Star*, approaching Hong Kong Island with what was later diagnosed as a faulty steering gear, struck a sister craft, the *Night Star*, amid-ships. The *Night Star* returned to the Hong Kong pier to allow her passengers to disembark, but continued to sink while tied at dockside. At a last moment, her crew slipped lines and she sank gracefully next to the pier. She was later recovered and thus became a *rising star*, if you will.

The fleet consists of 10 green and white, double-bowed vessels which can each accomodate 580 passengers and a 10-men crew. The Star Ferry Central to the (tourist district of Tsimshatsui (Kowloon) runs daily (except during the typhoon interruptions) from 6:30 a.m. to 11:30 p.m. (the Central-Hong Hon Service runs 7 a.m. to 7:20 p.m.) and is one of the world's greatest travel bargains. Its first-class one-way fare is only 70 Hong Kong cents (the lower deck second class fare is 50 Hong Kong cents).

Hong Kong Star Ferry crew at work.

TRIPPING BY TRAM

Slowly the kaleidoscope that is Hong Kong's urban theatre passes by: Hong Kong Island's north shore appears during abrupt stops and starts as the ancient vehicles jerk through some of the world's worst traffic.

Hong Kong's trams (or streetcars, if you prefer the American term) are an intriguing aspect of life in the colony. Though they serve as a prime form of transportation for many of Hong Kong Island's 1.5 million residents, they are also one of the best ways to enjoy a

can accommodate any pocketbook — hop on a tram. Unfortunately, there are no trams in Kowloon. You'll have to come across to Hong Kong Island to experience one.

A word of warning! The trams have a seating capacity of 28 on the upper deck and 20 on the lower deck. But about another 100 people can be stuffed — and are stuffed — into one during rush hours. Thus, it's no fun travelling by tram during rush hours. Not only is it uncomfortably crowded, but out-

charming do-it-yourself tour of the island — at the staggering price of only 60 Hong Kong cents per journey, regardless of distance travelled.

The normal tour of Hong Kong Island as packaged by travel agents usually consists of a bus trip up to The Peak, then to North Point and the Aw Boon Haw (formerly Tiger Balm) Gardens, on to Repulse Bay and Aberdeen on the south side of the island, and the journey back.

For a truly unique experience — one that

The view from one of Hong Kong's venerable trams is a popular transit view of the *real* colony.

side traffic is jampacked too. Aside from those two times during the day, and when there are major sporting events or horse-races, the trams are fairly uncrowded. All trams require exact fare change.

The trams are regularly spaced, one arriving every few minutes. Once you board a tram, head upstairs and, if possible, sit up front. The view up there, as you might imagine, is a scape of real life in the colony.

The Hong Kong Tourist Association has an excellent fact sheet on trams which, incidentally can be part of a posh dinner tour or, believe it or not, hired out by the hour for rolling cocktail parties.

RICKSHAW 'BOYS' — A DYING RACE

Some say they are a social embarrassment. Others feel they are an integral part of Chinese life in the Orient generally, and Hong Kong specifically. Regardless of where you ride on the matter, the rickshaw (or *jinriksha* as it is officially known) still survives (though barely) in this British Crown Colony.

Clustered around the Hong Kong and Kowloon entrances to the Star Ferry are the remnants of a once vast fleet of rickshaws that, as recently as post World War II, numbered about 8,000. Rickshaws then, as in the 19th Century, were an important form of Hong Kong transportation.

Today they number under 20 and owe their existence almost entirely to the tourist trade (Is there anyone who hasn't had or wants to have his/her photo taken in a rickshaw?). Hong Kong's rickshaw "boys" — average age about 60 — show a complete disdain for traffic signs and regulations, pulling their landcrafts in straight lines through pedestrain subways, onto pavements and in the wrong direction on one-way streets.

Naturally, in a bureaucracy like Hong Kong, you need one annual license to own a rickshaw and a second license to pull it. However, the Hong Kong government issued its last rickshaw license in 1975 when there were about 80 left in the colony. They don't intend to issue any more.

Though rickshaws were once commonly used as taxis, they were also used by wealthy families and businesses that needed or wanted a private and inexpensive form of transport. The last private or commercial license, held by a stationery company in Central District, expired in 1967.

These popular and private vehicles, known as *sze ka che* (which is also the Cantonese term for any private transport), have always been considered a snug and romantic travelling mode. Indeed, local records show that in 1917, 60 of Hong Kong's 1,750 registered rickshaws were operated by brothels.

Reverend Goble's Sedan Chair on Wheels

The rickshaw dates back to the 19th Century when an ingenious American Baptist missionary, Jonathon Goble, reportedly designed a rickshaw for his wife. It seems Mrs. Goble was reluctant to ride in a sedan chair carried by coolies, and she was determined to do something to relieve their difficult labour. Hence the Reverend Goble's rickshaw — a sedan chair on wheels.

The name comes from Japanese words: *jin* (man) *riki* (power) and *sha* (carriage). In modern Tokyo there are less than 100 *jinriksha* still operating, compared with some 170,000 a century ago. And to hire one these days (assuming you can find one) — costs about ¥250 for a short run. In Calcutta there are said to be 75,000 rickshaws still in running order, but only about 6,000 licenses have been issued. And due to traffic congestion there, the incidence of rickshaws is increasing because they are often faster than cars.

By 1863, some 22 years after Hong Kong was claimed by Britain, the colonial government saw fit to regulate road traffic, and Ordinance No. 6 — a statute pertaining to the licensing of public vehicles and chairs, drivers, bearers and horses — was passed. By 1895, there were about 700 licensed rickshaws and more than 8,000 registered pullers.

By 1924 there were 3,411 rickshaws registered. In that year a rickshaw could be rented for 28 Hong Kong cents and a puller could expect to net about HK$1.50 in a 12-hour day. But in those days a bowl of noodles with

Hong Kong's wily and charming Rickshaw "boys" don't legally exist in the colony anymore, but as one can see, their tradition does.

fish balls cost 3 Hong Kong cents and a labourer could support both a wife and concubine on HK$18 a month.

No More Rickshaws?

The rickshaw's decline began with the advent of the motorcar. There were only 218 rickshaws registered here in 1938 just before the Second World War started. There was a brief resurgence of popularity in 1945 when the number of rickshaws shot up past 8,000 due to a lack of vehicles, parts and fuel. But as soon as Hong Kong recovered from that occupation depression the final decline of the rickshaw started.

Believe it or not, there are legally "no" rickshaws now operating in Hong Kong be-

by posing for tourists who want a souvenir photo. That price is also negotiable, and can run as high as HK$20 to $25 a snap. However, beware of rickshaw pullers who skip away with an unsuspecting passenger and then try to charge HK$100 to $150 for a short ride. A quick run into Central or Tsimshatsui from the Star Ferry terminal should probably cost a good bargainer about HK$20 to $25.

Sometimes a bit of levity is inserted into the arduous life of a rickshaw-puller. During the 1970s R & R (Rest & Recreation) invasion by allied troops fighting in Vietnam, rickshaw races between inebriated members of the various countries' armed forces visiting here were run in the middle of the night down Lockhart Road through the Wanchai "Suzie Wong" bar district on Hong Kong Island, or

cause no annual licenses have been issued for the past eight years. The most-recent operator's fee was HK$50 per year — which allowed a rickshaw boy full run of Hong Kong Island and the Kowloon Peninsula. For an extra dollar he could add the entire New Territories to his service area.

The above rule means that the 18 to 20 rickshaws you see lined up daily on both sides of the harbour by the Star Ferry terminals do not legally exist because the Transport Department, under whose aegis rickshaws operate, has no record of them.

The Hong Kong Tourist Association, however, notes in its *Facts and Information Booklet* that the cost of a rickshaw ride in the colony is HK$20 per five minutes. In reality, bartering is the key. In fact, rickshaw boys seem to make most of their money these days

from the Star Ferry to a favourite bar in The Wanch. Much to the amusement of rickshaw-pullers, the soldiers would sometimes trade places with a puller and race away madly to the cheers of his mates.

During the year, you may occasionally hear of a Rickshaw Derby or Sedan Chair Race. These fun projects are for charity and usually attract great crowds. At one such event a couple of years ago, two Europeans convinced the Transport Department to "issue" them rickshaw licenses on the condition that their rickshaw would be auctioned off for charity. The request was granted.

Rickshaws even managed to survive a period a few years ago when they became an "*in*" gift for the person who has everything." They were literally being bought off the streets for about US$100 to $150 each.

216

CHINESE CUISINE – WHEN IN DOUBT, EAT

It has been said that when confronted with something they have never seen before or do not understand, the first impulse of a Chinese is to try eating it. As a result, this canon of Chinese folk philosophy has helped inspire the greatest cooking the world has known.

Standing as Chinese food does on five millenia of uninterrupted civilization, not much has been lost: rather, each generation of Chinese eaters has added great gustatory discoveries of the vast body of eating knowledge that preceded it.

then steamed for three days, thereby producing a layer of fragrant oil.

Rice was steamed in an earthenware vessel that had seven holes at the bottom and was lined with bamboo matting. Fish was steamed in a bamboo tube. Meat was preserved by salt curing, by grilling with spices and by fermentation with a yeast and wine mixture.

Early 'Barbaric' Tastes

Other culinary refinements came gradually as China's developing agriculture provided

Ancient Chinese cooking bears little resemblance to what you'll savour in Hong Kong today, but certain basic principles remain. Steaming, roasting, smoking and fermentation of meats were practiced at least as early as 1,000 B.C., as was the now forgotten practice of "scorched" pig roasting without evisceration.

Heavy, ornate, bronze cooking cauldrons and tripods from the Chou dynasty (1122-256 B.C.) have been unearthed intact. These items were used together as a double-boiler. Recipes of that time were also elaborate: a suckling pig, for example, was stuffed with dates, wrapped with hemp and mint and baked in a shell of clay. After the clay was removed, the pig was deep-fried until crisp,

steady supplies of new ingredients. Each region naturally evolved a distinctive cooking style that reflected its topography, climate, flora and fauna, the temperament of its people, and their contact with outsiders.

Foods of northern and western China, for example, developed apart from the mainstream of China's southern coastal rice bowl. This northern school, centered on the ancient and present capital of Peking, was heavily influenced by Mongols who swept into Han China during the late 13th Century. When the flat arid plain of northern China fell to these "Outer Barbarians" from the west, the exotic splendour of Chinese "agrarian cuisine" began a "new" taste odyssey.

This western Asia cooking — rooted in the hearty flavours of the wintry, simoom-swept steppes — was fine fare, but it was even further refined by China's indigenous Han chefs.

The Mongols, who founded the Yuan dynasty in 1279 A.D., were a nomadic tribe. They lived in tents and dressed in furs and their tastes — based on milk, butter and lamb — were quite different from the native Chinese.

These "uncivilized" wanderers preferred a rough and simple cuisine: whole animals were roasted in stone pits or steamed with rock salt.

kitchens. Southern Chinese (mainly the Cantonese, but including sub-groups such as the local Hunan, Chiu Chow and Hakka people) like to complain that Peking-based food lacks smoothness and subtlety. Pekinese, meanwhile, argue that southerners grind, chop and dilute the flavour out of their food.

'Have You Eaten?'

Whatever their regional and moot food points, Chinese everywhere talk about their food the way Westerners talk about art. This is

They made fruit preserves and used pine nuts, rosewater, almond oil and sugar for seasonings; lamb dumplings were made with bean paste and dried tangerine peel; and lamb cakes included innards, ginger, gourds, and eggs.

More than three centuries later, China was engulfed by yet another horde — this time by Manchurian warriors from the north who founded the Ching dynasty (1644-1912). Like the Mongols, the Manchus further influenced local Mongol-Han cuisine to suit their unusual tastes. The Chinese adapted well, but not completely.

Indeed, even today, 400 years after the Manchus and Mongols added new alien recipes to the vast Chinese menu, there are still great food preference battles fought in China's

probably because Chinese cuisine is indeed an art form.

But even if they aren't conscious of their food as a major cultural accomplishment, no Chinese can ever avoid talking about it. The most common Cantonese greeting, for example, is *Sik tzo fan mei?* — an expression which literally means "Have you eaten?"

Every Chinese dialect is rich in food symbolism. "You are breaking my rice bowl," wails the Chinese man whose livelihood is threatened. And even to simply learn how to say rice in Chinese, one needs an annotated dictionary. Consider the Cantonese linguistic

When in Hong Kong, don't be shy and eat. Ancient Chinese ritual of preparation, above.

variables for that common staple: plain rice is *mai;* cooked rice is *faan;* rice porridge (commonly called congee) is *juk*; and harvested but unhusked rice is *guk*.

Eating for the Chinese is also not just a bit of necessary metabolic bother — to be consummated as quickly as possible with great globs of starch three times a day. Granted, there has been a sad increase in Western or Western-style "fast food" outlets in Hong Kong, but when eating here, one is still expected to enjoy a measure of entertainment and, most important, a proper and tasty titillation of the palate.

The Chinese concept of a meal is very much a communal affair and one that provides a strong sensory impact. Dishes are chosen with both taste and texture in mind — a stomach-idea of creating one particular dish like a stew or roast; rather, he or she goes to the market to buy what is fresh and in season, and then creates the dish.

Monkey's Brain, Bear's Paw, Live Baby Mice and Lizards

To most Westerners, Chinese food is basically strange. In fact, many dishes considered rare delicacies by Chinese make the Westerner ill. For example, monkey's brain (eaten directly from the skull of a freshly killed monkey), bear's paw, snake, dog, pigeon, frogs, sparrows, live baby mice (good for ulcers) and lizards. Unfortunately for the average Hong Kong Chinese who savours such gourmet fare, many of these delicacies are

pleasing succession of sweet-sour, sharp-bland, hot-cool, and cruchy and smooth.

In a land which has experienced recurrent hunger and natural disasters, no wastage of foodstuffs is acceptable. Even today children are warned by their parents that if they leave any rice in their bowls they will marry a pock-marked spouse — and the more grains wasted, the more pock-marked their partner will be.

In spite of traditional poverty and privation, or maybe because of it, Chinese nearly always insist on fresh food. It is only very recently that refrigeration and freezing methods have been adopted by Asian households. Most traditional Chinese still shop three times a day for fresh meats and vegetables. A Chinese cook does not start a meal with the either banned by law or virtually impossible to obtain. Hence, they are rare and expensive.

Many Westerners also experience difficulty in eating with chopsticks. Small and loose rice grains are a particular *gweilo* menace. To accomplish the seemingly impossible, abandon self-consciousness, hold the rice bowl up against your lips in a drinking position and shovel the rice into your mouth with the chopsticks. Scraping and slurping are not considered a *faux pas* here or anywhere Chinese.

One mistake Westerners make, however, is the unseemly swamping of their rice with soya sauce, a crude act that robs it of its character and function. A meal should include enough spicy and savoury dishes to make the neutral blandness of steamed rice an essential balancing agent.

Chopsticks are thought to have been a-dopted for eating because of a Confucian distaste for knives — potentially dangerous weapons — on the dining table. In Hunan, China's agricultural rice bowl, curious extra long chopsticks are supplied in restaurants. Stories are told of people who feed each other across the table because the chopsticks are so long they can't manoeuvre the ends into their own mouths!

If chopsticks are impossible for you to coordinate, it is perfectly acceptable to use the porcelain spoon provided for soups as a scoop for other courses. And no one minds if you make a mess — it is even permissible to wipe your hands on the edge of the tablecloth. The object is to get the food into your mouth in the personal taste. However, since you are in Hong Kong, a colony largely influenced by Cantonese cooking, consider the following oft-repeated Chinese proverb:

> *"Live in Soochow* (a city noted for its refined manner and beautiful women), *die in Liuchow* (where teakwood coffins are made), *but eat in Kwangchow* (Canton)."

Indeed, if Chinese cooking is the world's finest, then judging by popular worldwide demand, Cantonese cuisine just may be the premier regional food of China.

The Cantonese live to eat and, at its most refined level, Cantonese gastronomy achieves a finicky discrimination that borders on cultism. Of these decadent gourmets, Confucius

most efficient manner.

A typical Chinese meal invariably starts with a cold dish, which is followed by other main courses. Soup — usually clear light broth — may be eaten after the heavier entrees to aid digestion. However, a thick full-bodied soup may be served as a main dish, and a sweet soup often serves as a dessert at meal's end. There are no inflexible rules when it comes to ordering. The main thing is to enjoy the food.

'Die in Liuchow, But Eat in Kwangchow'

As aforementioned, eating and enjoying of Chinese food is — given the diversity of foods one can eat in this region — largely a matter of once wrote:

> For him the rice could never be white enough and minced meat could never be chopped finely enough. When it was not cooked right, he would not eat. When the food was not in season he would not eat. When the meat was not cut correctly, he would not eat. When the food was not served with its proper sauce, he would not eat.

This gourmet syndrome is found wherever

For an initial dining experience in China's mandarin past and present: try one of fabulous Aberdeen's floating restaurants, above and right.

221

there are Chinese with the means to pursue it, but the Cantonese have pushed it to the extreme with dishes made of bear's paw, shark's fin, bird s nests, duck webs, deer tails, chicken testicles and the aforementioned live monkey's brain.

Gweilo 'Fortune Cookies'
Are a No-No in Hong Kong

Visitors to Hong Kong who think they are familiar with Cantonese food soon learn to their surprise that this discipline has little to do with sweet 'n sour pork — said to have been invented by ever resourceful inhabitants of Canton solely for sweet-toothed foreigners —

steamed. This discourages overcooking and preserves a food's delicate and "natural" flavours. Sauces are used to enhance flavours, not destroy them. The sauce usually contains contrasting ingredients like vinegar and sugar or ginger and onion.

A Cantonese restaurant is *the place* to eat fish, steamed whole with fresh ginger and spring onions and sprinkled with a little soy and sesame oil. Cantonese, unlike picky Western eaters, consider a fish's eyes and lips a delicacy. However, in keeping with a traditional superstition among fishing families, you will seldom see a Chinese diner turn over a fish to reach the meat underneath. He doesn't

or *chop suey* — said to have been invented in San Francisco when a customer entered a restaurant after closing, demanded service and the cooks threw their leftovers into a pot, served it up and in quiet jest called this Oriental goulash "*chop suey*." Also, despite Hong Kong's bent for things superstitious, "fortune cookies" do not exist here. They are another romantic *gweilo* ("foreign devil") invention.

In the Cantonese method of preparation food is cooked quickly and lightly — stir fried — in shallow water or an oil base, usually in a *wok*. The flavour of the foods is thus preserved, not lost, in preparation. Neither is the original taste of hot, spicy sauces. Many dishes, particularly vegetables or fish, are

want a capsized boat and drowned men on his conscience.

Prawns and crabs in various styles, steamed or in a black-bean sauce, are also popular Cantonese seafood dishes. If you hear the term "jumping prawns," this signifies that they are alive (therefore fresh), but doesn't mean you are expected to eat them that way! Shark's Fin Soup, golden threads of gelatinous-like shark's fin in a shark broth, is the centrepice of Cantonese banquets.

Chicken is the most widely-eaten fowl, and in keeping with the Chinese sense of economy and variety, a single chicken is often used to prepare several dishes. Chicken blood, for example, is cooked and solidified for soup, and the liver is used in a marvellous speciality called Gold Coin Chicken (*gum chen gi*). The livers are skewered between pieces of pork fat and red-roasted until the fat becomes crisp and the liver soft and succulent. The delicacy is then eaten with wafers of orange-flavoured bread.

Cantonese chicken dishes can be awkwardly bony for chopstick beginners, but lemon chicken is prepared boneless with the skin coated in a crisp batter and served in a lemon sauce flavoured with onions, ginger and sugar.

Anise-Flavoured Beans

For starters, choose something from the display of barbecued meats in the restaurant's

special winter eating tours into China, specifically to eat dogmeat, are popular.

'Buddha's Hand'

Yet another Cantonese dish to sample in the winter is a casserole of chicken and Chinese smoked pork sausage (*laap cheong*). These sausages are sold in pairs and usually are served steamed on a bed of rice. In autumn, restaurants serve rice birds, those tiny winged creatures who frequent paddy fields at harvest time. These are quite often eaten in concert with succulent Shanghai hairy crabs.

Frogs are also found in the rice paddies, and these "field chickens" are often served at ban-

display window. Cantonese barbecuing methods are unrivalled. Try goose, duck or, best of all, tender slices of pork with a gold and honeyed skin served on a bed of anise-flavoured preserved beans.

Also experience the taste sensation of double-boiled soups with duck, mushroom and tangerine peel, and a winter speciality called Monk Jumping Over the Wall. This is a blend of abalone, chicken, ham, mushrooms, and herbs that is so irresistible that monks are said to break their vows of vegetarianism if its fragrance is within smelling distance.

Snake is a traditional winter dish, but it is unfortunately a succulent food "misunderstood" by Westerners. Dogmeat is also a winter dish but is legally forbidden here, so

quets in South China. In Hong Kong markets they are sold live in plastic bags, and restaurants prepare them in many delicious ways. The best frog course is deep-fried frog's legs cooked in a crunchy batter mixed with crushed almonds and served with sweet and sour sauce.

More than 300 cooks were said to have been employed at the Imperial Palace in Peking before the fall of the Ching dynasty in 1912. It sounds like a severe case of overstaffing in the kitchens, but the Empress Dowager re-

Even in a year, a visitor would not be able to try all of the seafoods available and edible in the colony (sampler at left). Above, experts prepare swallow nests for Bird's Nest Soup.

portedly was accustomed to a main meal of 100 dishes to titillate her discriminating palate. She also maintained a platoon of eunuchs whose unsavoury job was to test each royal dish for poison.

Proper Peking Duck

Peking Duck is the most popular northern Chinese dish served in Hong Kong (and it is probably the most popular northern dish anywhere in the world). This duck dish is prepared by roasting it over an open charcoal fire and slowly basting it with syrup until the skin is crispy brown. In some sections of Hong Kong, you can actually see this meticulous cooking process being performed on the pavement over an earthenware brazier. Patient *foki*

spring onions and cucumber. The duck and sauce are placed on a wafer-thin wheat tortilla that looks like a thin, dry rolled crepe or pancake. This concoction is rolled up and eaten with the fingers.

The third course from the duck is the soup. Whilst you are busy with the first two courses, the duck's carcass is boiled with a combination of cabbage, mushrooms and herbs. Then a duck soup is served. When ordering Peking Duck, be sure to tell the waiter you want this soup. Some restaurants have been known to take advantage of visitors who do not realize there are three duck courses in a traditional Peking Duck meal.

Over the centuries, culinary elements from all over eastern Asia have been liberally adapted and absorbed, and it's difficult to trace

(waiters or assistants) slowly cook the duck, over and over again, all afternoon long, in preparation for the evening's repast.

When you partake of Peking Duck in a restaurant, part of the enjoyment of the meal is the "show" (there really is no other word for it) put on by the chef at your table as he swiftly carves the duck — *always* with a large razor-sharp chopper (butcher's cleaver) and *never* with carving or paring knives. In delicate cutting motions, performed at your table, the chef slices the skin off for the first of three duck courses with a quick succession of exact strokes, starting at the neck. After the crispy skin is served, the waiter quickly follows with the meat. The skin and meat are eaten with a mild, sweetish soya bean paste mixed with

the origins of some dishes. Peking Duck, for which the traditional recipe ran to nearly 15,000 words, was originally Mongolian, but it's now much more popular in Peking than in Ulan Bator.

Mongolian Hotpot

Mongolian hotpot, called "steamboat" in the Singapore-Malaysia region, is of central Chinese Moslem origins. It is probably the second best known of the northern dishes.

Mongolian hotpot is a winter food, served between November and March in northern-style restaurants. It is probably best described to Westerners as the Chinese version of *fondue Bourguignonne*.

The key preparation utensil for hotpot eating is a chafing dish with a small charcoal burning stove built-in underneath, and a chimney rising through its centre. A trough around this dish contains soup stock to which is added vegetables, cabbage and herbs. When the soup stock begins to boil, the entire stove is set into a hole cut in the centre of your table (Mongolian hotpot traditionally was a practical way to eat and keep warm at the same time).

Wafer-thin slices of various meats or fishes, previously ordered, are served raw, and you cook the meal yourself in small wire baskets dipped in this hotpot's bubbling broth. A spicy sauce, prepared to your taste by the waiter, adds to this the taste treat. The final course is the remaining soup broth.

longevity, and so is served at weddings and birthday festivities to ensure long life. Related Western egg noodles are descendents of Chinese noodles and were first introduced to Europe in the 14th Century by the explorer Marco Polo.

Bear's paws, another northern delicacy, is an esoteric banquet food available in Hong Kong. However, it is only available in certain restaurants and should be ordered well in advance because the paws require 16 hours of cooking to make them palatable.

For dessert, Peking restaurants offer irresistible toffee apples. These apple treats arrive at your table hot and syrupy and are then dipped in ice-cold water and transformed into a crackling, sesame-coated taste sensation.

Another version of this dish is Mongolian barbecue — a related eating system in which a hot griddle is placed in the same hole in your table. In this variation of the hotpot theme, meats and fish are barbecued instead of boiled.

A surprise for Westerners at their first Pekinese meal is that rice is not usually served (unless you request it). Wheat is commonly grown in the north so northerners traditionally eat steamed bread (*pao*) or tasty onion cakes instead of rice.

One of the spectacular treats at a Peking meal is hand-made noodles (at the table) called *lie mien*. The best quality vermicelli is produced in Shantung. A fine variety is made from flour dough, drawn out on a frame and dried in the sun. Vermicelli is a symbol of

Spicy Szechuan

Because Szechuan is one of China's westernmost provinces — and thus much exposed to the spicier delights of food in the Asian subcontinent — the cuisine of Szechuan is renowned for its spicy tastes and pungence.

The ultimate Szechuan dish is smoked duck, a crisp-skinned speciality with the aromatic flavour of camphor-tea. It is prepared with a seasoning of ginger, cinnamon, orange peel,

Ancient Chinese cooking bears little resemblance to what you'll savour in Hong Kong today, but certain basic principles remain, left; and above, the fish seller offers a catch that is temptingly fresh.

225

coriander and *hwa chiao,* pungent Szechuan peppercorns.

The duck is marinated in rice wine for 24 hours, steamed for two hours, smoked over a charcoal fire sprinkled with camphor wood chips and red tea leaves, fried briefly to crisp the skin, and finally served with lotus leaf pancakes.

Szechuan food is a richly-spiced cuisine with a distinctive chilli sting. Characteristic dishes are succulent prawns seasoned with garlic and ginger, chilli bean paste and wine, garlic-laced eggplant that's mashed and then braised, and *ma-boo* bean curd braised in a powerful chilli sauce.

The latter bean curd dish is a smooth-textured favourite known as "Old Ladies," because it is so soft you can eat it without

vinegar.

The tastiest vegetable dish is braised season beans cooked with minced pork and dried shrimps and simmered in soy. And a cooling dessert, perfect to quench chilli fires, is almond bean curd.

Chiu Chow cuisine is also known as Swatow food because this type of cooking originated in the administrative district around the city of Swatow in Kwangtung (Guangdong) Province.

Coastal Chiu Chow Cuisine

The coastal people of the southeast have an original method of harvesting oysters. They simply push bamboo sticks into oyster beds and the sticks gradually become encrusted with these molluscs. Harvesting is merely a

teeth. It is named after the wife of a 19th Century chef called Chen, and in the Chengtu region of Szechuan, Chen's descendants still operate a famous *ma-boo* bean curd shop.

Noodles or steamed bread are eaten in preference to rice, but Szechuan restaurants do specialize in a crispy rice dish made with the dried scrapings on the bottom of a rice pan. This crisply rice is deep-fried and covered with a rich and delicious sauce of meat, mushrooms, and abalone.

Minced beef with vermicelli is known in Chinese as "Ants Climbing a Tree." and steamed Szechuan pork is an expensive winter speciality that combines abalone, pork, chicken, sea cucumber, ham, mushrooms and bamboo shoots. One of the best Szechuan soups is sour pepper soup, prepared with bean curd, chicken's blood and shredded bamboo shoots seasoned with chillies, peppercorns and

matter of pulling up the sticks, and the cooking part is also just as simple: they hold the sticks over a fire and grill the oysters right in their shells.

In Chiu Chow restaurants the preparation is more sophisticated but equally tasty. Seafood addicts go for oysters fried in egg batter and clams served in a spicy sauce of black beans and chillies. Grey mullet is a favourite cold dish, and pomfret fish smoked over tea leaves and freshwater eel stewed in brown sauce are other recommended seafood wonders.

A Chiu Chow restaurant is also an appropriate place to try banquet-style food such as Shark's Fin Soup and Bird's Nest Soup. The dried saliva lining the sea swallow's nest pro-

If Hong Kong indeed has 5,000 Chinese restaurants, then food stalls that service those restaurants must number more than 10,000.

vides the magic base for the famous Bird's Nest Soup. The owner of one restaurant in Hong Kong reputedly rents a mountain in Thailand that is said to harbour the finest collection of sea swallow nests in Southeast Asia. The nest itself is virtually tasteless, but its nourishing saliva linings are believed to rejuvenate the old. This delicacy is also eaten as a dessert flavoured with coconut milk or almonds.

Baked rice birds are a seasonal fowl dish stuffed with chicken liver and served by the dozen. Minced pigeon, meanwhile, is cooked with water chestnuts and eaten wrapped in crisp lettuce leaves spiked with a dollop of plum sauce. Desserts — made from taro, water chestnuts and sugar syrup — are for the sweet-toothed only.

A Chiu Chow meal begins and ends with a thimbleful of "Iron Maiden," an excellent bitter tea drunk to aid digestion.

The Sung dynasty romantic poet and gourmet Su Tung Po invented one of the most satisfying Shanghainese dishes. Su Tung Po Pork uses humble ingredients and simple flavouring, but it's a memorable pork casserole which becomes as soft as bean curd after lengthy cooking.

These slow-braised Su Tung Po dishes are traditionally cooked in earthenware pots to enhance the flavour of the ingredients. The characteristic flavour of such eastern Chinese food is sweet. Soya sauce, rice wine and sugar go into a basic marinade. Fresh ginger root and dried tangerine peel are among secondary ingredients added later.

When ordering in a restaurant, it's wise to remember that portions are usually huge and you'll want to try plenty. Start the meal with a cold fish like smoked fish or the famous Drunken Chicken, a delicacy flavoured with Shao Hsing yellow rice wine and eaten cold with a garnish of coriander leaves.

Autumn is the time to sample hairy crab, a creature prized for its rich golden roe. There's an art to cracking the shell to get at the exquisite centre, and for your first hairy crab eating experience it's a good idea to go with someone who knows how it's done. Shao Hsing wine traditionally accompanies this hairy-pincered delicacy, and a cup of sweet ginger tea at the end of the meal aids digestion.

Other Shanghai specialities are sweet and sour carp, soya and spiced beef and braised bean curd with minced beef and chilli. Try jellyfish if you're feeling adventurous, or Lion's Head Casserole, which isn't as alarming as it sounds. It's an excellent dish of meatballs cooked with black mushrooms and bamboo shoots. Also recommended is the traditional sour and hot soup, a spicy blend of bean curd and blood, sea cucumber and mushrooms.

The best known dish from Hangchow is Beggar's Chicken. This succulent specialty is available at only a few Hong Kong restaurants. This chicken dish is served encased in a mud-pack that is cracked open with a hammer at your table. In the centre of this mud pack is a delicately baked chicken which has been stewing in its juices for more than eight hours.

Though its exact origin is unknown, this gourmet dish can be traced back to the time of the Ching dynasty Emperor Chien Lung (1736-1795).

The Hakka — or "guest people," because their long migrant path from the north eventually took them to the south — live in Hong Kong's New Territories. Theirs is a matriarchal society and because of this their women are noticed on just about every construction site in the colony. They are easily identified, because they wear black pajama-like clothes (called *samfoo*) and wide-brim straw hats with red and black tassles on the brim.

The Hakka main dishes are salt-baked chicken and stuffed duck. To prepare stuffed duck, the duck is first ingeniously deboned through a hole in the neck and then stuffed with a rich assortment of glutinous rice, chopped meats and lotus seeds. Perhaps because they are peasants, and were thus always on the run from war or famine, the Hakka have created unusual flavours from obvious but generally unused food sources such as braised chicken's blood or pig's brains stewed in Chinese wine. Though the last two might be a bit too much for the average Westerner's palate, at least try the bone marrow. It has a very delicate taste and is considered to be good for one's health.

Surprisingly, there is only one Hunanese restaurant in the colony so very few residents and visitors have tried this cuisine. The best known dish in this gastronomic discipline is preserved ham served in a sauce of honey and spices. These thick slices of ham are eaten in a steamed pancake. Minced pigeon soup cooked in a bamboo cup is another speciality.

Southwest Chinese cuisine includes steam pot chicken, a famous Yunnan dish cooked in a specially designed pot with an internal funnel which allows a regulated flow of steam to slowly cook the ingredients. Other Yunnan specialities are peach blossom rice and noodles cooked in chicken broth. The latter dish is called "Crossing the Bridge" noodles. There are no restaurants specializing solely in Yunnanese food in Hong Kong.

(See the restaurants section of the Guide In Brief section for further information about Hong Kong restaurants and their food specialities.)

DIM SUM—CHINESE PETIT FOURS

'Touching the Heart'

Dim sum is one of the great unheralded Chinese inventions, ranking with gunpowder and paper. Specifically, it is a Cantonese invention, and to say it is extremely popular with Hong Kong's Chinese population today would be an understatement. *Dim sum* to a Cantonese is what whisky is to a Scot or wine to a Frenchman. It is indispensible, and not having one's daily *dim sum* would make life indigestible.

This is not to say that non-Chinese visitors are not encouraged to partake of this taste treat. On the contrary, the Cantonese take pride in showing off this unique *petit cuisine*. Indeed, *dim sum* is so popular that if Hong Kong's tourist business magically declined overnight and nary a Westerner showed up for a *dim sum* lunch, their absence would not even be noticed. Which means that if you want to sample a *dim sum* lunch, make your decision before 10 a.m. and have your hotel book you a table.

Dim sum means "little heart" or "touching the heart" and it refers to food which comes in small portions on equally small plates. The official British word is "savouries," but this ancient fast-food is more reminiscent of a Scandinavian smorgasbord in reverse. In a *dim sum* house an infinite variety of Chinese hors d'oeuvres comes to you.

The first thing you'll notice about *dim sum* restaurants is how vast they are. Huge rooms, sometimes floor upon floor, are packed with hundreds of diners eating, reaching, shouting, and gesturing for *dim sum* which are wheeled to your table on trolleys pushed by serving girls. If they are true to Chinese tradition, these girls will sing traditional rhymes about the food. The trolleys are pushed through aisles which are jammed with waiters, other trolleys and, of course, people waiting for already crowded tables to be vacated.

Do not be put off by this lunch hour mayhem. The food is worth whatever minor annoyances you may have to endure, and if you reserve ahead, as suggested, the main annoyance at a *dim sum* palace will be alleviated.

On the trolley trays are steaming bamboo baskets. Visitors rarely understand what the trolley girls are chanting, but again, don't be shy. It is proper etiquette to take the tops off these baskets and marvel at the contents. Invariably, the girls, when serving a table of Westerners, will take the tops off all the baskets on her tray anyway.

Dim Sum Do's and Don'ts

A couple of *dim sum* points to remember:

Try to arrive for lunch about 12:30 p.m. At that time all the food is prepared and ready to go for early lunchers who come in between noon and 1 p.m. (Official lunch hour is 1 to 2 p.m.). Wait until after 12:30 p.m. and you may lose your table in seconds and suffer a long and hungry wait. Another reason not to eat late is

because you may miss out on the day's full range of *dim sum* selections.

Sit on or near a major aisle or intersection (make the request when reserving). Don't sit way in the rear, because back there it is difficult to attract the attention of besieged serving girls. Stop every girl as she passes by and question her about her particular fare.

Do not be afraid to question waiters who hover around the trolley girls if you want something. Ask them to suggest something. The waiters might try to feed you a regular dish (out of politeness, thinking you might not like *dim sum*), but stress that you indeed want *dim sum,* not sweet and sour pork.

Do not ask the waiters to clear off your table as the dishes and baskets stack up. In an ordinary Chinese meal, dishes are cleared after each course, but with a *dim sum* lunch the dishes are left on the table until it's time to tally up the bill; the waiter merely counts up the dishes, and each variably-sized dish is a certain price. The price can be as low or less than HK$2 for some items.

Lastly, stop by a Hong Kong Tourist Association office before you go "dim-summing" and pick up their *dim sum* brochure which has colour pictures and descriptions of the most popular dishes. Their Chinese names are transliterated into English for your easy pronunciation, and the Chinese characters are also there for waiters' reference.

Yum Cha

A *dim sum* lunch provides a daily opportunity (on Sunday it is traditionally a big family outing) to sample this treat, but it is possible to sample some of these dishes at any time of the day. This is made possible via another fabulous invention called *yum cha*, the Chinese version of a tea break.

Yum cha is a snack break featuring tea and *dim sum*. In a *yum cha* shop you will find not only people quietly relaxing in a traditional teahouse setting, but gentlemen out walking their pet birds. Bird connoisseurs commonly take their song birds out for a daily airing and a stop at their favourite teahouse for a bit of *yum cha, dim sum* and gossip. (These restaurants usually have poles strung across the length or width of their dining area — for hanging the bird cages on, of course.)

Dim Sum Savouries

Guon tong gau: Steamed dumpling stuffed with minced pork and chicken soup.
Har gau: Steamed shrimp dumpling.
Woo kok: Deep fried taro vegetable puff.
Shiu mai: Streamed minced pork and shrimp dumpling.
Tsing fun guen: Steamed rice flour roll filled with assorted meat.
Seen chuk guen: Deep fried bean curd roll filled with pork, shrimp and oyster sauce.
Au yuk: Steamed minced beef ball.
Nor mai gai: Steamed rice flour dumpling filled with assorted meat.
Chu yuen shiu mai: Sliced pork liver with steamed pork and shrimp dumpling.
Cha siu cheung: Steamed rice flour roll with barbecued pork filling.
Har cheung: Steamed rice flour roll with shrimp filling.
Au yuk cheung: Steamed rice flour roll with minced beef filling.
Jar fun gwor: Deep fried rice flour triangle filled with pork, shrimp, bamboo shoots.
Pai gwat: Steamed spare-rib with red peper sauce.
Fun gwor: Steamed rice flour triangle filled with pork, shrimp, bamboo shoots.
Ham shiu kok: Deep fried rice flour triangle filled with pork, shrimp and vegetables.
Gwor ching chung: Large glutinous rice dumpling filled with duck, preserved egg yolks, mushrooms and wrapped in lotus leaves.
Chai siu bau: Steamed barbecued pork bun.
Ho yip fan: Steamed fried rice in lotus leaf wrapping.
Gai chuk: Steamed chicken roll with bean curd wrapping.
Tsun guen: Deep fried spring roll filled with shredded pork, chicken, mushrooms, bamboo shoots and bean sprouts.

Dim Sum Desserts

Ng lau jar wan tun: Deep fried dumpling with sweet and sour sauce.
Daan sarn: Crisp and sticky sweet cake topped with almonds.
Hung dow sa: Sweat red bean paste soup.
Nor mai chi: Coconut snowball.
Daan tat: Hot custard tart.
Chien chang go: Thousand-layer sweet cake with egg topping.

ON MAINTAINING GOOD FUNG SHUI

It looked like a normal dedication ceremony. Gentlemen in fancy suits, shiny shoes and hard hats, had gathered around a construction site in Hong Kong. The chairman of Hong Kong's then new Mass Transit Railway (MTR) did the earthy honours and broke ground for the U.S. billion dollar venture.

That spade full of dirt would have been the

end of dedication ceremonies in most countries, but not in Hong Kong. It was now time for a Taoist priest to beat a gong and say prayers. He had to insure that the spirits disturbed during tunneling under the construction site would be placated.

Though physically Hong Kong looks like a modern 20th Century city in the best Western tradition, such temporal surface similarities

end there. In addition to written regulations and laws about construction of buildings, highways, bridges, tombs, homes, and whatever else goes into a modern concrete city, Hong Kong people also honour unwritten spiritual laws called *fung shui* (pronounced *fung soy*). After government departments have completed their building plans, architects and contractors consult a *fung shui* man, a geomancer. His job is to determine the most auspicious location for not only the building, but also its doors, windows and desks.

Wind-Water, Ch'i, Yin and Yang

Fung shui (which literally means "wind water") is practiced with a compass-like device which has eight ancient trigrams representing nature and its elements — heaven, water (the ocean), fire, thunder, wind, water (rain), hills and earth. These elements in turn represent eight animals (horse, goat, pheasant, dragon, fowl, swine, dog and the ox). This "science" is based on the principle of *ch'i*, the spirit or breath that animates *yin* and *yang*, female-passive and male-active elements. The *fung shui* geomancer's job is to put all these spiritual factors together to make a positive prediction.

Whether non-Chinese people here actually believe in *fung shui* doesn't matter. What is important is that this colony can't be run without Chinese; therefore, the Hong Kong government and private industry heed their ancient beliefs.

The MTR is not an isolated case. One of the most serious such incidents occurred at the end of 1976 when the colony's major airline, Cathay Pacific Airways, was digging a foundation for a new administration and engineering stores building. No preliminary *fung shui* ceremony was thought necessary despite the fact that a new air cargo terminal building (located nearby and partially-owned by the same company that owns Cathay Pacific) had observed proper *fung shui* ceremonies on March 4, 1975, well before the building's opening. Employees in the engineering division started to fall ill and word spread that the site's *fung shui* has been disturbed. A *fung shui* ceremony was held, thereby placating the disturbed spirits, and since then no one has been taken ill.

The mirror in the Pat Kwa is meant to repel evil spirits while the Fung Shui paper, right, to ensure peace, joy and health in the home.

In Central District, at the site where Hutchison House, Bank of America Tower and a multi-storey carpark stand, a mass execution was conducted by Japanese during their war-time occupation of the colony. When Hutchison House reached its full height, a Buddhist ceremony was conducted by the then deputy chairman of that giant conglomerate to appease the spirits of those who had died there. Across the road, in a government carpark and in government offices on a building's top floors, pencil-pushers in the Transport Department reported seeing ghosts. This unidentified flying spirits situation became so acute that the dapper Brit who then ran the Transport Department, Brian Wilson, led an exorcising procession of 70 chanting Buddhist monks and nuns through the carpark on February 8, 1974.

The Royal Hong Kong Police Force outwardly looks the same as any other law enforcement organization. But when morale dropped severely at the Wanchai Police Station in August, 1973, the then new divisional superintendant, Larry Powers, made concerned enquiries among his rank and file.

Powers' men believed the station had bad *fung shui* thrown on it because a building built opposite the station as part of a fair had a low slanting roof with two wooden spirals. Powers immediately called in a *fung shui* expert, and that geomancer concluded that the station's entrance facing the fair was in a bad place and susceptible to omens. His remedy? To keep the "two horn monster" at bay, he suggested that a pair of old cannon be put on either side of the entrance.

Some people and organizations try to ignore the superstitious and Chinese side of Hong Kong, but such ignorance nearly always leads to trouble.

The Royal Hong Kong Jockey Club is a case in point. Between 1960 and 1965, three jockeys accidentally died during races within three yards of the same spot. After ignoring this omen following the jockeys' deaths, the austere British gentlemen running the club finally brought in representatives of the Buddhist Association to exorcise that part of the racetrack. So far it has worked and there have been no more deaths.

Hong Kong's Chinese customs affect everyone, even progressive American businessmen. Before the Hong Kong Sheraton Hotel opened in 1974, its general manager, Robert Hamel, consulted a *fung shui* expert about the hotel's opening date; his local staff were reportedly very pleased. Another American hotel chain up the street neglected to do likewise and only after being plagued by bad *joss*

incidents did its management call in a *fung shui* expert to set things right.

The Regent of Hong Kong sheathed its lobby and mezzanine in 40-foot lengths of glass on a geomancer's advice. According to a *fung shui* source, the hotel rises at a site where "a dragon enters the harbour for his bath." By designing a see-through lobby, there was no chance of disrupting the dragon's ritual—a mistake which would have created inexpicable bad joss.

Octagonal mirrors or deflectors called *pat*

kwa are frequently hung outside windows of large office buildings and apartment houses. The deflectors protect their occupants by repelling evil.

Westerners might still be curious about the cause of Hong Kong film star Bruce Lee's death in 1973. But not Hong Kong's Chinese.

They *know* what happened to him. Typhoon Dot, they explain, ripped through the colony shortly before his demise and blew away Lee's *pat kwa*. He then became vulnerable and, naturally, died.

HONOURING WISE MEN AND HUNGRY GHOSTS

Noise, Illumination and Red

The people of Hong Kong live two lives. One is lived according to the Western solar calendar, which brings them the benefits of annual holidays such as New Year, Easter, and Christmas. The other is according to the Chinese lunar calendar, which involves a series of traditional family get-togethers throughout the year. On lunar holidays family members also visit temples and ancestral graves to make offerings to deities and forefathers. It is therefore not unusual for those

curately determine the solstices and equinoxes so that farmers would know when to plant their crops.

In addition to such ancient associations with the seasons, Chinese festivals also celebrate legends and historical events. Whatever the origins of these Chinese festivals, it should be noted that contemporary and practical considerations have influenced the nature of some traditional celebrations.

For example, fireworks, formerly an integral part of such festivals as the New Year and the Ching Ming spring celebration, have

who attend Christian Easter services also to observe traditional ceremonies with strong overtones of Chinese beliefs and customs.

Various festivals mark the passing of the four seasons. They follow the lunar calendar with its 12 months of 30 days each. An additional month occurs during leap years to make up for the uneven number of days in non-leap years. Because ancient Chinese civilization was agriculturally based, the lunar calendar was "naturally" calculated to suit agrarian realities.

It is believed that this calendar was first developed by one of China's legendary sage kings, Emperor Yao, who in the third millenium B.C. ordered his astrologers to ac-

been forbidden by law in Hong Kong since the colony's Red Guard political riots of 1967. As a result, devil spirits have to be scared away by other means, much to the celebrants' chagrin. On the other hand, papier-mâché Rolls-Royces, jumbo jets and television sets are burned as offerings to enrich the well-being of those in the afterlife.

Chinese New Year is the most important holiday on the calendar. Legend has it that in prehistoric times, when the Chinese had already settled in the basin of the Yellow River, their peaceful life was disrupted one wintry

An array of bright red *lai see* on display conjures up three words: Chinese New Year.

234

night when a mysterious monster attacked the citizens and destroyed their crops and homes. According to sages of the time, the appearance of this monster occurred after the sun had shown 365 times. It was found that this ferocious creature, called *Nein,* was afraid of three things: noise, illumination and the colour red.

Thus, on the 365th evening, vigilant Chinese had their houses brightly lit and made sure that 100 solid objects had been painted red. In addition, they struck drums and gongs and performed lion dances. As a result of these precautions, the monster disappeared. This tradition of celebration, now essentially a gesture of thanksgiving, has since been faithfully observed by Chinese on the 365th evening of every lunar year.

to children. The amount is theoretically insignificnt, because it is the act of giving that is important. It is a gesture believed to bring luck and prosperity to both the giver and receiver. The proper traditional Chinese New Year Cantonese greeting is *kung hay fat choi,* meaning "wishing you to prosper," and it is heard reverberating through homes and streets at this time.

In the People's Republic of China, the festival is referred to these days as the **Spring Festival** (*Chun Chieh*) because China has officially adopted the Gregorian or solar calendar. Therefore, the traditional lunar Chinese New Year is not "celebrated."

Two systems are used in naming and determining the character of every new year.

The first system names each new year after

'Kung Hay Fat Choi'

Traditionally, celebration of the New Year lasts 15 days. In some homes it is still fully celebrated, but modern-day responsibilities have caused it to be limited, in many Chinese families, to three days.

Some old Chinese customs, deliberately discarded or simply forgotten during the rest of the year, are revived during these New Year days. For example, the emphasis on respect for one's elders is manifested on New Year's Day when the younger generations kneel in front of (or bow their heads) and offer tea to their elders.

It is customary for married couples to give *lai see,* a red envelope containing lucky money,

an animal. There are 12 animals represented in the scale. In recurring chronological sequence the names of the years are Rat, Ox, Tiger, Rabbit, Dragon, Snake, Horse, Ram, Monkey, Rooster, Dog and Pig. This perpetual or cyclical system is called *kan tse.* (See astrology article in features section.)

The second system which determines the character of the new year is based on astrology, the *I Ching* (a complicated system of fortune telling), and on the Chinese view of heaven and earth.

The exact moment of the new year within a

Chinese New Year is the biggest holiday of the year for traditional Chinese; above, curious good *joss* constructions await festive buyers.

235

set period — the day and the time — is very important. The system of choosing it is called the *dou jien* and refers to the position of the handle of the Big Dipper (the seven principle stars in the constellation of Ursa Major). The compass is divided into 12 parts and the points around which this constellation revolves are designated by 12 characters. These points have been given animal names, but scholars also refer to them by their astrological character. The handle of the Big Dipper lands on a certain point on the compass which signifies something — good or bad *joss* (luck) — and that attribute is expressed as a year named after an animal.

The New Year festival is a happy time. Children run around with bright red packets of *lai see* — lucky money — and salaried people are

prosperous year (if it has indeed been one) and wish for another such year.

New Year's Debts = Bad Joss

It is bad *joss* to begin the year with outstanding debts, so this is an important time to settle accounts. However, Chinese pragmatism occasionally causes problems. The crime rate is always higher at this time of year because some Chinese will steal enough money to pay off their debts in order to begin the new year with good *joss*. Of course, modern Asia has proper billing procedures in business and a good accountant is usually careful enough not to let accounts mount up.

Another custom is the buying of peach blossoms (which bring good luck in male-female

happy because they have just received a year end bonus which, in some cases, represents two or three months' pay. Shop assistants and waiters, *foki*, are treated to a year-end feast by their bosses, *lo ban*. This feast is rich in food and symbolism. Chicken is always the main course and, in the manner of a good host, the boss serves his employees with his own chopsticks. If a *foki* receives the most succulent part of the chicken, it means he is being treated as a guest, not as part of the family, and is therefore out of a job for the coming year.

On the 16th day of the 12th moon (the last month), businessmen close their accounts and thank the three gods of wealth — Kuan Ti, Tusan Tan Shang Ti and Ts'ai Shen — for a

relationships), kumquat trees and narcissus flowers. These are indispensable decorations at this time of the year. Gardeners work very hard year round pruning leaves and buds so that these auspicious plants will bloom virtually overnight on New Year's Eve.

Tsao Wang's Sweetened Lips

New Year's celebrations actually begin about a week before New Year's Eve. This period is known as "Little New Year," and it is said that the "God of the Kitchen," Tsao Wang departs from his domain then for a yearly journey to heaven to report on all Chinese families.

It is of course desirable that Tsao Wang tell

only good things about the family or report as little as possible, so Chinese families guarantee that he bears good tidings by preparing a special sticky-sweet candy, *tang kwa,* which is smeared on the god's lips so that they are sealed or so only sweet words will be spoken. Naturally, most of the sweets find their way into the hands and mouths of the youngsters in the family.

Wine is also offered, and paper money burned, to assure Tsao Wang a comfortable journey. During his absence in heaven, the family turns his image around to face the wall and burns a caricature of him. Before he returns on New Year's Eve, the house must be thoroughly cleaned and each family member must help (if he or she wants to remain in Tsao Wang's good graces). Following this New

oysters are "splendour," melon seeds are "silver," and pig's trotters are "good luck in gambling."

Two traditional foods made especially for New Year are *gin tuy* and *yau kok.* The former looks like a softball; the latter has a triangular shape. Both are fried and made with glutinous rice flour. *Gin tuy* has sesame seeds sprinkled on the outside. *Yau kok* is stuffed with a filling of crushed peanuts, coconut shreds and sesame seeds. If you get the urge to try either of these, buy them at the nearest Chinese grocery store. They also serve as proper gifts if you are calling on someone. Cognac, however, is also an acceptable "modern" offering.

Tradition lives on and on. No one goes to sleep on New Year's Eve, and little children are discouraged from dozing off, in the belief it

Year's cleaning, the image is turned back around or a new image of Tsao Wang is placed above the stove. A feast is prepared to greet him after his long journey, and door gods are set up for the new year.

Eggs Are 'Silver Ingots'

As one would expect in any celebration where a kitchen god is honoured, food plays a big part in the Chinese New Year. Indeed, a virtual feast is prepared in the house to usher in the year. Certain foods are even renamed. Translated from the Chinese, eggs become "silver ingots," mushrooms are "opportunities," chicken is "the phoenix," kumquat is "gold luck," pig's tongue is "profits," dried

will shorten their lives if they are not awake for New Year's Day. After the new year has arrived, the head of the family presents all the children and juniors with *lai see* so they will have good fortune for another 12 months.

On New Year's Day ancestors are honoured at family altars, and red scrolls inscribed with characters signifying happiness, prosperity and long life are pasted on the walls. A basket of food is placed in the centre of the living room to guarantee that there will be enough to eat in the coming year, and knives and scissors

Hard-paddling dragon-boaters race to the finish line, left, to the sound of drumbeats and gongs; above, spirited fans cheer their teams. This festival honours wise minister Chu Yuan.

are hidden away so that no one will cut luck's continuity.

The second day is known as *Hoi Nien* or "The Opening of the Year." The most important event of this day is a banquet-style dinner. The third day is commonly regarded as one which might induce quarrels, so people avoid social visits. The seventh day is called *Yan Yut* or "Everybody Birthday." Though now observed only in a modified way, it is a day on which smiling faces are expected.

In Honour of Wise Chu Yuan

The Dragon Boat Festival (*Tuen Ng* in Cantonese, *Tuan Yang* in Mandarin) has been celebrated on the fifth day of the fifth moon (early June) for the past two-and-a-half millenia. Its

To express his concern for the old ruler, Chu Yuan wrote a poem called *Li Sao*, the classical Chinese version of a political speech. (Because of the poem, the festival is sometimes called **Poet's Day** or **Patriotic Poet's Day**.) This angered the new king who ordered Chu Yuan's exile. But instead of leaving, Chu Yuan jumped into the Mi-Lo River, a river in the present Hunan Province. Today's dragon boat races symbolize the vain attempts of friends who raced to this spot to save unfortunate Chu.

Another tale has Chu Yuan despairing that his good counsel was being ignored. While wandering alone one day he composed *Li Sao* and then became so disgusted at the human world of intrigue and deceit that he committed suicide.

exact origin is unknown, but legend notes that this festival commemorates the tragic death of the honest and learned minister of state, Chu Yuan, who died in 288 B.C. in the ancient Kingdom of Ch'u during the time of the Warring States (403-221 B.C.).

At that time, Chu was the true and dedicated power behind the throne; he was a wise man who advised the ruler correctly for the good of his people. Other envious advisors, however, didn't appreciate Chu's influence, so they encouraged his disfavour with the king. Consequently, the king's *joss* failed him because he took bad advice (which resulted in a disastrous losing war with his neighbour). To make matters worse, the old king was captured during the fighting.

In mourning for their honest statesman, the people threw rice in the river to feed his ghost. One bright day Chu Yuan's ghost (or spirit) appeared to the people on the river bank and said: "You made offerings to me for which I am thankful, but the rice was all devoured by turtles and fish. I hope you will offer me rice again, but this time, please wrap it in bamboo tubes, close the openings with leaves and bind them with different coloured thread so that the turtles and fish will not dare to eat it." This appearance was supposed to have happened quite a time after his demise in 40 B.C.

A full harvest moon rises over lamplit Victoria Park at Causeway Bay during a Chung Chiu celebration; right, Chang-O, Queen of the Moon.

Yet another version of this honourable Chu tale has him instructing that silk be used (not bamboo) and that the silk rice packets be bound with fine threads, each of a different colour. Such rice packets are now the standard offering made during this festival.

A dragon boat is like a huge war canoe with a dragon's head carved at the bow and a dragon's tail at the stern. Depending on their size, they are manned by 20 to 80 paddlers accompanied by a drummer at mid-canoe who sets the timing of oar strokes with a huge drum.

There are half a dozen Hong Kong sites where these day-long races are held. These venues change occasionally, but Tai Po and Yaumatei usually host the biggest dragon boat events. Stanley Village is another popular site. (Check the newspapers, your hotel or call on the Hong Kong Tourist Association to find out the exact sites and times.)

'Lady Dragon-Boaters'

Various organizations, both European and Chinese (such as the police, firemen, army, embassies, bars, restaurants, clubs, Boy Scouts, welfare groups, and even the local journalists' union) enter teams. Elimination heats are held and the final championship race is run by the three fastest boats. For the past two-and-a-half millenia it has been exclusively a man's sport, but in 1971 Hong Kong's first women's team entered these races; now, ladies' teams are quite common.

Each race site is crowded with people who watch from the shore and from the decks of every conceivable type of boat. The course itself is usually surrounded by hundreds of junks of all sizes, each one covered with bunting indicating team affiliations. Numerous pleasure boats, warships, police launches and ferries are also gathered nearby.

A gunshot signals the start of a race and immediately an unbroken cadence of drums aboard the dragon boats and the clanging of cymbals aboard spectator junks (to ward off evil spirits) fills the harbour with noise.

This holiday has also developed over the years into another celebration — this one dedicated to the Goddess of Heaven (*Matsu* in Mandarin and *Tin Hau* in Cantonese). Though this goddess has her own special day, she is *the* goddess of fishermen and, by logical watery extension, also a patron of swimmers, lifeguards, sailors and, in the case of this holiday, dragon boaters.

A glutinous rice concoction, called *ch'un tse* in Cantonese or *tsung tzu* in Mandarin, is sold during this festival. In North China and Taiwan, the *tsung tzu* are triangular shaped, but in the south they are square.

About a week after local dragon boat races, special **International Dragon Boat Races** are held in which teams from all over Asia, and some from as far away as the United States, compete.

A Harvest Moon Cake Festival

A Mid-Autumn (Chung Chiu) Festival, the third major festival of the Chinese calendar, is celebrated on the 15th day of the eighth month. This festival corresponds to harvest festivals observed by Western cultures (in Hong Kong it is also combined with an annual **Lantern Festival**).

Contrary to what most people believe, this festival probably has less to do with harvest festivities than with the philosophically

minded Chinese of old. The union of man's spirit with nature in order to achieve perfect harmony was the fundamental canon of Taoism, so much so that contemplation of nature was a way of life.

This festival is also known as the **Moon Cake Festival** because a special kind of sweet cake (*yueh ping*) prepared in the shape of the moon and filled with sesame seeds, ground lotus seeds and duck eggs is served as a traditional Chung Chiu delicacy. Nobody actually knows when the custom of eating moon cakes to celebrate the Moon Festival began, but one belief traces its origin to the 14th Century. At that time, China was in revolt against the Mongols. Chu Yuen-chang, and his senior deputy, Liu Po-wen, discussed battle plans and de-

239

veloped a secret moon cake strategy to take a certain walled city held by the Mongol enemy. Liu dressed up as a Taoist priest and entered the besieged city bearing moon cakes. He distributed these to the city's populace. When the time for that year's Chung Chiu festival arrived, people opened their cakes and found hidden messages advising them to coordinate their uprising with the troops outside. Thus, the emperor-to-be ingeniously took the city and his throne. Moon cakes, of course, became even more famous. Whether this sweet Chinese version of ancient Europe's "Trojan Horse" story is true no one really knows.

The real moon plays a significant part in this festival. In Hong Kong, any open space or mountain top is crowded with people trying to get a glimpse of this season's auspicious full moon.

First Lady on the Moon

It is generally conceded that Neil Armstrong, the American astronaut, was the first man on the moon (in 1969). But that's not necessarily the truth to Chinese, who believe that the first person on the moon was a beautiful woman who lived during the Hsia dynasty (2205-1766 B.C.).

This somewhat complicated moon landing story goes like this: A woman, Chang-O, was married to the great General Hou-Yi of the Imperial Guard. General Hou was a skilled archer and one day, at the behest of the Emperor, he shot down eight of nine suns that had mysteriously appeared in the heavens that morning. His marksmanship was richly rewarded by the Emperor and he became very famous. However, the people feared that these suns would appear again to torture them and dry up the planet, so they prayed to the Goddess of Heaven (*Wang Mu*) to make General Hou immortal so that he could always defend the Emperor, his progeny and the country. Their wish was granted and General Hou was given a Pill of Immortality.

Another version of this story notes that Chang-O, the wife of the Divine Archer, I, shot down nine of ten suns plaguing the world and received the Herb of Immortality as a reward.

Whoever the hero was, Chang-O grabbed the pill (or the herb) and fled to the moon. In some versions it is uncertain whether she ever actually got there, because on opera stages she is always portrayed as still dancing-flying towards the moon.

When Chang-O (according to positive accounts) reached the moon, she found there a tree under which there was a friendly hare.

Because the air on the moon is cold, she began coughing and the Immortality Pill came out of her throat. She thought it would be good to pound the pill into small pieces and scatter them on Earth so that everyone could be immortal. So she ordered the hare to pound the pill, built a palace for herself and remained on the moon.

This helpful hare is referred to in Chinese mythology as the Jade Hare. Because of his and Chang-O's legendary importance, you will see — stamped on every mooncake, every mooncake box, and every Moon Cake Festival poster — images of Chang-O and sometimes the Jade Hare.

The Old Man on the Moon

In Western mythology, the moon is considered to be inconsistent. Shakespeare, in *Romeo and Juliet,* for example, said, "Swear not by the inconsistent moon." However, in the East, the Chinese believe the opposite.

There is a saying in Chinese that marriages are made in heaven and prepared on the moon. The man who does the preparing is the old man of the moon (Yueh Lao Yeh). This old man, it is said, keeps a record book with all the names of newborn babies. He is the one heavenly person who knows everyone's future partners, and nobody can fight the decisions written down in his book. He is one reason why the moon is so important in Chinese mythology and especially at the time of the Moon Festival. Everybody, including children, hikes up high mountains or hills or onto open beaches to view the moon in the hope that he will grant their favourite wishes.

To celebrate this sighting of the moon, red plastic lanterns wrought in traditional styles and embellished with traditional motifs are prepared for the occasion. It is quite a sight to see Victoria Park in Causeway Bay, or Morse Park in Kowloon, alight with thousands of candlelit lanterns. These "Lantern Carnivals" also occur spontaneously on most of the colony's beaches.

The lanterns are made in such traditional shapes as rabbits, goldfish, carps, butterflies, lobsters and star-shaped fruits. However, in modern Hong Kong you will also see lanterns in the shape of missiles, airplanes, rockets, ships and tanks. In Chinese mythology, the butterfly is the symbol of longevity and the lobster the symbol of mirth. Star-shaped fruit is the seasonal fruit in the autumn, and the carp is an old symbol of the Emperor. The carp-

During the colony's annual Tin Hau Festival, junks crowded with brilliantly-painted flags and enthusiastic devotees brighten the harbour.

Emperor symbolizes strength, courage, wisdom and, of course, power.

Tin Hau Observances

On an island such as Hong Kong, it is natural that legendary deities related to the sea should figure prominently, at least among the boat people, in traditional observances.

The **Festival of Tin Hau** (also spelled T'ien Hou), dedicated to the Mother-Goddess of the Sea, takes place on the 23rd day of the third month. On this occasion fishermen make offerings to their popular protector.

Tin Hau's origins are nebulous. However, it

with streaming multicoloured pennants and crammed with people, fill Hong Kong's waterways as they head for one of the many temples. The biggest Tin Hau temple — and festival — is at Joss House Bay in the New Territories.

Cheung Chau's 'Bun Festival'

Hong Kong's Cheung Chau Island is a living picture postcard of a quiet fishing and rural community, but during the four days of its annual **Bun Festival** it is inundated with thousands of visitors. This festival begins on the eighth day of the fourth moon (usually early May).

is said that she was the sixth and youngest daughter of a Sung dynasty (960-1279 A.D.) mandarin who lived in the fishing village of Pu Tien in Fukien Province. She was born Mo Niang in the eighth year of Emperor Yuen Yan's reign (1098). Even as a child she was adept at forecasting the weather, a talent which endeared her to fishermen.

She is said to be able to walk on water if supplied with a straw mat. Tin Hau also calms the waves, helps fishermen make bountiful catches and protects them from shipwreck and sickness. Her apotheosis took place during the early days of the Ch'ing dynasty (1644–1911 A.D.) when the Emperor K'ang-hsi beatified her by edict and conferred upon her the title of Heavenly Queen.

Tin Hau festivities begin at dawn when junks, sampans and lighters, all gaily bedecked

The Autumn Bun Festival is not a traditional Chinese celebration. Rather, it is a *ta chiu* or spirit-placating observance. Depending upon whom you hear the origin story from, this festival commemorates the victims of a plague which swept the island some 75 years ago, or it commemorates the hundreds of brutally slain victims of pirate Pak Pai, who ruled Cheung Chau and its surrounding waters before the British presence. It is his temple which is the focal point of the festival.

The actual festival began after Cheung Chau residents discovered human bones in areas where they wanted to build houses. To

A filial son, above, scrubs a forefather's earthly remains during annual ancestral rites on Lantau Island.

allay any misfortune that might occur here — and to placate the spirits of the dead whose remains and resting place they were about to disturb — three prominent Taoist priests were brought in for consultation with gods and the island's elders. Though nobody was certain who the remains belonged to, it was thought best to have a spirit-placating festival to rid the site of bad *fung shui*.

This observance is commonly referred to as the "Bun Festival" — which is an English nickname, not a translation from the Cantonese — because of the grand finale.

At midnight between the third and final day of the four-day festival, there is a free-for-all, quaintly described as a race, for symbolic offering buns, or *pao*, which are mounted on bamboo towers that rise some 60 to 80 feet.

The object of this free-for-all is to grab as many buns as you can once a signal has been given. He who accumulates the most buns and/or buns from the highest points on the towers will enjoy the best *joss* during the coming year. Because of a series of gang fights during recent over-enthusiastic climbs up these towers, this bun-tower climbing ritual has been abandoned. (Incidentally, the buns are perfectly edible and are not unlike the type Chinese eat with coffee for breakfast.)

Presiding over this four-day Cheung Chau festival are three deities: Shang Shaang, the red-faced god of earth and mountains; To Tei Kung, a household god who brings good luck; and Dai Sze Wong, the God of Hades. Effigies of these three gods are built and villagers pay homage to them.

The third day of the festival is highlighted by a grand procession. Near the end of the procession come colourful parade floats borne on long support poles by lines of bearers. Usually each village street or organization on Cheung Chau enters a float. They depict the various vices and virtues of mankind. The key characters on these floats are always portrayed by children, who wear colourful, traditional costumes and kneel, stand or balance themselves on their hands. A stunning frozen tableau effect is achieved by the use of invisible wire and metal support frames.

Graveside Picnics

The **Ching Ming Festival** — "The Clear and Bright Festival" — is related to the solar calendar. This seasonal festival marks the beginning of spring and is held on the 106th day after the winter solstice and is celebrated here in April.

On this day observants customarily visit ancestral graves where traditional rites and offerings are made to honour one's ancestors. The event, however. has the atmosphere of a picnic because the offered food is eaten at the various gravesites. It is not a solemn occasion, but rather, a time for happy communion with one's forefathers.

This unusual ancestral observance is related to the traditional Chinese need to receive blessings from previous generations at the onset of a new undertaking.

On the Care and Feeding Of Hungry Ghosts

The **Festival of Hungry Ghosts** occurs on the 15th day of the seventh moon, and is the closest Chinese equivalent to Christianity's All Souls Day.

Taoists and other Chinese religious sects (as well as superstitious people from the Chiu Chow region of Kwangtung Province) take this festival seriously and actively participate in it. Depending on individual preference, donations from the human world may or may not benefit the ghosts; however, in the human world one group that benefits greatly from this holiday are papier-mâché craftsmen. They fashion complete wardrobes, cars, airplanes, furniture, money, and other necessities of life, out of paper, and these folk art forms are all burned as offerings during the Festival of the Hungry Ghosts. The act of offering gifts to the ghosts by burning such paper replicas generally takes place on the pavements and is quite a colourful scene.

Cheung Yeung Mountain-Climbing

The **Cheung Yeung Festival** is observed on the ninth day of the ninth month (in October). This festival is related to a disastrous incident that occurred during the Han dynasty (206 B.C. — 221 A.D.). According to legend, a gentleman, upon the advice of a soothsayer, sought to avoid calamity by taking his family to the mountains for 24 hours. Upon returning to his village, the gentleman found that disaster had indeed struck. Thus, a custom of leaving one's home and going off to a higher location continues today, and roads up to Victoria Peak are jammed at this time as modern-day doomsdayers follow that ancestor's example.

To the boat people, Tam Kung, a local boygod capable of raising and quelling tempests, is the most important deity after Tin Hau. Therefore, a **Tam Kung Festival** in his honour is held on the eighth day of the fourth month in the district of Shaukiwan on the eastern tip of Hong Kong Island in an area known as Ah Kung Ngam or "Ancestor's Rocky Hill."

HONG KONG TEMPLES – A SPIRITUAL SPECTRUM

Much as Hong Kong's modern life-style offers continual diversification and variety, religion remains an unchanging, integral part of the life of its people. Despite the fact that practically every denomination of the Christian faith — as well as Judaism, Islam, and other Oriental religions — are represented here, the bulk of Hong Kong's people still practice traditional forms of Chinese religion.

Hong Kong's homes, streets and countryside are dotted with literally hundreds of small to huge Confucian-Taoist-Buddhist temples and shrines, and by numerous other religious structures maintained by Middle-Eastern and Western religious faiths. All practice their religions freely here — with little or no interference, intolerance or discrimination.

In countries which are substantially nurtured by only one faith — such as Italy by Catholicism or Saudi Arabia by Islam — the multi-religious practices tolerated here must verge on sacrilege. Hong Kong Chinese, however, take for granted an eclectic worshipper who goes into a Taoist temple to burn incense after having attended Sunday services in a Christian church.

Chinese Religious Ways

Specifically Chinese customs, superstitions, cultural preferences and traditional ways of life here are not necessarily results of strict religious beliefs, but are dependent on a number of external factors. In the case of China — and by extension, Hong Kong — they are integrated with religion, whether indigenous or imported, to such an extent that it may be hard to identify the subtle differences.

Confucianism was originally a way of life; its essence was based on the concept of propriety in human relationships. This involves a pious attitude toward one's superiors, and respectful behaviour towards living parents. Confucian doctrine is basically coloured by social overtones. Therefore, it encourages hierarchism, both metaphysical and spiritual, and its natural outcome is evidenced by the elevation of Confucianism in China to the status of religion.

Taoism, on the other hand, is introspective; its ideal aims at perfection through complete conformity with *The Way,* or principle (*Tao*), of nature. For a sage to understand his own nature, an understanding of the nature of all things is very important. Hence, unity with all things in a pantheistic identity of spirits becomes the goal. Assuming such unity is within human reach, a search for immortality through the use of alchemy and a search for harmony with all living things are its guiding principles.

Most Taoist gods, therefore, are legendary figures whose earthly existence is considered to be worthy of imitation. The jurisdiction of their spiritual powers is directly related to special or outstanding aspects of their former earthly forms. Visual evidence of this phenomenon are specific attributes associated with each deity. The God of Literature, *Man,* for example, always holds a brush. Much as Taoist canons are philosophically based, Taoist religious practices are coloured by mythology and pantheism.

'Foreign' Buddhism

Unlike China-born Confucianism and Taoism, **Buddhism** is a "foreign" religion imported to China from India during the first Century A.D. The branch of Buddhism which thrives in China is known as the Mahayana School. This is a Buddhism which focuses on the achievement of enlightenment in order to reach *nirvana,* or the state of extinction of self, as exemplified by Gautama Buddha, a historical figure who lived in the Sixth Century B.C. in northern India. Buddhism involves a set of rules whereby a faithful person is guided toward release from the sufferings of physical existence to the attainment of the Buddhist goal of extinction of self.

A peculiar and interesting aspect of Chinese religious practices is the recognition and acceptance of deities historically foreign to the basic tenets of a particular religion. Kuan Yin (the Goddess of Mercy), for example, is a Buddhist deity worshipped in Taoist temples. This cross-pollination spiritual device is often used to overcome the competition different temples face when they attempt to attract faithful followers. The idea is to appeal to the widest audience possible.

The following prominent temples and shrines are only samples of Hong Kong's innumerable "Chinese" places of worship, but each should provide the casual visitor with fascinating insights into Chinese people and their multi faceted religious faiths.

Petite brass deer, traditional paper lamps and bright fluorescent fixtures glow in the fine old Man Mo Temple on Hollywood Road, Western.

A Patron of Police and Criminals

The Man Mo Temple, on Hollywood Road, near "Cat Street," is the colony's oldest still-standing temple, dating back to 1842 or 1847, depending on which history you read. It is also the colony's largest. This temple is dedicated to the god Man (born Cheung Ah Tse in 287 A.D.), who is the God of Literature. Man also controls the destinies of civil servants (mandarins) who in ancient times were the hierarchy of the Chinese intelligentsia. (Unfortunately, the status of such civil servants has deteriorated since those days.)

The temple is also dedicated to the God of Martial Arts or War, Mo, who was born Kuan Yue in A.D. 160. (He is also known as Kuan Ti or Kuan Kung.) Mo is best known for the

number and predict the future. The principal goddess here is Kuan Yin.

Popular Tin Hau Temples

The grandest, most spectacular celebration dedicated to Tin Hau, the colony's popular Goddess of the Sea, takes place at Da Miao ("The Green Temple") in Joss House Bay when tens of t ousands of people aboard hundreds of junks and public ferries converge on the hilltop temple to the accompaniment of gongs and drums. It's a memorable experience to see this colourful fleet assembled off the remote Fat Tong Mun Peninsula in the New Territories.

The entryway to this temple is painted with a pair of door gods whose task is to guard

protection he gives people from the deprivations of war and is said to be a favourite of members of Hong Kong's underworld. Ironically, he is also found in virtually every police station. The police worship him for the same reasons criminals do. Mo is also a patron of pawn shops and curio dealers.

Guarding the temple are The Eight Immortals and inside are two sacred brass deer, each about three feet high. They symbolize longevity. Inside is also a smaller shrine to Pao Kung, the God of Justice. If you choose to have your fortune told here, shake the bamboo sticks inside a *chum* (a canister) until a number is chosen, then go next door to the adjacent Litt Shing Kung (All Saints) Temple to consult a soothsayer. He will read your

against any mischief-making evil spirits who might attempt to enter. Legends indicate that this pair of gods represents two generals of the T'ang dynasty (618-906 A.D.), Chiu Shu-pao and Hu Ching-tai, who were able to protect the Emperor from demons by posting themselves outside the palace gates.

The main part of the temple (which houses statues of the guardian gods) is separated from an antechamber by an open court. Of particular interest here is a statue under a canopied shrine representing the god Wong Tai Sin. He is one of the most popular gods in Hong Kong because he is known to gener-

The much-revered wine jar-bearing goddess known to the Chinese as Kuan Yin, above.

ously grant the wishes of his many devotees.

The **Tin Hau Temple in Aberdeen,** meanwhile, dates back to 1851 when the present temple site was still on the seashore. Its last renovation was in 1898, but it is still in good antique repair. Like most traditional Taoist temples, its rooftop is bordered by miniature figures from Chinese legend and mythology.

The central shrine contains two statues of Tin Hau. The smaller one is carried in processions on festival days. This duplication of the principal deity is a common practice in Taoist temples. Numerous statues here, representing a pantheon of minor deities, illustrates the flexibility of Taoism and reflects the diverse needs, both material and spiritual, of Hong Kong's true believers. Each demi-god is responsible for answering a specific request. A wrestler, for example, would be praying at the wrong door if he sought the help of a demigod known as **The Unpredictable Ghost** (whose main function is to escort souls to the underworld and is usually shown carrying gold or silver). One of the **T'u Ti,** or **Local Gods,** most of whom are related to the soil or earth, might be a more suitable benefactor. Such a patron would be specifically empowered to ensure that the wrestler experiences a soft landing when thrown to the ground.

Merciful Kuan Yin

The incorporation of gods of different faiths under one roof is also illustrated by the presence of **Kuan Yin,** the merciful goddess who is able to deliver people from misery by granting them one of her compassionate glances. A large screen, known as the **spirit screen,** blocks the way from the main entrance to the central shrine and functions to keep evil spirits out of the temple. Because it is believed that such spirits can only move in straight lines, their negative presence here is thus deflected by placing a spirit screen at strategic locations in a temple (or home).

Another notable object within this temple is a drum and a bell (cast in 1726) which used to hang in another nearby temple long since demolished.

Though Tin Hau's name graces the complex of four temples on Public Square Street in Kowloon's Yaumatei, only the main temple (third from the left) is hers. This temple was built more than a century ago at another temple site on the seashore. The more recent temple has a modern concrete ceiling that seems out of place in an old-fashioned building. It is the practical result of a fire that destroyed the old traditional roof.

The temple-keepers here wear rich, red robes and black silk hats as they lead worshippers from one altar to the next and call out incantations and prayers.

There are five large altars. The goddess herself is at temple centre, flanked by four large ceramic figures. One holds a large pen, supposedly to record people's good or bad habits. A second holds the goddess's gold seal. The other two characters are known as "**Favourable Wind Ear**" and "**Thousand-Li Eye.**"

On a side wall are three shelves holding 60 tiny figures known as **Tai Sui.** They are the **Gods of the Year.** The Chinese calendar has a 60-year cycle and, appropriately, when people worship they pray to a god that corresponds to their age. Parents bring newborn infants (who are considered to be a year old when they are born) to worship at the **Number One God.** On Chinese Lunar New Year, everyone becomes a year older, so the same child, after New Year festivities, will be presented to the **Number Two God,** and so on. Being 60 years old is a great honour; for a person to live through the entire 60-year cycle and start a second round is quite an achievement.

The City God

Next door (to the left) is the temple of **Shing Wong,** known as **The City God;** he is a spiritual magistrate whose responsibility is to care for the dead. He is also expected to dole out rewards or punishments to every city dweller — an onerous task, considering the several million people who live in this city. He is also responsible for those who have already died, so Shing Wong has the needed assistance of **Ten Judges of the Underworld.** Anyone who dies has to pass the judgement of these Ten Judges, who decide whether one should be punished for wrongs done. Some of the grotesque penalties meted out are graphically depicted on wall murals here.

Next to Shing Wong is the **Fook Pak Temple** (on the far left as you enter the complex) where **To Tei (The Earth God)** and **Kuan Yin** share the places of honour. Gods of justice, war and happiness are also present. There are lots of shiny brass and redolent clouds of incense here. Out in a courtyard, under a palm tree, is an unusual icon. It is small and simple, a square-cut stone with a few carved figures near it and a box of sand for the placing of joss sticks. This is **The District God.** It attracts many worshippers, who tell it all their personal news. Folks unburden their hearts here.

Another important deity is **Kam Fa, The Goddess of Pregnant Women.** With her are 12 assistants, each of whom has a special spiritual power related to the raising of children.

The temple to the right as you face the Tin Hau Temple is the temple of **Shea Tan,** a shrine dedicated to the local community. By the entrance of this temple are sketches of a palm and a face which remind worshippers that this particular temple is for the deliverance of oracles. The shrines inside this temple belong to **Shea Kung,** a local earth god, who is a "landlord" charged with the safe-keeping of districts, villages, towns and other residential zones. Shrines are also dedicated to **The God of Wealth, The Unpredictable Ghost,** the 60 **Tai Sui, The God of War, The God of Literature, The Goddess of Mercy, The God of Justice** and another local deity, **Wong Tai Sin.**

A Supernatural Tipster

One of Hong Kong's newest temples is Kowloon City's **Wong Tai Sin Temple,** built in 1973. The first temple on the site dates only to 1921, and for its first 50 years it was private.

This temple was erected in honour of **Wong Tai Sin** who has the best reputation of all the Taoist gods for the best of all reasons: he grants advice to devotees about useful horse-racing tips and he cures illness.

Another interesting thing about this temple is that more than 100 fortune tellers' stalls are permanently set up along an alley leading to it. Worshippers who want their future forecast are therefore readily served by either a palmist or physiognomist.

At the **Temple of Ten Thousand Buddhas** are literally thousands of 12 inches high, gold and black buddhas that line this temple's 45 feet high walls from base to ceiling. According to accurate counts made here, there are 12,800 buddhas altogether. Dedicated to Kuan Yin, this temple's main complex was built in 1950. Located in what was once the tiny New Territories fishing village of Shatin (and now the site of one of the government's "new towns" housing more than 100,000), this temple is located on a hillside and is reached after climbing more than 400 steps.

There are four other temples in this complex, but they are located another 60 to 70 steps up the hill. The temple at the extreme left is dedicated to **The Jade Emperor,** the highest of all Taoist gods. The next temple has a large statue of **The God of War** and in the next shrine is a statue of Kuan Yin.

Ching Chung Koon Temple at the 21 milestone on Castle Peak Road in Castle Peak in the New Territories comprises a Taoist temple complex and a home for the aged. Its main temple was built in 1853 and is dedicated to **Lui Tung-pin** (also known as **Lui Tung Bun** and, in Cantonese, **Liu Shui**), one of **The Eight Immortals** of Taoism.

A brief history of Taoism's spread to Hong Kong and a record of its two branches under **Chung Yuen** and **Chung Chuen** is recorded in writing on pillars in this temple.

An ancestral hall containing thousands of ancestor tablets is one of the most sought after places for the repose of the soul. Places can be reserved for someone who is still alive and well so that upon death his name may be entered in a reserved slot. His soul is thus given a place among the perpetual prayers and offerings of the resident monks.

Other notable features of this temple compound are large murals depicting various Taoist deities such as **Wong Mo** or **The Mother of the Jade Emperor.** Outdoors, stately archways, lily-ponds, willows, and rock gardens all frame a gracious and traditional Chinese garden. There is also a library here that documents the 4,000 year history of Taoism.

Ching Shan or **Castle Peak Monastery** was originally established in 428 A.D., but the present monastery was founded by a Buddhist monk in 1918. Of particular interest here is a **fish tomb** which signifies the Buddhist belief that no form of life should be destroyed. A stone inscribed with the characters *Ko Shan Tai Yat,* "The Best Among High Mountains," rests on a peak that rises above the monastery.

Ling Tou Monastery is situated on the northern slope of Castle Peak. It is nearly 1,500 years old, but the present buildings in the Ling Tou complex are only about 200 years old.

On outlying Cheung Chau Island, the **Temple of the Jade Vacuity** is a place of note. It was built in 1783 in grateful homage to the god **Pak Tai** who drove a plague away.

Pak Tai was a Chinese prince who practised perfection nearly 3,000 years ago. When he died he was invited to become a god and was appointed **Commander of the Twelve Heavenly Legions** to fight against **The Demon King.** The most impressive feature of this temple is its characteristic Chinese roof of green concave tiles and circular ridges. It is the main rallying point during Cheung Chau's annual Bun Festival (see feature article on festivals).

Po Lin Monastery on Lantau Island has perhaps the colony's most imposing traditional Chinese architecture. Its 60 feet high main temple establishes a tone of beauty and serenity and reigns architecturally in this monastic compound. This is in keeping with the name of the monastery — *Po Lin* — which means "Precious Lotus." Its main attractions include the marble sculptures of 500 *lohan* followers of Buddha, and the icons which relate the life story of Buddha.

A monk offers daily prayers, right, at the impressive Po Lin Buddhist temple on Lantau Island. Po Lin is Chinese for "Precious Lotus."

MAD MAHJONG — ANCIENT CHINESE THERAPY

Mahjong to the Chinese is not just a game. It is a habit-forming social event, a virtual way of life, which can be as addictive as cigarettes, alcohol or opium.

Mahjong also drives Westerners mad. Not the game, but the noise accompanying it. *Mahjong* is a game that is virtually impossible to play quietly. If you're near a *mahjong* game, you're involved in it whether you want to be or not.

The sounds of *mahjong* — the clickity-clacking of the tiles rubbing against each other during the shuffle, sharp banging noises as tiles are slammed on the table top with each call, and loud shouts announcing each call — seem to pervade much of the normal din which is life in this modern Chinese metropolis. *Mahjong*, besides being a popular social function, is also an opportunity for skillful gambling. Some *mahjong* fans insist there's as much skill involved in betting during a *mahjong* game as there is in backgammon or bridge. And in Hong Kong, where most gambling is illegal, betting on *mahjong* takes on added significance.

Unseemly Behaviour?

A Westerner, who finds himself competing for existence in a *mahjong* game, is usually aghast at the loud and seemingly "unsocial" (in the Western sense) behaviour that punctuates a typical *mahjong* game. Westerners do not realize that the cacophony indicates the level of excitement. To a non-*mahjong* freak, the game smacks of being an antisocial contest instead of a competition between friends. This is a false impression. The Chinese, you'll discover, express themselves in a manner quite unlike a typical Westerner. And indeed, any qualitative judgments should be based on local values, not Western ones. But even if you are an adaptable sort, *mahjong* games can be intolerably loud.

In Chinese cities, *mahjong* is played almost everywhere and at any time. At the beach, while children swim, parents set a table up right on the sand. At building sites and in factory canteens, workers with the "habit" while away their lunch hour and sometimes their lunch money. Tales abound in Hong Kong of people — from *taitai* (rich house-wives) to *amah* (maids) — who have made and lost fortunes in an afternoon's *mahjong* game.

Mahjong is also ever-clacking at dinner parties, banquets, and wedding celebrations. Bilingual wedding invitations may announce a wedding banquet at 8:30 p.m. in English, but the Chinese side of the invitation often asks the guests to come at 6 p.m. The time differential indicates the duration of a traditional prefeast *mahjong* game.

No Dilly-Dallying Allowed

The game originated during the Sung dynasty (960-1279) when it was played with 40 pieces of paper, each with a picture on one side. As the game was played then, each of the four players received eight opening cards, leaving eight for exchanging.

During the Ching Dynasty (1644-1912), at the time of the Taiping Rebellion during the middle of the last century, soldiers popularized the game by playing for a flagon of wine. By this time principles of the game had changed and the paper *mahjong* cards had metamorphosed into more durable bamboo, ivory or bone tiles, some of them elaborately carved.

Mahjong as it is played today in Hong Kong is much more complicated than the original game. The tiles are brick-shaped, about an inch long, and are hand-engraved with Chinese characters and patterns. The first time you watch the game, you will be amazed by the speed in which players make moves and bets. There is no dilly-dallying or stalling in *mahjong*.

To begin play, the leader throws the three game dice. The rolled number is then translated into an exact positioning of the tiles in a square arrangement. The leader takes four tiles, and each player in turn (and in a counter-clockwise sequence, beginning with north) also takes the next four from that position. On the fourth round, the leader takes two and each player one. The leader now has 14 tiles while the other three players have 13 each. The leader then discards one tile (by slamming it on the table, naturally) and play commences counter-clockwise. If north does not want the discarded tile, he chooses another from the tiles still remaining on the table, but only from where the last person left off. (Are you still with us?)

The object of the game is to "go out," much as in rummy, by matching up tiles of similar values or suits. The winner is the first player to line up four sets of three tiles (either as three-of-a-kind or as three-tile straights) plus an additional pair (which is the 13th tile plus one picked tile which must fit in to make a pair or, if such a pair exists, form a set), thereby adding up to a total of 14 tiles. (Are you still with us?)

Each player also has a packet of betting chips worth 100 points. Before a game, the players decide what a betting point will be worth — anywhere from one cent to $10. When a player "goes out" successfully, he is awarded points based on the combination of tiles he went out with. Each player gives the winner "X" points (chips) and the leader gives double. If the leader wins, he receives double from each of the three players. When a player loses his packet of chips worth 100 points, the

ly, social event.

Much of the excitement of the game is due to the pace at which it is played — the faster the moves, the more thrilling the action. Tiles are not merely put down politely on the table and picked up, but are slammed down and grabbed up midst a great clatter and loud exclamations. As the excitement builds and money changes hands, a sort of frenzy seizes the players and — like the neck-to-neck finish of a horse race — the table appears to be the scene of pandemonium.

Multiply that mad scene by 10,000 or 100,000 and you have a good audio-visual

game is technically over, unless of course he starts borrowing to prolong it (a fairly common practice). And occasionally, by common agreement, each player starts out with more than 100 points.

Frenetic But Friendly

To a Westerner, just about every game of *mahjong* is "heated," and this of course is what drives non-*mahjong* players to distraction. A typical friendly neighbourhood *mahjong* game is more like a kung fu fight scene than a friend-

Keep your eyes on the *mahjong* hands. The action is frenetic, but relaxing, Chinese-style.

image of Hong Kong on a typical afternoon or evening. Even as you read this story there are *mahjong* games going on *everywhere* in the colony — in workers' flats, on sampans, in tea shops, in mansions, in factory canteens, at the seaside — everywhere!

The game of *mahjong* appears to be anything but a game of leisure and relaxation. But that, of course, is exactly what it is.

Mahjong also is used as a conclusive Chinese test of an unknown man's or woman's mettle. Indeed, an old Chinese saying advises that if one wishes to find out what kind of man his daughter is going to marry, the best way to find out is to invite him over for a "friendly" game of *mahjong*.

LUCKY NUMBER 222 — 'EASY-EASY-EASY'

A Spiritual Sequence?

Would you pay US$132,000 for license plate number 3? An anonymous businessman did just that in Hong Kong. He thought the number plate "lucky," because in Cantonese the number can symbolize "living or giving birth."

As of December 1985, Hong Kong's Transport Department had held 101 auctions for "lucky" numbers. Number 3 drew the highest bid. By contrast, the lowest bids allowed were HK$1,000 — the reserve price. However, there is one unconfirmed story 1479 on his car. The car had been bought a few years before that encounter, with the number, for HK$1,000. The car number was (and still is) considered "lucky" because it is also considered an antique. Having been issued chronologically in 1959 well before the big car boom of the Sixties and Seventies, it has no prefix. It is the lack of a prefix that makes it even more valuable. If it were a three-digit or two-digit or even one-digit license number, it would be worth many thousands of times the amount offered by the superstitious pump attendant.

that a mere HK$250 was once paid for number 913 (whose homophones mean "everlasting life"). It true, 913 was one of the best bargains ever bought.

From the time lucky number auctions began in May, 1973, until December 1985, HK$36.4 million has been raised for the government's charity lottery fund.

Prior to May 1973, there was already a profitable trade in numbers considered to be "lucky." At that time, the government issued the numbers as they came up in sequence. You can imagine the surprise of a foreign car-owner when in 1970 he drove his dilapidated 1959 Sunbeam Rapier convertible into a petrol station and the station owner offered him HK$2,500 in cash for the "lucky" number

For ordinary car registration, Hong Kong has an ascending scale of charges. Cars with motors under 1500 cc can be registered for HK$2,500 while the most expensive registration is HK$7,400 for cars over 4500 cc. For the official fee, you get whatever number is next in sequence.

The government has designated about 400 "lucky" numbers and carefully restricts their sale at regularly spaced auctions of 15 numbers at a time. Before the auction scheme, sought-after numbers were freely traded on

These license-plate numerals borne by opulent 20th Century carriages are among the colony's most sought-after "lucky numbers." All were parked at Shaw Brothers Movie Town.

the open market and numbers were allotted sequentially with no restrictions. Now, all numbers considered lucky in Cantonese, and prestige numbers in single, double, triple and quadruple digits without prefixes, are reserved and available only through auctions.

Those who possessed "lucky numbers" prior to May 1973, had their car registration books marked "non-transferable," meaning that the number must be returned to the government for auctioning upon death or de-registration. The "lucky" number cannot be transferred to another person — even to a

162: 'Easy All the Way'

Naturally, a black market has developed for the numbers, usually based around scrapped cars. There is also supposed to be a numbers syndicate which through a cumbersome process of buying and selling vehicles secures various "lucky" numbers as they come up in sequence.

Ads sometimes appear in the Chinese press offering lucky numbers, though such trans-actions are illegal and technically impossible. An advertisement in the Chinese press once

relative — or be made part of an estate. It can only be transferred by the owner to another of his vehicles. A lobby effort is now in progress to allow the legal transfer of "lucky numbers" upon death — along with other willed pro-perty and possessions.

The Hong Kong government allows "lucky" numbers to be reserved for auction with a deposit of HK$1,000. This has the effect of allowing people to choose their numbers instead of just waiting to see what new num-bers come up in sequence (since there are few numbers ever returned). The amount also serves as a reserve price in the auction, and it secures the number's placement in the next auction. And presumably the reserve amount is returned if the bidder is unsuccessful.

offered BH8222 (signifying prosperity-easy-easy-easy) for HK$2,500; a real bargain if the deal was actually clinched, because this same number at an auction would fetch three times that sum.

Lucky numbers include: 2 for "easy," 3 for "living or giving birth," 6 for "longevity," 8 for "*baht*" "prosperity," and 9 for "per-petuity" or "eternity."

Combinations of numbers can also be im-portant. For example, 162 means "easy all the way," 163 means "live all the way" or "give birth all the way," and 168 "prosperity all the way." This spiritual numbers awareness also has been adopted by nightclubs, boutiques and companies here — all with proper lucky number names.

CHINESE OPERA

Chinese opera is an integral part of Chinese cultural entertainment and originates from China's earliest folk music and dances. Historically, the form of modern day Chinese opera — a definite story put to music and dance — emerged during the Sung dynasty (960-1297 A.D.). During the 18th Century, Chinese opera came to be associated with festivals and state occasions at the Imperial Court in Peking. It would be a mistake, however, to think that the enjoyment of Chinese opera was monopolized by royalty and the intelligentsia.

On the contrary, its very form explains its popularity among common folk. This custom survives in Hong Kong so much so that during any important festival on the Chinese calendar, a performance of Chinese opera is obligatory.

Performances of Chinese opera are usually held in informal bamboo and mat theatres temporarily erected in public areas. This has less to do with the lack of accommodation than with a tradition of building such mat-shed structures in the large patios of old Chinese homes. A natural result of the universal popularity of Chinese opera is its cultural and regional variations. Cantonese operas, for example, are quite different from Chiu Chow operas, and due to its development under imperial patronage, Peking opera is characterized by the court's official dialect, Mandarin.

Shrill Falsettos

The backbone of Chinese opera is the actor-singer. Not unlike Western opera stars, Chinese operatic singers undergo many years of intensive training. To achieve a proper high-pitched falsetto, for example, requires strenuous discipline.

Singing artists are in turn accompanied by a traditional Chinese orchestra. Musicians playing percussion instruments occupy one side of the stage while others responsible for wind and string instruments sit on the opposite side, leaving the main area of the stage clear for the performers. To the novice Westerner, Chinese music seems incomprehensible, partly because little obvious melody seems involved in the instrument-playing, and also because the actors' shrill vocals usually dominate the performance. As in Shakespearean theatre, there were no actresses during Chinese opera's early development. The stage was regarded unsuitable for women, so female roles were portrayed by male actors. As in the West, however, that tradition has died.

Makeup, movements, props and specific costume colours identify an actor's age, sex

On preceding pages, left and right, Chinese opera at its Hong Kong best, including a makeup portrait of the late master Leong Seng Poh.

and personality the moment he or she appears on stage. Actors in Peking operas wear extremely heavy makeup, a cosmetic style derived from the use of painted masks in older operatic forms. Cantonese and Chiu Chow operas do not feature such heavily painted faces, but makeup is still very important for dramatic effect and role identification. In Peking opera a white patch on the nose indicates a comic character of low rank; a completely white face suggests an evil and treacherous character; a red face identifies a courageous but dim-witted man; and a black faced actor is a normal, thinking person.

Headdresses are also a vital part of the Chinese opera costume: the more important the character, the more elaborate it is. There are no less than 18 types of opera beards, each symbolizing a different personality. Costumes are understandably very exaggerated in style. Though based on historical dress, they are created to achieve as great a theatrical effect as possible.

Props are normally sparse, but brilliantly painted scenery background panels are usually used. And though intricately carved furniture is sometimes used, a great deal of the enjoyment of a performance is left to the audience's imagination. For example, an actor taking measured steps behind two squares of embroidered silk placed before him on the stage is indicating that he is seated in a sedan chair.

Purple For Barbarians

The colour code is rather important because each colour identifies the rank, status and personality of the different operatic roles. Yellow is the colour of emperors, green represents a person of high rank and purple is the mark of a barbarian general.

As in Western operas, Chinese ones incorporate a lot of mime, dance, sword-playing, and acrobatics. And, for the principal artists, gesture, movement and attitude are all as important as vocal lines. Folklore, legends and historical incidents are the dramatic sources from which Chinese opera's vast repertoire is drawn.

In the West, audiences are urged to be seated at show time, but for Chinese opera it is perfectly acceptable for members of the audience to arrive late for a performance, leave early, walk around and chat, or even eat during a show, which may run anywhere from three to four hours to an entire day. Sometimes one wonders how the actors can be heard over the audience din, but when a good line is sung, the recognition is there instantly. However, in keeping with the universal desire to be appreciated and praised, performers of Chinese opera do line up on stage to acknowledge applause at the end of a performance.

TAILORING TIPS, OR HOW TO FEEL FIT

Made-to-measure items are still consistently at the top of every Hong Kong visitor's shopping list, and tailoring is a very important part of the touristic economy.

The problem for most shoppers, regardless of destination, is time. There is just not enough of it. Therefore, if first-rate made-to-measure clothes are anywhere on your shopping list, move that must-do item to the top of the list. Yes, you can probably find a tailor willing to sell you a 24-hour suit, but like most things done in a rush, it would no doubt prove to be a shoddy and disappointing production — if not today, then next week when the buttons fall off and threads begin to unravel.

Give yourself plenty of time for tailoring by immediately getting on with the labourious task of choosing a tailor. The difficulty is not with physically finding a tailor shop — Hong Kong boasts more than 4,000 — but with finding one that has quality materials and proven suit-building skills. Shop location and, of course, price, are also among important considerations.

If you have a reliable business or social contact in the city in which you are planning to buy something, by all means consider their advice.

Everybody in the colony, of course, has a favourite tailor but a visitor should seriously weigh his choice after considering the proximity of the tailor's shop to his hotel. True, you may be able to find a tailor who's slightly cheaper or even better on the back streets and you might even have the address of one recommended by somebody who was here five or 10 years ago; but before you make a decision, remember the hassle of travelling to an out-of-the-way shop. Time, money and convenience factors may inspire you to patronize a shop closer to where you live or perhaps in your hotel arcade.

Sewing Down a Deal

All tailor shops will ask for a down payment and here you can put Apa's First Rule for Tailor Shops into practice: "The amount of personal service received is inversely related to the down payment." In other words, the smaller a down payment you can get away with the more attention you will receive at the end of

"Pants are troublesome because they are deceptively easy to fit." As our sage advises, be wary of the tape.

the project.

Be explicit in your directions. In most cases, the salesman who has taken your measurements and to whom you are meticulously rattling off your specific instructions is not the tailor. Most tailor shops give the cloth to members of the tailors' union, who then do the final cutting and sewing. Obviously, it is at this transfer point where there is mis-communication. Perseverance is the key. It is your suit and those specific details you requested are important. Quite obviously, if you can find a shop with its own in-house tailor, you are ahead of the game. However, in most Indian shops the tailor is not on the premises.

Most tailor shops will try to get by with one fitting. It is easier for them. Demand as many fittings as you desire, but remember that a minimum of three within a three to five day period is the norm: one when the material is basted up, one when it is partly finished, and a final fitting.

It is a good idea to reiterate any special requests (number of pockets, flaps, etc.) during these fittings, because the tailor himself will usually do these fittings, in consultation with the sales clerk. If the tailor is not there to fine-focus your fitting, complain. One last word of warning: tailor shops in Hong Kong are hospitable — sometimes too hospitable. Remember, alcohol complicates this made-to-measure exercise.

If you are going back to a colder climate (like Europe), you might consider advising the tailor to leave the waist a little bit looser, because it is likely you'll put on more weight in the colder climate. Or you might ask him to leave a little extra material in the waist or crotch so that you can easily have the trousers let out later if necessary.

Mail Order

All tailors keep records of clients' measurements, so it is theoretically possible to re-order by mail. Whether a thus commissioned suit will fit you is another matter. When ordering by mail bear in mind — and body — how many fittings it took when you were last in the shop. If the shop outfitted you right off, maybe you can chance an order via mail and be satisfied. On the other hand, if it took them a week to make a presentable suit when you were physically here to inspect the work, that problem will only be aggravated when dealing via post.

259

WILLIAM
HOLDEN

in

Ray
Stark's

THE
WORLD
OF
SUZiE
WONG

co-starring

NANCY
KWAN

as SUZIE WONG

NEW WORLDS OF SUZIE WONG

Hong Kong's nightlife image is perhaps best personified by author Richard Mason's famous character, Suzie Wong. In spite of the fact that "The World of Suzie Wong" has undergone drastic changes since the Fifties when the book and subsequent movie twitted the outside world's romantic imagination, Mason's now stereotypical image of a gentle Chinese bar girl still attracts the bachelors.

These days, however, a more accurate local nightlife image might be a Japanese businessman being teased by a topless hostess in a

Tsimshatsui, are still attractive haunts. Somehow, both visiting GIs and civilians manage to find a respite in the bars, brothels, pubs, nightclubs, and restaurants that dot these neon nightscapes.

Suzie Wong may be pushing 40, even 50, but her female heirs are still young and nubile. You often have to chat and drink your way through some very hard birds to find her, but that Chinese girl flashing long white legs through a slit *cheongsam* is still out there.

In spite of its "Suzie Wong" reputation, Hong Kong does have enough nightlife to

pseudo-plush but very expensive Wanchai or Tsimshatsui gawk-bar.

Hong Kong tomcatting is an expensive proposition these days, but the high prices seem to be ignored by the platoons of sailors, soldiers, airmen and marines from many nations who still march into the "The Wanch" — as Suzie's world is endearingly called by residents. Gone are the heady R & R days of the Vietnam war when whole fleets would sail into "Fragrant Harbour" for a brief and raucous visit, but The Wanch, and her Kowloon sister,

Yes, Suzie Wong times are a changing. Above, black "Velvet" at Tsimshatsui's Bottoms Up.

please anyone. From straight in-and-out porn and hardcore girlie bars — to pleasant pubs and discos to which you could even take your mother — they're all here.

Suzie Suzuki Bars?

Hong Kong not only has a variety in kind, but in price. There are still bars where you can quietly nurse a beer for under HK$15, while on the other side of the same street a "Japanese-style" club can set you back HK$25 for that same amber bottle of San Mig (but they have minimums from HK$80-100). In the former, you can either choose to be alone or invite a "luverly" to join you for about the same price per drink. But in the Japanese clubs (Suzie Suzuki bars?) you'll pay about HK$70-100 for a quarter hour of a hostess's company, *plus* HK$20 to 25 for her quickly quaffed drink.

The following is an after-hours survey of some of the more popular places, identified according to categories (so you don't take your wife to the wrong place):

Girlie bars can be divided into two types — topless or non-topless, and (*à la* Suzie Wong) where you pay hostesses by the quarter hour, or where you don't.

In case you imagined that because times have changed in Wanchai there are fewer bars — fear not. Stand on Lockhart Road any evening, look through that avenue's neon col-

the circuit. It is not. But it looks like it is, probably because the luverlies there have not changed since the bar opened. If you are a connoisseur of bar scenes, a trip to the Red Lips is a must. To complete this trip into the colony's sensual past, also visit the **Red Lion** and **Four Sisters**. They are also "old," but their "girls" are a bit younger — reminiscent perhaps of Hong Kong in the Fifties and Sixties.

The best, most popular (with women as well as men) and oldest topless bar is the **Bottom's Up**, where four hexagonal and interconnected bars are surrounded by mirrors (so you are never quite certain whether you are coming or going). Topless barmaids sit in the middle of these six-sided "bars" on very large swivel

lage of innumerable bar signs, and you'll find whatever or whomever your Asia dream may be, and then some; indeed, Wanchai is still alive and Suzie Wong-ing.

"True" girlie bars still offer beer for under HK$10 and girls' drinks for under HK$20. Good examples are the **Pussycat, Club Washington** and **Makati Inn** (with Filipino girls) in Wanchai, which are not topless, and the **Suzie Wong, United, Panda, Popeye** and **Hignway** which are. Across the pond in Kowloon, meanwhile, the **Red Lion, Four Sisters** and **Red Lips** are also not topless.

The Aging Red Lips

There are some Hong Kong hands who say the Red Lips is the oldest "true" girlie bar on

stools that look more like sunken swivel-beds. The **Kismet** and the **New Lido** are other places in this genre. But be warned that most of the topless bars in Kowloon, perhaps with the exception of the Bottom's Up, are designed with the rich Japanese businessman's pocketbook in mind.

The hostess clubs are definitely aimed at big spenders, which means the majority of their patrons are Japanese. Indeed, many of these even have Japanese names, such as the **Ginza,**

The Red Lips — one of the original girlie bars and a must for anyone who wants to savour something of the colony's sensual history.

Danshaku, Kokusai and **Hollywood Club** (all in Kowloon). The **Copacabana, New Playboy** and **Latin Quarter** are somewhat more universal in appeal, as are Hong Kong's **Mitoro Fujiya** and **Dai-ichi**. The **Korea Palace** — with Korean hostesses — is a favourite hang-out for Japanese and Korean businessmen.

Pre-Fab Pubs

One of the more pleasant nightlife changes in Hong Kong has been the rebirth of more pubs or taverns for those who prefer a type of conviviality which was previously only available in more expensive and subduced hotel bars. That's probably because a

Filipino dance bands are standard fare here, as they are throughout Asia, but beyond such *mabuhay* sound spots there are only a few bars in Honkers where you can hear live rock or jazz. These few, however, should not be missed. The **Dicken's Bar** in the Excelsior Hotel has jazz, mostly on Sundays (on off-days it's proper pub). **Haley's** features oldtime rock'n roll nightly, and **The Godown** is one of the first clubs to schedule folk and jazz nights. In Kowloon, **Ned Kelly's Last Stand** swings to everything from folk to jazz and rock, while **Rick's Café** has jazz-rock, while Hardy's is known for its folk music.

For wine bars try **Coates Wine Bar, Brown's Wine & Cheese, Rumours** or **1997.**

group of pre-fabs pubs—direct from England—have hit Hong Kong and have set the colony's newest getting-pissed style. The first of these were the **Bull and Bear** and the **Jockey,** both in Central. It was just a matter of time until a pub or tavern hit The Wanch and within staggering distance of each other are now the **Old China Hand, Horse and Groom Bell Inn, Rock Exchange**. Three other Hong Kong taverns are the **Shakespeare, London Price** and **Mad Dogs**.

Back across the harbour are the **Cutty Sark** (one of the most expensive), the **White Stag,** the **Brewery** and the **Blacksmith's Arm,** plus three distinctively Aussie pubs— **Ned Kelly's Last Stand**, the **Stoned Crow** and the **Waltzing Matilda Inn**.

Piano Bars, Pulsing Discos And Taxi-Dancing Halls

True cocktail lounges and piano bars exist here too, but virtually all are in hotels. Some of these bars are pure piano bars; others have a husky-voiced female vocalist accompanied by a small combo or solo guitarist. All are pleasant and quiet places to to meet a friend or simply be left alone. Recommended are **L'Aperitif** in the Peninsula, **Great Wall** in the Sheraton, the **Inn Bar** in the Holiday Inn-Golden Mile, **Royal Falcon** in the Royal Garden, **China Coast Pub** and **The Flying Machine** in the Airport Meridien, the **Chin Chin** in the Hyatt Regency and the **Gun Bar** in the Hong Kong Hotel. All are in

Kowloon. The **Dragon Boat** in the Hilton, **Captain's Bar** in the Mandarin, **Yum Sing** in the Lee Gardens, and **Lau Ling** in the Furama Intercontinental are, likewise, all in Hong Kong.

And what would Hong Kong's nighlife be without a pulsing disco scene? Hong Kong's rather late answer to Studio 54 or Regine's is **Canton** where the "chic seek to meet" as the saying goes. Vying for the colony's best boogie bar title are **Hot Gossip**, **Chicago**, **Shesado**, **Apollo 18**, **New York New York** and **Today's World** (complete with a robot greeter). Disco records also spin eternally at the **Polaris** (Hyatt-Regency), **Another World** (Holiday Inn-Golden Mile) and **Hollywood East** (Regal Meridien). The **Polaris** is on a

Likewise, Chinese ballrooms, in which you buy tickets to taxi-dance with painted and powdered ladies, can be a language problem. Count your fingers when you leave such establishments.

'No Touchee'

Another pleasant diversion are the colony's floating supper clubs. Entertainment isn't all that great, but the scenery from these air-conditioned nightclubs that cruise through the harbour is superb and they can make for a memorable and romantic evening.

The same prudent rules of common sense apply in Hong Kong's bar as they do in any other fun-loving country. Don't flash

top floor where grand views can be enjoyed once your eyes have recovered from the very flashing strobelights.

Hong Kong discos, however, can be expensive boogie experiences. Entrance fees (which include two drinks) range from HK$50 to $100.

There are not many Western-style supper clubs left. In fact, the **Pink Giraffe** in the Sheraton is one of the few left. However, the Hilton often hosts special dinner theatre shows in their ballroom, so keep an eye on nightlife ads to find out what's scheduled there. There are also a few Chinese supper clubs still operating, but these are usually not very popular with Western tourists.

all your cash. Perhaps it is even wise to leave most of it in a hotel safe deposit box with your passport. Though most bars have credit card decals, you'll find it is difficult to pay with them because cashiers will keep saying things like "cash discount." A little perseverance and plastic payments should work.

Though there is a saying referring to yachts that "if you have to ask the price, it isn't for you," that advice could apply to women. However, it saves a lot of hassles if you know the score before you tuck in. Most Wanchai/Tsimshatsui bars have a sign posted

Sophisticated hostesses indeed! As our man in Tsimshatsui advises, "Lookee, yes, but no touchee" — unless all social systems are go.

264

somewhere advertising the cost of drinks for you, and for her, plus the escort rental time and fees. Look for this sign or ask, to avoid later arguments over your bill.

Beware of piling on drinks (unless you can afford it, of course) when a hostess brings her lovely friend over to your table. It is good for the ego to be surrounded by caressing women, who laugh at your every bad joke, but the pleasure clock is ticking doubletime and you can't plead later that "I didn't ask for her, and her, and ..."

In the topless bars, the local rule is "no touchee," unless of course you have an inspired gift of gab — and grab. A hint: barmaids usually do not have drinks bought for them, because they are not, strictly speaking, hostesses. But they rarely refuse the gesture.

On 'Buying Out'

A "buying out" fee may top HK$250 in some of the cheaper girlie bars, and can be as high as HK$1500 to $2500 in classier hostess joints. If you are considering a "buy out," you might consider sleeping during the day so you can leave with the girl after work hours, and after serious negotiation, of course.

Which leads us to the subject of guest houses. Some of the conservative hotels don't allow a man to toddle in with a rent-a-bird in the middle of the night. But as you can imagine, there are plenty of "cheap guest houses" in both Wanchai and Tsimshatsui which will cater to your every impetuous need. These places usually rent rooms by the hour, or two, but an all night price can be negotiated during low-occupancy periods. The highest class "guest houses" are in Kowloon Tong and easily found by taxi from Tsimshatsui (or, for that matter, from Hong Kong Island). Here, depending on your pocketbook's bulge, you can rent anything from a straight room to one with a heart-shaped vibrating bed surrounded by mirrors — by the hour or all-nightee. Your choice.

The biggest problems for foreigners out on the town are encountered in Chinese ballrooms. Some are straight, but many are "controlled" by alleged local triad heavies. Therefore, any argument which develops is quickly subdued by efficient "enforcers." Of course, if you have a Chinese mate to assist, most problems are diplomatically solved. Girls who join your table and with whom you dance (to abbreviated dance numbers) cost about HK$10 to $15 for a 10 minute long tete-a-tete. Customer drinks cost about the same as in other bars. Dance hostesses make their money by time, not by the drinks they sell, so they often drink along with their customers, at the same price. Local intelligence indicates that ballroom girls are an easier "buy out" than those in other bars, but the buying out fee is around HK$250 to $300 in the swankier ballrooms (and language may prove to be a problem).

If you *really* get into Hong Kong's nightlife, you may be offered a psst-psst chance to experience a "floorshow" in a "private club." These clandestine shows feature simulated sex, and their cost is relative to their eroticism. However, the shows are quick (usually about 20 minutes) and you pay between HK$25 to $50 per act. Drinks are extra, usually around HK$10. These shows, however, are said to be not nearly as good as those staged in other parts of the Wicked East.

For nighthawks who can't be bothered with a bar, club or restaurant ambience, female company, an "escort" if you will, is as close as your hotel phone. There are a dozen or so escort agencies which will supply you with a companion for about HK$100 an hour, they require a five hour minimum companionship.

Rent-a-Bird

If you drop by an escort agency, you can thumb through photo books there and choose the lady of your dreams. If not, it is a potluck escort affair. Rent-a-birds come in all shapes, sizes and nationalities so that Europeans can fulfill their fondest cross-cultural fantasies with Asians, and vice versa. Officially, of course, you are just hiring a woman for her charming conversation, good looks and to accompany you to dinner or a party. Any other conquests are subject to negotiation.

If you have just come from Bangkok or Manila and the word "massage" brings back idyllic fantasies of those kneady Thai or Filipino establishments, Hong Kong will be a rude awakening: Most of the colony's massage "parlours" are mobile — meaning the lasses come to you.

However, by making a modest reservation, you can still get your tired and harried bod back on the right path *chez vous*. The cost for a massage is about HK$300 for 1½ hours and usually includes a bath like mommy used to give you. There does not seem to be any difficulty for the masseuse to gain entrance to hotel rooms during the day. If you are interested in a straight sauna and massage, most Hong Kong hotels have health club facilities which are excellent.

Guide In Brief

Travelling to Hong Kong

By Air

The colony is served by more than 30 airline companies, plus another dozen charter and cargo airlines. Kai Tak will reach its air traffic saturation point by the mid Eighties, but various expansion plans are in progress to extend the life of the airport.

Kai Tak is one of the few airports still located virtually within a city—less than 5 kilometers and about 10 minutes away from Kowloon's Tsimshatsui hotel district, 20 minutes from Causeway Bay and about 25 to 30 minutes from Central District (both on Hong Kong Island).

No airport handling more than 12 million passengers a year is fun. Kai Tak has been expanded—and expanded—but at times when a half-dozen 747s are arriving and departing at the same time, the runway and skies are like an airborne cattle yard. However, Hong Kong maintains one of the world's most efficient runway-to-hotel gauntlets.

The terminal building doesn't win architectural awards, but recent massive renovation efforts have eased many former traffic bottlenecks. Upon arrival, jumbo aircrafts park alongside modern passenger bridges. Immigration, customs and baggage check points are all within a short walking distance, and free baggage carts are available. You can push your carts past customs, or hire a porter (they are free, but a tip of HK$2 per piece of baggage is normal). A Hong Kong Hotel Association's reservation desk is available to assist travellers. The foreign exchange window, which, along with others in the airport, give the worst rates in town. (Therefore, just change a wee bit to see you through.) Free phones are in the buffer hall immediately past customs. There are well-marked, but still confusing, exits: left is the greeting area if you are being met; straight ahead are hotel buses and city-bound tour coaches.

Security:

Security is very rigid at Kai Tak. Some airlines—Cathay Pacific Airways in particular—X-ray all baggage before it is checked in. All hand carry items are either X-rayed or manually inspected. The X-ray machines at Kai Tak do affect film. Amateur and professional photographers should *always* take their exposed and unexposed film out before they go through the X-ray machine because though one particular machine might not harm the film (assuming the warning sign is correct and the machine functions correctly), the cumulative effect of X-rays on film can damage your photographs.

Announcements:

Silence now reigns supreme, so check flight boards or ask ground hostesses about arrival-departure information.

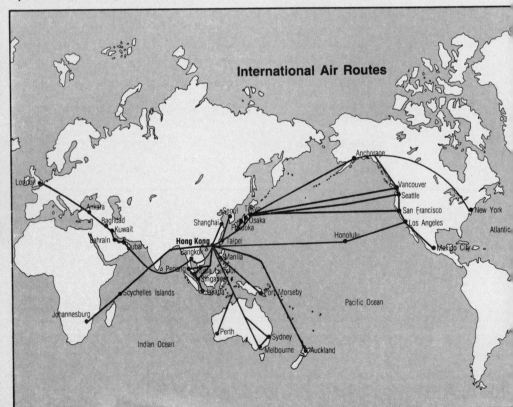

International Air Routes

Left Luggage:

The left-luggage counter is on the far left side as you enter the departure area.

Airport Transportation:

There is a special airport bus service — both to and from the airport — to and from Tsimshatsui and Hong Kong Island. Route 201 to Tsimshatsui costs HK$2.50 and Route 200 to Hong Kong costs HK$5 (exact fare change only). Both bus routes stop at all major hotels. Route 200 operates from 7:25 a.m. to 10:30 p.m. from the airport, and 7:30 a.m. to 10:40 p.m. from Hong Kong Island.

Route 201 operates from 7:30 a.m. to 11 p.m. from the airport, and 8 a.m. to 10.30 p.m. from Tsimshatsui.

Metered taxis are available and are somewhat cheaper on long runs. There is a HK$20 surcharge on any trip through the Cross-Harbour Tunnel, and HK$3 for the Aberdeen and Lion Rock Tunnels, plus a HK$1 charge on each piece of baggage. Taxi drivers are usually honest, but some try to overcharge on the very short trip (under HK$10) into Tsimshatsui so just pay whatever is on the meter (which is obviously ticking over in H.K. dollars, not the U.S. ones that some wily taxi drivers would have you believe). (See section on **Transportation** for what to do about taxi complaints.) Avis self-drive cars are also available at HK$200-490 per day.

Porters:

Porters are available at the airport arrivals area, and are at your service whether you arrive privately or by hotel transport. Though this service is free, they do appreciate a gratuity, normally about HK$2 per piece of baggage.

By Sea

For those with plenty of time and very ample means, a half-dozen cruise lines include Hong Kong on their "Exotic East" or "Round-the-World" grand tours. Most have recently added a Chinese port — but few give enough time in any one place for more than a cursory view. Among the current fleet that tie up at Ocean Terminal (Hong Kong's shamefully well placed and serviced passenger wharf) are ships from **Norwegian America Line, Royal Viking Line, Holland-America Line, Cunard** (very occasionally in the sleek form of the *QE2*) and of course **P & O**, whose steamships once ruled the England-to-Far East run.

Only slightly more direct and less expensive are passenger-carrying freighters. **American President Lines** (San Francisco) and **Glen & Shire Lines** (London) are the only ones that make anything like frequent Pacific or European runs, stopping as well at various ports along the way. Either the *ABC Shipping Guide* (available at most libraries) or one of the several "freighter travel" services can often pinpoint others. There is, of course, always the possibility — fairly slim in most places — of talking tramp skippers into taking extra crew. Newspaper shipping pages around Asia or in any major port city are the best places to start.

For those who really want a ship and don't mind not being fawned over, the easiest, cheapest option is **Golden Line/Guan Guan Shipping** (23 Telok Ayer St., Singapore), which runs every three weeks Penang/Singapore/Hong Kong return. The Hong Kong leg takes about four-and-a-half days either way, and even in first class costs less than the place.

Finally, on the American West Coast, around the Pacific and in most ports in Asia, even marginally experienced sailors can sometimes pick up an empty spot on a private sailing boat. In Hong Kong, the best places to ask are the **Royal Hong Kong Yacht Club** (at Kellett Island, Causeway Bay, across from the Excelsior Hotel) and the various anchorages in Stanley and Deep Water Bay.

Travel Advisories

Visas and Health Documents:

Most visitors need only a valid passport to enter Hong Kong. Also, in keeping with recent trends worldwide, vaccination certificate for cholera are waived *except* for arrivals from officially declared "infected areas." Youthful and visibly less well-heeled arrivals will probably be asked to show onward tickets, "sufficient means" or references in the colony, but few *bona fide* tourists are ever turned away.

Visitors are not allowed to take up employment, paid or unpaid, to establish or join any business, or to enter school as a student. And except in unusual circumstances, visitors are not allowed to change their citizenship status after arrival.

Without a Visa:

The maximum stay varies according to nationality: six months for British subjects (United Kingdom passport holders only); three months for other British passport holders (Commonwealth countries) and citizens of Andorra, Austria, Belgium, Brazil, Chile, Colombia, Denmark, Ecuador, Eire, France, Israel, Italy, Liechtenstein, Luxembourg, the Maldives, Monaco, the Netherlands, Norway, Portugal, San Marino, Spain, Sweden, Switzerland, and Turkey; one month for citizens Bolivia, Costa Rica, Dominican Republic, El Salvador, Finland, Mexico, Morocco, Nepal, Nicaragua, Pakistan, Panama, Greece, Guatemala, Honduras, Iceland, Paraguay, Peru, Tunisia, the United States, Uruguay, and Venezuela; 14 days for citizens of Thailand and seven days for nationals of other countries, including the Vatican and the U.S. Trust Territory of The Pacific Islands (American Micronesia), but excluding exceptions listed below.

Must Have a Visa:

Visitors from the categories listed below ALWAYS REQUIRE A VISA: (1) Nationals of Afghanistan, Albania, Argentina, Bulgaria, the People's Republic of China, Cuba, Czechoslovakia, the German Democratic Republic, Hungary, Kampuchea, Laos, Mongolia, North Korea, Poland, Rumania, the Soviet Union, Vietnam and (North) Yemen; (2) holders of

Taiwan passports; (3) all "stateless" persons; and (4) holders of Iranian and Libyan passports.

Transits:

Visas are not normally required for transit stays if valid onward booking (by air) is held and travel documents are in order, or if onward or return bookings (by sea) are held for the same vessel, travel documents are in order and carrier accepts responsibility for removal of passenger. (In other words, you *can* get off your cruise ship when it is in port.) Sea/air or air/sea transits are governed by normal visa regulations.

Applications For Visas:

If a visa to visit Hong Kong is required, apply at the nearest British Embassy, Consulate General or High Commission (in Commonwealth countries), or write directly to the Immigration Department, Mirror Tower, 61 Mody Road, East Tsimshatsui, Kowloon, Tel: 3-733-3111. Allow at least eight weeks for an answer.

Extensions of Visas:

It is extremely rare for a person on a visitor's visa to change his or her visa status category without first leaving the colony. However, visa extensions are usually given freely provided you have the means to stay here (without working) and onward ticketing. Address all queries to the Immigration Department, Mirror Tower, 61 Mody Road, East Tsimshatsui, Kowloon, Tel: 3-733-3111. (Visa extensions cost HK$100.)

Macau-China Trips:

If admitted to Hong Kong with a multiple-entry visa, you will not need another Hong Kong visa to return from Macau or China. If you have a single-entry visa, you will need a re-entry visa (obtainable from the Immigration Department) to come back.

Check-in:

Though most airlines at Kai Tak Airport have computerized booking facilities, they still request check-in at least two hours before flight time because of the airport's burgeoning crowds. Most airlines begin their check-in three hours before flight time, but **Jardine Airways**, which handles quite a number of flights (see airlines listing), allows a same-day check-in at any time before the flight, which means you can drop your bags off and receive a boarding card any time during the day at your convenience. This system is especially popular with persons booking late-night long hauls to Europe, Africa or Australia.

Departure Tax:

The airport's departure tax is HK$120 for adults and HK$60 for children two to 12 years of age. Travel agents may include this in your ticket price. If not, you pay at check-in and a receipt is attached to your ticket.

Hand-Carry Baggage:

The size of hand-carry items allowed on aircraft is more strictly controlled in Hong Kong than at most other airports. As you go into immigration security sectors, uniformed personnel will inspect hand-carry items. There is a box there measuring 22 x 14 x 9 inches (56 x 36 x 23 centimetres) and all your baggage must fit into it (with the exception of garment bags.) Additional "hand baggage," however, can be purchased in transit area duty-free shops.

If you have items that cannot be checked as baggage—such as baby bags or strollers or large camera bags, etc.—ask for the airline's supervisor. (The check-in girl will call her.) They are strict but fair and often will either escort you through customs or give you a red baggage exemption tag.

Unaccompanied Baggage:

Over-weight charges for accompanied baggage are quite expensive. At Kai Tak Airport, however, there is an **Unaccompanied Baggage Service** in the Passenger Terminal and near the check-in counters. This service will forward your excess baggage by air freight. (Alternatively, you can either take it to the **Air Cargo Terminal**—about a mile from the Passenger Terminal—or leave it with a commercial air freight forwarder.) Arrive at Kai Tak long before your normal check-in time, because it takes time to complete the various airway bills. Payment for such services is required in advance and credit cards are accepted. Your bags will not accompany you on your flight but will usually arrive at your destination 24 hours later. If you want the bags to be on your flight, to avoid two trips to the airport, go to the airport at least 24 to 48 hours before your flight to make such arrangements. Note: Your bags, regardless of when you send them, are collected in the Air Cargo Terminal, not in the passenger baggage collection area.

Departure Transport:

Hotels and travel agents offer regular airport transportation services. Any metered taxi will also gladly make the run to Kai Tak. (See **Transportation** section for charges.) An airport bus service stops every 10 to 20 minutes at major hotels in Central District and Causeway Bay (on Hong Kong Island) and at Tsimshatsui in Kowloon. Some hotels are reluctant to dispense airport bus information because it is the cheapest way of getting to the airport and would interfere with their own airport transportation services. On airport buses, however, there are no individual luggage racks (just a communal baggage bay) and the buses' steps are steep. Travellers with a lot of baggage would probably prefer a taxi or hotel service, because there is no porter service from the curbside bus stops. Route 201 serves Kowloon and the fare is HK$2.50. Route 200 serves Hong Kong Island and its fare is HK$5. Exact change only.

Customs:

Though Hong Kong is a well-known duty-free port, arriving non-resident visitors still face the usual limitations on consumable luxuries: 200 cigarettes, 50 cigars or 250 grams of tobacco; a quart of liquor or spirits; and cosmetics "in reasonable quantities for personal use". The only import duties levied here are on petroleum products and alcohol products (both grog and perfumes). Everything else is duty-free. (The allowances for returning residents is half that of non-residents — 100 cigarettes or 25 cigars or 125 grams of tobacco — plus one bottle of still wine — i.e. no liquor or spirits.)

Hong Kong is also a free money market, so there are no restrictions on the type or amount of money brought in or taken out. (Warning: the next countries you visit might have special monetary rules, so check their restrictions before you leave Hong Kong.

Airport customs officers take a very active interest in drugs and firearms. The worst most tourists can expect is a very stern glance and a few pointed questions, but this interrogation frequently includes full-scale searches, particularly of suspicious young arrivals from Thailand or India. Prescription medicines should always be carried in their original containers. Firearms, live ammunition, knives, spears, bows and arrows must be declared immediately and left in customs custody until departure.

Currency and exchange:

The financial arts are Hong Kong's stock-in-trade. Because it's a strategic centre for international transactions, the colony has banks of every description and there are no local restrictions whatsoever on the import, export, purchase or sale of foreign currency. Anything from credit cards to "black" or "hot" cash can be handled — but there are clearly better and worse ways to go about such money dealings.

Businessmen and tax fugitives notwithstanding, most visitors need not get too bogged down in the esoterica of floating exchange exchange rates. Though the Hong Kong dollar fluctuates, its value is usually around HK$7.80 to a U.S. dollar. Hotel cashiers are handy, often open 24 hours, and as a rule they change either traveller's cheques or major foreign currencies, usually at a slightly higher rate than financial institutions or money-changers.

Legal Tender:

The Hong Kong dollar has a singular distinction: it is the world's last major currency issued not by a government but by local private banks. With unflagging free enterprise, the two leading financial houses here — **The Hongkong and Shanghai Banking Corporation** and **The Standard Chartered** — issue all the colony's paper money, emblazoning notes with grandly stylized views of their own headquarters. The British Queen is confined to coins and one cent notes.

The Hong Kong dollar is divided into 100 cents. There are seven standard bills. Each bank uses a different motif, but all share similar denomination colours: $1000 (gold), $500 (brown), $100 (red), $50 (blue), $20 (orange) and $10 (green). (Note: Due to the changeover of the paper currency, you will find some notes in different sizes and colours.) There is also a small and rarely seen one cent (1¢) note that's only slightly larger than a subway ticket. They are blank on one side and make unique souvenirs. Coins include 5¢, 10¢, 20¢, 50¢, $1, $2 and $5.

Money-Changers:

Many licensed money-changers, usually open from 9 a.m. to late at night, will often accept more obscure foreign notes — at a substantial markdown. Nevertheless, their traveller's cheque and banknote rates are considerably better than those offered by hotels. For large transactions — US$250 or more — exchange rates often can be negotiated to even greater advantage.

Traveller's Cheques:

They are sold here by foreign exchange dealers and banks. European or Japanese traveller's cheques are as acceptable as U.S. dollar cheques. Many small merchants here prefer traveller's cheques to credit cards or hard currency, so hold out for more than the going bank rate during any negotiations involving traveller's cheques.

Credit Cards:

All major cards are accepted. (See section under **Shopping**).

Getting Acquainted

Climate:

A historian recently noted that Hong Kong's weather is "trying for half the year". Foreign residents might agree, but few visitors stay long enough for the weather to become truly oppressive.

In meteorological terms, the climate is tropical (just barely) and monsoonal. Two seasons dominate the year — one consistently hot, wet and humid (the **Southwest Monsoon,** corresponding very roughly to spring/summer), and the other cool and dry (the **Northeast Monsoon,** corresponding to fall/winter). The colony can, however, experience great variations in this general pattern — notably in periods between successive monsoons — and dramatically during **typhoon season.** (The word "typhoon" is derived from Cantonese *dai foo* which means "big wind." It is Asia's version of a Western hurricane.)

Typhoons:

If you are unlucky enough to be here when a full-scale **typhoon** sweeps in from the South China Sea, you will find out first-hand why it was named *dai foo,* or "big wind," in Cantonese. There is not much you can do except slink back to your hotel and have a typhoon party, which is precisely what many Hong Kong residents do in their homes during these Asian hurricanes.

The **Royal Observatory** is modern enough to have early-warning computers and a weather satellite ground station, so no more does the weatherman stand out on the RO's lawn to see which way the clouds are moving. When a typhoon or **"Severe Tropical**

Storm" (which may escalate into a typhoon) comes within a 400-mile radius of the colony, storm signal #1 goes up. The populace is quite blase about a number one signal. A #1 signal can remain aloft for days — sometimes during beautiful pre-storm weather, or be quickly changed to the next important signal #3. Number three is the first real alert because it signifies that winds are reaching speeds of 22 to 33 knots with gusts up to 60 knots.

Never underestimate a typhoon. Too many visitors, mostly from the United States and the Caribbean, probably do because they have seen so many hurricanes. They tend to think typhoons are nothing more than severe rainstorms. A few statistics for the disbelievers. Typhoon Hope in 1979 left 12 dead and 260 injured. Severe Tropical Storm Agnes in 1978 left three dead and 126 injured, and Typhoon Rose, which left the harbour a shambles, claimed 130 lives, 80 on a capsized Hong-Macau ferry. Typhoon Ruby in 1964 killed 120 and Typhoon Wanda in 1962 killed 138.

For information about a typhoon, call the **City & New Territories Department's Typhoon Emergency Number** (Tel: 3-692-255), but do not ring the Royal Observatory, the police or the first brigade, who all are on busy full alert. To find out if the airport is closed, phone 3-769-7531, but rest assured that individual airlines will regularly update you on the details of their own typhoon-disrupted flights.

Dry Monsoons:

The dry monsoon season begins sometime in September, and brings three months of warm (rather than hot) days and usually clear blue skies. Nights are cool, humidity low, and day-to-day temperature changes are slight. October and November are the best months to visit here, and the colony is predictably chock-a-block with visitors at that time. From December through early January, it is still sunny during the day and cool at night. This period signals a gradual shift to less predictable weather.

Beginning with Chinese New Year — late-January to mid-February — the temperature and clear and dry skies alternate with longer spells of cold wind and dank mist that can run unbroken for weeks. Mountaintops occasionally show night-time frost (the appearance of frost is always a headline story in local tabloids), and beaches at this time of the year are largely deserted.

Hong Kong's **rainy season** arrives in earnest about the middle of March, when the temperature rises, humidity thickens and trees grow green. Skies can be consistently gray, and heavy afternoon rainstorms become increasingly common. Though quite changeable, this "spring" season generally stays cool enough to be agreeable with visitors.

Mid May to September is high summer, and also the unpredictable typhoon season. Punctuated by cloudbursts, intense tropical sunshine scorches open land and broils even well-tanned skin. Humidity rarely falls below 90 percent, but temperatures rarely top 32-34°C. Airconditioning eases this steamy torpor, so much so that sweaters are sometimes required indoors.

Average Temperatures and Rainfall:

	Average daily Maximum °F/°C	Average daily Minimum °F/°C	Average daily Rainfall (in./mm)
January	64/18	56/13	1.2/30
February	63/17	55/12.5	1.8/45
March	67/19.5	60/15.5	2.8/70
April	75/24	67/19.5	5.3/133
May	82/28	74/23	11.4/285
June	85/29.5	78/25.5	16.0/400
July	87/30.5	78/25.5	14.5/363
August	87/30.5	78/25.5	14.4/360
September	85/29.5	77/25	10.9/272.5
October	81/27	73/22.5	3.9/98
November	74/23	65/18.5	1.7/43
December	68/20	59/15	1.0/25

For temperature (and time) dial 5-1152

What to Wear and Bring:

Clothing should follow seasons not unlike those in the American Deep South. Dank winter months (January and February) require sweaters, heavy jackets or even a light topcoat. A fickle, cool-to-warm spring (March and April) is best handled with adaptable, all-purpose outfits. High, emphatically tropical summer (May through September) demands the lightest cloths, umbrellas (traditional local models are superb, raincoats a steamy washout) and some sort of protection against fanatic air-conditioning. Much-favoured and dry and temperate fall (October through December) is best suited by middle-weight clothes with perhaps a sweater for cool nights during the later months.

Style of dress is happily more a matter of personal taste than public acceptability. The odd habits of visiting "barbarians" long ago ceased to startle residents, and shorts, sandals and haltertops are as popular locally as they are, for most of the year, practical. Obvious opulence, on the other hand, will impress hotel room-clerks — and inspire pajama-clad merchants to new heights in "tourist" pricing. Any semblance of skirt or coat-and-tie mollifies the handful of hotel restaurants requiring "formal dress".

As in most of the world, working businessmen in Hong Kong wear business clothes. Short-sleeved, perm-prest "safari suits" have taken up some of the slack left by the decline of the rumpled linen suit, but otherwise a crisp, cravatted globetrotter look is — sometimes sweatily — *de rigueur*.

Time Zones:

The International Dateline puts Hong Kong resolutely ahead of most of the world. There is no daylight savings here so Hong Kong remains GMT +8 all year. Go back or forward the specified number of hours to determine standard time (and in some cases today's date) in other places:

Auckland	+4	Mexico City	−14
Athens	−6	Moscow	−5
Bangkok	−1	New Delhi	−2½
Buenos Aires	−11	Ottawa	−13
Cairo	−6	Peking	same
Dacca	−2	Rangoon	−1½
Europe	−7	Singapore	same

Honolulu	−18	Seoul	+1
Jakarta	−1	Sydney	+2
Johannesburg	−6	Taipei	same
Karachi	−3	Tehran	−4½
Kuala Lumpur	same	Tel Aviv	−6
Lagos	−7	Tokyo	+1
London	−8	USA (East)	−13
Macau	same	USA (Central)	−14
Manila	same	USA (Pacific)	−16

Example: If it is noon in Hong Kong, in New York it is midnight the previous evening (−12 hours) in summer or 11 p.m. in winter (−13 hours).

Weights and Measures:

Hong Kong is still making the complicated transition from the Imperial to the metric system of weights and measures. Also, the Chinese have their own methods of weighing and measuring — which are still very much in use today. The following are Chinese-Asian weighing and measuring terms you may encounter here.

Weight

Daam = 100 Catties
Catty (prronounced *gun* in Cantonese) = 16 taels
Tael (pronounced *leung*) = 10 chins
Chin = 10 guns

The terms *catty* and *tael* are quite commonly used in market places. They are equivalent to 1⅓ lbs, and 1⅓ oz respectively. The latter term is also used in gold and silver markets instead of ounce.

Measures

Fortunately, Chinese terms are rarely used here; residents prefer mile, foot and inch, and are gradually accepting kilometre, metre, and etc. For the record, the Chinese version of a mile or kilometer is *lay* (equivalent to 0.3107 mile); a foot is *tchek* (1.0936 feet); and an inch is *tchuen* (1.312 inches).

Electricity:

A 200 volts/50 cycles current will make a fiery mess of the wrong shaver or hairdryer. Most hotels have all-purpose adapters, but be certain before you plug in.

Drinking Water:

The true colonial prefers stronger stuff, the Chinese stick with tea, and many (possibly nostalgic) Western residents insist on boiled or bottled. Nevertheless, both officially and in fact, straight from the tap is perfectly harmless. It's still not a good idea to ask for a glass of water at a street stall in the New Territories, but several decades have passed since hotel guests had to brush their teeth with gin.

Pets:

No animals are allowed into the colony without having them spend half a year in private or government guarantee kennels.

The problem does not usually affect short-time visitors. All queries or pleas should be posted to the

Agriculture & Fisheries Department, Canton Road Government Offices, 12-14th floors, 393 Canton Road, Tsimshatsui, Kowloon, (Tel: 3-688-111, Ext. 255).

Law Enforcement:

The local legal system is very British, but different from Britain's. Its most notable anachronism is punishment by caning for minor offenders. Also, capital punishment is still permissable.

Lawyers here are called barristers and solicitors, due process works as well as in most places and, despite historical precedent by Hong Kong's founding fathers, drug smugglers should not expect particularly kind treatment. The legal languages are English and Cantonese.

The British-administrated Royal Hong Kong Police wear light green uniforms in summer, blue ones in winter, and carry handguns. English speaking officers have a small red tab below their serial numbers.

In emergencies phone 999 — and ask for the police, fire department, or ambulance, as required.

Identification Cards:

In 1980, the Hong Kong government passed legislation requiring everyone to carry a Hong Kong identity card. If you are going to remain here for more than 180 days, you must register for a Hong Kong identity card within 30 days of arrival. Such ID cards are issued by the Immigration (see Appendix A for address).

As the law is now written, visitors are required to have some form of identification. If you prefer to keep your passport in the hotel's safe deposit box, some other document with a photo (driver's licence or the like) will suffice. This is especially necessary if you are going out to the New Territories or one of the outlying islands.

Banks:

Local banking hours are now in the process of gradual extension, but 9:00 a.m. to 4:30 p.m. on weekdays, and 9 a.m. to noon Saturdays (closed Sundays) are normal business hours for foreign exchange services.

Personal Cheques:

Personal cheques will be of little use here, even at a local branch of the issuing bank back home (unless prior arrangements have been made). There are some shopkeepers who won't let such paper complications stand in the way of a good sale, but most will probably laugh.

Overseas Remittances:

Receiving money from overseas is a minor but sometimes unavoidable hassle. The simplest, fastest and surest money transfer agents here are the major international banks — preferably one from the traveller's home country, and ideally one where a regular checking or savings account is maintained (see the "Commercial" phone book's yellow pages). Your bank's local staff can explain various options, but the easiest procedure is to have a friend or relative make a deposit in your home bank and instruct that institution to relay funds to a particular bank or related bank branch in Hong Kong. To avoid delays, your full name, passport number and address should be included with the transfer document. You also should know to which bank the money is coming and should inform the bank of your pending cash transfer. If you accept all or part of your money in Hong Kong dollars, and the rest in traveller's cheques, you will get a better deal than if you receive all the money in foreign currency. (A minimum surcharge of HK$25 is usually charged for the latter.)

Passport Photos:

Need a quick passport photo? Though there are many photo shops which provide half day or one day service, you will soon discover there are handy coin-operated photo machines at most major Mass Transit Railway Station. The three most well-known ones are in the **Transport Department,** Murray Road, Hong Kong, the **Immigration Department,** and the **YMCA Salisbury Road** (near the Star Ferry, next to the Peninsula Hotel), Tsimshatsui, both in Kowloon. Price: HK$5-10 for four photos.

Embassies and Consular Services

Aside from complaints regarding lost passports, vanished funds and assorted legal troubles, foreign embassies also provide the only authoritative advice on what you can buy and how much you can take back home. They can advise you about duties, tariffs and how much that "bargain" jade necklace you covet is likely to cost.

These embassies are also the all-important dispensers of visas, a bureaucratic shoal on which more than one unplanned trip has foundered. Those travelling on in Asia will do well to utilize efficient and business-like Hong Kong for setting passport matters in order.

Because Hong Kong is a colony, not a country, demanding to speak to the "ambassador" will require a phone call to another country. However, the consulates and, for British Commonwealth countries, commissions listed in Appendix A can handle most normal problems raised by travellers.

The only exception to the above is the British. Because this is their colony, there is no Britannic diplomatic mission, as such, Holders of United Kingdom passports, or those planning to visit England or any British possession or Commonwealth country not represented here, should refer visa and other travel queries to the **Overseas Visa Section** of the **Hong Kong Immigration Department.**

For a list of foreign embassies, their addresses and telephone numbers, please refer to relevant section in Appendix A.

Tourist Information

The Hong Kong Tourist Association:

The Hong Kong Tourist Association (HKTA) is a bubbling fount of information—verbally or in the form of numerous brochures advising about everything from eating and shopping to hiking and horseraces. Frontline HKTA staff seem genuinely interested in helping visitors.

For brochures, maps or basic questions-and-answers, as well as souvenirs and gifts, the HKTA has walk-in visitors' centres at Kai Tak Airport (just outside customs) at the Kowloon Star Ferry Concourse (8 a.m. to 6 p.m., weekends till 1 p.m.), Empire Centre, East Tsimshatsui, Kowloon (9 a.m. to 6 p.m. daily) and in Connaught Centre, 35th floor (8 a.m. to 6 p.m. Saturdays till 1 p.m.) on Hong Kong Island. The centre at the airport stays open from 8 a.m. to 10:30 p.m. daily. For elusive addresses, lost directions and train or ferry schedules, there is also a telephone enquiries service: Tel: 5-244-191 or 3-722-5555 (from 8 a.m. to 6 p.m. weekdays, 8 a.m. to 1 p.m. Saturdays and Sundays). For really serious questions—notably shopping complaints—the best bet is to contact HKTA Headquarters on the 35th floor of Connaught Centre.

The HKTA *Official Guidebook* (updated monthly) is a bit commercial, but is still a good information source (for HK$10). Many hotels also offer this book free with their own name and logo printed on the cover.

Overseas, the HKTA maintains offices in Chicago, Frankfurt, London, New York, Osaka, Paris, Rome, San Francisco, Singapore, Sydney and Tokyo, plus all Cathay Pacific Airways offices.

Information Sources

Other sources of information on Hong Kong are the **Hong Kong Publications Centre** in the General Post Office Building, Hong Kong Island (9 a.m. to 6 p.m., Saturdays till 1 p.m.) and the **Urban Council Publication Centre** in Club Lusitano, Ice House Street, Central, Hong Kong (9 a.m. to 5:30 p.m., Saturdays till 12:30 p.m.)

Other information lodes are the **Community Advice Bureau,** (St. John's Cathedral, Garden Road, Central, Hong Kong, Tel: 5-245-444). This association is normally for residents, but they will assist if they can. Also try the **Trade Development Council** (Great Eagle Centre, 31st floor, 23 Harbour Road, Hong Kong. Tel: 51-1833-4333), used mainly by businessmen, but helpful.

Royal Hong Kong Police Force officers who speak English wear red tabs under their numbers (worn on the shoulder). The RHKRF officers wear light green uniforms in summer, blue in winter.

For emergency assistance, the **telephone numbers for Police, fire or Ambulance is 999.**

For serious problems that may require a friend rather than a police officer, call the **Samaritans** at

Tel: 5-278-484 or 5-278-489. They speak English and answer phone calls 24 hours a day. The Alcoholics Anonymous branch in Hong Kong can be reached on 5-812-7244 and 5-225665. If you are a serviceman, the **Sailors and Soldiers Home** is on the 3rd floor, 22 Hennessy Road, Wanchai, Hong Kong.

For time and temperature dial 5-1152. The Consumer Council (Asian House, 3rd floor, 1 Hennessy Rd., Tel: 5-748297) may be of help in altercations with shopkeepers. So may the Tele-Law Service (5-213333/7).

Transportation

Getting around Hong Kong is much easier than it seems. Though Cantonese is the language spoken by 98 percent of the population, English is also widely used (if only for English place names which differ from their Cantonese counterparts). It helps, however, to have an address or item written out in Chinese characters by a friend or hotel employee.

Transportation to Shenzhen Special Economic Zone & Port of Shekou, P.R.C. For tourists heading to Shenzhen (also called Shum Chun), China's first and largest and wealthiest Special Economic Zone (SEZ), and the adjacent oil port of Shekou, is dead easy because the travel agency does all the work. However, if you prefer to go on your own, whether as a tourist or a businessperson, it can be done.

Buses:

Hong Kong has numerous scheduled buses and bus routes to just about every corner of the colony. **China Motor Buses** are blue whilst **Kowloon Motor Buses** are red. With the advent of the cross-harbour tunnel routes, however, they commute on each other's turf. Bus fares range from HK$1 to $4. There are too many routes to list here, but two that are used frequently by tourists are the two airport buses (see **Airport Transportation** notes) and buses to Repulse Bay Beach and other places on the South side of the island. The deluxe (no standing) buses to Repulse Bay Beach are numbers 260 and 262 and cost HK$4. (There is a convenient bus stop in front of the Hong Kong side Star Ferry Terminal.) The number six bus plies the same route for HK$2.50, but they are regular buses, usually packed like sardine cans during the summer. For either bus, sit on the top deck and enjoy the scenic and swaying ride. Exact change only.

For buses to Shenzhen, the Chinese Special Economic Zone on the border, contact Citybus (China) Ltd., 3-722-4866. They run both double-decker buses and air-conditioned coaches (HK$17-40, depending on the day destination within the SEZ). They also run day tours (HK$385 including visas and lunch). Hong Kong's Kowloon Canton Railway runs to the border (Lo Wu) many times daily for HK$10 second class, HK$20 first class. (Call 0-606-9600 for information.) Here, you cross the border on foot. Be prepared for crowds whose pushing and shoving is so renown they may make it an Olympic sport. The border is at Shenzhen and you take a bus or taxi to

Shekou, about 30 kms away. Citybus (China) Ltd. runs both double-decker buses (Route 500) and all-conditioned coaches daily to Shenzhen (HK$17-40, depending on the day and destination within the SEZ). They also run day tours (HK$385 including visas and lunch). 24 hour visa service. Call 3-722-4866 for information.

The Miramar Hotel has a fleet of 10 chauffeur-driven, seven-seater/cars which run between Hong Kong and Shenzhen (2 hours)/Shekou (3 hours). Hire car rates are HK$830 one way, HK$1,180 same day return and HK$2,150 overnight return. To Shekou, the fees are HK$900, $1,250 and $2,250 respectively. The service is not restricted to hotel guests and you have to make your own visa arrangements. Call 3-681111 ext. 2 for information.

The resorts in the SEZ, which are well off the beaten track, often have their own buses direct from Hong Kong or which meet the public transport in the SEZ.

There is also a hovercraft service from Hong Kong departing from Kowloon's Taikoktsui Ferry Pier (three sailings, call 3-929345 for information) or the old Macau Ferry Terminal on Hong Kong Island (four sailings, call 5-448052 for information). The one-way fare from either terminal is HK$35.

Transportation to Port of Zuhai Special Economic Zone (SEZ):

The Special Economic Zone of Zuhai is another oil exploration port, like the aforementioned Shekou, only this one is near Macau. There is a six-time daily "jetcat" service leaving from Hong Kong Island's old Macau Ferry Terminal, next to the Shun Tak Centre, direct to this SEZ. The one-class fares are HK$70 on weekdays, HK$80 on weekends and public holidays. Daylight service only. Call 5-232136. It is only a 30 minute ride from Zuhai to Macau.

Minibuses and Maxicabs:

Yellow 14-seater vans with a red stripe—called minibuses here—ply all the main routes and make unscheduled stops and charge variable fares. There is a sign in the front indicating their destinations and fare charges. To complicate matters, other yellow 14-seater vans with a green stripe and roof—called **maxicabs**—run on fixed routes at fixed prices. There is a special maxicab to The Peak (HK$3) and another to Ocean Park (HK$3). The maxi-bus terminal in Central is on the eastern side of the Star Ferry carpark.

Trams:

On Hong Kong island there are trams running along the north shore from west to east (and vice versa) which pass through the main tourist areas of Central, Wanchai, Causeway Bay and Taikao Shingui Quarry Bay. The cost is only 60 Hong Kong cents (exact change). Sit on the upper deck and watch the real Hong Kong bump and grind by. (See "Tripping By Tram" feature article.)

The Peak Tram:

Hong Kong's other "tram" is the **Peak Tram**, which is not a tram at all but a funicular railway up to The

Peak. It is a form of regular local commuter transport and a favourite "tourist attraction." The funicular rises 1,305 feet above sea level in about 10 minutes on a steep journey over 4,500 feet of track. The fare is HK$4 and travel hours are from 7 a.m. to midnight. The **Lower Peak Tram Station** in Central District is on Garden Road, up from the Hilton Hotel and across from the U.S. Consulate. A free topless double-decker shuttle bus service operates between the Lower Station and the Star Ferry from 9 a.m. to 7 p.m. daily at 20 minute intervals. There are five intermediate stations before you reach the **Upper Peak Tram Station** nestled underneath the **Peak Tower,** a futuristic building on stilts that houses a European restaurant and the Peak Tower Village with stalls full of Chinese handicrafts.

The Mass Transit Railway (MTR):

The most dramatic change in Hong Kong's public transportation scene is the fully air-conditioned **Mass Transit Railway,** commonly called the **MTR,** which in other countries might be called and Underground, Tube, Metro or Subway. The 38.6 kilometer system has three lines with 37 stations, stretching from industrial Kwun Tong (Kowloon) land Tsuen Wan (New Territories) through some of Kowloon's most populated areas, underneath Nathan Road to the Tsimshatsui tourist and entertainment district, and under the harbour to Central, the governmental and financial centre of the colony and along the north shore of Hong Kong Island. (With the MTR, it is easy to reach many of the favourite tourist areas on the island, particularly Wanchai, Causeway Bay and Taikoo Shing.) The longest trip takes less than 60 minutes and fares range from HK$2-5. The four minute cross-harbour trip is only HK$3.50. You can use the MTR for shopping or sightseeing trips that previously could only be made on crowded and hot buses. The MTR is open 6 a.m. to 1 a.m. the following morning daily. See the *MTR Guide* for subway directions. For tourists really on the go, the HK$15 "Tourist Ticket" is good value.

A few points before you go charging underground. First, there are no toilets down there, and smoking, drinking and eating are prohibited. The ticket machines take exact change, but there are change booths where you can break notes. After placing money in a ticket machine, you receive a magnetic plastic card about the size of a credit card. This is placed in a slot by the turnstile for entry. Upon departure, the card is again placed in a turnstile. The amount you paid is electronically calculated, and if you paid enough, you may pass through the exit turnstile.

You will see signs warning about HK$1,000 fines for "ticket flickers" caught in the act. Ticket flickers are people who flick the plastic cards on their nails. In case you thought that Hong Kong has been forced to do something about noise pollution (imagine thousands of commuters ticket-flicking during rush hour), you are wrong. "Ticket-flicking" is banned because the MTR found it damaged the fare cards. A last MTR warning: the MTR's shiny metal seats are slipper so be prepared to slide when the train starts up. The crossover with the railway is at Kowloon Tong Station.

The Kowloon-Canton Railway:

The old **Kowloon-Canton Railway** is now a modern electrified commuter train because the three through trains to Canton are now Chinese-operated. There are nine stops on this 22 mile segment through Kowloon and the NT. Fares range from HK$1.50-10 second class, double for first class. Don't worry about inadvertently chug-chugging into China. Before the train enters the (Hong Kong) restricted zone after the Sheung Shui Station, police check to see if you have a China visa. Note: There are no toilets on the Hong Kong trains, but there are such facilities on Chinese trains. The main railway station is in Hung Hom, Kowloon, and there is direct passenger ferry service to that station from the Star Ferry in Central District. Tel: 0-606-9600 for information.

The Star Ferry:

You can always tell the tourists from the residents on Hong Kong's most famous mode of transportation, the **Star Ferry.** The tourists are agog at the magnificent site of the world's third busiest harbour—and one of the best natural harbours in the world—as the double-bowed, green and white, two-decker ferries weave their way through the 0.8 nautical mile course between Hong Kong and Tsimshatsui (Kowloon).

The residents, on the other hand, are quite content to spend the seven minute sea voyage with their noses tucked into their newspapers or racing sheets. Upper deck, first class seats cost the princely sum of 70 Hong Kong cents and the view of the harbour from there will delight any shutter-bug. A more exciting ride (because you are closer to the water racing past) is in second class seats on the lower deck; a ride there costs only 50 Hong Kong cents.

Walla-Wallas:

After the MTR closes at 1 a.m. and the Star Ferry at 11:30, you can still ride across the harbour in a small motorboat called a **walla-walla** (supposedly named for the hometown—Walla-Wall, Washington, USA—of this craft's original owner. You can also take a taxi or bus through the cross-harbour tunnel, but if you are staying in Tsimshatsui and end up in Central—or vice versa—the direct cross-harbour water route by Star Ferry, MTR or walla-walla is the fastest and cheapest means of transportation. On Hong Kong Island, walla-wallas are located at Queen's Pier to the East of the Star Ferry concourse (to the right as you face the harbour, in front of City Hall) while in Kowloon, they are located at Kowloon Public Pier, (to the left of the Star Ferry as you face the water, opposite the Ocean Terminal). The cost is HK$4.50 per person or HK$45 for an entire boat if you are impatient.

Local Ferries:

There are other ferry services from the Star Ferry, Wanchai and North Point Piers (on Hong Kong) to various destinations in Kowloon, but these are primarily commuter ferries, rarely taken by visitors.

Inter-Island Ferries:

There are 236 islands in the colony (Hong Kong Island of course is just one of them). A convenient **inter-island ferries** transportation system is in operation here to service many of them. At the **Outlying Districts Ferry Pier,** Connaught Road, Central, Hong Kong, you'll find double and triple-decker ferries — some with air-conditioning — that regularly travel to the outlying islands. The routes and times are too numerous to mention here, but there is regular service — quite crowded during weekends and holidays — to Lantau, Cheung Chau and Lamma islands (the big three) and many of the colony's smaller isles. Fares range from HK$4-11, Fare charges vary from children prices to adult ordinary and deluxe.

The Hong Kong Tourist Association has a complete schedule of all ferry services and will answer telephone queries at 5-244-191 or 3-722-5555 or The **Hong Kong and Yaumatei Ferry Company's** enquiry number is 5-423081.

Taxis:

Have you been introduced to Hong Kong's "national flag" yet? Facetious local wags, tired of fighting for taxis — and being extorted by them during rush hours or holiday periods or late at night — have nicknamed the dirty "vacant" ragflag (supposedly signifying the driver is off duty) as Hong Kong's national standard because of its pesky ubiquitousness. Metered taxis in urban areas are red with silver roofs and the dome atop the roof is lit at night when the taxi is unoccupied. (There are also green and white taxis restricted to the New Territories (NT) and these run on a different — and cheaper — fare system.)

The taxi flagfall costs HK$5 for the first two kilometers and 70 Hong Kong cents for each subsequent 266 metres. Waiting time is 70 Hong Kong cents for every two minutes. (The green and white NT taxis have a HK$3.30 flagfall with a subsequent rate of 70 Hong Kong cents for each 400 metres.) Urban taxis are allowed to charge a HK$20 surcharge for passage through the cross-harbour tunnel, plus HK$1 for each piece of luggage or large package. There is a HK$3 surcharge for the Aberdeen Tunnel. Note: If you have any trouble with a taxi — say you are victimized, overcharged or you have left your wallet in the back seat — contact the Royal Hong Kong Police special "taxi hotline" at Tel: 5-277-177. (Don't forget to record the taxi's number!) If a complaint is not resolved, you must be prepared to appear as a witness to the police prosecution. In most cases, the courts will push a tourist's case to the front of its judicial queues to make an example of the offender. The Hong Kong Tourist Association has a bilingual "Communication Card" to make life easier.

Some taxis are equipped with mobile telephones to phone anywhere in the colony. Charges are HK$2 per minute , in addition to the fare.

Self-Drive and Chauffeured Cars:

Rental cars, with or without drivers, are also available. The familiar self-drive names of **Avis, Hertz** and **Budget** are here, along with a couple of dozen

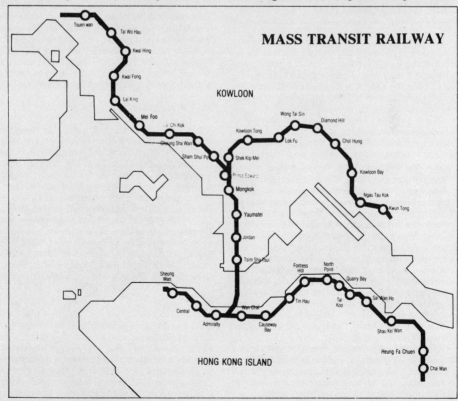

MASS TRANSIT RAILWAY

KOWLOON

HONG KONG ISLAND

local firms. Those under 18 cannot hire any motor vehicles (including cycles and scooters). All visitors with a valid overseas driving licence, however, can drive here for a year. Hotels, through their own transportation services, can usually handle requests for **chauffeur-driven cars.**

Rickshaws:

Hong Kong still has a small number of **rickshaws** that congregate around Star Ferry concourses on both sides of the harbour. Tourists hire the rickshaws more to pose for pictures than as transportation, but the unofficial "official" rate is HK$20 for five minutes. However, because rickshaw-pullers refuse to budge without a round of bartering, the price extracted from visitors is usually more. In one recent incident, a wily puller dashed off with someone who only wanted to have a picture taken. He ran once around the Star Ferry car park, demanded HK$160, and was supported by loud shouting and intimidation by other rickshaw lads. Such intimidation usually happens to elderly tourists. If such problems occur in Kowloon, go to the Police Reporting Centre in the Star Ferry Concourses on either side of the harbour. The price for posing for a picture is between HK$20 to $30, depending on how hard you bargain.

Accommodation

Whether to stay in Hong Kong or Kowloon is a long-standing debate with die-hard aficionados of both harbour sides. Money is not a factor. The best-heeled (at The Peninsula) and shoestring travellers (in the YMCA or Chungking Mansions) are next-door neighbours in Kowloon, though these digs are decidedly, well, different.

Access to shops and restaurants is also not a consideration. Both sides of the harbour are commercially endowed. The Mass Transit Railway (MTR) connects various parts Kowloon and Hong Kong Island in minutes, as does the Star Ferry.

Despite certain Hong Kong advantages, most people end up in Kowloon's Tsimshatsui District — probably because it has most of the colony's hotels. Kowloon also has the gaudiest, most aggressive and sexually free tourist ambience (almost 24 hours a day).

Hong Kong's Central District is considerably more restrained, because it is the business, financial and government centre. Though there is good shopping in Central, it closes at dusk. Hong Kong's Causeway Bay, however, features a wide range of accommodations, late-night shopping and eating. And between Central and Causeway Bay is the "Suzie Wong" bar district of Wanchai, rife with honky-tonk local colour and just down the tram-line from either Central or Causeway Bay.

A listing of hotels complete down through the ranks is found in Appendix A. Rate categories are based on the cheapest single rates, but remember that all hotels add a 10 percent service charge and five percent room tax to all quoted room tariffs.

Cheap Sleeps:

Like the Amir Kabir in Tehran or Bangkok's Malaysia Hotel, Hong Kong has its place that is *the* place for impecunious travellers: the **Chungking Mansions.** At 40 Nathan Road, Tsimshatsui, Kowloon — in the shadow of the lordly Peninsula — the CM rabbit warren offers a huge, sometimes strange, "high"-rise collection of hostels, dormitories, "guest houses" and mini-hotels. None are rock-bottom cheap, except in the peak visitor season (roughly June through September). Fierce intramural competition for guests gives the footloose considerable bargaining power.

The cream of the Mansions' crop are in "A" block, the first of four crash complexes encountered past the dingy, arcaded front entrance. **International Guest House** (9th & 10th floors, Tel: 3-664-256) and **Chungking House** (4th & 5th floors, Tel: 3-665-362) are both quite respectable, offering optional air-con, TV, room service and laundry. Doubles at either start around HK$130, with lower rates for longer terms.

Prices tend to drop moving further back along the line of lifts. "B" and "D" blocks have dozens of small places with names like **Astor, Columbia, Boston** and **New York,** and room prices in the HK$35 range. Cheapest are the hostels, notably **Woodstock** (7th floor, "D" block), where a bed in a sex-segregated dorm room goes for about HK$10. Although many of the places offer cooking facilities (including refrigerators), throughout the Mansions there are numerous small, cheap eating places, including some quite authentic Indian "messes."

There are six youth hostels, four in the New Territories, one each on Lantau and Hong Kong Islands. The cost is only HK$10. See the **Hong Kong Youth Hostel Association,** A Block, 14th floor, Rm. 1408, Watson's Estate, North Point, Hong Kong. Tel: 5-700-985. (Note: The hostels are quite full during the summer school holidays and you must be members of the International Federation of Youth Hostels.)

Student Amenities:

In addition to discount air tickets, the **Hong Kong Student Travel Bureau** offers limited accommodation services. Holders of official international student, teacher or youth identity cards can get advice, assistance in booking, access to local university facilities and, occasionally, preferential hotel rates by visiting the bureau's office at 1024 Star House, 10th floor, just off the Star Ferry Concourse in Kowloon (Tel: 3-721-3269). If you have an **International Youth Hostel** card, you will be eligible for their accommodations and activities. Write c/o Hong Kong Youth Hostel Association. A Block, 14th floor, Watson's Estate, North Point, Hong Kong (Tel: 5-700-985). (Note: facilities are quite crowded during the summer.)

Island Sleeps:

Lantau Island is a favourite place for the Hong Kong people to get away from it all. Visitors, if they visit the island at all, usually do it in one day. However, there are a variety of places to stay on the island, two in monasteries. Some of these "sleeps" are quite cheap — under HK$50 — and some are hotels offering cottages or full "units" (suites sleeping four or six with kitchen facilities). Note: Reserve well in advance.

Cheung Chau Warwick – Tung Wan, Cheung Chau Island, Hong Kong. Tel: 5-981-0081. For those who really want to get away from it all in first-class style. About HK$400 upwards.

Cheung Sha Resort – c/o Wah Nam Travel Service, 3rd fl., Eastern Commercial Centre, 397 Hennessy Rd., Hong Kong. Tel: 5-891-1161. (units sleeping six – HK$200-350.)

Lantau Tea Gardens – Tel: 5-985-8161. (units sleeping 2-6, HK$120-230).

Po Lin Monastery – Nong Ping, Lantau Island, Hong Kong. Tel: 5-985-7426. (dormitory accommodation HK$70, including three vegetarian meals.)

Sea Breeze Hotel – Pui O Village, Lantau Island, Hong Kong Tel: 5-984-7977 (rooms only HK$160-270.)

Silvermine Beach Hotel – Silvermine Bay, Mui Wo, Lantau Island, Hong Kong. Tel: 5-984-8295. About HK$242-368.

Warwick Hotel – BF East Bay (Tung Wan) Cheung Chaw, Hong Kong, Tel: 5-981-0081 (HK$250-350).

Communications

Mail:

Hong Kong's post offices feature portraits of the Queen and reliable, usually efficient service. Air letters normally take four or five days to Europe or Australia, six to eight to most destinations in the United States and Canada. Surface packages can vary anywhere from three weeks to three months.

The most complete and convenient facility is Hong Kong-side's **General Post Office**. Located just off the Star Ferry Concourse, the gleaming white G.P.O. has a full range of package and letter services, including a philatelic window and a ground-floor "General Delivery" counter (Poste Restante, G.P.O., Hong Kong). Outside working hours (8 a.m. to 6 p.m. daily, closed Sundays and public holidays), the G.P.O.'s stamp machines and letter slots are open round-the-clock.

For large and delicate items, there are reliable commercial packing and shipping firms, with **Crown-Pacific** perhaps the best-known. For those doing things themselves, the G.P.O. information number (Tel: 5-231071) can detail the various regulations on packaging, contents and size.

1st class airmail (letter & postcards)

	First 10 grams	Each Additional 10 grams
Asia west through Afghanistan	HK$1.30	80¢
Rest of the world	HK$1.70	90¢

2nd class airmail (unsealed letters & printed matter)

	First 10 grams	Each Additional 10 grams
Asia west through Afghanistan	HK 80¢	50¢
Rest of the world	HK$1.20	70¢

Airletters (Aerogrammes)
Anywhere: HK$1

Air Parcels (excluding insurance, registration etc.)

	First 500 grams	Each Additional 500 grams
USA (excluding Hawaii)	HK$37	$26
Australia (excluding W.A.)	HK$51	$20
UK	HK$63	$21

Registration: HK$5
Express (Special Delivery): HK$4
Speedpost (guaranteed 24 hour delivery): On demand to certain countries at varying prices. Check at the General Post Office or the Kowloon Central Post Office.
Surface Parcels (excluding insurance, registration etc.)

	1 kilo	3 kilos	5 kilos	10 kilos
U.S.A.	HK$30	$65	$105	$190
Australia	HK$40	$55	$80	$115
U.K.	HK$55	$75	$100	$140

Phones and Cables:

Communications to, from and within the colony work with commendable efficiency. Geared to the needs of an internationally oriented business community, the completely – if at times somewhat halting – bilingual systems are all operated by **Cable & Wireless Ltd.**, with offices all over Hong Kong.

Local Calls:

Phone numbers have five, six, seven or even eight digits plus an area code: "3" for Kowloon, "5" for Hong Kong and most islands, "0" for the New Territories. The outlying islands use the "5" prefix plus "981" (Cheung Chau), "982" (Lamma) and "984" or "987" (Lawtan). As in most places, *the area code is dropped when calling within a given area.*

For directory listings, the English-language phonebooks – three residential (one for each area code), one commercial, including standard-model "Yellow Pages" – are often a better bet than wrangling with the information operators (dial 108). In a pinch, the Hong Kong Tourist Association's enquiries service, Tel: 5-244191 or 3-722-5555, can handle many local problems. For operated assisted calls (plus direct dial to China) dial 011; collect, conference or ship to shore 011; book or delayed international calls 015; and direct dialling enquiries 013.

Because there is no long-distance within the colony and subscribers get unlimited free calls, most restaurants and shops allow use of their phones without charge.

Pay phones, which are pink and quite rare outside hotel lobbies and the Star Ferry terminals, take one **HK$1** coin for the first three minutes.

The emergency police/fire/ambulance number is 999 – no coin needed from public phones.

An ear-rattling *wai* is the standard Cantonese telephone greeting. Though seemingly rude to most Western ears, the nearest translation is simply "Hello?"

Overseas Calls:

International calls can be placed through hotel switchboards (which usually add a 10 percent service fee unless they are direct dialed) or directly with **Cable & Wireless** at one of its several public offices:

Central District: Exchange Square, Connaught Place (near the Furama Hotel). Open 24 hours, Tel: 5-237939.

Tsimshatsui: Ocean Terminal (just off the Star Ferry Concourse, Kowloon). Open 8 a.m. to midnight, Tel: 3-676-901. Hermes House, 10 Middle Road. 3-732-9293 Open 24 hours daily.

Causeway Bay: Lee Gardens Hotel, Hysan Avenue. Open 10 a.m. to 1 p.m., 2 p.m. to 6 p.m. Monday through Friday: 10 a.m. to 3 p.m. Saturday. Tel: 5-770-577.

Kai Tak Airport: Passenger Terminal Building. Open 8:30 a.m. to 10 p.m. Monday through Saturday, noon to 7 p.m. Sunday. Tel: 3-769-7914.

Minimum three-minute calls to the United States, Canada, and Australia cost HK$63, France and West Germany HK$72, and the United Kingdom HK$60. *Since overseas connections are often delayed 15 minutes to an hour, calls for a particular hour should be booked in advance.*

Cables and Telex:

As with overseas phone calls, these may be placed either through hotels or at any of the Cable & Wirless offices listed above.

And page 282 for the proverbial "Singing Telegram" dial 5-245-109. This will let loose a gorilla or a Playboy bunny or Rambo or Chippendale-type or a leopard lady vamp—the list goes on and on—to personally sing your greetings to the lucky recipient, be it birthday or otherwise. The cost is HK$400 (plus transport).

News Media

Newspapers:

There are 51 Chinese newspapers—though most are referred to as the "mosquito press" and concentrate on either horseracing or sex—and two English local dailies—**The South China Morning Post and Hong Kong Standard.** Two international English-language dailies—**The Asian Wall Street Journal** and **The International Herald Tribune**—are also printed here.

The SCM Post and **The Standard** publish a great deal of international news, more than you would expect for a daily in Hong Kong, and the two international dailies contain almost all the worldwide news.

Magazines:

Hong Kong is one of Asia's major printing and publishing centres, so you will find a plethora of magazines—495 to be exact; 322 in Chinese, 126 in English and 47 bi-lingual. Asia editions of **Time** and **Newsweek** are printed here, as is the **Reader's Digest.** Regional news magazines such as **Far Eastern Economic Review** and **Asiaweek** also originate here.

Foreign Media:

If that is not enough to keep you informed, overseas editions of many foreign papers and magazines are flown in daily. Unfortunately, they are quite expensive.

The best way to beat exorbitant print media prices is to go to the Star Ferry Concourse, Kowloon-side. As you face the entrance, turn left and walk along the row of news vendors there. You will soon find a woman who has an excellent selection of used foreign newspapers in all languages—most only slightly crumpled, perhaps only a day old and available by late evening on the same day they arrive. This lady, according to local rumour, has a contact with the cleaners at Kai Tak Airport. Her cleaners remove already-read foreign papers from the planes, iron them and pass them off—freshly re-pressed—for re-sale.

Television Stations:

There are two television stations—**Asia Television Ltd. (ATV)** and **Hong Kong Television Broadcasts Ltd. (TVB)**—broadcasting on four channels. Each has an English-language and a Cantonese-language channel. Overseas news—including daily satellite feeds—is commonly included in their news programmes. The weekly guide to events and TV in Hong Kong is called **Television & Entertainment Times.** (HK$6).

Radio:

There are only three radio stations: the government-operated **Radio-Television Hong Kong (RTHK)** (which carries **BBC** world service feeds), **Commercial Radio** and the **British Forces Broadcasting Services (BFBS).** Hong Kong has a total of nine commercial radio channels that programme everything from contemporary pop on AM bands to magnificent interludes of classical music on FM. RTHK has five channels—two in Englsih, two in Chinese and one bilingual. (Two of RTHK's stations are FM.) Commercial Radio has three AM channels—two in Chinese and one in English. BFBS has only one channel; it broadcasts two-thirds of its programmes in Nepali, one-third in English.

Health and Emergencies

Hong Kong's once well-deserved reputation as a "Whiteman's grave" went out with pirates and the end of the opium trade. Standards of health and medicine today compare fully with the West, and aside from the obvious (see **Gastric Unrest** below) travellers need take no particular precautions.

Chemists (Pharmacies):

Don't panic if you have suddenly discovered that you've run out of your urgently needed prescription medicine. Hong Kong has modern chemists or dispensaries (as they are called here), and you will not have to make do with ground seahorse or some other traditional remedy. The main Western pharmacies are **Watson's The Chemists** (Melbourne Plaza, Hilton

Hotel and Hutchison House, all in Central, Hong Kong, and at the Ocean Centre and New World Centre in Tsimshatsui, Kowloon), **Manning Dispensary** (Perkins Road, Repulse Bay, Causeway Bay and the Landmark, all in Hong Kong), **Colonial Dispensary** (Landmark, Central, Hong Kong) and the **Victoria Dispensary** (Theatre Lane, Central, Hong Kong).

There are also hundreds of Chinese medicine companies which accept prescriptions and usually stock both Western and Asian medicines. These, however, should not be confused with traditional herbalists (with whom they sometimes share premises). Herbalists will happily sell you a dried sea-horse, a bit of rhinocerous horn, deer's antler, tiger's penis and a selection of special herbs—all prepared while you wait.

Hospitals:

In descending order of price, the most notable private hospitals are **Matilda** (on Mt. Kellett Road, The Peak, Hong Kong), **Canossa** (1 Old Peak Road, above Central District, Hong Kong), **The Baptist Hospital** (222 Waterloo Road, Kowloon, Tel: 3-374-141), and the **Adventist**. None are cheap, but all are comfortable and offer highest quality specialists and facilities.

For serious accidents or real emergencies, 24-hour casualty wards are operated by **Queen Mary** (Pokfulam Road, Pokfulam, Hong Kong, Tel: 5-819-2111), **Queen Elizabeth** (Wylie Road off Gascoigne Road, Kowloon. Tel: 3-710-2111), **Princess Margaret** (Lai King Shan Road, Laichikok, Tel: 3-742-7111) and **Prince of Wales** (Shatin, New Territories. Tel: 0-636-2211) hsopitals, the four leading government-run institutions. Stays at either, though a bit rough-and-ready, are again in the bargain class.

Clinics:

For the walking wounded, clinics are a practical and economical alternative, most offering the basic range of specialists in-house. The **Hong Kong Adventist Hospital** (40 Stubbs Road at Wongneichung Road, above Happy Valley, Hong Kong, Tel: 5-746-211) operates an expat-staff out-patient department Sunday through Friday-noon, and also has a good dental clinic with 24-hour emergency service. **Anderson & Partners** and **Vio & Partners, Drs. Oram & Howard,** all have clinics on both sides of the harbour. (See telephone directory.)

The undoubted bargain ($5 for consultation, $5 for treatment, plus a few hours' waiting in line) are the more than 50 **government clinics** (also called **Jockey Club Clinics**) scattered around town (see Medical & Health Department in official government listings at the start of the telephone directory).

Private Practice Physicians:

Though many people still prefer traditional cures for minor ills, modern Western practices dominate the field. Most doctors took all or part of their training overseas (usually in Britain, north America, Australia or New Zealand), and the medical and dental professions together include several score expatriates. Private physician's fees as well tend to be internationally scaled, particularly room visits by hotel doctors (either resident or on-call at most), which can

run to $100 or more. Office consulations are generally less than half of that, specialist treatment (normally by reterral only) sometimes more.

Acupuncturists:

Not every one accepts this traditional type of Chinese medicine so you will have to make up your own mind whether the needle treatment is for you. There are many clinics in Hong Kong, but few practitioners who speak English or take the time to explain the treatment to a visitor. One who does is Robert Cheung, Room 322 Caroline Mansion, 4 Yun Ping Rd., Causeway Bay, Hong Kong. Tel: 5-767789. He practices both acupunction and acupressure, and in fact runs courses on them in English.

Gastric Unrest:

In hotels and main-line restaurants (including all those named in these pages), health standards hold up well against any in the world. Order what you like, and worry more about the various glutton's maladies than some indescribable Oriental dysentery.

Off the beaten path, things predictably become more problematic—but rarely exceed even the newest China hand's powers of discretion. Assuming one conquers the obvious oddities (the shirtless chef, the shoeless waiter, the chicken gizzards *et al*), an obvious question arises: how much local colour is too much? The buzz of a hundred flies is one standard bad sign, as is food served tepid rather than steaming hot. Lack of a refrigerator means nothing in itself, because most Chinese prefer "warm" (freshly killed) meat. A quick glance at the raw ingredients never hurts. As more positive steps, go where the locals seem to go, do as they do by rinsing chopsticks and bowls in hot tea, and drink either more hot tea or anything from a bottle—without ice. Fruit—with the usual tropical caveat about avoiding pre-peeled items—is fine for dessert, but the cautious might stick to ice cream.

In the end, though, getting sick results more from bad luck than from anything one does or doesn't do. The hapless—and most travellers to most places seem doomed to this at some point—can minimize debilitation by:

1) *Eating nothing solid* for 24 hours, then starting slowly on soups and noodles; 2) *Drinking copiously* (bland liquids only) to stave off dehydration; and 3) *Going as easy* as it seems reasonable. For persistent diarrhoea or vomiting, obviously seek medical attention.

Innoculations:

For travellers heading off to more exotic locals, two **Port Health Innoculation Centres** give any and every shot at bargain prices: at second floor, Centrepoint, 181 Gloucester Road, Wanchai, Hong Kong (5-722-056) and New World Centre, Tsimshatsui, Kowloon, (3-681601). Hours are 9 a.m. to 1 p.m. and 2 to 5 p.m. Monday through Friday, and 9 a.m. to 1 p.m. Saturdays. (There is also a centre at the airport.)

Drugs:

Hong Kong has recently tightened up its former *laissez-faire* approach to prescription drugs. Although birth-control pills and the sometimes-crucial lomotil diarrhea pills can still be bought over the counter anywhere, things like Valium and tetracycline will require a bit of persuasive talking — and bargaining — at one of Wanchai's "medicine companies." Otherwise, **Watson's** (Des Voeux Road at Pedder Street, Central District, Hong Kong) and **Victoria Dispensary** (Theatre Lane, next to Queen's Theatre, off Queen's Road Central, Hong Kong) are among the more complete and easily accessible pharmacies.

Dining Out

No one has ever contradicted the guesstimate that there are more than 5,000 restaurants listed in the colony's telephone directories. The exactitude of that figure is debatable, but a hungry fact remains: anywhere you turn in the colony, there is a restaurant.

Chinese Food:

Hong Kong, like Paris, is a place where conversation invariably involves the current merits and demerits of restaurants. A new restaurant discovery by an old Hong Kong hand is such important intelligence that the "discoverer" often is rewarded with extra rounds of pink gin. Restaurants in Hong Kong, like those in France, tend to be extensions of one's living room, places where friends and families gather for celebrations and feasts.

The Restaurants listing found in Appendix A is an abbreviated sampler of renowned local restaurants. One would require a separate book to list every restaurant in a particular category, but those listed are generally considered to be good representative places. Most Chinese restaurants in hotels have been omitted. They are usually better than average Chinese eating places, but they tend to tailor their food for outsiders who know little about Chinese cuisine. Their dishes — with the exception of those prepared for pre-arranged banquets — are hence rather ordinary, even though they are elegantly served and quite expensive. However, if you prefer a secure hotel ambience, the two best Chinese restaurants in local hotels are probably the **Man Wah** in the Mandarin and the **Rainbow Room** in the Lee Gardens Hotels. They are mentioned because they specialize in seasonal dishes usually unavailable at other hotel restaurants.

Hong Kong's first eating rule is *be adventurous;* get out of your hotel and sample some of the best Chinese, Japanese, Korean, Singaporean, Malayan, Indonesian, Filipino, Thai, Indian and Vietnamese foods in the world. But don't be too surprised if the local Cantonese cuisine (or any other Chinese foods served here) looks and tastes different from hometown "Chinese food." It is the real thing here! It is your favourite Chinese restaurant dishes back home that are, well, different.

The **Yung Kee** in Central is one of the colony's famous **Cantonese** eateries because once — many years ago — it was named one of the 10 best restaurants in the world by *Fortune* magazine. Regardless of its place in the dining Olympics, this Cantonese restaurant is justifiably famous for its goose dishes. It is also one of the few restaurants that uphold local tradition and still serve *pay daan* (hundred year old eggs) as an un-asked-for appetizer. Other reputable Cantonese food palaces are the **Lychee Village**, **Sun Tung Lok** (for shark's fin), **Ocean City**, the **Riverside**, the **King Bun** and **Tao Yuan**. (The **Riverside** also serves Cantonese and Japanese versions of traditional Mongolian hotpot and Szechuan dishes).

A few special categories: for vegetarian Cantonese food try the **Wishful Cottage** or the **Vegi Food Kitchen**. For Cantonese snake dishes (during winter months) try the **Yip Lam Kee**, the **Patek** or the **King of Snakes**. And, if you are here at any time but winter, dine out on a floating sampan restaurant on Causeway Bay for fresh Cantonese seafood. Lastly, the **North Garden** specializes in game dishes.

When one sees a sign advertising "Northern Chinese Food," one's mind usually conjures up images of crisp Peking Duck. Which is quite right, but remember that there are other types of northern prepared duck quite different from the usual barbecued Peking Duck. The **Pine & Bamboo**, the **American Restaurant**, the **New American Restaurant, Peking**, **Spring Deer**, **Kowloon Peking** and **North China** and the several **Peking Gardens** should satiate any duck-craving palate. These northern-style places also feature **Mongolian hotpots** and barbecues. Some of the above, like the Kowloon Peking, feature both; others, like **The Mongolian Barbecue** and the **Genghis Khan** serve only that speciality.

Spicy **Szechuanese** food, usually only popular with serious Chinese food gourmets, has an ardent cult following of fire-breathing afficionados. The **Red Pepper** in the Causeway Bay area is a particularly popular Szechuanese restaurant, especially with expatriates, but purists contend that the Red Pepper's food is not as hot as it should be, or used to be. Therefore, you might want to patronize the **Kam Chuen Lau** which has a no spices barred reputation. The **Cleveland Szechuan**, **Sichuan Pep 'N Chilli**, **Unicorn Szechuan** and **Sze Chuen Lau** are also guaranteed to keep you crying for more.

Shanghainese food is not nearly as spicy as Szechuanese cuisine, but it is not very well known either. The **Great Shanghai**, **Four Five Six Grand Shanghai** and **Yick Heung** are recommended. A note about Four Five Six: Shanghainese restaurants all over the world have that same numerical name because that was the name and address of the most famous restaurant in Shanghai before 1949.

Chiu Chow food is primarily known for its "Iron Maiden" tea, which precedes the meal and is so strong it is served in thimble-like cups. The **Carrianna Chiu Chow** and **Siam Bird's Nest** are the two most popular Chiu Chow restaurants here but you might also try the **Golden Red Chiu Chow**, **Tsui Hung** or **Pak Lok**.

For **Hakka** food drop by **Franho**, **Tsiu King Lau**, **Home** or **Fu Dao**. Hakka Chinese are people indigenous to Hong Kong's rural New Territories.

Hangchow food is probably the rarest in Hong Kong and its *entreé de resistance* is Beggar's Chicken. Try the **Tien Hung Lau**.

And a mention of the superb seafood restaurants (Cantonese) along the waterfront of Lamma Island: succulent and fresh. Just about one will do but the **Shum Kee (Lamma Hilton)**, **Chow Kee**, **Peach Garden** and the **Fu Kee** are the most popular. The Sampan restaurants in the Causeway Bay Typhoon Shelter provide another Cantonese seafood taste treat. (October-April only.)

A word about the colony's big restaurant chain called **Jade Garden** or **Maxim's, Peking** or **Princess** or **Sichuan** or **Shanghai Garden**. They are in a variety of locations throughout the colony and in most of them you can get anything from a Peking Duck or Szechuan Duck or Cantonese Duck to a Beggar's Chicken. It takes a bit of work to get past the usually polite waiters who try to make things easy by having you order what he things all foreigners like — sweet'n sour pork, fried rice, and the like. But persevere. The food is worth any diplomatic hassling involved.

For more Chinese food details and suggestions see the features section essay on **Chinese Cuisine**.

Vietnamese Food:

Vietnamese refugees have encouraged the growth of small establishments specializing in the delectable mint-flavoured food of their country.

The distinctive fish sauce called *nuoc mam* is an important flavouring element in Vietnamese food. This pungent sauce is made from the juices of rice fish that have been salted and fermented in the sun; it's the main source of protein for poor Vietnamese. You need not ask for it in restaurants 'it's always on the table, mixed with chillies and grated vegetables.

Most Vietnamese food portions are small and spicy and always accompanied by a colander of lettuce and mint. Vietnamese spring rolls are eaten wrapped in lettuce leaves and dunked in *nuoc mam*. *Chao-tom*, a shrimp delicacy moulded round a stick of sugar cane is eaten in a sheet of rice paper with mint. Also good is sliced beef in vinegar, a do-it-yourself hotpot.

An essential course during a Vietnamese meal is *pho tai*, a sustaining soup of noodles and rare beef slices with *nuoc nam* stirred into it. *Seven-style Beef* is a speciality, and *nem chua* is a raw pork delicacy marinated in wine. It's excellent as a starter. If you want to drink beer ask for "33," a French lager brewed in Ho Chi Minh City. Vietnamese restaurants also serve good filtered coffee and a refreshing iced drink, *che dau sanh*, made with yellow beans and sago.

Hong Kong probably has the best Vietnamese restaurants outside of Vietnam because all the above ingredients are easily obtainable. For those who think all Asian food is Chinese, try the **Saigon, Golden Bull, Yin Ping, Perfume River** or **Vietnam City**.

Filipino Food:

Only a few restaurants specialize in Filipino food, but here you can sample the much-loved *sinigang*, sour soup seasoned with tamarinds, mangoes and limes. Filipinos are also fond of *dinuguan*, a rich casserole of pork stewed in blood, and the national beverage is *halo halo*, a lush concoction of cooked fruit in milk and sugar topped with crushed ice. You can also find the Filipino aphrodisiac, *balut*, which is a crunchy and unhatched duck embryo eaten straight from the shell. For the latest in *mabuhay* mumchies, try the **Little Manila, Mabuhay** or **Luneta**.

Indian Food:

Most of Hong Kong's Indian restaurants specialize in north Indian dishes, and sometimes the meal is served in the traditional way in small bowls assembled on a brass tray called a *thali*. This is a good way to experience many flavours.

Several of these dishes are named after Shah Jehan, who built the Taj Mahal at Agra. Rice dishes are often flavoured with saffron, the most expensive spice in the world. One ounce of pure saffron is said to be made from 75,000 flowers. You might like to try Bombay Duck, which is not a bird at all, but a small curried fish delicacy. Try all the Indian foods above and more at the **Shalimar, Ashoka, Maharaja, Woodlands** (which is vegetarian), **Viceroy of India, New Delhi, Gaylord, Mayor** or **Cosmo**.

Burmese Food:

Non-aficionados will classify the cuisine as some form of "Indian". There are of course many similarities due to proximity of the two countries, but also many differences in the cuisines. Try the *khaukswe*, a chicken and noodles dish prepared with coconut milk, or *mohinga*, a fish soup with rice noodles served traditionally at lunch. **Khih's Burmese Kitchen.**

Sri Lankan Food:

Another country whose cuisine is dismissed as "Indian". Lots of hot curries of course, but also such favourites as *hoppers* (string — a type of noodles made from rice flour — flat, rice flour *pancakes*, or egg — same as pan but with a fried egg added), the ancient Cutch dish of *lumprais*, curry steamed n a banana leaf and *sambol*, which is very different from the South Indian variety, at the **Club Sri Lanka**.

Indonesian Food:

Several restaurants feature highly-seasoned food from the Spice Islands of Indonesia. One of the most popular dishes is *satay*, skewered meats marinated and basted with pungent sauces, grilled on a charcoal burner at your table, and the dipped into a peanut sauce spiked with hot peppers. They also serve *rijsttafel*, a "rice table" buffet of 16 dishes or more said to have been invented because Dutch settlers couldn't decide which local dishes they liked best. For the most *bagus* (good) local Indonesian *makan* (food) try the **Indonesian, New Indonesian, Shinta, Jaya Indonesian, Jaya Rijsttafel, Ramayana, Indonesian Satay House** or **Cosmo**.

Straits Malay Food:

That *nonya* and other Straits fare favoured down south can be enjoyed at the **Sampaguita** or the Satay **Hut** (Coffee House). Malayan food can also be had at the **Marseille** or the **Merlin**. For a one-stop Straits-style eating binge, try the **S.M.I.** Curry Centre or **Cosmo**.

Japanese Food:

Japanese restaurants here are more expensive than Chinese restaurants — or any other Asian restaurant for that matter — but they are still half the price of counterparts in Tokyo. Try the **Yagiu, Nagoya, Kanetanaka, Osaka, Benkay, Okahan, Yamato, Nadaman, Hooraiya Teppanyaka, Ozeki, Sui Sha Ya** or **Shiki**. For just sushi, try **Ah-So**.

Thai Food:

Meals in ancient Siam were eaten lounging on floor cushions. Some restaurants in Thailand still honour that comfortable custom, but Hong Kong's Thai eating places have standard tables, chairs, spoons and forks. The central flavour of this chilli-based cuisine is packed in a powerful shrimp soup called *tom yam kung*. Watch out for the tiny red chillies. Some gourmets consider Thai cuisine to be the hottest in the world. For dessert try *songaya*, an ambrosia baked inside a coconut husk. Savour same at the **Bangkok Hotel Restaurant, Golden Thai** or **Sawadee**.

Korean Food:

The spicy and pungent cuisine of Korea is characterized by a much-loved condiment called *kimchi*. Various vegetables, but usually cabbage, are preserved in a brine of salt, ginger root, garlic and hot peppers. It's as essential a part of a Korean meal as salt and pepper are in the West.

Most Korean restaurants serve meat barbecues *(bulgogi)* as a set meal, and *kimchi* is always included. *Bulgogi* dishes include a variety of meats and fishes which arrive at your table finely-sliced, marinated and ready for cooking.

Korean ginseng has legendary pepper-upper and aphrodisiacal qualities and some restaurants offer ginseng specialities for those seeking such sensations. Ginseng soup is made of a whole chicken stuffed with glutinous rice, red dates and that magic root. It's boiled for six hours until it becomes an "invigorating" broth. It must be ordered in advance. If you forget, take your ginseng in a vodka cocktail. Encounter the above at the **Koreana, Manna Korea, Korea Barbecue, Korea Garden** or **Go Ju Jang**.

French Cuisine:

Top of the line for pure and opulent French cuisine are **Le Pierrot, Plume** and **Le Restaurant de France**. It is expensive, but superb. The favourite local *provencale* French restaurant is **Au Trou Normand**, complete with proper shots of Calvados to fill the *trou* (the between courses "hole") Normandy-style. A lesser known *provencale*-style restaurant is **Stanley's**. And for **French** seafood, **The Mistral** and **La Brasseries** (there are two); are also good choices.

Continental Cuisine:

Continental cuisine is the most popular form of European cuisine served here and hotels compete bitterly for customers. The famous **Gaddi's** is certainly on top, but don't discount such restaurants as **Napoleon, Margaux, Belvedere, Park Lane, La Ronde** and **Lalique**. Also recommended in hotels are the **Sheraton Grill, Mandarin Grill, Hilton Grill** and **Rotiserrie**.

Outside the hotels, one of the most famous, venerable and oldest eateries is **Jimmy's Kitchen**, a pleasant place (with branch restaurants) that features reasonable prices. Another good spot, **Landau's**, is part of the Jimmy's group.

For steaks, try the **Palm, San Francisco Steak House, Louis' Steak House**, the **Texas Rib House** and the **Steak House**.

German food, including game, is the speciality of **Hugo's** and the **Baron's Table**, but the latter also has the best **smoked food** in the colony, direct from its own smokehouse. Less expensive is the **Old Heidelberg**.

For **Austrian** food, **Mozart Stb'n** while the **Dutch** are catered for at the **'Dutch Kitchen**. For **Swiss** Fare, the **Chesa** (winter *fondues* only) is top of the line, followed by the **Swiss Inn**.

Rigoletto and **Primavera** have the best **Italian food**, followed by **La Taverna, La Bella Donna** and the **Vini Salumi Delicatessen**. The **Spaghetti House** and **Pizza Hut** are good and cheaper.

Good old **American** food is served at the **California** while for Mexican fare, try **Casa Mexicana** or **Something Else**.

The **Beverly Hills Deli** and **Lyndy's** will guarantee you an instant food trip back to New York with your first chomp into a corned beef on rye or hot pastrami. The **delicatessen Corner** is more European-style and features excellent smoked meats.

Hungarian food? The **Paprika, Goulash** and **Bull's Blood**.

And for the **Scots** who miss their haggis, **Mad Dogs** will ease the pangs of hunger.

Middle Eastern food — including everything from Greek *dolmas* to Algerian *couscous* — is on the menu at the **Sheikh** or the **Omar Khayyam**.

You can have **Russian** food at the **Czarina**. It is out of the mainstream of tourist traffic, but has the best borscht in town.

Those from Down Under who are experiencing Vegemite withdrawals and craving a meat pie with a tube of Fosters should try the **Stoned Crow** and **Ned Kelly's Last Stand**. Both serve **Australian** plonk (wine), and the former has a pretty decent menu once you get past the pies. And speaking of meat pies, all the pubs and taverns listed in the nightlife listing feature traditional pub meals.

For the best **cheap eats**, excluding fast food outlets and street stalls, you can't beat **Sammy's Kitchen**, well known to those on the road, or the **YMCA** or **China Fleet Club**.

Fast Food:

How can Hong Kong be "Chinese" with more than a dozen **MacDonald's**, plus **Burger King, Orange Julius, Shakey's, Mr. Donut, Pizza Hut** and other quickie eateries.

What Westerners do not realize, and rarely partake of, is the traditional Chinese version of a fast food outlet, the **dai pai dong** (street stall). Street stalls are everywhere and it is at these little venues that a good percentage of the population eats.

These are not to be confused with Chinese Western-style takeaways — aptly named **Wong's Fast Foods** or **Whispering Brook** which specialize in inexpensive Chinese dishes which are extremely popular and served fast. They also carry Western items. All of the foods at these places are served as "lunchboxes," regardless of the time of day.

Ice Cream:

Despite a very suitable climate, this deep Western mystery remains only partly slurped. Pushcart men and grocers do a fair business in mass-produced, on-the-stick varieties, most at least okay—but beware the red-bean popsicle! For serious students, though, the only recourse is a specialist:

Colorado Meat Co. 14 Wellington St, Central, Hong Kong. Solid, made-in-U.S.A. takeaways.

Dairy Fram Creameries which are scattered around the colony and **Swensen's.**

Also try cooling ice cream fantasies served at hotel coffee shops among which the Hilton's **Cat Street** and the Excelsior's **Windmill** stand out. More elegant will certainly be an afternoon cooler at the Peninsula's **Lobby,** the Mandarin's **Clipper Lounge.**

For a Proper Cuppa:

Hong Kong's most well-known place for high tea during the past half century has been the colonnaded lobby of the **Peninsula Hotel.** Anyone who *is* anyone passes through the Pen's gilded lobby. High tea there is a good place to watch the world go by: "What ho! I say old chappie," and colonial *et al.*

Unfortunately, these days Asian and American tourists seem to outnumber the faithful old Brits at tea time; but it is still *the* place for this British ritual.

One of the newest places for high tea is the lobby of the Regent of Hong Kong. Opened only in late 1980, this hotel is still "new," but while sipping a traditional cuppa in its 40-foot high glass-walled lobby you can marvel at life sailing by in Hong Kong harbour.

Relics, Vestiges:

Confucius and the British Empire are paid their respects in institutions such as the **Luk Yu Tea House** 26-42 Stanley Street, Central, Hong Kong. Tel: 5-235-464—in Chinese, please. Three thousand years of civilization haven't quite ended yet. No fluorescent formica flashes here; black-wood tables, marble-backed benches and brass spittoons do graceful justice to classic Cantonese food and 30-year-old teas. Un-Foreign tongues are almost insistently not spoken, and the English menu is pointedly brief. Without a Chinese speaker, there isn't much point—but afternoon *dim sum* and a pot of Cloud Mist tea might warm even an antique dealer's otherwise pitiless heart. Go calmly with humility and a working knowledge of chopsticks. Centrally located, open 7.30 a.m. to 10 p.m., and less expensive than it looks.

The Hows and Whys of Chopsticking:

The ongoing chopsticks mystery is like the old story of the chicken and the egg. Which came first in Chinese customs—chopsticks or the Chinese system of cutting food into tiny pieces and cooking it so it is soft enough to be devoured without a knife?

The answer is lost to history, but chopsticks have been handed down through the Chinese ages as their most efficient cooking and eating utensils. Alas, many uncoordinated Westerners can't ever master the art of eating or cooking with chopsticks, and there is nothing more embarrassing than to watch a couple of five year old Chinese kids at the next table deftly manoeuvr their chopsticks while you are fumbling about foolishly.

Chopsticks serve as a combination of fork, knife and (when used to shovel food) spoon. Indeed, eating soup with chopsticks is a bit much, but Chinese normally drink their soup and pick up the morsels with chopsticks (if porcelain spoons are not available).

Chinese chopsticks are blunter than their Japanese counterparts, and are made of ivory, bone, wood and (most commonly) plastic. Highly decorated ivory and bone chopsticks are mostly decorative souvenirs these days, plastic ones are used in nearly all local restaurants and wooden ones are used in kitchens. Chopsticks are used for either grasping or separating a morsel. If you think you're a "Grand Chopstick Master" the final test is getting a peanut or slipper button mushroom into your mouth. And for true chopsticking mastery, try passing that peanut or mushroom to a nearby friend!

If you master this art, stop by a market and buy a packet (six pairs) of cheap wooden chopsticks and a few pairs of the longer serving chopsticks. Take them home for your kitchen and use them when you want to turn or stir something frying or grilling. You'll be surprised how useful they are.

For chopstick novices, the more than helpful Hong Kong Tourist Association has published a special "How to use Chopsticks" diagram. For the convenience of "Outer Barbarians," we herewith republish this step-by-step diagram with the HKTA's blessings:

The thin ends of the chopsticks should point towards the food, with the tips exactly together. Here's how to handle chopsticks in 3 easy lessons:

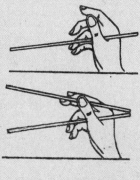

Hold one chopstick firmly between the joint of your thumb and the tip of your third finger.

Then hold the second chopstick between the tip of your thumb and the tips of your first and second fingers.

The lower chopstick remains rigid while you move the upper chopstick in a pincer movement to pick up the food.

The whole action can only be perfected by practice in your own style. But once you can lift a peanut up and deliver it safely to your mouth without losing control—then you are a real expert and ready for anything!

The 'Hong Kong Cheongsam':

What elbow bender or bartender in the world has not heard of a Singapore Sling? For half a century, this alcoholic propaganda (in the eyes of Hong Kong) has been doing Hong Kong in. Not any more.

After a series of top-level discussions—which rumour has it went all the way to the Queen—it was decided that Hong Kong's honour was at stake and something had to be done.

So in 1979, a Hong Kong cocktail competiton was launched, and the eventual winner was Leung Shiu-fai, a ginslinger from the elegant (and now demolished) Repulse Bay Hotel bar.

Leung's creation, the **Hong Kong Cheongsam** was named after that high-necked, skin-tight dress with the revealing and seductive slit. His drink is a subtle mixture of gin, maraschino, white *cream de menthe*, fresh lemon juice, egg-white, Seven-Up, cherry, lemon slice, cucumber slice and a sprig of mint. Incidentally, Leung experimented with 60 other concoctions before settling on this one.

Ask for one.

Shopping

Shopping, of course, is what Hong Kong is all about. It is a gigantic bazaar and, in spite of a few other tourist attractions, people with money flock here to spend it. You can probably find *anything* in Hong Kong if you look hard enough, but it can be an exasperating and exhausting experience—exasperating because of language difficulties, and exhausting because of the heat and the constant go-go-go. Hopefully this shopping guide will save you time and hassle, thereby leaving you with more free hours to enjoy Hong Kong.

Note: Military or diplomatic personnel, or anyone with permission to shop in the **China Fleet Club's** collection of stores (China Fleet Club, Fleet House, Arsenal Street, Wanchai, Hong Kong), will find the same brand names and items there as in the rest of Hong Kong, but prices are between 10 and 25 percent cheaper.

The Hong Kong Tourist Association has several publications just on shopping which you will find useful. The **Official Guide to Shopping, Eating out & Services, Shopping in Hong Kong** and **Shopping Guide to Video Equipment.** (The HKTA's shops also carry a good selection of souvenirs and gifts or another handy book is the one **The Complete Guide to Factory Bangains.**) The back page of the **South China Morning Post** classifieds is a useful source as is the Hong Kong Tourist Association's free factory shopping list although a more comprehensive one may be purchased (HK$10) from The American Women's Association, Flat C-7, Monticello, 48 Kennedy Road, Hong Kong, Tel: 5-272-961.

Duty Free Shopping:

Hong Kong is a duty free port where only a few commercial items are taxed. The two that affect tourists directly are alcohol (perfumes and spirits) and tobacco (cigarettes, cigars and loose tobacco). Industrial and private petroleum products are also taxed, but that's it. All other goods are duty-free anywhere in the colony. The same goes for items on sale in the many airport shops. But if you delay some of your shopping till the last minute and are forced to buy at the airport (a camera, a watch, a stereo, even a magazine or a newspaper, anything except the duty-free items mentioned above), be advised that "duty-free" prices there will probably be more than at similar shops downtown.

However, the **Duty Free Stores**, in addition to airport outlets, has stores in various locations—in Kowloon's J. Hotung Centre (Tsimshatsui) at Ocean Terminal (called the **Wine Cellar**), **Harbour Crystal Centre** and **Tsimshatsui Centre** (Both in East Tsimshatsui). These outlets have duty-free items and a large selection of other things, such as designer brand luxury goods.

Department Stores:

Wing On, Sincere and **Shui Hing** are among the oldest and largest chain department stores, with branches throughout the colony. Posher **Lane Crawford** (three locations) is the oldest European store here, and among popular others are the **Da Da, Ding How** and **Klasse** department stores.

The Japanese department stores **Daimaru, Matsuzakaya Sogo** and **Mitsukoshi** (located near each other in Causeway Bay, Hong Kong)—have such drawing power that they have virtually pioneered Causeway Bay's shopping image. In Kowloon the **Tokyo** is in the **New World Centre** and **Isetan** next to the **Sheraton Hotel.**

Evergreen's a smaller chain store at several locations, is favoured by Europeans living here for its hard-to-find hardware items (though they stock a myriad of other items too). The **Taiwan Man Sang** stores, meanwhile, are the Taiwanese version of the various **"China Products"** stores that stock mainland Chinese goods.

A word of warning. If "sale" signs are posted, stand back or be prepared for Hong Kong's famous pushing and shoving shopping scenes.

Credit Cards:

Some of the glass doorways to hi-fi and camera shops are so plastered with credit card decals you can't see in or out. Yet, when you try to pay with one, clerks mumble and grumble. The basis of all arguments by credit card-shy shopkeepers who want to avoid taking your card is that your agreed to "bargain" price is a "cash discount" price (a condition never mentioned during negotiations). There's not much you can do to counter that excuse. Threats to report them to the credit card company are invariably shrugged off or laughed at. The credit card companies know about this rip-off, but cannot or will not do anything to discourage it, even though contracts with the stores state they must honour credit cards like cash. This is because legal action would spoil the local credit card office's highly competitive numbers game geared to collecting signatures and selling as much as they can.

Sometimes, if you have bargained for a large enough sale, you can force the shopkeeper to accept your card. Sometimes you have to accept a seven percent card fee the shop will have to pay, or you can bargain for a split of the fee. But in many cases, you'll have to leave or pay as they demand. In short, if you really want to pay with a credit card, shops will usually add seven percent onto the price you had previously negotiated. So much for plastic purchases.

"Made In China" Goods:

There's no need to cross the border into China to inspect or acquire things Chinese. A string of decidedly capitalistic **"Communist" department** stores offer Hong Kong shoppers a sometimes stupefying range of basic and luxury goods, usually in greater variety and, often, for identical items, at better prices than those in Peking or Canton Friendship Stores. For anything from proletarian plastic chopsticks to silk brocades, the places listed in Appendix A are among the last reliable Hong Kong haunts for truly spectacular bargains.

Visitors (particularly those short of either time or money) will almost certainly find communist Chinese stores unbeatable for memorable gifts and unusual personal acquisitions. Though they are vast and often—especially at lunch hour—bargain-basement jammed, they conveniently feature fixed prices and glass-counter, Western-style displays. Most are open seven days a week, and several are open until 10 p.m. nightly. All provide packing, mailing, and even mail-order services. Though their sales staffs generally speak workable English, their marketing style, exhibited toward locals and foreigners alike, is laconic.

Sound Equipment:

Unless you know exactly what you want to buy in the hi-fi and stereo field, the purchase of sound equipment can be a troublesome affair. There is no scarcity of hi-fi shops that stock the latest gear, but testing and comparing is troublesome because most shops are small retail establishments with boxes piled upon boxes, usually in a tiny room. Clerks always seem to be too busy to spend a few minutes with a foreigner. They seem to expect visitors to just come in, plop money down and walk out. Therefore, any extra effort by a salesman is wasted. It's a discourteous sales style, but it happens time and again here. And shops rarely have, or part with, information on the various systems they stock.

Another difficulty is that audio gear brand names are not always listed in shopping directories. They are usually identified by the agent's name, not the brand name. This makes shopping difficult if you want to check components of a particular brand. (Note: prices charged in shops are always cheaper than those publicized by agents.)

Camera Gear:

Probably every known type of camera gear is sold all over the colony. The rule, again, is to compare prices and bargain. Quite often, camera shops sell other things such as calculators and electronic goods, and by buying other items in the same shop you may be able to earn an overall discount. It helps to know exactly what you want, but most camera stores will allow you to examine a couple of cameras before they get bored with you. Be honest; tell them you are comparing prices, mark their prices down on their calling card and, later, after you've had a chance to compare several shops' goods, make your choice.

A word about guarantees. With some products, especially Nikon gear, there are authorized agents here who are allotted only a certain quota of cameras. This is because there is always a big buyers' demand for new items that hit the market—as when lightweight, electronic and automatic cameras debuted a few years back. "Authorized" decals mean only that Nikon has allowed that shop to sell their gear on behalf of the official Hong Kong Nikon agent. However, there is no law preventing other shops from buying gear in Japan, shipping it to Hong Kong and displaying it in shop windows. One would think that these stores would be more expensive, but usually the opposite is true. That's because they are free of restraints put on them if they are "authorized" retailers. Therefore, good bargains can be had. However, these stores probably will not be able to offer you one year world-wide guarantees that authorized Nikon dealers can endorse.

Clothes:

Gone are the old Hong Kong days when you could get only made-to-measure hand-tailored clothes here (which were carbon copies of more expensive Saville Row, Champs Elysees or Fifth Avenue designs). In Hong Kong it is still possible to find a Chinese tailor who makes custom Western suits and dresses (including the traditional, high-necked, skin-tight *cheongsam*). Indeed, tailored clothing (see feature article on **Tailoring Tips**) is one of the things Hong Kong is traditionally famous for. However, few people realize that many of the ready-to-wear garments they bought back home were made in Hong Kong under licence to trendy big name designers. Calvin Klein, Gloria Vanderbilt, Charlotte Ford, Pierre Cardin, Yves St. Laurent, Levis, Britannia and Bang Bang products, to name but a few prominent labels, are all manufacturers of Hong Kong.

Visitors are quite often surprised to find how many ready-to-wear garments residents buy. High fashion boutiques are found in just about all the main shopping arcades on both sides of the harbour. (One good concentration of chic boutiques is found in the **Wellington-On Lan-D'Aguilar Street** area, Central, Hong Kong). There is no pretense, however, that these designer fashions are any cheaper than the same goods back home. Indeed, the *latest* styles cost bucks. Unknown designers' goods are probably slightly cheaper, but not the status brands.

Counterfeit Designs:

You'll find lots of these pirate fashions in the various shopping lanes and with the ubiquitous street vendors in Causeway Bay (around the Daimaru Department Store and the Excelsior Hotel Shopping Arcade). There are also particularly good buys in the two **"clothing alleys"** in Central—**Li Yuen Street East** and **Li Yuen Street West**—which run between Queen's Road and Des Voeux Road. There are also a couple of alleys on either side with good buys too.

Clothes For Tots:

Further west, past Central Market, and exactly parallel to the two Li Yuen Streets, is Hong Kong's most famous "alley" **Wing On Street,** which is a cloth (not clothing) alley. Continuing further west is **Baby Lane** (Fat Hing Street), so-called because of its vast selection of traditional Chinese baby clothing—everything from silk-embroidered capes and padded Chinese jackets and vests *(mien lap)* to quilts and unique Chinese backpacks.

Factory Outlets and Street Markets:

It is possible to get genuine designer clothes—some with exclusive boutique labels in whatever language—at market prices. Overruns or seconds (which may or may not be damaged) are sold off in **factory outlets** at very discounted prices.

It is always wise to call first because some of the factory outlets do not keep regular hours or do not have regular stocks.

Several of the colony's fascinating **street markets** have even greater discounts. The two main markets for clothing are **Stanley Market** in Stanley Village (Hong Kong) and the **Kowloon City Market.** They are packed on weekends. You have to dig around a bit, and be discerning, but pushing and shoving and fighting for bargains is what makes for good shopping stories back home.

The two biggest **night street markets** are the **Macau Ferry Carpark** (Connaught Road, Central, Hong Kong) and **Temple Street** in Kowloon. There you can get everything from longjohns to sweaters, shirts, jeans and made-to-measure suits.

For a list of the colony's most well-known factory outlets, please refer to relevant section in Appendix A.

Art:

Art market goods include everything from expensively faded Confucian watercolours to five-a-dollar "New China" papercuts. The so-called "old"

scroll paintings stocked by the various China Products Stores and by most antique dealers are perennial favourites but casual browsers will see more of them—as well as other examples of Eastern and Western arts—at **Sun Fung,** 35 Queen's Road, Central, Hong Hong, **Tsi Ku Chai,** South China Building, 1st floor, 1 Wyndham Street, Central, Hong Kong, or **Pok Art,** 18 Granville Road, Tsimshatsui, Kowloon. Also check the Chinese "village", the Peak Tower.

Though most dealers will offer to arrange framing, going directly to a specialist will afford you a wider choice of styles and often saves money. The owners are usually quite knowledgeable, particularly with Chinese pictures, and will give you sound advice on possible choices for matting and frame styles. By American or European standards, prices are low. Try **Gallery,** Admiralty Centre, Hong Kong, **Man Fong,** 41 Wellington Street, Central, Hong Kong, **Timarie,** 43-55 Wyndham Street, Central, Hong Kong, and **Wah Cheong,** 7 Wellington Street, Central, Hong Kong.

Hong Kong is also a good place to buy prints and paintings from other parts of the world. Among international galleries are **Asian-African Arts,** 1A Humphreys Ave., Tsimshatsui, Kowloon, **Galerie de Monde,** 26 Hollywood Road, Central, Hong Kong and **Alvin Gallery,** 30 Hollywood Road, Hong Kong.

The Asian Collector Gallery, 19-27 Wyndham St., Hong Kong, specializes in old maps and engravings, as well as rare 19th- Century prints of the South coast of China, Hong Kong and Macau. Occasionally this shop has available pictures by masters such as George Chinnery and Auguste Borget.

The **South China Morning Post Family Bookshops** (at various locations throughout the colony) sell a variety of framed reproductions. The best buy of all, however, is the set of 19th Century Hong Kong and South China prints sold by the Hong Kong Government in their **Government Publications Centre** (General Post Office Building, by the Star Ferry Concourse, Hong Kong). Look for the display there. These prints sell for the remarkable price of HK$3 each. Fine postcards are also available for HK$1. These are some of the best bargains in town.

Antiques:

Hong Kong, appropriately, is still one of the world's foremost centres for the acquisition of Chinese antiques. Antique stores here range from very posh places with branch galleries in the United States and Europe to tiny, hole-in-the-wall shops well off culture vulture migration routes.

True antique hounds—not unlike anthropologists and fossil hunters—like to do a lot of walking up and down Central District's urban hills and into the colony's back streets. For them the many tiny shops along **Hollywood Road** (on Hong Kong Island), and the various **"ladder streets"** leading further up the mountian toward Mid-Levels, are a rich source of old collectibles. (On the Western side of Hollywood Road are some of the colony's older shops that specialize in blackwood furniture, and in the area between Lyndhurst Terrace and a little past the Central Police Station—47 Hollywood Road—you'll find mostly "modern" shops.)

For persons without much time, will (especially during summer's heat) or expertise, there are many more expensive and easily accessible antique shops in the colony's many air-conditioned private and hotel shopping arcades. Shops like **Charlotte Horstmann & Gerald Godfrey Ltd** (at Ocean Terminal, Ocean Centre Harbour City in Kowloon), **Eileen Kershaw** (Peninsula Hotel) and **Lane Crawford's** (Queen's Road Central) are top of the line—with prices to match.

Smaller shops like **Honeychurch** (29 Hollywood Road, Hong Kong), **Banyan Tree** (Edinburgh Tower and Harbour City),**Gallery 69** (123 Edinburgh Tower, Hong Kong, and Regent Hotel),**Ian McLean Antiques** (73 Wyndham Street), **Mingei** (26 Wyndham St., Hong Kong) and **Amazing Grace** (6 locations) are among the more popular antique shops. But there are many more. Start walking and ye shall find them.

But if you don't like walking, there may be a way to have some of the antiques come to you. How? Read the newspapers and check for auction announcements (the classified section in *The South China Morning Post* is best). There are two local auctioneers— **Lammert Brothers** (Sutherland House, Central, Hong Kong) and **Victoria Auctioneers** (38 D'Aguilar Street, Central)—who specialize in local antique auctions. Successful purchasing depends on how you pick your goods and how well you bid, but bargains are there to be had. Admission to these auctions is free.

If you want to tuck in with the big boys in international collecting circles, check the papers to see if your visit coincides with a periodical **Sotheby's** or **Christies'** auction. These sales are usually held in a Central hotel. Invitations are either sent to select big spenders or can be purchased for about US$40; the admission charge is to discourage onlookers and non-spenders.

If you are here in May, check out the **International Asian Antiques Fair** or write to **Andamans East International,** Wilson House, 19-27 Wyndham St., Central, Hong Kong, Tel: 5-221-518, for further information.

Snuff Bottles:

Snuff bottles are still one of the hottest items on the collector's and souvenir market. A tourist looking for an inexpensive and small souvenir of his or her trip to Hong Kong can buy a small porcelain hand-painted snuff bottle in just about any tourist shop in Hong Kong for between HK$5 and $25. Snuff bottle afficionados may look down their noses at such "instant" collector items, but these little bottles do make nice mantle knick-knacks. But don't judge the entire snuff bottle *genre* by those roughly painted bottles usually found in markets and sidewalk stalls. Indeed, some snuff bottles are magnificent works of art.

Serious collectors of Chinese *objects d'art* have a snobbish attitude toward snuff bottles; they consider them "pop art" not worthy of consideration. Museums, if they give them space at all, usually relegate them to a dark corner or back room. However, this attitude doesn't deter avid collectors.

Silk:

Silk is one of the colony's great buys. Chinese silk is both beautiful and expensive, but it's still a bargain here and there are numerous colours, designs and textures of silk available. **China Arts & Crafts** or the **Yue Hwa Stores** have the best selections. Because Chinese garment styling is still rushing headlong into the early Fifities, most women prefer to purchase lengths of silk and have modern-style garments made by a favourite tailor.

Thai silk (and cotton) is also available here. Many of the designer shops have fashions made of Siamese silk, but the **Thai Shop** (Silvercord and Houston Centre, both in Kowloon) specializes in Thai goods.

Embroidery:

Most of the **China Products Stores** have embroidery departments, but their selections are not always up to par. If you do not find what you like there, try the half-dozen or so tiny shops on **On Lan Street** (a tiny cul-de-sac off Wyndham Street in Central, only one block up from the main China Arts and Crafts Store on the corner of Wyndham Street and Queen's Road Central). Also try the row of shops at the top of **Wyndham Street,** Central and **Swatow Drawn Work** in World-Wide House (Central).

The Hong Kong Tourist Association sells a small booklet on Swatow embroidery that's packed with useful information. If you are planning to make large purchases, you might want to read that booklet first.

Carpets:

Hong Kong is also an excellent place to buy woolen or silk Chinese carpets. As with other shopping items, the various **China Products Stores** have rug departments with varying prices and qualities available.

The most famous carpet manufacturer here is **Tai Ping Carpets** (also listed as **Hong Kong Carpet Manufacturers Limited**) which has a showroom in Hutchison House, Central, Hong Kong, and a factory at Tai Po in the New Territories (see **Shopping Places** listing in Apppendix A). Also check the morning papers, especially classified ads in *The South China Morning Post* for occasional Tai Ping Carpets sales. Another carpet manufacturers is **Sammy Y. Lee & Wangs,** Windsor Mansions, 29 Chatham Road, Tsimshatsui, Kowloon.

Hong Kong is also a good place for Persian,Turkish or Afghan rugs (which unfortunately have increased in price due to political problems in those countries). Try your bargaining luck at the **Mir Oriental Carpets** 30 Hollywood Road, Central, **Oriental Carpet Trading,** 42 Wyndham Street, Central. Hong Kong or **Tribal Rugs,** Admiralty Centre or 41 Wyndham St., Hong Kong.

Porcelain:

Full dinner ensembles or smaller tea and coffee services are some of the top items on visitors' shopping lists. **Royal Crown Derby** (at **Craig's** , St. George's Building, Hong Kong, or Ocean Centre, Kowloon), **Wedgewood** (Ocean Terminal, Kowloon), **Royal Worcester** (also at **Craig's**) all have retail outlets here and do good business.

However, the best dining service buys are to be had in the various **China Products Stores** or at the few local porcelain factories. At the former, you have to take whatever is in stock. Their method of stock selection for all items is haphazard and, at times, it is quite difficult to buy additional matching pieces.

Ivory:

Hong Kong is the world's largest market for ivory. There are numerous shops here selling everything from inexpensive ivory toothpicks to magnificent *mahjong* tiles, chess sets and meticulously carved whole elephant tusks. Ivory is another material that the Chinese have revered for centuries.

Many of the colony's antique shops sell magnificent ivory brush-holders, snuff bottles, bracelets, etcetera, so there is no shortage of such things to buy. (Note: just because an ivory piece has browned does not mean it is old. Staining ivory so it looks old is a favourite sales trick here.)

Before you fall in love with a piece of ivory, make certain the shop or factory gives you a Certificate of Origin issued by the Department of Trade, Industry and Customs. Most European countries and the United States have limited ivory imports in an attempt to protect the unauthorized slaughter of elephants in East Africa (from where most ivory comes).

Crystal:

Bargains in fine Western crystal such as **Rosenthal, Waterford** or **Danish** exist in some of the posh emporiums like **Lane Crawford's** (Queen's Road, Central, Hong Kong), **Town House** (Ocean Terminal, and Ocean Centre, Kowloon), **Town & Country-Georg Jensen** (30 Queen's Road, Cental, Hong Kong), **Art Universe Company** (Royal Garden Hotel) and **Hunter's** (Peninsula Hotel and Ocean Terminal).

The best bargains in crystal, however, exist in the various **Chinese Emporiums** where stylish wine glsses are sold for as little as US$2.

Jade:

Just about every visitor to Hong Kong, or the Orient for that matter, has heard of jade, and many intend to buy some while here. Though "jade" trinkets, costume jewellery and figurines are found everywhere in the colony, good quality jade is relatively rare and pricey.

If you were to determine the scarcity of this Oriental stone after an initial shopping survey of Hong Kong, you would probably conclude that the entire jade business is a colossal blue-green joke. Nearly everyone has "rare" jade for sale—at very low prices. Like most of Hong Kong's "tremendous bargains," they aren't. However, "jade" represents the mysterious East and most travellers who come here feel they must possess a piece of the stuff to prove they've been here.

An unlucky combination of natural and political forces have melded together to cause prices for this medium-rare stone to soar. Unfortunately, most good jade is found only in China and Burma, so access to such jade is physically and politically difficult. Hence its exorbitant cost.

The word "jade" comes from the Portuguese word *mijada,* which means *kidneys.* The first jade was brought back to Europe by early Spanish and Portuguese explorers who had been informed by Chinese vendors that it was a curative stone capable of relieving colic and pain and warding off kidney diseases.

The art of jade carving, as we know it today, began under the Emperor Chien Lung (1736-1796) during the Ching dynasty.

Two substances are called jade: nephrite, or "soft jade," called *yu* by Chinese, and jadeite, or "hard jade" (called *fei tsu* or *tsu*).The former was the only type known in ancient times and was used for decorative *objets d'art.* The latter is a "newer" jade of recent discovery and is the green Burmese type commonly used as jewellery.

Jade comes in many colours—varying shades of green, purple, orange, yellow, brown, white, and even violet. The most expensive colour is imperial jade, a deep translucent shade similar to the deep green of an emerald. Good jade should be even in colour, not mottled or cracked.

Jadeite (or "hard jade"), also called Burmese jade, now seems to be the most expensive of the various jades. Nephrite ("soft jade") is similar in appearance, but is more common and therefore cheaper. Nephrite is also known as Taiwan jade, New Zealand jade, or New Zealand greenstone. There is also "new jade," which is bowenite, a form of serpentine, Indian jade (aventurine, a green quartz) and Australian jade (which is chrysoprase, another form of green quartz). Obviously, with so many "jades" about, you must know what you are looking for and buy only from reputable shops. If you want a quality piece of jade jewellery or carving always patronize only reputable dealers. Contact the Hong Kong Tourist Association (HKTA) for a list of reputable firms. The HKTA also has a handy publication called *A Shoppers Guide to Jewellery in Hong Kong,* which will not make you a jade expert but will provide some useful hints. Also see *Gems & Jewellery in Hong Kong: A Buyer's Guide.* At most antique and jewellery shops, bartering is always the rule. Be sure to compare the prices and artworks as much as possible. The **Jade Market** is in Yaumatei (Kowloon) and is open from 10 a.m. — 4 a.m. daily.

Silversmiths:

The colony's silverware specialists stock both imported sterling silver items and locally made ones. Try **De Sillva's** (World-wide House. Central Hong Kong), **Town & Country-Georg Jensen** (30 Queen's Road Central, Hong Kong).

Metalware:

Something of a luxury in most places are handcast or worked brass, bronze, copper and pewter that are produced in unpretentions Hong Kong workshops. The places below stock lamps, bells, candlesticks, pots and metal whatever in both Western and Oriental styles.

Fook Ngai — 23 Wellington Street, Central, Hong Kong.

Ho Kwong Kee — 1st floor, A1-2 Tung Nam Factory Building, 40 Mataukok Road, Tokwawan, Kowloon.

Hung Tai Brassware Factory — 8th floor, Wai Shun Industrial Building, 5 Yuk Yat Street, Tokwawan, Kowloon.

Sum Ngai Brassware Mfg. — 195B, Kamtin, Kam Sheung Road, Yuen Long, New Territories.

The adventurous should try the small brassware stores/stalls around the corner of **Hi Lung Lane** and Reclamation Street (# 182) Yaumatei, Kowloon. For pewter, try **Selangor Pewter** in Swire House, Kowloon.

Jewellery:

Being a free market with no customs duties on luxuries such as jewellery, it is no wonder that Hong Kong seems to have a goldsmith/jeweller on every street corner. Combine Hong Kong's entrepôt status with the tragi history of wars and famines in China, and one understands why the majority of Hong Kong's fiscally aware population prefer something solid — like real gold and jewellery. Consequently, there are thousands of jewellery shops here. But despite laws that allegedly guarantee that you get what you pay for, gold-buying can be a problem.

Big name local jewellers such as **Kevin's** (Hilton Hotel, Hong Kong), **Chow Sang Sang and King Fook** (the latter two have various locations around the colony) are among the largest and most prestigious. Also opulent are **Dickson Watch & Jewellery** (in the Landmark, Hong Kong), **De Silva's** (World-Wide House, Hong Kong), **House of Shen** (Peninsula Hotel, Kowloon), **Manchu Gems** (Ocean Terminal, Kowloon) and **Dabera** (Swire House, Hong Kong).

Big, international jewellers also have outlets here. **Van Cleef & Arpels** (Landmark, Hong Kong, and the Peninsula Hotel, Kowloon) and **Cartier** (Prince's Building, Hong Kong, and Peninsula Hotel, Kowloon).

Jade, that stone to which the Chinese attribute so many mysterious powers, can be coveted and bought at **Jade House** (Regent and Hong Kong hotels, Kowloon) and **Jade Creations** (Lane Crawford House, 4th floor, Queen's Road, Central, Hong Kong), and many other places. Also have a look in the various **China Arts & Crafts** jade jewellery sections. China Arts & Crafts also has various types of porcelain jewellery. (For more information see section on **Jade.**)

If you have complaints about a jeweller, or doubts about the stones or gold you've purchased, follow the advice in the **Complaints** section.

Watches and clocks:

Watches for sale, like cameras, sound systems and jewellery, are ubiquitous here. On just about every corner of the colony there is a shop selling watches. But indeed, this is a good place to buy that once in a lifetime Rolex, Cartier, Patek Philippe, Seiko or Omega timepiece. They come in all shapes and sizes, big name and unknown, Swiss and Japanese. But like most things one buys, you get what you pay for. So if someone offers you a "solid gold Rolex" for half the going price, the case will probably not be gold, and the movement may be a cheap Russian substitute.

Sometimes your Cartier watch, which was a super bargain, becomes a "Carter" watch in better lighting conditions. And those unknown "ASEIKONS" magically become SEIKOS when the jeweller removes the "a" and "n" decals. Let the buyer, again, beware.

Luggage:

The **China Products Stores** have a large selection of inexpensive suitcases. And there are dozens of little bag shops in just about every corner or every shopping arcade. Street vendors in **Causeway Bay** parade up and down walks there with handfuls at substantial discounts. The two "clothing alleys" in Central — **Li Yuen Street East** and **Li Yuen Street West** — have several bag stalls (at the Des Voeux Road end) and several bag shops inside.

Shoes:

Be wary of superb bargains in locally-made or Philippines-made shoes. Sometimes, depending on the wearer's grace, they fall apart after a few wearings, especially during the rainy season. Many people, however, frequent the long row of shoe shops in Happy Valley on **Leighton Road**, those along **Prince Edward Road**, near the Kowloon MTR station of the same name. Slippers or sandals are best bought in the open market. International labels like Clark's and Bally are available in all the major department stores. **Shellbrook Shoes** in the Ocean Terminal has a good selection of foreign-made shoes and electronic foot-measuring equipment, an ankle-grabbing rarity in this colony. There are also a variety of bootmakers in both Wanchai and Tsimshatsui. Always give custom leather folks enough time for adjustments and don't expect perfect-fitting shoe or boot miracles overnight.

Lamps:

Real antique vases deserve better than having light fixtures jammed down their throats. To avoid aesthetic murder and to save a lot of money, visit several of the colonys shops that carry wide-ranging stocks of new porcelain lampstands and fittings. They can also arrange for shades to be made in any shape, size or fabric (though silk is the obvious favourite for local lamp coverings). Try **Fook Wing**, 16 Wo On Lane, Central Hong Kong), **Henry Lampshades** (Ocean Terminal, Tsimshatsui, Kowloon) or **Magnificent Company** (Battery Path and Ice House Street, Central, Hong Kong).

Musical Instruments:

China's melodious workshops turn out a complete range of standard Western and Chinese musical instruments, most at a much lower cost than Western counterparts. The various **China Products Stores** have the best selections. For Western instruments and music, the two biggest Hong Kong music stores are the **Tsang Fook Piano Company** and the **Tom Lee Piano Company.** Both have various locations of both sides of the harbour so check the telephone directory.

Smoker's Supplies:

A flash cigarette lighter is Hong Kong's status symbol *de rigueur.* But appearances can be deceiving.

For every US$500 European model there are dozens of Asian-made clones that cost as little as one-tenth the original's price. By sticking with the main-line imitation brands — **Win** is a particularly good brand — the differences in reliability and servicing will be negligible when compared to name brand lighters.

The lowest smokers' gear prices are usually awarded by tiny shops in Tsimshatsui, Wanchai and Causeway Bay. But for everything from Cartier lighters to obscure brands of cigarettes, excellent selections of pipes, cigars and pipe tobaccos, and other smoking paraphernalia, try the **Tabaqueria Filipina** (various locations on both sides of the harbour). For those with more expensive tastes. there's **Dunhill** (Prince's Building, Central, Hong Kong, or the Peninsula Hotel, Kowloon), and the **Davidoff Cigar Boutique** (Peninsula and Regent Hotels, Kowloon or the Landmark, Hong Kong).

Buttons and Bows:

Need a button or a zipper urgently to repair that "catastrophe" from the night before? **Buttons & Bows** (Prince's Building, Central, Hong Kong) has a modest selection of sewing accessories, and so do the sewing sections in department stores. But for one of the world's greatest selections — at street market prices — walk along Queen's Road, Central West, Until you come to **Pottinger Street** (opposite Central Market and between Lane Crawford's and the China Emporium),a ladder street due north and away from the harbourside. Starting at the corner of Pottinger Street and Queem's Road, you'll see dozens of stalls stocking thousands (millions?) of buttons, zippers, beads and sewing supplies. If something is not available there, these shops will make it for you.

Stamp and Coins:

Serious numismatics and philatelists can check the yellow pages of the telephone directory. There are dozens of dealers. Collectors however might try:

Commonwealth Stamp Co. — Shing Lee Commercial Bldg, 1st fl., 6-12 Wingkut ST., Central Hong Kong.
Commercial Press — 35 Queen's Road, Central, Hong Kong, and other locations. Recent stamp issues from the People's Republic.
Taiwan Man Sang — Various locations. Stamps from Taiwan.
General Post Office — Philatlic window, 1st floor, G.P.O. (off Star Ferry Plaza), Central, Hong Kong.
Cat Street junk shops — Strange specimens of every description.

Many of the **Hollywood Road** curio dealers also deal in both stamps and coins, principally issues from China.

One Cent Hong Kong Notes:

The cheapest souvenir in Hong Kong costs one Hong Kong cent! That's HK1¢ or 1¢ Hong Kong, just to make certain everyone understands. And with due respect to inflation, this price has remained steady for more than a century.

Historic Bonds:

One of the hottest souvenir items to hit Hong Kong in a long time has been historic bonds. Some of these old Chinese bonds date back to the early years of this century and were used for funding projects such as the Hukuang Railway (loan of 1911) or the Canton-Kowloon Railway (1907). They were issued during a time of great expansion in China. As in many countries today, the Chinese floated bonds on the world's money markets. With the abrupt change of government in 1949, and th strokes of a new Communist Chinese legal pen, these bonds were declared null and void (because they were issued by former "imperialist" governments). They have always been around Hong Kong, but usually in safe deposit boxes or buried in long forgotten bundles of paper.

These bonds have also become a chic gift item in Hong Kong. Like lottery tickets given as gifts, they satiate one's gambling desire. Also, they look beautiful framed and one's office wall.

Prices for these bonds range from HK$90 to HK$15,000. Though you will find them in many antique shops, the prime fount of such paper is **Dollarsaver**, 30 Queen's Road East, Hong Kong (Tel: 5-280-825). A tiny nameless antique shop at 47 Hollywood Road, Hong Kong, also has a few bonds tucked away on back shelves.

Sporting Goods:

Hong Kong might seem like a strange and claustrophobic place to buy sporting goods, but indeed there are some very good sporting life bargains to be had here. The cheapest gear is in the various **China Products Stores** where you can buy everything from tennis rackets to sleeping bags and hiking boots. For better, top quality, international gear try the following shops:
Golf Clubs — The pro shops at **golf clubs.**
General Sports Gear — **Tokyo Sports**, Tsimshatsui Centre and Ocean Centre, Kowloon, and **New Sport**, Marco Polo Hotel.
Scuba Gear — **Bunn's Diving**, 188-E Wanchai Road, Wanchai, Hong Kong.
Camping Gear — **Mountaineer & Traveller Service**, 38A Boundary Street, Mongkok.
Jogging-Running Gear — **Marathon Sports**, various locations on both sides of harbour.
Sailmakers also prosper here because of cheap labour and low overheads. Chinese lofts are best for working sails — particularly the extra-heavy-duty cruising sorts. They are very inexpensive and give one good service but you should always provide complete design specifications. If you're looking for sails, try **De Vries**, 10 Kwai Ting Road, Kwai Chung or **Gaastra International**, 28A Hung To Road, Kwun Tung, or **Neil Pryde**, 77 Ping Che Road, Fanling, New Territories. There are dozens of other sail manufacturers here, so also check the yellow pages in the phone directory. Neil Pryde specializes in top-quality racing sails.

Yacht supplies can be found at the **Boating Centre**, Edko Tower, 32 Ice House St. Central, Hong Kong.

For British Admiralty Charts and other nautical reference works go to **George Falconer Nautical Limited**, Hong Kong Chinese Bank Bldg., 61 Des Voeux Road, Hong Kong.

Boats:

Hong Kong's most famous yard for **pleasure craft** is **Cheoy Lee**, 863 Laichikok Road, Kowloon, Tel: 3-743-7710, which welcomes interested visitors and would-be yachtsmen.

Junks, of course, are the hometown favourite and even considering shipping costs they give good value per foot. There's no one left who builds sailing types, but the **Sau Kee Shipyard**, 1 Shui Sau Street, Applichau (Tel: 5-527-219), still builds diesel-powered 25 footers for a lot less than anywhere in the West. The yard and its neighbours also make for an interesting visit, and nearby Aberdeen Harbour is a good place to watch the boats in action.

Marine and Yacht Supplies:

Hong Kong is very much a working harbour, with hundreds of yards and ships' chandleries dealing every sort of Western or Oriental marine equipment. Although fancy electronics and yachting supplies are not notably cheap, if you scrounge through piles of filthy gear, you'll inevitably turn up buried treasure such as brass portholes, handcarved blocks, old binnacles and the like. The best hunting is in **Western District** (along the waterfront past the Western Market), and at **Yaumatei** (on Canton and Shanghai Streets north of Jordan Road). Quick sketches of what you're looking for and a confident sleeves-rolled-up demeanor will usually overcome language problems.

Old-style copper or brass **ships' lamps** — either kerosene or electric — are still standard issue gear on the South China Sea, but their discovery by European residents has led to "special" pricing, so shop around and bargain firmly. Try **Hop Lee**, 18 Peel Street, and **Hop Fat Cheong**, 25 Tung Man Street, Central, Hong Kong for fascinating nautical lamps.

Boat Models:

For scale model, precision-crafted models of boats and ships, try **Zakaske (Scale Models) Limited** 124 Bedford Rd., Kowloon, Tel: 3-960951.

Model Soldiers:

Scale models of such fine regiments Seaforth Highlanders or the 2/7th Duke of Edinburgh's Own Gurkha Rifles, and many more. Precision made and the prices will forever cure you of calling them 'toy soldiers'. **King & Country**, 31 Wyndham St., Central, Hong Kong. Tel: 5-258603.

Ethnic Shops:

As one would expect in this international bazaar, there are quite a few "ethnic" shops.
Mountain Folkcraft (Ocean Terminal, Kowloon, and at 12 Wo On Lane, Central, Hong Kong), **Banyan** (Edinburgh Tower, Hong Kong and Harbour City) and **Nic Nac Shop** (Harbour City) all have ample supplies of Indian, Kashmiri and Nepali handicrafts. The **Amazing Grace** outlets in Landmark and Excelsior Hotel (Hong Kong), and Ocean Centre and Ocean Terminal (Kowloon) have a wide cross-cultural selection.

Vietnamese porcelain and lacquerware can be found at the **Vietnamese Import/Export Shop** (Asian House Arcade, 1 Hennessy Road, Wanchai, Hong Kong, on the Lockhart Road side of the arcade). Just the place to buy one of those lovely porcelain elephants (all sizes), known as BUFE's to allied GIs who served in that war. And for one of the best selections of Korean goods, try for one of the best selections of Korean goods, try **Gallery 69** (Edinburgh Tower, Hong Kong and Regent Hotel).

Chinese handicrafts can be found in the **Welfare Handicrafts Shop** (Connaught Centre, Central, Hong Kong, Salisbury Road, between Star House and the YMCA, and at Ocean Terminal, Kowloon). These shops have superb selections of items made especially for the shops. (All profits go to charity, and the women working there are volunteers.) Available are items such as *mien lap* (Chinese padded coats), baby backpacks and "bronzes" (patterned after ancient bronzes). If you are stuck for a gift idea and do not fancy charging through the colony in search of something, try this place, especially if you have kiddies on your shopping list. One price, no bartering, everything is marked, and the folks there are courteous.

Junk Gods:

The fisherfolk of Hong Kong display these icons in their rather cramped galleys. They represent an assortment of Chinese gods, deities and revered ancestors.

You'll find these greatly over-priced "antiques" in antique shops throughout the colony and in tiny shops on **Cheung Chau Island** (where many are made). At one time during the Seventies these images were quite cheap on Cheung Chau.

At 182 Reclamation Street (at the corner of Hi Lung Lane) Yaumatei, Kowloon, you will find the **Sun Hung Hing** altar shop (and three other such places a few yards away). Prices for icons there range from HK$30 to $300. These shops are also good places to buy *Pat kwa*, hexagonal mirrors used to deflect bad spirits. Brassware shops also abound there. Take the MTR to either Jordan Road or Yaumatei stations. The shops are about halfway between those MTR stops.

Chops:

Most visitors look upon the meticulously carved Chinese chops (also called seals or stamps) as quaint little remnants of the past. However, though most people in Hong Kong these days are literate and can sign their names, chops are still used here for official and/or legal business.

Most visitors buy chops as inexpensive souvenirs. These chops are usually made of sandstone or bone. Some of the more expensive ones are made of ivory, and the most expensive are carved from jade or other precious stones. If you feel adventurous, find **Man Wah Lane**, off Bonham Strand East, Hong Kong, and there you will find a little alley full of chop-carvers. Some of them speak enough English to translate your name phonetically into Chinese characters, though this is probably best written for you beforehand by a clerk at your hotel.

If you don't have much time, the indoor air-conditioned **Chinese "villages"** at Peak Tower, Hong Kong, has chop-makers who speak decent English.

The average price for a name chop is between HK$60 and HK$100 for just the chop. They cost more if they are in a small container with the ink (always of imperial red) and stamping pad.

Also study the valuable collections of chops for sale in the various **China Arts and Crafts** stores. Some are blank and some have an original inscription on them. If the latter is the case, the chop will be ground down or sawn off, and your characters will be carved or gouged on the now blank chop.

Remember when buying one that there are male and female chops. The male chop, *yang wen,* has elevated characters with the background cut away. When inked, the letters take the ink and the background is white. An opposite effect—with the characters gouged out so that the back ground is inked and the characters are white—is the female chop style *(yen wen).* Chop-makers will, if you prefer, carve your name in Roman letters instead of traditional Chinese characters.

If you have an interest in astrology, **Mountain Folkcraft** (Ocean Terminal, Kowloon, and 12 Wo On Lane, Central, Hong Kong) has chops ready-made with Chinese animal zodiac signs.

Mien Lap:

Mien lap is the Cantonese term for padded coats. If you are here in the winter, you cannot help but notice them on people in the streets or in store windows. They come in short jackets, long gowns or vests (waistcoats) and are made to fit men, women or children. They are the Chinese answer to a padded quilt, only this quite can be worn. Traditional *mien tap* colours are brown, black or blue for older persons and bright pink or red for babies (of either sex). But in Hong Kong, you will also find beautiful floral patterns in different designs and colour combinations. They are made with Western tastes in mind.

The best ones are on sale at the various **China Products Stores**. These are made of silk stuffed with high quality kapok or cashmere. They usually cost around HK$200 to $300 for an adult jacket. *Mien lap* sold in lanes and markets are cheaper—between HK$60 to $100—but they are stuffed with cotton padding. But they are all warm and just the thing to ward off damp chills in a far corner of the world. Baby *mien lap* are perfect gifts and cost under HK$50.

Chopsticks:

The ubiquitous yellow-plastic restaurant ones are definitely third-rate. The **China Products Stores** housewares departments have much more refined—but nevertheless very inexpensive—black-lacquered models. For out-and-out opulence, most ivory shops sell sets almost too well carved to be used for mere food.

Tea:

One way to tell just how Chinese Hong Kong really is, by her teashops. Having tea, *yum cha,* with small savouries, *dim sum,* is a way of life here, a relaxing bit of lifestyle which will never be replaced by coffee shops.

Tea is not just a thirst quencher here. The Chinese feel it has medicinal qualities as well. Herbal medicine

shops and teashops have medicinal herbal teas prepared for common problems such as colds, or specially made up for more serious maladies. There is even ginseng tea available for enhancement of sexual prowess.

The formal drinking of tea is said to date back more than 2,000 years and is another of those original Chinese social customs which has successfully infiltrated the Western world. Tea was introduced to Japan in the 7th Century and to Britain in the 18th Century. There is even a patron saint of tea, Luk Yu, who wrote a book in 780 on the subject called *Cha Ching* (Book of Tea). His name graces Hong Kong's most famous teahouse, the half-century old **Luk Yu Teahouse** on Stanley Street (a place said to serve Hong Kong's greatest selection of teas). Most Chinese like their tea slightly scented, hence the popularity of jasmine, chrysanthemum, rose and narcissus teas.

There are three main types of teas: green or unfermented tea, black or fermented tea (which the Chinese call "red" tea) and oolong tea, which is semifermented. The Chinese do not ruin their tea with milk, sugar or lemon, but rather savour its taste by drinking it straight. Depending on the type of tea, it is described by Chinese as delicate or quite strong. **Chiu Chow tea** is so strong it is drunk out of thimblesized glasses. It is an oolong mixture called **Tit Kuan Yin Cha,** Iron Goddess of Mercy Tea, and is powerful enough to keep you awake through a full night of Hong Kong's dated television programmes.

Chinese tea is always served by the pot, not, repeat not, by the teabag (even though those wretched little things are on sale here for Westerners). Traditional Chinese tea cups, meanwhile, come without handles and with small lids. To avoid getting a mouthful of tea leaves, adjust the lid so that just the hot—never warm or cold—liquid passes into your mouth. If you run out of tea in a Chinese restaurant, don't waste your energy by flagging down a waiter. Merely use the secret Chinese sign—turn the pot's top upside down and rest it on the pot's handle. Magically, a passing waiter will whisk away the pot and bring you another. And if you have a mouthful of superb Chinese food and want to tell the waiter to stop pouring, tap two fingers on the table.

There are dozens of little teashops in the colony, but two other well-known ones are the **Yung Wah Kee** and the **Chan Chun Lan Tea Co.** Each has locations on both sides of the harbour. Also, the **China Products Stores** always have a tea counter. Other interesting tea houses you might want to visit (since the Luk Yu is alway full) are the **Wan Lai** (484 Shanghai Street, Yaumatei, Kowloon) or the **Hing Wan** (119 Queen's Road Central, Hong Kong). Both are favourite hangouts of bird-walkers, who gather for a modest cuppa after taking their pet birds for a walk.

If you find yourself on Lantau Island, visit the **Lantau Tea Garden,** Hong Kong's only tea plantation, near the popular Po Lin Buddhist Temple. The Hong Kong Tourist Association sells a lovely package of various Chinese teas for HK $79.

Photo Film:

Unlike much of southeast Asia (onward travellers, particularly to China, take note), Hong Kong boasts ample stocks if amateur and professional photographic films. With all major world brands widely available—at prices often below home-country—there is little reason for camera-carriers to multiply the risks of airport X-ray damage by bringing in their own. The major downtown suppliers—notably any of the numerous branches of **Stereo Ltd**. or **Asia Photo Supplies**—are a better source than sun-baked souvenir stands that sell two rolls of film a year.

Processing is also quite cheap, but again, as anywhere, mass production tends to diminish quality. Except for **Kodachrome**, which is sent to Australia and returns processed in about two weeks, **Fotomax** offers one-hour service while the places above offer same-day (if you bring the film in before 10 a.m.) or overnight service for most films at no extra cost. Special or professional needs are best met at the specialist labs: **The Lab**, 34 Wong Chuk Hang Road, Aberdeen, Hong Kong. Tel: 5-550-351; **Robert Lam Colour**, 24 D'Aguilar Street, Central, Hong Kong. Tel: 5-296-807; or **Ray Cranbourne** Photography for black and white film only (61 Wyndham Street Central, Basement, Hong Kong, Tel: 5-248-482).

Tours, Special Attractions

The Hong Kong Tourist Association's *Sightseeing* pamphlet (given away at most hotels) lists the several dozen options. The brief descriptions include routes, times, prices, and whether any meals or drinks are included. Bookings are best handled through hotel reception desks.

Tour Tips:

1) The best trips are usually the simplest, notably **hald-day circular tours** of Hong Kong or Kowloon and the New Territories.

2) Particularly with three or four people, the higher priced **limousine tours** are well worth the extra flexibility and speed. Most will happily alter itineraries to suit particular tastes.

3) **Outlying island excursions** are just as easily and comfortably done by ordinary ferry—at as little as one quarter the cost, even including a splendid gourmet-shop picnic lunch.

4) **Tour-group dinners** and **nightclub shows** are invariably awful, doubly so at Aberdeen's infamous floating restaurants. Save the often considerable sums and have a first-class meal at a real restaurant. But by all means take the pleasant **sunset cruise** which ends up in Aberdeen Harbour. Just refuse to be pressured into dinner on those floating restaurants and return to shore.

5) Avoid Saturdays and Sundays, when time spent sitting in traffic is subtracted from already too-short stopovers.

The "Shopper's Paradise" is a tough place to be down and out. Though the *laissez-faire* economy spawns millionaires and bargain-happy tourists, it also leaves luckless tens of thousands in the overworked hands of hard-pressed private charities. One of these, the **Hong Kong Christian Service**, raises money

running instructive, sobering tours for visitors with an interest or a conscience. The three-hour trips (usually including a housing estate, an addicts' halfway centre and homes for the aged or retarded) leave Mondays and Fridays at 10 a.m. from the Tsimshatsui Y.M.C.A. (next to the Peninsula Hotel, Tel: 3-670-071, Ext. 271). A standard donation is $20.

Hong Kong's three most unique tour attractions—**Ocean Park**, the **Sung Dynasty Village** and the new **Space Museum** and **Planetarium** are described in the **Hong Kong For Children** section. That does not mean, however, that adults will not enjoy them. On the contrary, more adult visitors go to Ocean Park and the Sung Dynasty Village than children.

China Tours:

Hong Kong is *the* place to book one of those "fully booked" China tours which have recently been heavily advertised in your home country. Time and again, visitors who wanted to visit the Middle Kingdom and were turned down in London, New York or Paris because those city's China tour quotas were used up, arrive here and find out—*after* their travel plans have been made—that had they booked in Hong Kong, they would have found space on a China-bound excursion.

If you want to tour China write ahead. **Swire Travel** (c/o Swire House, second floor, Hong Kong, Tel: 5-844-8448) is one of the largest and most reputable agencies dealing in China tours, but there are many others available. You will need to send a deposit—a minimum of US$60 for the cheapest Canton tours—which is non-refundable if you cancel. The deposit, however, is applied to the full tour cost when you finally book and pay. Also send a photocopy of *every* page in your passport—not just the page with identity data.

If you are in Hong Kong shopping for a China tour (there are dozens advertised in the papers daily) and you find that the particular time you want to go is fully-booked, or if it is a public holiday in Hong Kong (especially the Chinese New Year period, or during a Canton Trade Fair held in April or October), you will probably not make it. But at other times, there often is space available on China tours. After trying a couple of agents with no success, trot along to the **China Travel Service** (77 Queen's Road Central, Hong Kong) before giving up hope. It is better to go in person, but you can also inquire by phone (5-259-121).

Persons with limited time here can peek at China from the **Lok Ma Chau Lookout point** (in Hong Kong's New Territories) or take a day trip just across the border into **Shenzhen** (which you will also see advertised as **Shum Chun**). This industrial area has vastly expanded from a little border village into a new joint venture economic zone. The Shenzhen trip is not an exciting China sojourn, but if you only have a day, it is the best available. The itinerary includes a visit to the **Shenzhen Reservoir**, adjacent **parklands**, a **kindergarten** and an **Arts & Crafts Centre**. Lunch is served at the reservoir. These tours leave from the **Hung Hom Railway Station** (Kowloon) for the 75 minute ride to **Lowu**, the border crossing with the famous-covered wooden railway bridge. You walk over this bridge into busy Shenzhen "on the other side."

Note: Many of the Communist Chinese goods available in various "official stores" that service quickie tours to Canton and Shenzhen are also available in Hong Kong and usually are cheaper here. Also, there are no toilets on the Hong Kong trains. There are, however, toilets on Canton-bound Chinese trains.

China and "China" Notes:

Hong Kong steers pragmatically clear of the two-China problem: neither the **People's Republic** nor **Taiwan** has official diplomatic representatives in the colony. Nevertheless, barring major shifts in policy, travel difficulties—including visas—can be handily resolved at the following two Chinese offices:

China Travel Service (People's Republic of China) 77 Queen's Road Central, Hong Kong, Tel: 5-259-121. Hours: 9 a.m. to 1 p.m. and 2 to 5 p.m. Monday through Saturday.

Chung Hwa Travel (Taiwan) 1009 Tak Shing House, Des Voeux Road Central at Pedder St., Hong Kong, Tel: 5-258-315. Hours: 9 a.m. to 12:30 p.m. and 2 to 5 p.m. Monday through Friday and until noon Saturday.

Cultural Activities

The Hong Kong Arts Centre, located on a site in Wanchai donated by the government, was opened in 1977. Built at a cost of HK$30 million, it is a private enterprise maintained by the donations of individuals and corporations. It houses a theatre, recital hall, studio theatre, exhibition galleries, a sculpture terrace, libraries, rehearsal rooms and facilities for workshops and experimental productions. It is a venue where the arts can be performed, displayed and developed. Since its opening, the Centre has mounted an extensive programme of concerts, recitals, plays, poetry readings, exhibitions and, in conjunction with the **Studio One Film Society,** screening of fine foreign films for cinema afficionados. Local individual performers and theatrical groups contribute to activities there, as well as internationally renowned artists.

Hong Kong Island's **City Hall** also has hosted thousands of international performances. A new cultural centre for Tsimshatsui (near the Star Ferry) is planned for the near future.

There are also local symphonic orchestras, such as the **Hong Kong Philharmonic** and the **Hong Kong Chinese Music Orchestra,** plus several amateur and professional theatres which employ full-time professional musicians and actors. These arts organizations reflect Hong Kong's cosmopolitan and international cultural life.

Twice annually, Hong Kong indulges in not one, but two, **international arts festivals.**

The **Hong Kong Arts Festival,** in January and February, features an intriguing programme of Western and Eastern art. Renowned orchestras, dance companies, drama groups, opera companies and jazz ensembles are invited to perform here alongside talented local artists. Traditional Chinese arts blend with Western cultural fare to create a uniquely Hong Kong arts extravaganza.

Another annual arts affair, the **Festival of Asian Arts,** is sponsored by the Urban Council and invites artists

and performers from various cultural regions in Asia to introduce to Hong Kong audiences their indigenous art forms. During this cultural orgy, Hong Kong is represented by groups that perform traditional Cantonese and Peking opera, Cantonese drama, multi-regional Chinese folk dance and music. Also included are performances by the Hong Kong Philharmonic Orchestra and the Hong Kong Chinese Music Orchestra. This festival takes place during October and November.

Chinese operas, puppet shows, dancing and other "local" cultural fare occur regularly throughout the year, especially during traditional festival periods. There are **free Chinese cultural performances** weekly sponsored by the Hong Kong Tourist Association.

See the feature section article **"Honouring Wise Men and Hungry Ghosts"** for details about Hong Kong's major annual religious festivals.

Museums and Art Galleries:

Museums are a usual tourist attraction rarely considered in a frantic shopping bazaar like Hong Kong. But the colony supports five, divided into two administrative categories—those under the joint management of the Urban Council and the Urban Department of Services, and those attached to universities.

The Hong Kong Museum of Art has a diversified collection, including contemporary and classical paintings, calligraphic scrolls, ceramics, sculpture, lacquerware, jade and cloisonné. Its most distinctive holdings are an extensive collection of oil paintings, drawings, prints, lithographs and engravings of historical Hong Kong. They provide a vivid pictorial record of Sino-British contacts in the 18th and 19th centuries. Contemporary works by Hong Kong artists are also regularly exhibited in this museum.

The Museum of Art is located in City Hall, near Hong Kong Island's Star Ferry Concourse. Admission is free. Hours: from 10 a.m. to 6 p.m. Monday through Saturday (except Thursday) and from 1 to 6 p.m. Sunday.

The Hong Kong Museum of History has in its permanent collection fine model junks that illustrate the colony's traditional fishing industry and one of the most comprehensive collections of late 19th and early 20th Century photographs of Hong Kong that document Fragrant Harbour's historic realities. Also significant is a collection of Hong Kong's coinage and the currencies of nearby Kwangtung Province. With the co-operation of the Hong Kong Archaeological Society, excavated objects, representative of the colony's earliest prehistoric periods, are on display in the museum's archaeological section. Disappearing local arts and crafts, traditional agricultural and fishing implements and rural architectural displays reminiscent of the old New Territories are an important part of the museum's ethnographic collection.

The **Museum of History** is at 58 Haiphong Road on Kowloon side. Admission is free. Hours: from 10 a.m. to 6 p.m. Monday through Saturday (except Friday) and from 1 to 6 p.m. Sunday.

The **Lei Cheng Uk Branch Museum** is at the site of a Later Han dynasty (25 to 220 A.D.) tomb. In its display halls are funerary wares and models of clay houses typical of that period. (See the Kowloon travel section for details.)

This museum-tomb is located at 41 Tonkin Street, Kowloon. Admission is 10 cents. Hours: from 10 a.m.

to 1 p.m. and 2 p.m. to 6 p.m. daily (except Thursday), and 1 to 6 p.m. Sunday.

The Fung Ping Shang Museum at Hong Kong University is the oldest museum in Hong Kong, founded in 1953. Its excellent bronze collection is divided into three groups: Shang and Chou era (15th-3rd Centuries B.C.) ritual vessels which testify to the superb achievement of early Chinese metallurgy; decorative mirrors from the Warring States period (480-221 B.C.) to the T'ang dynasty (618-906 A.D.); and 966 Nestorian crosses of the Yuan dynasty (1260-1368 A.D.), the largest collection of its kind in the world. Ceramics including simple pottery of the Third Millenium B.C., a number of Ming (1368-1644 A.D.) and Ch'ing (1644-1900 A.D.) dynasty paintings and specimens of Buddhist sculptural art from India are also on permanent display.

This musuem is located at 94 Bonham St., Pokfulam, Hong Kong. Hours: from 10 a.m. to 6 p.m. daily (except Thursday) and from 2 to 6 p.m. Sunday.

Museum of Tea Ware, Flagstaff House, Victoria Park, Hong Kong. A branch of Museum of Art, it contains more than 500 pieces of tea ware.

Museum of Chinese Historial Relics service as a permanent exhibition site for cultural treasures from China. Twice yearly exhibits. Causeway Centre, 1st. fl., 28 Harbour Rd., Wanchai, Hong Kong. Adults HK$15. Children HK$10.

Hong Kong Space Museum — Not really a museum but "they" named it. The 'Space Theatre,' known as a planetarium in other lands, offers five shows daily (2:30, 4, 5:30, 7:30 and 9 p.m.) The English-language shows are at 4 p.m. on Mondays and Fridays, 9 p.m. Sundays and Wednesdays. However, a simultaneous translation service is available (for an extra HK$5) in English, Japanese and Mandarin, should you find yourself at a Cantonese show. Arrive 30 minutes ahead to make arrangements. There are also an Exhibition Hall and Hall of Solar Sciences with excellent exhibitions. Open daily except Tuesday from 2-10 p.m., Sundays and public holidays 10:30 a.m.-10 p.m. Space Theatre tickets HK$15 adult, HK$10 children. Exhibition Hall and Hall of Solar Sciences *free*. Enquiries: 3-721-2361.

The **Art Gallery of the Chinese University** is relatively new, but houses an important collection of paintings and calligraphy by Kwantung artists from the Ming period to modern times. Other impressive items are a collection of 300 bronze seals of Han and pre-Han provenance, and stone rubbings from monuments of the Han and Sung dynasties.

The Art Gallery is located on the campus of the Chinese University in the New Territories. Admission is free. Hours: from 10 a.m. to 4:30 p.m. daily.

Pao Sui Loong Galleries of the Hong Kong Arts Centre. Changing exhibitions Open 10 a.m. to 8 p.m. daily. Free

There is also a wax museum with life-like wax figures from Chinese history in Kowloon's **Sung Dynasty Village** and is only accessible during a commercial tour of that visitors' attraction.

Libraries:

Borrowing books is normally impossible for short-term visitors, but most libraries here have reading rooms where you can relax or do scholarly research. The best libraries are:

Urban Council Public Library — City Hall, Edinburgh Place (off Star Ferry Concourse), Hong Kong. Large, comprehensive and usually crowded. Hours: 9 a.m. to 8 p.m. weekdays except Thursdays, 9 a.m. to 5 p.m. Saturday, 9 a.m. to 1 p.m. Sunday.

British Council Library — 255 Hennessy Road, Wanchai, Hong Kong, Tel: 5-756-501. British books, magazines and newspapers. Hours: 7:30 a.m. to 10:30 p.m. weekdays, and from 7:30a.m. to 7:30 p.m. Saturday.

American Library — Pacific House, third floor, Queen's Road Central, Hong Kong. U.S. books, magazines, newsapapers, telephone directories and college catalogues. Hours: 10 a.m. to 6 p.m. weekdays.

Universities Service Centre Library — 155 Argyle St., Mongkok, Kowloon. Useful collection for China scholars. Open business hours daily, but prior permission usually required.

Hong Kong Tourist Association Library — Connaught Centre, 35th floor, Connaught Road, Central, Hong Kong. Principally a working collection for travel writers. Hours: 9 a.m. to 5 p.m. weekdays, and 9 a.m. to 1 p.m. Saturday.

Note: The three major universities — the **University of Hong Kong**, the **Chinese University** and **Hong Kong Polytechnic** — all have comprehensive and large libraries, but special permission is required before outsiders can use these facilities.

Booksellers:

Hong Kong patronizes some of Asia's best overseas book-sellers, even though their price mark-ups are quite high (but less than at hotel bookstands). Among the principal ones are:

Harris Book Company — Prince's Bldg. Arcade, first floor, Central, Hong Kong; **Hong Kong Book Centre**, basement, 25 Des Voeux Road Central, Hong Kong; **Kelly & Walsh**, 10 Ice House St. Central, Hong Kong; **SCM Post Family Bookshops** at Star Ferry (Hong Kong), Ocean Centre (Kowloon) and at various Mass Transit Railway stations; **Swindon Book Company**, Ocean Terminal, second floor (near Star Ferry, Kowloon), Ocean Centre, next to Ocean Terminal, and at 24 Ashley Road, Kowloon; and **Times Book Centre**, Hutchison House, Central, Hong Kong.

Movies:

Hong Kong movie houses also offer a spectrum of foreign languages besides those in Mandarin and the few in Cantonese: Indian and Japanese films are regularly shown, and the foreign community has an ample selection of American and European movies to choose from.

The biggest deterrents to good commercial films here are the government censors and distributors, the latter being the worst culprits. The distributors arbitrarily cut (not edit) films to fit neatly into a convenient time frame (usually two hours) so they can cram in five or six showings a day. *A Bridge Too Far* is a classic example. Sir Laurence Olivier's visage and name were posted over the marquee (along with the other stars) but his one cameo appearance in the film was completely cut out. To combat this clip-clip mentality, theatres now have to advertise the time length of a flick. Therefore, if *The Longest Day* is shown in 120 minutes, you know that 60 minutes have been chopped.

Nearly a hundred theatres here screen everything from demure Chinese costume dramas to gory "spaghetti" Westerns. Most screen for shows daily—usually at 2:30, 5:30, 7:30 & 9:30. Some add special morning, noon or midnight showings, especially during holidays or weekends, and all include 20 to 30 minutes of often amusing pre-film advertisements. Though programmes can change without warning virtually overnight. The *Hong Kong Standard's* day-to-day listings are generally accurate and complete.

Because of frequent crowds, most theatres sell reserved seats only. During the week, or in the case of more obscure offerings, simply show up at screen time and you should be able to secure a seat. It's always better, however, to arrive at least a few hours before a screening to buy a reserved seat ticket. You can also make a reservation over the phone. The latter allows you a chance to reconfirm the programme. A concierge's Cantonese can be helpful, and remember that tickets are held only until **15 minutes** before the start of scheduled show.

Ticket prices follow an old-style, three-tier system. The top-end prices are: "Loge" or "Dress Circle" at HK$20-22 for all but the biggest-name imports. "Back Stalls" and "Front Stalls" are cheaper. (Except at the **Palace**, the largest, most comfortable and expensive theatre here.)

Festivals, Holidays

The principal Chinese festivals listed below are described in detail in the feature section article on "Honouring Wise Men and Hungry Ghosts." On public holidays (indicated by asteriks), banks and offices close. The quiet Chinese New year, however, usually does not affect tourist-area restaurants and shops.

Undated listings below are normally set at least six months in advance: contact the Hong Kong Tourist Association for precise information.

January 1	**New Year's Day***
January-February	**Chinese New Year***
February-March	**Hong Kong Arts Festival**
March	**Yuen Siu** (Lantern Festival)
March-April	**Ching Ming* Easter Holidays"** (Good Friday, Easter Sunday and Monday)
May	**Birthday of Tin Hau** **Buddha's Birthday** **Tam King**
May	**Horse-Racing Season ends**
June	**Tuen Ng*** (Dragon Boat Festival)
July	**Queen's Birthday** **Birthday of Lu Pan**
August 25	**Liberation Day***
September	**Mid-Autumn Festival** **Horse-racing Season begins**
October	**Birthday of Confucius** **Chung Yueng***
October-November	**Asian Arts Festival**
December 25	**Christmas***
December 26	**Boxing Day***

Sports

Martial Arts:

Several local martial arts institutions welcome interested visitors, whether you are skilled or a novice. Both the **South China Athletic Association** (particularly for *tai chi chuan, shiu lam, judo* and *yoga),* and the **YMCA International House** for *judo, tae kwon do, hung kuen* and **hak kei do**) teach regular, inexpensive classes at all proficiency levels.

Specialized kung fu schools include **Luk Chi Fu** (446 Hennessy Road, third floor, Causeway Bay, Hong Kong, Tel: 5-891-1044), the **Hong Kong Chinese Martial Arts Association** (687 Nathan Road, ground floor, Blocks A & B, Mongkok, Kowloon, Tel: 3-944-803) and the **Kung Fu Association** (174 Tung Lowan Road, first floor, flat C, Hong Kong, Tel: 5-715-056). (Chinese speakers may be necessary for effective communication at the latter two associations.)

For the simply curious, parks throughout the colony (notably **Chater Garden** in Central, the **Botanical Gardens** above Central, **Victoria Park** in Causeway Bay and **Kowloon Park** in Tsimshatsui) are alive just after dawn every morning with mass displays of *tai chi chuan.*

Boating:

So-called **"pleasure junks"** can be found and hired through the classified listings in *The South China Morning Post's* classified section. You might also try the **Hong Kong Boating Centre**, Edko Tower, 32 Ice House St., Centre, Hong Kong, Tel: 5-223-527. Prices vary, but begin at about HK$400 per hour for a minimum of two or three hours.

More colourful are motorized sampans, which can accommodate up to a dozen people. Sampans can be rented dockside in Aberdeen or at the **Causeway Bay Typhoon Shelter.** The owners tend to view tourists as easy money, so hire sampans at Aberdeen will often demand up to HK$100 for an hour's swing through the anchorage. Barter aggressively.

Swimming:

Can be quite good, particularly at the colony's more isolated beaches. Many of the top hotels—and the Tsimshatsui Y.M.C.A.—have pools.

Beaches:

Hong Kong is not known as a beach resort, but the island does have a number of beautiful beaches which are accessible by public land transport. Additionally, a great number of beaches on the outlying islands are accessible by inter-island ferry and private boats.

On Hong Kong, Kowloon, Lantau, and Cheung Chau islands, there are 38 **gazetted beaches.** "Gazetted" means the beaches are under the care and protection of the Urban Council and have lifeguards and changing facilities, barbeque pits, restaurants and other amenities.

Water-Skiing:

Very popular in summer at the more fashionable beaches. Skis and a boat with driver can be rented for HK$220 per hour from several companies in **Deep Water Bay**, notably the **Deep Water Bay Speedboat Co.**, Tel: 5-812-0391.

Sailing:

Members of yacht clubs with reciprocal privileges can usually find a crew slot or rent dinghies from the **Royal Hong Kong Yacht Club**, at Kellett Island (opposite the Excelsior Hotel), Causeway Bay, Hong Kong, Tel: 5-790-2817.

Scuba Diving:

There are interesting scuba sites here, but often the water is less than perfectly clear. Unless you have an "in" to one of the many underwater clubs here, your best bet is to contact **Bunn's Diving Shop**, 188 Wanchai Road, Wanchai, Hong Kong, Tel: 5-721-629. Note: If you are a British Sub-Aqua Club member, there are more than a half dozen club branches here. Check the club list or write to the headquarters in London for specific addresses in Hong Kong.

Windsurfing:

There are four windsurfing centres here which rent surfboards or give lessons. **Stanley Main Beach**, Hong Kong (5-223-316); **Cheung Chau Island** at Tung Wan Beach at the **Surf Hotel**, **Sha Beach**, **Sai Kung** and at Silver Mine Beach, **Lantau Island**.

Rugby:

League play occurs at various locations, generally during the cooler months. Contact the **Hong Kong Rugby Football Union**, G.P.O. Box 1088, Hong Kong, Tel: 5-660-719.

Football (Soccer):

Professional and semi-professional matches are held at various stadia in the colony. Check the newspapers' sports sections.

Cricket:

Both the **Hong Kong Cricket Club**, Wongneichong Gap Road, on the way to Repulse Bay, Hong Kong, and the **Kowloon Cricket Club**, Cox's Road, Tsimshatsui, Kowloon, host league games on weekends during cooler months. But these are private clubs. If you belong to a cricket club at home, check to see if there are reciprocal rights to these clubs.

Golf:

The **Royal Hong Kong Golf Club** has three 18-hole courses at **Fanling**, New Territories (about 70 minutes by train from Kowloon), and a nine-hole course at **Deep Water Bay**, Hong Kong (between Aberdeen and Repulse Bay, about 20 minutes by cab from Central). Visitors may pay these courses on Monday through Fridays only. Green fees are HK$360 per 18 holes or HK$480 per day at Fanling, HK$100 per round at

Deep Water Bay. (Phone 0-901-211 for Fanling or 5-812-0088 for Deep Water Bay.

Squash:

Not yet the vogue in hotels (and a fair hassle for those without an acquaintance in one of the several private clubs). **Victoria Park** in Causeway Bay, Hong Kong, has a handful of public courts open from 7 a.m. to 9 p.m. daily. Fee: HK$16 per hour. Booking, however, is often difficult (Tel: 5-706-186 after 10 a.m.).

Tennis:

Like the problem of booking a squash court, reserving a tennis court is easier said than done. Try **Victoria Park** in Causeway Bay, Tel: 5-706-186, open from 7 a.m. to 11 p.m., or scenic **Bowen Road**, in Hong Kong's Mid-Levels, Tel: 5-282-983, open from 7 a.m. to 6 p.m. The newest courts are on **Wongneichung Road** enroute to Repulse Bay, open 7 a.m. to 11 p.m., Tel: 5-749-122, but **Kowloon Tsai Park** in North Kowloon, Tel: 3-367-878, open 7 a.m. to 7 p.m., also has public courts. The cost for courts ranges from HK$12 to $24 per hour depending on the time of the day. Booking is always heavy, particularly on weekends. The easiest places to play — and the nicest locations — are the Bowen Road or Wongneichung Road Courts (on weekday mid-mornings).

Table Tennis:

Ping pong isn't quite up to Mainland "diplomatic" standards, but is very good here nonetheless. There are public tables at Morse Park Indoor Games Hall in Hong Kong. Fees are a nominal HK$4 per hour.

Bowling:

There are three modern bowling alleys in Kowloon: the **Brunswick Bowling Centre**, Middle Road, and **Four Seas Blowing Centre** on Castle Peak Road or at **Cityplaza**, Taikoo Shing, Hong Kong. The best alleys in Hong Kong are at the **South China Athletic Association** on Caroline Hill Road, Happy Valley.

Hiking:

Serious trekkers might want to tackle the 62-mile **MacLehose Trail** (named for the current governor, an outdoorsman who was the official impetus behind the establishment of many new parks and trails in Hong Kong) in the **New Territories**. Though it has been navigated in less than 54 hours, the less energetic can opt to hike any of its 10 segments.

Hong Kong has "protected" some 70 percent of its 1,067 square kilometers and calls these countryside areas **"country parks."** Trails have been cut out of the rugged countryside, camping places built, and they are guarded by police patrols. There are a total of 21 such country parks, five on the south side of Hong Kong Island, two on Lantau island, one in Kowloon and the rest in the New Territories. There is a handy brochure distributed by the Government Information Services called *How to Get to Hong Kong's Country Parks*. However, the bible for anyone who wants to really enjoy the Hong Kong countryside is *Selected Walks in Hong Kong* by Ronald Forrest and George

Hobbins which details more than 75 rural walks. (Note: There are snakes in Hong Kong, so a sturdy walking stick can prove handy.)

Jogging:

A better urban bet than cycling, but still a bit awkward. Runners staying in Tsimshatsui or Causeway Bay can try, respectively, **Kowloon** or **Victoria** parks, neither of them terribly exciting. More expensive, flat, scenic and for most of its length carless is **Bowen Road**, a five-minute cab ride—or serious climb—above Central District. Peak jogging experiences can be enjoyed on The Peak's flat, car-free, two-mile loop along **Harlech** and **Lugard roads**. It is well worth the hardcore ascent/descent efforts required. The Hilton Hotel, Central, offers its visitors an early morning jogging programme, as does the Regent of Hong Kong in Tsimshatsui, Kowloon. Also try the Adventist Hospitals **jogging clinic** each Sunday (5-746211). The Hash House Harriers are also prevalent.

Cycling:

Traffic, narrow roads and hills make this sport a problematic one, but bicycles can be rented at the less harrowing **Silver Mine Bay** on Lantau Island.

Ice Skating:

At **Laichikok Amusement Park** (near the Mei Foo Sun Cheun apartment complex), Kowloon, from 11 a.m. to 10:30 p.m. It is HK$22 for two hours, skates included. Travel there by the Mass Transit Railway or bus from the Kowloon Star Ferry. Laichikok is a complete amusement park. At the ice rink at City-plaza, Taikoo Shing Quarry Bay, Hong Kong, it costs HK$20 including the use of skates for every session. The hours are from 7 a.m. to 10 p.m.

Roller Skating:

The charges of rinks at **Cityplaza**, Taikoo Shing, Hong Kong 5-670391 and **Telford Gardens**, Kowloon (3-757-6611) vary with time of day.

Horseback Riding:

Try the **Jockey Club** stables in Pokfulam, Hong Kong (5-501359). They teach everything from beginners' classes to proper show jumping.

Horseraces:

Horseraces are Hong Kong's Roman Circus, an orgy of money-letting for everyone from the poorest day-labourer to the haughtiest *taipan* (top executive). Annual meeting dates—some 60 in all, and more than 400 actual races—take place on Wednesday nights and Saturday and Sunday afternoons, September through May. They alternate weekly between two courses— the uniquely urban original course in **Happy Valley**, Hong Kong, and a massively modern new facility, at **Shatin** in the New Territories. Betting, controlled by the **Royal Hong Kong Jockey Club**, follows (more or less) standard parimutuel rules and includes both on and off-course wagering. Hong Kong is so mad about the "sport of kings" that more than HK$100 million is turned over on a typical race day.

Tickets to the exalted **Member's Enclosure** are available at the RHKJC Off-Course Betting Centre at the Star Ferry (Hong Kong) or the Membership Department Office, RHKJC Building, 12th floor, 2 Sports Road, Happy Valley, Hong Kong (the tall building by the grandstands at the Happy Valley track), from two days before a race meeting. (Telephone 5-790-4827 for enquiries.) Guest badges are HK$50 and valid for that day only. Bring your passport to prove you are a visitor. If you miss the above two outlets, apply at either track on the day of the races (from noon for day races; 6 p.m. for night meetings) at the Badge Enquiry Office located inside the main entrance to the member's enclosure of either track. At Happy Valley, however, the stands often fill up early, so go to the track at least an hour early. Special buses and trains run to the more distant Shatin course. Private cars are not allowed there.

Tip sheets and complete racing forms are published for each meeting in all four English-language newspapers and are also broadcast on the radio.

The Hong Kong Tourist Association operates a horseracing tour which includes transfers, meals, guides and entrance to the members' enclosure for HK$200. Telephone 3-722-5555 for details.

Special Betting Terms

Quinella	—1st and 2nd in one race.
Double Quinella	—Pick one of the first two horses in two specific races.
Six Up	—Choosing one of the first two horses in *each* of the days six races.
Triple	—Pick three winners from three specific races.

Hong Kong For Kids

What about kids who accompany their parents on a trip here?

Ocean Park, and its neighbour, Water World, are natural attractions for kids who are fed up with flying or hotel rooms or shopping in hot humid weather. The Ocean Park is a combination marineland and amusement park. The former is on quite a large scale while the latter, though smaller than those giant parks back home, is still spectacular. And, of course, fun.

The Ocean Park is divided between two levels and it is on the headland—connected to the lowland by a 1½ kilometer cable-car system—where you will find the Ocean Theatre, a 3,000-seat aquatic theater for performing dolphins and a killer whale. (There is also an occasional high dive act to enliven things.) The Wave Cove with its rocky shoreline is home to a variety of seals and penguins and birds. Viewing is above and below the waterline. The Atoll Reef is the three-level aquarium housing some 30,000 fish, including sharks which are hand fed.

On the same level is the amusement section featuring, among other rides, The Dragon, one of the longest (840 meters) and most spectacular roller coasters in the world. There is also an escalator leading to yet another amusement section which, according to the *Guiness Gook of Records* is the longest in the world.

On the lower level are the children's play area and petting zoo, dolphin feeding pools, trained bird and seal shows, plus delightful gardens.

Adjacent to the Ocean Park, yet distinctly separate is, Water World, which, as the name implies, is a water play park, complete with five slides, a beach, and a variety of other aquatic attractions.

Both Ocean Park and Water World are easily accessible, even though they are on the south side of Hong Kong Island, near Aberdeen and you are in a hotel in Kowloon. (It is also a good opportunity to combine a trip to Aberdeen or the floating restaurants or Stanley Market with a stop at these two attractions). Both venues are served by special Citybus transport from Central and tickets can be purchased in the Mass Transit Railway stations which include the round trip bus fare. The buses, incidentally, are often topless double-deckers which makes the trip a nice sightseeing one too.

Tickets to Ocean Park cost HK$77 for adults and HK$38 for children, including round trip bus transport. (It is HK$70 and HK$35 without.) The park is open all year. For information and show times call 5-550947.

Water World is only open from May through October. The cost is HK$40 for adults and HK$20 for kids with special lower prices for evenings. (If you take the bus, add HK$7 and HK$3 onto the tab.) Call 5-556055 for information and also check the weather.

Another great place for kids is the **Aw Boon Haw** (formerly Tiger Balm) **Gardens** on Tai Hang Road, also on Hong Kong Island. This is a Chinese version of Disneyland with weird sculptured and painted monsters and demons from Chinese mythology. Besides these, the **Space Museum** (which is actually a **Plantetarium** and **Museum**) is another good place for children (over 6). Sitting in the **Space Theatre** watching skies whiz by makes one feel like he's on a hyper-speed space journey in *Star Wars*. There are five scheduled "trips" a day, each lasting for about an hour, but only four in English per week (Call 3-721-2361 for times.) In the **Exhibition Hall** there is an *Apollo 7* space capsule from the United States Mercury Space Program, a piece of the moon and other space exhibits brought back to Earth by American astronauts. Book your tickets early (up to four days in advance is allowed) at the Space Museum itself in Kowloon, just across from the Peninsula Hotel.

In the Laichikok area of Kowloon is the **Sung Dynasty Village**. China's Sung dynasty began 1,000 years ago, and this village is a "living" replica of a small Sung community. Passing through the village gates is like stepping out of a capsule after a trip through time. One second you're in modern Hong Kong—and the next you're 1,000 years back in time on the main street of a Chinese village, surrounded by acrobats, kung fu artists and shops selling traditional Chinese goods. When you buy tickets you are given a packet of Sung dynasty paper money, invented during this era, which you use to buy things. At the village's **wax museum**—which of course would not have existed 1,000 years ago—there are life-like figures from Chinese history; one of the two guards at the entrance is real, the other is wax—which one? Phone 3-741-5111 for opening hours and show times. Travel agencies arrange tours, which include lunch or a snack, for HK$120 to $155. The local entrance fee is

HK$30 but doesn't include transportation or food.

The Sung Dynasty Village is just adjacent the **Laichikok Amusement Park**. This park is not as glamorous as those in the United States, but it's still fun, especially for children. Laichikok has an ice-skating ring (HK$22) for a two hour skates rental), a small zoo and numerous carnival-style rides. The **Peak Tower Village** on The Peak is Hong Kong's air-conditioned "village" with traditional "street stalls," fortune tellers, calligraphers, acupuncturists and shops where small traditional trades are plied. Try a special candy there called "Dragon Beard."

There are Chinese shadow-boxing, or *tai chi chuan*, demonstrations every morning in the parks (7:30 to 8:30 a.m. Monday through Saturday) at **Chater Gardens**, Central, and **Victoria Park**, Causeway Bay, both in Hong Kong. Also from 7 to 8 a.m. Monday through friday at **Kowloon Park** and **King George V Park**, Kowloon. The Hong Kong Tourist Association sponsors free kung fu demonstrations, puppet shows, acrobats, jugglers at **The Landmark** and **Cityplaza** on Hong Kong Island and at the Ocean Terminal and New World Centre in Kowloon. Telephone 3-722-5555 for the times.

Hong Kong's main zoo is in the **Botanical Gardens** in Mid-Levels, across the street from the Governor's mansion. There are more than 300 different kinds of birds, many monkeys, a lynx, even a jaguar.

Horse Riding? Ring the **Jockey Club** stables in Happy Valley, Hong Kong (5-501359).

The **YMCA** on Salisbury Road, Tsimshatsui, Kowloon, has youth activities scheduled all year, but especially during the summer. Pop in and see what's going on. You might also want to check the **Girl Guides** (Girl Scouts), the **Brownies** (3-325523), the **Boy Scouts** (3-673-096) or the **Outward Bound School** (3-281-6346) to see what is planned for children.

One of the best sources of kids fun information is the *Children's Guide to Hong Kong* by Ellen O'connor and *Enjoy Hong Kong with Pre-schoolers* by Lindsay Hasell.

Doing Business Here

Working:

Most foreigners who work here are professionals, "expats" who were hired back home. Menial or temporary jobs are invariably filled by locals for pay per month what most from the West would expect per week. The only real exception are girlie bars, escort services and British-style pubs, where foreign females command a distinct premium and may or may not be on a "work visa."

Teaching languages, though, is one good possibility, particularly for native speakers of English. The commercial language schools and occasional private students advertised in *The South China Morning Post* classifieds are okay for a start, but the first can be depressing and the second few and official national programmes: the **British Council**, Alliance Francaise, and the **Goethe Institute** (see phone book), but they do not hire visitors. Stopping by to chat with the teachers is a good beginning, but a university degree, prior experience and reasonably long-term plans are essential.

Without solid professional qualifications or an inside track, the only other halfway decent chance are the English-language media (see **Media Section**). Whether from liberal outlook or desperation, the lower-prestige print and broadcast organizations occasionally give a chance to simple energetic enthusiasm. More than one career has started at *The Hong Kong Standard,* but nevertheless this is strictly hit or miss; the days are long gone when you could arrive on a tourist visa and start working for a paper the next day. Phoning around to ad agencies will sometimes turn up modelling or soundtrack dubbing assignments.

Except for British (U.K.) passport-holders, official policy on work permits for foreigners is somewhat exclusionary. Those still overseas with a firm commitment *on paper* from an established local company will have no problems: any British embassy or consulate will clear a residence visa in a few days. But within the colony on a visitor's pass, it is technically illegal to even *seek* employment. And unless a prospective employer is willing to go through a lot of bureaucratic hassling, this means having to leave for a week or so and apply for the visa at an embassy elsewhere, say Manila. Short-timers can and do—illegally, of course—work under-the-table by stretching out a visitor's pass (see **Travel Formalities** above). But they also tend to get increasingly hostile questions when applying for extensions.

Those with seriously imperial aspirations should contact the **Hong Kong Government Office Recruitment Department**, 6, Grafton St., London W1X3LB. Offical jobs for expatriates run the gamut from police officer to film director, and include all sorts of anachronistic perks and benefits. Everyone, though, pays salaries tax, up to a maximum of only 17%.

Legal Requirements:

If you want to do business here, consider the following basic new business procedures:

Registering a **limited company** in Hong Kong requires little paper work and very little money. The standard business **Registration Fee** is HK$600 plus HK$6 for each HK$1,000 of nominal capital. A **name filing fee** costs HK$30 per name (which is reserved for three months if acceptable). **Sole proprietorships** cost only HK$600 (annually) to register and are simpler to set up. (Free brochures are available from government departments involved.)

There are solicitors and accountants here who specialize in such things, but the legal procedure is really quite painless. If you wish, you can register your company at your accountants' or solicitors' office and keep your actual "office" in your briefcase and hotel room. For **limited companies**, contact the **Registrar General's Office** and, for **sole proprietorships, the Business Registration Office**. **Factory registration** is handled by the **Labour Department** and **work permits/visas** are the concern of the **Immigration Department**. (All addresses are listed in Appendix A.)

Identity Cards:

By law, everyone must carry some form of identification and identity card must be presented before any Government service—business or otherwise—is performed. (See earlier section on *Identification Cards* in these pages.)

Taxes:

Limited companies pay **basic taxes** of 18½%, sole proprietorships, 17%. **Interest tax** is 17%. **Property tax**—the English term is rates—comes with your rent and is usually excluded from most rental agreements. (The property rates are set by the government and are periodically updated.) There is a simplified **graduated salaries tax**, with few deductions allowed, but a salaries tax cannot exceed 17% of one's total salary. There is no capital gains tax *(per se),* dividend tax or a tax on income or profits earned overseas or offshore.

Money, Remittance and Investment:

Hong Kong is a **free money market**. Any amount of any currency can be moved in or out of the colony. There are controls on capital or profit remittances.

Special Economic Zone:

Lately, an additional trading venue has been established in a **Special Economic Zone** on the Chinese side of the Sino-British border at **Shenzhen** (also called **Shum Shum**) where more than 1,000 co-ventures between Hong Kong and Chinese companies were in full operation at the end of 1982. The Chinese usually supply land—which is scarce and expensive in Hong Kong—and labour—which is cheaper than in Hong Kong—in exchange for modern manufacturing and marketing skills.

Other Useful Information:

Readers who are interested in more detailed information about making an investment in the colony are referred to Appendix A where lists of useful business publications and organisations are given.

Complaints

Though Hong Kong's laws are fairly strict when compared with those enforced by other Asian countries, there is always somebody in the colony ready to fleece a bewildered visitor. The Hong Kong Tourist Association (HKTA) has a wide-ranging and reputable membership but they cannot vouch for every member firm; they can, however, exert a certain amount of pressure in a dispute. If you have a legitimate complaint, see them (at Connaught Centre, 35th floor, Hong Kong, Tel: 5-244-191), especially if the firm has the HKTA decal (a junk logo) on its door or window.

Gold Purchases:

Hong Kong's jewellers have since 1972 been legally required to adhere to a gold hallmark (if they sell a gold bracelet at 18K, it must really be 18K and so marked) and since 1981 the parts-per thousand gold content of a piece is also guaranteed by law, so you should get what you pay for. This is an elementary safeguard, because Hong Kong jewellers have long felt it is "against Chinese tradition" to properly hallmark jewellery. Also, when called on the carpet for dishonesty a jeweller usually blames "language problems" — even if a tourist or resident testifies that a sales clerk spoke English better than he or she did. Let the buyer beware, because occasionally this causes problems when gold purchases are made. Again, call the HKTA, or perhaps the **Consumer Council** (Asian House, 3rd flr., 1 Hennessy Rd., Hong Kong, Tel: 5-200511) to air such complaints.

Diamond Purchases:

If your complaint deals with diamonds try the **Diamond Importers Association** (Hong Diamond Exchange Bldg. Duddell St., Central, Hong Kong, Tel: 5-235-497). This association polices its members.

Identifying Gems and Metals:

If you want your gem's identity and value confirmed, go to the **Gemological Laboratory of Hong Kong** (802 Luk Hoi Tung Building, 31 Queen's Road, Central, Hong Kong, Tel: 5-262-422). To assay gold, visit Hong Kong's mint (**Zenith Refinery**, 213 Wai Yip Street, Pioneer Industry Building, 5th Floor Kwun Tong, Kowloon. Tel: 3-890-223).

Taxi Complaints:

Taxi complaints are usually the most common made by visitors and they fall into two categories — overcharging or attempts to claim lost property left in a vehicle. The Royal Hong Kong Police Force has a **Taxi "hotline"** (Tel: 5-277-171) to assist. If a constable is nearby, take your complaint directly to him (or threaten to). Such tactics are a marvellous cure for obdurate drivers.

Copyright Infringements:

For copyright violations — if you happen to be Messrs. Cartier, Gucci, Lanvin or the likes address your complaints to the **Trade Department** Ocean Centre, 5 Canton Road, Tsimshatsui, Kowloon, Tel: 3-722-2333.

Fraud:

To complain about out and out fraud, contact the RHKPF "Fraud Squad" (Commercial Crimes, RHKPF, Block "O" Victoria Barracks, Hong Kong, Tel: 5-271-416).

If you find out about a fraudulent sale after you have departed, write to the HKTA or the Consumer Council.

Money Thefts:

This is a complaint most consulates don't like to hear, but they are usually quite helpful and sym-

pathetic to theft victims. The Royal Hong Kong Police Force is also efficient and helpful. If your hotel is reluctant to assist because of the bad publicity, go to the police directly. Also, the Hong Kong Tourist Association will gladly assist travellers who have been robbed or swindled.

Courtesy

One would think that a territory immersed in the diplomatic business of selling would realize the importance of being polite. The reverse, unfortunately, is often true. Hong Kong deserves its dubious reputation, as "the rudest place on earth."

The Hong Kong government is aware of this protocol problem and constantly exhorts (through media campaigns) its 150,000 plus civil servants to be polite. The Hong Kong Tourist Association is also concerned.

Tipping

Though a 10 percent gratuity is added to most hotel and restaurant bills, you are still expected to tip. If the service has been bad, however, collect every penny from the change tray. If the service has been abominable, go to the restaurant manager and demand that the automatic 10 percent service charge — in your case, non-service charge — be deducted from your bill.

Most Chinese restaurants add on a service charge, but some of the smaller, traditional ones do not. Ask and you shall find out.

Bellboys, porters and doormen usually receive about HK$20 per piece. Cloakroom and lavatory attendants, HK$1. Taxi drivers, barbers and hairdressers, about 10 percent. Tourist guides — if good — HK$10. Nothing to cinema usherettes or petrol station attendants.

Religious Services

There are numerous houses of worship besides Buddhist temples, the Royal Hong Kong Jockey Club, and the Hongkong and Shanghai Banking Corporation. Although many are mission-oriented and therefore Chinese-speaking, the principal places (below) conduct all or most of their services in English. With the possible exceptions of **St. John's** and the **Shelley Street Mosque** (both built in the 1840s), none are either as old or notable as those in Macau.

Protestant (Church of England — Episcopalian):

St. John's Cathedral (Anglican), Garden Road (behind the Hilton Hotel), Central District, Hong Kong.

St. Andrew's (Anglican), 138 Nathan Road, Tsimshatsui, Kowloon.

English Methodist Church (Methodist), Queen's Road East, Hong Kong.

Church of All Nations (Lutheran), 8 South Bay Close, Repulse Bay Road, Hong Kong.

Truth Luthern Church, 50 Waterloo Road, Kowloon.

Union Church (Interdenominational), Kennedy Road, above Mid-Levels, Hong Kong; and 4 Jordan Road, Yaumatei, Kowloon.

Hindu and Sikh:

Temple, Queen's Road East at Stubbs Road, Happy Valley, Hong Kong.

Zoroastrian:

Zoroastrian Church, Leighton Road at Caroline Hill Road (near Lee Gardens Hotel), Happy Valley, Hong Kong.

Roman Catholic:

Cathedral, 16 Caine Road (up Glenealy Path), above Central District, Hong Kong.

St. Joseph's, 7 Garden Road, Mid-levels, Central District, Hong Kong.

St. Theresa's, 258 Prince Edward Road, Kowloon Tsai, Kowloon.

Rosary Church, 125 Chatham Road, Tsimshatsui, Kowloon.

Islamic:

Mohammedan Mosque, Shelley and Mosque Streets (off Robinson Road), Mid-Levels, Hong Kong.

Kowloon Mosque, Nathan Road at Cameron Road (in Kowloon Park), Tsimshatsui, Kowloon.

Jewish:

Ohel Leah Synagogue, 70 Robinson Road, Mid-Levels, Hong Kong.

Language

Speaking:

Hong Kong is officially bi-lingual (English & Cantonese), which means more on paper than it does on a street corner in North Kowloon. Many residents, of course, can hold their own in one or several of the other Chinese dialects. There is no such thing as spoken "Chinese," only various Chinese dialects. The written language is the same for all areas, which means if two Chinese cannot speak to each other, they can write each other a note, even though each character has a different dialectical pronouncication for the same meaning.

For most of the population, though, English is at best a few numbers, the ubiquitous "hello," "bye-bye" and a few street and place names.

Fortunately for visitors, most of the million or so effective English-speakers are concentrated in and around the downtown business and tourist districts. Even fairly far afield shops and restaurants invariably have a resident linguist able enough to get things done. Often this will be a teen-aged or younger student, who together with red-badged cops and more fashionable dressers are the most dependable targets for on-the-street queries.

Even gestures, though, usually go a lot farther than phrasebook attempts at Cantonese, universally acknowledged as one of the world's most difficult languages for foreigners. The reason is tones—low, middle and high, and rising neutral and falling, used in every combination—which are both absolutely crucial to meaning and next to imperceptible to unpractised Western ears. As one of literally hundreds of examples, the word written in English *ma* varies according to pronunciation from "rope " to "mother" to "horse" (the written characters, of course, would all be different—and intelligible to any literate Chinese, no matter what his dialect).

Survival Cantonese

For those who insist, though, what follows is a list of what might otherwise be called "Useful Phrases." Particularly the numbers are within most people's grasp, but without fluent coaching from the start—something for which cab drivers are well suited—the result will inevitably be hopeless mispronunciation.

Numerals:

In Cantonese, counting is based on the pattern of numbers from "one" to "ten." The following is a list of basic numbers and their pronunciation in Cantonese:*

1	Yāt	一	20	Yih-sahp	二十
2	Yih	二	30	Sàam-sahp	三十
3	Sàam	三	40	Sei-sahp	四十
4	Sei	四	50	Ńgh-sahp	五十
5	Ńgh	五	60	Luhk-sahp	六十
6	Luhk	六	70	Chát-sahp	七十
7	Chát	七	80	Baat-sahp	八十
8	Baat	八	90	Gáu-sahp	九十
9	Gáu	九	99	Gáu-sahp Gáu	九十九
10	Sahp	十	100	Yāt-baak	一百
11	Sahp-yāt	十一	1,000	Yāt-chihn	一千
			10,000	Yāt-mahn	一萬

* The romanization system used here is the Yale System.

Greetings:

Hello! (only for answering telephone)	Wai!	喂！
How are you?	Néih hou ma?	你好嗎？
What's your name?	Gwai sing a?	貴姓亞？
Good morning	Jóu Sahn	早晨
Good night	Jóu Táu	早抖
Good-bye	Joi Gin	再見
Thank you (for a service)	M̀gòi	唔該
Thank you (for a gift/dinner)	Dò jeh	多謝
You're welcome/Not at all	Hóu Wah	好話
I'm sorry	Deui M̀jyuh	對唔住
Can you speak English?	Néih wúih m̀wúih góng yìng màhn?	你會唔會講英文
Yes	Haih	係
	or Hou	好
No	M̀haih	唔係
	or Mhou	唔好

Orientation Directions:

Hong Kong	Hèung góng	香港
Kowloon	Gáu lùhng	九龍
The New Territories	Sàn gaai	新界
The Peak	Sàan déng	山頂
How far is A from B?	A lèih B géi yúhn?	距離幾遠？
Where?	Bīn-douh?	邊度？
How long does it take?	Yiu géi nói?	要幾耐？

Commerce:

How many?/How much?	Géi dō?	幾多？
How much is it?	Géi dō chín?	幾多錢
Dollar $	Mān	文
One dollar	Yāt mān	一文
Ten dollars	Sahp mān	十文

Transport:

Bus	Bā-sí	巴士
Peak Tram	Laahm chè	纜車
Tram	Dihn chè	電車
Mini-bus	Síu Bā	小巴
Plane	Fèi gèi	飛機
Taxi	Dīk-sí	的士
Mass Transit Railway (MTR)	Deih hah tit-louh	地下鐵路
Train station	Fó-chè jaahn	火車站
Pier	Máh-tàuh	碼頭
Airport	Fèi gèi chèuhng	飛機場
Cross-harbor tunnel	Hói dái seuih douh	海底隧道

Etceteras:

May I ask	Chéng mahn	請問
Bring me the menu please.	Chāan Páai M̀gòi	茶牌唔該
I'd like to drink "Jasmine" tea.	Ngóh yám hèung pín chàh	我飲香片茶
To drink	Yám	飲
To eat	Sihk	食
Tea	Chàh	茶
Report to the police.	Bou gíng	報警
What time is it?	Géi dím jūng?	幾點鐘
o'clock	Dím jūng	點鐘
3 o'clock	Sàam dím-jūng	三點鐘
Minute	Fàn	分

Guide In Brief

Travelling to Macau

You will not believe the number of ways you can get from Hong Kong to Macau by sea. You could spend a little less than an hour crossing that 40-mile stretch of the Pearl River Estuary on a jetfoil or hoverferry, 70 minutes on a jetcat, 75 minutes on a hydrofoil, 90 - 100 minutes on a high-speed ferry, and 2½ - 3 hours by ferry. With all that sea transportation, you would reckon there would always be empty seats. Well, the old timers will tell you how drastically things have improved, but somehow Macau's 4.5 over million visitors annually usually manage to grab every seat, especially on weekends and public holidays. However, with the advent of computerized ticketing, there are less "full boats" sailing with empty seats. Another innovation which veteran Asia hands just love is the night jetfoil service, this means Hongkongers can whip over after work for a Macanese meal washed down by an inexpensive bottle of Portuguese wine (it is the cheapest *vinho* in all of Asia, including Australia) and return the same night. Regardless of when you go, make certain you have your return tickets in your possession *before* you go. Just about all the Macau ferry sailings use the Macau Ferry Terminal in the Shun Tak Centre, Connaught Road, Central, Hong Kong with the exception of the hoverferries (and a very, very limited jetfoil service) which sail regularly from the Shampuipo Ferry Pier in Kowloon. Note: Baggage on the "foils" and "cats" is limited to 20 lbs. — but there is no real "check-in" in an airline sense. The main problem is not weight, but space. There just is not much room for large suitcases.

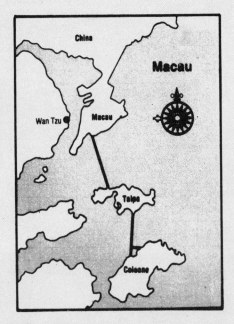

Jetfoils

Jetfoils carry 240 people in two classes and leave either destination for the 55 minute journey at half-hourly intervals from 7 a.m. till 5 p.m. in the winter, 6 p.m. in summer, when the less frequent night jetfoils take over till 2 p.m. Upper-deck, first class fares (same airplane seats as lower deck passengers, but free coffee and newspapers, slightly better service, and first crack at exiting upon arrival) are HK$66 on weekday, daylight sailings, HK$72 on weekend and all public holidays, daylight hours, and HK$88 for the night service, any day. Lower deck economy fares are HK$57 for weekday, daylight trips, HK$63 on weekends and all public holidays, daylight hours, and HK$77 for all night sailings. Most departures are made from Hong Kong, and three from Kowloon's Shamshuipo Ferry Pier. For information on Hong Kong sailings call 5-859-3333; Kowloon sailings 3-866818.

Computer booking service

There is a computer booking service called Ticketmate with 11 outlets in Hong Kong (many of which are in the major mass Transit Railway stations) and three in Macau where you can buy a passage up to 28 days in advance. Holders of American Express, Visa or Diners Club credit cards can book by phone up to 28 days in advance by dialing 5-859-3288 in Hong Kong. (The service is not offered in Macau).

Jetcats

These one-class, jet-propelled catamaran ferries carry up to 215 people and make ten 70-minute return trips daily (only daylight hours) for HK$46 one way on weekdays, and HK$58 on weekends and public holidays. American Express cardholders only can reserve and charge tickets by telephoning 5-232136, but must collect tickets within 24 hours of the booking. Ticketmate computer bookings available. For information, call 5-401882 (same day sailings only), 5-232136 (advanced sailing). Departure from Hong Kong.

Jetcats also sail five times daily (daylight hours only) to the Special Economic Zone of Zuhai, an oil exploration port, which is only 30 minutes away by road from Macau. One-way fares are HK$70 weekdays, HK$80 weekends and public holidays. Departs from old Macau Ferry Terminal, next to the present one, on Hong Kong Island.

Hydrofoils

They depart half-hourly for the 75 minute crossing beginning at 8 a.m. with final departures at 5 p.m. in winter and 6 p.m. in summer. The one class fares are HK$46 on weekdays, HK$58 on weekends and public holidays. Only American Express cardholders can reserve and charge tickets by calling 5-232136, but must be collected within 24 hours of the booking. Ticketmate computer bookings available. For information call 5-401822 (current sailings), 5-232136 (advanced sailings). Departures from Hong Kong.

High-speed Ferries

These 690-passenger vessels make the 40-mile trip in 90 - 100 minutes, 5 roundtrips daily (an extra during the weekend) between 8 a.m. and 11 p.m. Tickets are HK$35 economy, HK$45 first class and HK$55 in the VIP lounge. Same fares 7 days a week. The ferries are completely air-conditioned with aircraft seating, luggage racks, snack bars and slot machines. For information call 5-815-2789. Departures from Hong Kong. Ticketmate computer bookings available.

Hoverferries

Eight 60-minute trips daily during the daylight hours for HK$45 one way on weekdays, HK$56 on weekends and public holidays. These 250-passenger vessels leave from the Shamshuipo Ferry Pier in Kowloon. For information call 3-862549.

Ferries

For those who enjoy a more leisurely trip -- the proverbial "slow boat to Macau" -- try the old-fashioned regular ferries which chug along, twice daily, making the crossing in 2½ to 3 hours. Prices begin at HK$12 for a deck chair, dormitory bunk bed HK$23 (day) and HK$30 (night), aircraft seat HK$30, deluxe cabin for two HK$120 and VIP cabin for two HK$150. Children over 1 year HK$8. For information call 5-859-3333. Departures from Hong Kong.

Tax

There is a HK$15 embarkation tax levied by the Hong Kong Government on all tickets to Macau.

Travel Advisories

Visas

Visas are NOT required by nationals of the United States, Philippines, Japan, Australia, Canada, New Zealand, Malaysia, Thailand, Brazil, Austria, Belgium, Denmark, Spain, France, Greece, Italy, Norway, the Netherlands, the United Kingdom, West Germany and Sweden (up to six months stay), or Hongkong residents (British Commonwealth subjects for up to seven days, other nationalities for up to three days).

Getting a visa is usually painless. It is stamped into your passport upon arrival for HK$50. A family visa (HK$75) covers an individual or husband traveling with wife and children on the same passport, and is valid for a visit of 20 days or two visits within a 20-day period. (Group visas cost only HK$25 per person in bona fide groups of 10 or more).

Visas obtained from Portuguese consulates (including the one in Hong Kong which is located at 1001-1002, Two Exchange Square, Connaught Place, Central Hong Kong. Tel: 5-225789) cost HK$48.10 per person.

Nationals of countries which do not have diplomatic relations with Portugal must obtain their visas from Portuguese missions overseas. They cannot obtain them upon arrival in Macau.

If you have entered Hong Kong on a visa, traveling to Macau, or to China (on a day or overnight tour) via Macau, does not affect your Hong Kong visa. If you are on a single-entry visa, however, you will need a re-entry visa (obtainable from the Hong Kong Immigration Department) before leaving.

Health

International innoculation certificates are not normally required, unless cholera has been detected either in Hong Kong or Macau or in the area recently visited by the arrival.

Customs

Aside from normal restrictions on drugs, firearms, ammunition and explosives, Macau allows nearly any other items in-or-out. There are no restrictions on exports and no export duties on Macau purchases.

Hong Kong customs, in addition to restricting drugs, firearms, ammunition and explosives (the last three should be declared upon your original arrival in Hong Kong and left in bond), halves the duty-free tobacco allowance for returnees from Macau to 50 cigarettes, 25 cigars or a quarter pound of tobacco. And the grog allowance is cut to one bottle of wine.

You'll fare better by going into China. There you can have two to three bottles of grog and 400 cigarettes. Cameras, watches, radios, tape recorders and the like, and all currencies, have to be declared and are audited on departure. The usual prohibitions against drugs, firearms, ammunition, explosives and certain printed material apply.

Money, the Macanese Pataca

Macau's **pataca** is a sort of shadow version of the Hong Kong dollar, the two normally differing in value by less than five percent. Hong Kong notes and coins traditionally enjoy a slight premium and (except at the post office and telecoms) circulate freely -- with the spender thus taking a slight loss on pataca-denominated transactions. Changing money is the obvious solution, but to avoid double-costly reconversion -- pataca are not acceptable in Hong Kong, except at banks or money-changers -- the best policy is to change enough for basic expenses and cover any excess with HK dollars. (Note: in addition to being roughly equal, both currencies are usually symbolized by "$".) There are no restrictions on the amount or type of currency brought in or out.

Avos and Pataca

The **pataca** is divided into 100 *avos* (¢), with coins and bills as follows: 5, 10 and 50 *avos* in brass, 1, 5 and 20 *patacas* in nickel, and 5, 10, 50, 100 and 500 pataca denominations in paper bank notes.

There are no restrictions on moving money in and out of the territory, but the *pataca* is rarely used outside of Macau, even in Hong Kong.

Exchanging Money

Exchange windows at the ferry pier are the simplest place to get reasonable rates for major foreign currencies and traveller's cheques. A dozen-odd banks along Avenida Almeida Ribeiro offer more complete services — 10 a.m. to 1 p.m., and 3 to 4 p.m. business days. There are also the five casinos and cashiers at most of the major hotels. Major credit cards are accepted in hotels and some of the larger restaurants. Traveller's cheques are accepted everywhere.

Getting Acquainted

Climate

Forty miles isn't much as a swallow flies, so Macau's weather differs little from its larger colonial neighbour. Climate, though, is a different matter: whatever the skies are doing, Macau's relative lack of grit, noise and towering concrete make the place at least *feel* pleasant.

Spring and fall, though, are clearly the best times for leisurely visits. the worst times to visit are weekends, when seasonless gambling hordes descend on this Asian Monaco. From May to September, however, there is always the chance of being stranded when a typhoon keeps the ferries in port — but one could certainly suffer a worse fate.

Language

Officially it's Portuguese. In practice it's Cantonese and English — though the latter is generally neither as common nor as fluent as in Hong Kong.

Given the difficulty of pronouncing correctly most Portuguese place names (which differ in Cantonese), taxi drivers will appreciate being shown a note in Chinese or the tri-lingual tourist map published by the Department of Tourism. Ask a tour agent or hotel clerk to help you with this. Restaurant and hotel reservations will similarly be streamlined by having a Cantonese or Portuguese speaker do the phoning for you.

Taxes and Tipping

Prices in Macau — particularly for food and accommodations — run somewhat lower than in Hong Kong. A few restaurants and most hotels add a 10 percent service charge, and all but the smallest villas add a five percent government "tourism tax." Tips of 10 percent are standard for residents, but the mostly amiable — and underpaid — waiters are said to be disappointed if visitors don't leave slightly more.

Water

Tap water is usually boiled and provided to hotel rooms by the pitcher — less for safety than to minimize chlorine bouquet. Many residents and visitors nevertheless prefer the local custom of drinking wine.

Electricity

Power in most hotels is **220 volts,** but some of the older parts of the territory still use 110.

Tourist Information

In Hong Kong, the **Macau Tourist Information Bureau (MTIB)** — at 1729 Star House, 17th floor next to the Star Ferry Concourse, Tsimshatsui, Kowloon, Tel: 3-677-747 — is the principal clearing house for questions, recommendations, maps and free publications. (Note: The MTIB is scheduled to move to the Macau Ferry Terminal at the Shun Tak Centre) 3rd floor, Room 305) sometime before mid-1986.

In Macau the **Tourist Department** is located at Travessa do paiva (Tel: 77218) or at the Macau Ferry Pier.

Overseas, Macau maintains information offices in Manila, Sydney, Tokyo, London, Los Angeles, Toronto, Honolulu, New York and Vancouver, or c/o any Portuguese embassy or consulate. Any *Portuguese National Tourist* office will also be able to answer queries.

The following countries with consulates and commissions in Hong Kong are also accredited by Macau: Austria, Belgium, Brazil, Britain, Canada, West Germany, France, Greece, Italy, Japan, Mexico, Norway, Pakistan, Philippines, Sweden, Thailand and the United States.

Transportation

By Foot

On foot is in fact the undisputedly the best way around. Other matters to consider are summer heat and the several notable hills (**Gulia, Penha,** the **Monte Fort** and the **Camoes Gardens,** together roughly bounding the city's old quarter). Fortunately, siestas will preclude the worst of the first, while taxis and buses can handily surmount the others (see below).

Bicycling

Off the main streets, a possibly more aesthetic choice is bicycling. Several places around the intersection of Rua do Campo and the Praia Grande, and on Avenida D. Joao IV alongside the **Sintra Hotel** rent out very basic models (and occasionally, motorcycles) for about Ptc. 3 to Ptc. 5 per hour, depending on the day of the week and time of day. Bikes can also be hired at the Hyatt-Regency and Oriental Hotels. (Bicycles are not allowed to cross the bridge to Taipa.)

Pedicabs

The greatest languor will certainly be encouraged by **pedicabs,** three-wheeled, two-passenger rickshaws that are pedalled rather than pulled. Still very much in day-to-day use (unlike Hong Kong's rickshaws), their drivers nevertheless — and with some justice — view tourists as walking goldmines. Firm, often largely non-verbal bargaining *beforehand* is the rule, about Ptc. 10 (for two) for a short ride (say, along the Praia Grande) or HK$25 to $30 an hour, usually enough to keep both sides happy. (Like bicyles, pedicabs cannot cross the bridge and aren't much on hills.)

Taxis

Taxis will of course go anywhere, at rates as cheap as any in the world (Ptc. 4 at flagfall, 50 avos each additional 1/5 mile — or a highly negotiable Ptc. 70 or so per hour). The driver's English abilities (or tourist Portuguese) vary enormously: a few can almost manage guided tours, while others will need to be shown notes in Chinese characters for destinations other than the major hotels. You will have to barter with them to go across to the islands, though the official surcharges are Ptc. 5 to Taipa and Ptc. 10 to Coloane.

Buses

The islands — Taipa and Coloane — are a special case. With the demise of ferry runs from the Inner Harbour, the only other access is by public bus. Not all are the splendid, open-top doubledeckers, but fairly frequent runs are scheduled from 7 a.m. to 11 p.m. The plaza opposite the **Lisboa Hotel** is the simplest place to wait. Fares are: Taipa, Ptc. 1, Coloane town, Ptc. 1.50, **Hac Sa beach**, Ptc. 2.

In-town Macau has five meandering bus routes, the most useful being perhaps the **No. 5**, which runs from the **Temple of A-Ma** out to the **Barrier Gate** via Avenida Almeida Ribeiro. The No 3 runs from the Macau Ferry Pier to the city centre. Hours again are 7 a.m. to 11 p.m., fares a flat 50 avos.

Mini-Mokes:

You will no doubt have a ball seeing Macau in these zippy four-seaters, the only rent-a-car service available. Rates range from HK$220 to HK$270 per day, depending on which day. Special hotel/moke rates are available with the Hyatt-Regency Hotel or Pousada de Coloane. Bookings can be made in Hong Kong at Macau Mokes Ltd., 1701 Hollywood Centre, 233 Hollywood Rd., Hong Kong. Tel: 5-434190. Telex: 76444 MOKES HX or in Macau at the Macau Ferry Terminal, Room 202. Tel; 78851. Telex: 88251 MBC OM. Credit cards accepted. Note: Only drivers holding driving licenses recognized in Portugal or International Permits are permitted behind the wheel in Macau. Hong Kong driving licenses are not acceptable.

Accommodation

Most visitors on tours to Hong Kong usually enjoy at least a day trip to the Portuguese territory. Some stay overnight. In such cases, the trip is quite pleasant because tour companies prearrange everything.

For those interested in making a quick and independent visit to Macau, whether for a day or overnight, arrangements are a bit more difficult. You have to secure two sets of reservations — transportation and hotel — to coincide with your particular needs. A tourist agency should be able to assist you, but of course they charge more, and may want you to include a lot of "options" like organized tours or meals. For a "one-shot" approach (transportation and hotel) try a local Hong Kong travel agent or check the *South China Morning Post* classified for tours.

Many of the major hotels in Macau have Hong Kong reservation offices (see Appendix B) to facilitiate matters, but if you choose a smaller hotel or boarding house, you'll have to ring Macau (HK$10.80 for three minutes). You should realise that Macau does tend to be filled up with ardent Hong Kong gamblers during the weekends and on public holidays. If you have a credit card, you can make telephone reservations. If not you will have to scamper down to the **Macau Ferry Pier** on Hong Kong Island or at any Mass Transit Railway station to get your ticket (see **Transportation**).

But don't let logistical problems discourage you. The visit is worth all the trouble. The **Macau Tourist Information Bureau's** office — in Hong Kong (1729, 17th floor, Star House), next to the Kowloon Star Ferry Concourse, Tel: 3-677-747, and Department of Tourism offices at the Macau Ferry Pier (in Macau) and on Travessa do Paiva, Tel: 77218 — can be very helpful. Note: The **MTIB** office in Hong Kong is scheduled to move to the Shun Tak Centre, (Room 305, 3rd floor), where the ferries depart, sometime before mid-1986).

Communications

Telephone Services

Macau offers the standard range of modern international services, albeit with characteristically restrained efficiency. Calls and cables can be placed round-the-clock, either through hotel front desks or from the General Post Office on Avenida Almeida Ribeiro just off the main downtown square, or from the Central Post Offices on Taipa and Coloane islands.

In telephone terms, Hong Kong is considered overseas, and three minutes cost just over HK$10. Local calls — including Taipa and Colane islands — are 30 *avos* (three ten-*avos* coins) from public booths or free on hotel or private lines. Use area code 070 for Taipa Island and 080 for Coloane Island. Service numbers include:

Directory Information:	73001
Fire Department:	72222
Police:	73333
Ambulance:	73366 or 73870

Dining Out

Macanese Food

It is this liberal use of spices that distinguishes Macanese food from normal Portuguese cuisine. The most famous local dish served in Macau is African Chicken. The name, of course, imples that it originated in Mozambique or Angola, where it was called Chicken Biri-Biri (or Piri-Piri, depending on which account you read). Biri-biri is the spicy sauce that enhances food in that part of the world. The chicken itself is spiced, peppered and grilled (properly over charcoal) until dry so that the spices are virtually baked hard by the flames. Another recipe calls for the marination of the chicken in coconut milk mixed with a strong preparation of spices. Despite its name, some gourmets insist that African Chicken is more closely related to Indian tandoori chicken (presumably served in old Goa). Though the origins of spiced chicken are in doubt, it is a taste treat not to be missed. The same goes for the less popular spiced prawns (Prawns Biri-Biri).

The Portuguese also have adapted Chinese salt and pepper prawns to suit their taste. Yet other treats are prawns, chicken or fish baked in garlic. Some restuarants have also taken succulent crabs found in the area, applied the **biri-biri** treatment and created a spicy crab dish that's **very different** from the Chinese version. Quail and pigeon Chinese dishes have also been improvised **A La Macanese**.

The following is a glossary of basic Macanese food and wine terms to use when ordering at a local Macanese-Portuguese restuarant:

camaroes — shrimps, prawns
peixe — fish
soupa — soup
carangue jos — crabs
feijoadas — beans
cabrito — lamb
coelho — rabbit
galinha — chicken
bacalhau — cod, the most common fish served
carne de vaca — beef
vinho — wine
vinho tinta — red wine
vinho branco — white wine
vinho rose — rose wine
vinho verde — young wines (both red and white)
porto — port
coziedu — meat soup
cabidela — duck stew

Restaurants

Low overheads and cheap, family labour, have kept prices here well below those for Western food in Hong Kong. For under HK$50 per person you can enjoy a good meal that includes a modest quantity of sturdy Portuguese wine. Portuguese wines, brandies and ports in Macau are the cheapest in Asia. Restaurant reservations are usually required only on weekends and holidays, but even during the slower winter, or at smaller places, calling ahead to book a table is both prudent and polite.

To the occasional rue of the unsuspecting, Macanese dinners (outside of hotels) tend to be eaten early. An arrival at 8:30 p.m. is about the limit, but 7 or 7.30 p.m. will make local restaurateurs much happier. If you want to dine on Coloane or Taipa, you should remember that after-dark taxis normally ask more than the HK$5 and HK$10 surcharges. (To Taipa and Coloane respectively). Furthermore they may be hard to find on the return trip. Buses, however, run until 11 p.m. (restaurants will know the schedule), and riding back in an open-topped double-decker on a warm night is certainly no hardship.

Some of Macau's more prominent restaurants are listed in Appendix B. Besides the restaurant's name and address, a brief, subjective critique is given.

Shopping

Macau is rarely thought of as a shopping mart, except for her magnificently-priced wines, brandies and ports (which are restricted upon return to Hong Kong). Though it is a duty-free port like Hong Kong, the array of goods available is not nearly so elaborate. Some items, such as cameras or hi-fi systems are more expensive at Macau because of the smaller number sold. Like Hong Kong, Macau is a clothing manufacturing centre, especially of knitwear, but what little is on display is not very fashionable.

Antiques and Artifacts

But all is not lost if you prefer shopping to gambling. Macau is a good place to buy Chinese **antiques** and **artifacts**. The main street, **Avenida Almeida Ribeiro,** has a few antique shops on both sides of the street as you walk from the Outer Harbour (near the Lisboa and Sintra Hotels, and the hydrofoil/jetfoil piers) towards the Inner Harbour (near the Floating Casino).

There are also concentrations of "antique" stalls at the **Bishop's Palace,** the **Portas do Cerco** (border gates) and at the ruins of **St. Paul's.** These are basically souvenir dealers who try to palm off freshly painted Ming-style plates as genuine "Ming." But if you fancy something and the price is about right, bargain for the best price.

For the more adventurous, there are literally dozens of tiny little antique shops and even junk shops located between St. Paul's facade and Avenida Ribeiro. **Rua da Palm,** the road leading up to St. Paul's, is another place. Also, at a fork in the road, where the right hand street leads up to St Paul's massive ruins and the new plaza, go left along **Largo Rua de Estalagens.** Along here curio shops will pop up as you get into the older part of the city. You are walking roughly parallel to Avenida Ribeiro. There are also tiny shops on several side streets to your left. Take your camera along. This area's sights are as interesting as antique-hunting.

Other Shopping Venues

Beacuse Macau is a gambling town, you might try browsing in the town's various pawn shops and second hand shops.

The Department of Tourism, in collaboration with the **Goldsmith's & Jeweller's Association,** has published a **shopping guide** and each member shop is identified by a decal on its shop door. These shops should given you a warranty card and proper receipt for each purchase. If you encounter any shopping problems, take your complaints to the Department of Tourism on Travessa do Paiva, Tel: 77218.

Tours and Attractions

Guides and Tours

Small as it is, Macau is serviced by several commercial sightseeing firms. In addition to multilingual conducted tours, most travel agents will arrange ferry and hotel bookings and complete one or two-day Macau tour packages, some of which may include day trips to China. By using these companies' services, you save the hassle of making such arrangements independently.

Licenced Macau tour operators are listed below, but remember that many of the same tours can be arranged from Hong Kong by Hong Kong travel agents.

Tour Agencies

Able
5-9 Travessa do Padre Narciso. Tel: 89798.
Asia
23-B Rua da Praia Grande. Tel: 82687.
Cable: ASIA-TOURS.
Hongkong office — Tel: (3)693847
China Travel Service (Macau)
63 Rau da Praia Grande. Tel: 88922, 88812, Cable: 9999 MACAU
Estoril
Ground floor, Hotel Lisboa, Avenida da Amizade. Tel: 73614. Cable: ESTOURS. Telex: 88203 HOTEL OM.
Hongkong office — Tel: 5-591028
Guangdong (Macau)
37-A Rau da Praia Grande, 1st floor. Tel: 88807, 78475. Cable: MYCM 9889. Telex: 88451 MANYU OM.
HI-NO-DE CARAVELA
Ground floor, 6A-4C Rua de Sacadura Cabral. Tel: 566622. Telex: 88771. CRTSZ OM. Facsimile: 566622.
Hong Kong Office — 3-686181.
H. Nolasco, Lda
20 Avenida Almeida Riberiro. Tel: 76463. Cable: POPULAR.
International
9 Travessa do Padre Narciso, Loja B, ground floor. Tel: 86522, 87884, 86567. Hongkong office: Tel: 5-412011.

Lotus
Edificio Fong Meng, ground floor, Rua de Sao Lourenco. Tel: 81765. Cable: LOTUSTOUR.
Macau Star
Room 511, Tai Fung Bank Building, 34 Avenida Almeida Ribeiro. Tel: 558855, 558866. Telex: 88590 STAR OM. Hongkong office — 3-662261, 3-662262
Macau Tours
9 Avenida da Amizade. Tel: 85555. Cable: MAC-TOURS. Hongkong office — Tel: (5)422308
MBC Tours
7-9 Rua Santa Clara, Edificio Ribeiro, Loja D. Tel: 76422. Telex: 88251 MBC OM. Cable: MACAU BUC.
F. Rodrigues
71 Rua da Praia Grande. Tel: 75511.
Sintra
Hotel Sintra, Avenida Dom Joao IV. Tel: 86394. Cable: HOTELSINTRA. Telex: 88324 SINTA OM. Hongkong office — Tel: 5-408028.
South China
15 Avenida Dr Rodrigo Rodrigues, Apt A-B, 1st floor. Tel: 87211, 87219.
STDM
Hotel Sintra, Avenida Dom Joao IV Tel: 85878, 77718, Telex: 88324 SINTA OM. Hongkong office — Tel: 5-408028.
T.K.W.
27-31 Rua Formosa, Apt 408, 4th floor, Tel: 76200.
Wing On
303-4 Edificio Tai Fung, 3rd floor, 32 Avenida Almeiro. Tel: 77701.

Macau-China Tours, Resorts

These modern China days, you can almost go up to Macau's ornate 19th Century **Portas do Cerco** (border gates) and get a visa. It is easier, though, to go through a travel agency. These days it takes one day for an individual or a group to process China travel documents at the Chinese frontier post of **Gongbei.**

Many visitors travel from Macau because China has created a **Special Tourism Zone** in the **Zhongshan county area** immediately adjacent this Portuguese territory. The area is open for day tours or for longer trips to three resorts that opened in this zone in 1980.

These day trips are made under Chinese supervision with organized tour groups. Travel agents in Macau and Hong Kong arrange everything and, for those really short of time, it is probably the best way to get a quick look at China.

Day tours usually follow two basic itineraries. Both start in **Cuiheng Village,** the birthplace of Dr. Sun Yatsen, the founding father of modern China who was the first president of the Chinese Republic in 1911 after the Manchus of the Ching dynasty were overthrown. In this village you can visit his residence, a Sun Yatsen exhibition hall and a memorial school. From there the tours split up and go either to **Shiqi City** or **Zhuhai City.** After lunch in one of those "cities" there are visits to Chinese communes, schools or, possibly, a fishing village. It is possible to do the entire trip in one day which doesn't leave you much time to see Macau en route. The cost starts around HK$350 and includes all transportation to and from Macau.

There are, however, more elaborate tours including, believe it or not, golfing tours (where you do your

18 in China), which have time for visiting Macau. These usually feature an overnight stay in Macau and are available via usual travel agencies.

Chinese Resorts

— To just Tour or play golf —

Persons who have more time should visit one of the new resorts just adjacent the China-Macau border. The **Shi Ching Shan Tourist Centre** is the closest, only 10 minutes by car from the border gate and offers complete tourist facilities, including air-conditioning, swimming pools, restaurants and local tours. Doubles around HK$170.

The **Chung Shan Hot Spring Golf Club** is a little farther away — 30 minutes by car — and in addition to usual tourist conveniences, it offers therapeutic spa waters from the nearby **Iong Mak Hot Springs**. These mineral waters are piped directly into the hotel. (According to the Chinese, the medicinal qualities of Iong Mak's water are especially good for "joint" or "skin" problems) At Chung Shan you can book normal double rooms (HK$210 per night, weekdays, HK$230 weekends) or villas. Make reservations at least 24 hours in advance.

Chung Shan's main attraction for foreigners is not so much the medicinal hot springs as the Arnold Palmer-designed, 18-holed, par 72, 5,991-metre championship golf course. Paddy fields into golf courses? Sounds almost biblical, but there it is. Green fees are HK$100 weekdays, HK$150 weekends Golf clubs can be rented for HK$50 and caddies are HK$40.

Transport to Chung Shan is not difficult once you reach Macau, it costs HK$15 for a scheduled bus or if you prefer, there are private cars and coaches available. Contact the Chung Shan office in Macau on the first floor of the Ferry Terminal. The Hong Kong office is in Room 504, Pedder Bldg., Pedder St., Central, Hong Kong. Tel: 5-234942. Telex: 75050 WINGS HX. In China, the address is Sanxiang Commune, Zhongshan City, Guangdong Province. Tel; (Zhongshan) 22811 (ext. Hot Spring Golf Club). Telex: 44828 CSHS CN. Cables: 3306. At least 24 hours is needed to obtain a visas.

Lest you think you misread the previous paragraph about golfing in China, brace yourself for another course in the same area. This one is called the Zuhai International Golf Club and sports an 18-holed, par 72, 6,380-metre course. Managed by Japan Golf Promotions Ltd., it also has the adjacent Pearl Land Amusement Park, a 122,000-square metre complex with, among other attractions, a kilometre-long go-kart track and roller coaster. Bookings can be made in Hong Kong via Zuhai Tours (5-232136).

This course can also be reached via Macau and a 30-40 minute car or bus ride. Alernatively, you can take a pleasant jetcat ride (about an hour) direct from Hong Kong. (See Macau transportation, "jetcats".) The Hyatt Regency Hotel on Taipa Island runs Golfer's Getaway special package which includes return transportation between Hong Kong and Macau, transfers in Macau and China, all golfing and visa fees, plus an American breakfast and one night stay, for HK$777. Call 5-463797.

Nearby resort is in **Shiqi**. It is designed not only for tourists, but as a rest stop for persons travelling between Canton and Macau.

At the visa facilities at Gongbei, it is also possible to obtain permission to visit Canton or other parts of China without having to go via Hong Kong. The road to Canton is a bit rough, however, a regular bus service runs to Canton from Macau.

Macau Beaches

Macau itself does not have much in the way of beaches, but the islands of **Coloane** and **Taipa** do. The best known resort is the **Pousada de Coloane** on **Cheoc Van Beach** on Coloane Island. The *pousada* (inn) does not really advertise itself as a "resort," but it is on the beach. Also on Coloane is **Hac Sa Beach**, a much larger and popular public beach.

The Camoes Museum

The building housing the **Camoes Museum** dates from the 1770s, when it was used by the East India Company. It first re-opened as a museum in 1960, and was completely renovated and re-opened yet again in December, 1980.

Holidays and Festivals

More than 400 years of survival have left Macau plenty of causes to celebrate. With the zeal of true believers on a heathen sea, the Portuguese and their converts to the Roman Catholic faith honour saints' and feast days in high Iberian style, replete with pageants, bright costumes and processions through the streets. And not to be outdone by Christian foreigners on their home turf, traditional Chinese festivals here turn out throngs armed with crates of local fireworks, traditional Chinese noise-makers that have been banned in Hong Kong since 1967.

But, pyrotechnics aside, Macau's moon-determined Chinese festival calendar is nearly identical to that of Hong Kong (see festivals and temples feature article). Public holidays have little effect on shops or restaurants, but those celebrated in Hong Kong (notably Chinese New Year) invariably jam Macau with gamblers, which makes room reservations here even more difficult.

Among Macau's major holidays are:

January—February

New Year's Day (January 1)
Chinese New Year*
Lantern Festival

February—March

Feast of our Lord of Passos (Evening procession from St. Augustine's Church to Macau's Cathedral where a night-long vigil is kept. The next day his statue is carried through the streets of Macau — to the Stations of the Cross — and returned to St. Augustine's)

March—April

Feast of the God Tou Tei

April

Ching Ming Festival*
Easter Weekend, including **Good Friday** and **Easter Monday***

Anniversary of the 1974 Portuguese Revolution*
(April 25)

May

Labourers' Day* (May 1)
Feast of our Lady of Fatima (May 13) (procession from Santa Domingos Church to Penha Church, celebrating the 1917 religious miracle that took place at Fatima, Portugal)
Feast of the Bathing of Lord Buddha
A-Ma Festival (Tin Hau Festival in Hong Kong)
Feast of Tam Kong

June

Camoes and Portugal Communities Day* (June 10)
Dragon Boat Festival*
Feast of St. John the Baptist* (June 10)
Feast of Kuan Tai*
Feast of St. Anthony of Lisbon

July—August

Feast of Na Cha (July 13)
Battle of July 13th (islands only)
Feast of Lovers
Feast of the Assumption of Our Lady
Festival of Hungry Ghosts

September

Mid-Autumn Festival*
Confucius Day

October

Portuguese Republic Day* (October 5)
Chung Yeung Festival

November

All Saints' Day (November 1)
All Souls' Day (November 2)

December

Portuguese Independence Day* (December 1)
Feast of the Immaculate Conception* (December 8)
Winter Solstice (December 22)
Christmas* (December 24—25)

An asterisk (*) above indicates that this is a local public holiday.

Nightlife

Bars, Nightclubs

Macau in recent years has rarely lived up to its sinful reputation. Most foreigners consider nightlife here outside the casinos a rather tame scene.

Day or night, the Hotel Bela Vista's **Verandah** is a good first choice for a quiet drink — notably from chilled bottles (or half-bottles) of dangerously inexpensive Portuguese wine. Other well-shaded places include the **Matsuya Hotel's Terrace**, the seaside **Pousada de Coloane**, and any of several sidewalk cafes along the Praia Grande.

Virtually all the slick and aggressively cosmopolitan spots are lodged in the major hotels. Indeed, a decent "pub" crawl could be manged without ever leaving the **Lisboa Hotel**. As for night clubs, the Lisboa offers **Portas do Sol** (dinner, a show and dancing).

the Lisboa's competition is the **Estoril Hotel** where there is a **Cabaret** on the ground floor (Cantonese entertainment, plus hostesses). The Western hostess bar in the Estoril is the **Paris Night Club. Disco,** something of a newcomer to Macau, can be found in the Hyatt Regency's **Green Parrot**. The Pesidente Hotel's **Skylight**, the Royal Hotel's **Royal Disco** and the Lisboa Hotel's **Mikado**. Prices vary greatly from place to place — and tend to go up on weekends — but even at the top they do not exceed moderate by world standards. One or another credit card is usually acceptable.

Macau's professional girlfriends require the same caveats given to their sisters in Hong Kong. Without a good-sized jackpot in hand, visitors might better pass up the opportunities who present themselves around the casinos in favour of the aptly-named **Red Lantern** tavern, in the **Wing Hang Bank Building** on Avenida de Almeida Ribeiro.

Macau's massage parlours (in the Estoril, Lisboa Royal and Sintra hotels) are famous in Hong Kong because of the Thais and Filipinas who work in them. A brief wisp of Patpong is felt at **Santos Bar** which has Thai bargirls.

For pub drinking, try the Bar dos Cavalheiros, 95A Rva da Praia Grande. The most exciting show in Macau is the long running Crazy Paris show, a classy French strip extravaganza (a la the Crazy Horse Saloon previously in the venerable Dom Pedro V Theatre and now in the new wing of the Lisboa Hotel. It is as incongruous a show as could be had in Macau. There are two shows nightly, three on weekends and public holidays at HK$50 and HK$60 respectively.

Suggested Readings: Fiction, Non-Fiction

Hong Kong and Macau have inspired everything in print from weighty research tomes to three-inch-thick historical novels and mysteries. Opinions vary as to which novels are fact or fiction, but any of the following are informative and exciting enough to be good company.

Fiction

Clavell, James, *Tai-Pan* New York, Antheneum & Dell, 1966; and *Noble House,* London, Hodder & Stoughton, 1981. *Tai-Pan* is a fictional account of the founding of Hong Kong, and *Noble House,* a sequel to historic *Tai-Pan.*
Coaes, Austin, *City of Broken Promises,* Hong Kong, Frederick Muller of Heinemann Asia, 1967 and 1977.
Rags to riches love story set in Macau in the mid-19th Century.
Cooper, Anthony, *The Sanctuary,* Hong Kong, Communication Management Ltd., 1984. Once again, Hong Kong is on the verge of chaos, this time because a beautiful Vietnamese assassine hopes to kill a visiting Chinese Minister of State.
Elegant, Robert, *Dynasty*, (Glasgow,) Wm. Collins & Sons, 1977; and *Manchu,* New York, McGraw-Hill 1980, and Penguin Books, 1981. In *Dynasty,* Elegant

recounts the lives of one of the colony's premier Chinese families during the years 1900 to 1970. In *Manchu,* Jesuit-educated Francis Arrowsmith penetrates the Middle Kingdom and its Imperial Court during the mid-1660s and proceeds to make a fortune in Macau.

Gall, Sandy, *Chasing the Dragon,* London, William Collins Sons & Co., 1981 and Pan Books, 1982. The trail of opium leads from Hong Kong to the Golden Triangle and involves a CIA plot.

Gordon-Davis, John, *Typhoon,* London, Michael Joseph Ltd., 1978. Nature and the triads direct Jake Macadam's life.

Hurd, Douglas and Osmond, Andrew, *Smile on the Face of the Tiger,* Glasgow, Wm. Collins & Sons, 1969. Britain is faced with a Chinese ultimatum for Hong Kong's return.

Le Carre, John, *The Honourable Schoolboy,* London, Hodder & Stoughton, 1977. George Smiley, acting head of the British Secret Service, the "Circus," and his ace KGB enemy Karla, fight it out again in Hong Kong.

Lee Ding Fai, *Running Dog,* Hong Kong, Heinemann Asia, 1980. The story of Hong Kong society through the lives and times of an average, Hong Kong Chinese family.

Maitland, Derek, *The Firecracker Suite,* Hong Kong, CFW Publications, 1980. Comic tales of an Australian expatriate's life in Hong Kong.

Marshall, William, *Yellowthread Street,* London, Pan Books, 1977. Hong Kong's version of Ed McBain's *7th Precinct* mysteries by a former Australian resident.

Mason, Richard, *The World of Suzie Wong,* Glasgow, Wm. Collins & Sons., 1957. The bestseller that established Hong Kong's contemporary romantic image.

Stewart, Ian, *Peking Payoff,* London, Hamlyn Paperbacks, 1978. With China and Russia about to have at it, the pressure builds for Hong Kong to be taken back.

Thursby, Geoffrey, *Miller,* Hong Kong, Communication Management, 1983. A European taipan tries to buck the system by falling in love with a Chinese girl.

Van Lustbader, Eric, *Jian,* London, Granada Publishing, 1985. The master of the Oriental potboiler uses Hong Kong as well as Japan for this thriller.

Specialist and Reference

Asia Yearbook, Hong Kong, Far Eastern Economic Review. The FEER's annual wrap-up on Asia which has an excellent chapter on Hong Kong.

Berger, Bob, *Hidden Treasure,* Hong Kong, Macmillan, 1977. A guide to hidden shops with special and unique Chinese treasures.

Bernstein, Ken, *Hong Kong,* Lausanne, Editions Berlitz, 1979. A pocket guide to Hong Kong.

Boschman, Roger *Hong Kong by Night,* CFW Publications, 1981. All there is to know about Hong Kong's varied entertainment scene.

Clemens, John, *Discovering Macau,* Hong Kong, Macmillan, 1977. A comprehensive guide to the 400-plus year old Portuguese territory.

Clewlow, Carol, *Hong Kong, Macau and Canton,* Melbourne, Lonely Planet, 1981. How to tour these three areas on the cheap.

Crisswell, Colin, *The Taipans,* Oxford University Press, 1981. A look at the merchant princes who made the colony.

Doing Business in Hong Kong, Hong Kong, Amcham Publications. Everything you ever wanted to know about setting up shop in Hong Kong.

Flux, David, *Hong Kong Taxation: Law and Practice,* Hong Kong, Chinese University Press, 1983 A comprehensive, easy-to-understand guide to all taxes.

Forrest, Ronald, and Hobbins, George, *Selected Walks in Hong Kong,* Hong Kong, S.C.M. Post, 1979. Marvelous for anyone—who wants to get away from ubanity for a short while

Goetz, Dana, *The Complete Guide to Hong Kong Factory Bargains,* Hong Kong, Dana Goetz Publishing, 1986. As the name implies, the book is the key to bargain shopping.

Hong Kong, Hong Kong, Hong Kong Government, Hong Kong's annual "official" yearbook.

Hong Kong for the Business Visitor, Hong Kong H.K. Trade Development Council. A businessperson's guide through the bureaucratic maze.

Hong Kong Guide 1893, Oxford University Press, 1982. A delightful reprint. Compare this with the Insight Guides and see where the colony has gone.

Hong Kong's 100 best Restaurants, Hong Kong, Illustrated Magazine Publishing Co. Ltd.; 1984. The *Hong Kong Tatler's* compendium of eateries.

Living in Hong Kong, Hong Kong, Amcham Publications, 1982. All you want to know about settling in Hong Kong.

Malloy R., and Ahrens, J., *Gems & Jewellery in Hong Kong: A Buyer's Buide,* Hong Kong *South China Morning Post,* 1984. A guide to shops and factories plus tips on what to look for.

Matyeh, Joe, *Bachelor's Guide to Hong Kong,* Hong Kong, Ted Thomas Ltd., 1981. A, well, different and comprehensive guide to Suzie Wong's domain.

O'Connor, Ellen, *Children's Guide to Hong Kong,* Hong Kong, S.C.M. Post, 1981. What to do with the kiddies when visiting Hong Kong.

Okuley, Bert, and King-Poole, F., *Gambler's Guide to Macau,* Hong Kong, S.C.M. Post, 1979. The authors returned poorer after completing their research, but it is still a good book.

Post Guide to Hong Kong Restaurants, Hong Kong, *South China Morning Post,* 1984. A handy book to help you select the restaurants of our choice out of Hong Kong's 5,000 eateries.

Savidge, Joyce, *Temples,* Hong Kong, Hong Kong Government, 1977. A guide to and history of Hong Kong's many Chinese temples.

Sebastian, Evelyn, and Leung, Betty, *Hong Kong from A to Z,* Hong Kong, Guiller Books, 1978. Hong Kong in alphabetical order.

Sinclair, Kevin, *Who's Who in Hong Kong,* S.C.M. Post, 1982. A compendium of Hong Kong's finest.

Tobias, Mel, *Flashbacks,* Hong Kong, Gulliver Books, 1979. History of Hong Kong cinema.

Autobiographical/Biographical

Coates, Austin, *Myself a Mandarin,* Hong Kong, Frederick Muller Ltd. & Heinemann Educational Books, 1968 and 1975. In 1949, the author, then a 26-year old British expatriate in the Hong Kong government, relates his trials, tribulations and education as Her Majesty's all-powerful magistrate in the New Territories.

Han Suyin, *A Many Splendoured Thing*, London, Jonathan Cape & Triad Panther, 1952 and 1978. One of the original love stories.

Hughes, Richard, *Foreign Devil*, London, Andre Deutsch, 1972. The former doyen of the foreign press corps in Asia reminisces about 30 years of reporting in the Far East, thereby linking Richard Sorge, the Russian spy in pre-war Tokyo, to his world scoop interview with spies Guy Burgess and Donald Maclean.

Historical/Political

Bonavia, David, *Hong Kong 1997: The Final Settlement*, 1985. A concise history and analysis of the Sino-British negotiations (1982-84), the signing of the agreement (1989) returning all of Hong Kong to China in 1997 and the simultaneous setting up of the autonomous Special Administrative Region which Hong Kong is to become.

Boxer, C.R., *Seventeenth Century Macau*, Hong Kong, Heinemann (Asia), 1984. A reprint of rare documents and illustrations.

Cameron, Nigel, *The Cultured Pearl*, Hong Kong, Oxford University Press, 1978. A history of Hong Kong's swashbuckling, opium-running days of the last century.

Carew, Tim, *The Fall of Hong Kong*, London, Anthony Blond Ltd. and Pan Books, 1960 and 1963. The hopeless but heroic defence of Hong Kong as the Imperial Japanese war machine plods on, beginning on Christmas 1941.

Coates, Austin, *A Macao Narrative*, Hong Kong, Heinemann Educational Books Asia, 1978. A history of Macau from its founding in the mid-16th Century until the present day.

Davies, Shann, *Chronicles in Stone*, Macau, Department of Tourism, 1985. An exploration of some of Macau's historical buildings and the part they played in the life of the community through the generations.

Endacott, G.B., *A History of Hong Kong*, London, Oxford University Press; Hong Kong from its beginning to the middle-Sixties; and with Birch, Alan, *Hong Kong Eclipse*, London, Oxford University Press, 1978. A history of Hong Kong from pre-World War II to after liberation.

Graca, Jorge, *Fortifications of Macau*, Macau, Department of Tourism 1984. Survey of all Macau's architectural structures with details of their design, construction and history.

Guillen-Nunez, Cesar, *Macau*, Hong Kong, Oxford University Press, 1984. Part of the *'Images of Asia'* series, it deals with Macau's rich artistic heritage.

Harris, Peter, *Hong Kong: A study in Bureaucratic Politics*, Hong Kong. Heinemann Asia, 1978. An explanation of how this anachronistic, *laisez-faire* colonial government works.

Hughes, Richard, *Borrowed Time-Borrowed Place*, London, Andre Deutsch, 1968, revised 1976. Analysis of Hong Kong "Yesterday, Today and Tomorrow" by the former dean of Asia's foreign correspondents.

Hurd, Douglas, *The Arrow War*, New York, Macmillan, 1967. An in-depth look at the 1856—1860 Anglo-Chinese war.

Luff, John, *Hidden Years*, Hong Kong, S.C.M. Post, 1967. History of 1941-1945; and *The Hong Kong Story*, Hong Kong, S.C.M. Post. A history of the colony from 1841—1900.

Mattock, Katherine, *Story of Government House*, Hong Kong, Hong Kong Government, 1978. A history of Hong Kong through the colony's varied inhabitants and the colony's premier abode, the Governor's residence.

Montalto de Jesus, C.A., *Historic Macau*, Hong Kong, Oxford University Press, 1984. A facsimile reprint of a 1902 History of Macau.

Robertson, Frank, *Triangle of Death: Inside Story of the Triads, the Chinese Mafia*, London, Routledge and Kegan, 1977. A veteran foreign correspondent — 30 years on the Asia beat — traces the drug scene through Asia to the West.

Waley, Arthur, *The Opium War Through Chinese Eyes*, London, George Allen and Unwin Ltd., 1958. The "other side" of the opium wars (1839—1842).

Things Chinese

Baker, Dr. Hugh, *Ancestral Images*, Hong Kong, S.C.M. Post, 1979. Collections of Dr. Baker's studies of traditional Chinese village life and more.

Bloomfield, Frena, *The Occult World of Hong Kong*, Hong Kong, Hong Kong Publishing Co. Ltd., 1980. The netherlands of East and West meet in this brief tome, complete with addresses and phone numbers.

Burkhard, V.R., *Chinese Creeds & Customs*, (Vols. I, II and III), Hong Kong, S.C.M. Post, 1953, 1955 and 1958. Still *the* work about Chinese traditions.

Colonial Comics/Cartoons

Hacker, Arthur, *Hacker's Hong Kong*, Hong Kong, Gareth Powell and Ted Thomas, 1976. A talented British civil servant sketches the Hong Kong government's view of the other side of colonial life.

Zabo, *Hong Kong Sweet & Sour*, Hong Kong, Lorraine Langridge, 1968. A French cartoonist's line drawings of life in this improbable place.

Art

Hutcheon, Robin, *Chinnery*, Hong Kong, S.C.M. Post, 1974. The biography of the British artist George Chinnery (1774—1852) who painted life on the South China Coast, especially at Macau and Hong Kong, in those early days.

Photographic

Barrett, Dean, and Hahn, Werner, *Aberdeen: Catching the Last Rays*, Hong Kong, Perennial Press, 1974. A study of the fishing village of Aberdeen.

Davies, Shann, and Brazier, Mark, *Viva Macau*, Hong Kong, Macmillan, 1980. An historical one-day look through Macau's four centuries of history.

Elegant, Robert, and Brake, Brian, *Hong Kong (Great Cities of the World series)*, Amsterdam,

Time-Life, 1977. The colony described as one of the world's major urban centres.

Fischbeck, Frank, *Face of Hong Kong,* Hong Kong, Libra Books, 1970. Hong Kong depicted by its people. Some 27 different portraits, ranging from rickshaw pullers and coolies to a Communist millionaire in full Red Guard regalia waving a Mao-book.

Roberts, Lew, *Over Hong,* Hong Kong, *South China Morning Post,* 1982. 97 spectacular colour plates of Hong Kong through the eye of a bird.

Warner John, *Fragrant Harbour,* Hong Kong, John Warner Publications, 1976. A superb collection of very early photographs of Hong Kong.

Wilshire, Trea, and Fischbeck, Frank, *Hong Kong: An Impossible Journey Through History,* Hong Kong, Serasia, 1971. An excellent history of the colony from 1841—1971, supplemented by photographs of modern Hong Kong.

Appendix A

ACCOMMODATIONS

Luxury — Over HK$1,000 Per Day

Mandarin—5 Connaught Road, Central, Hong Kong. Tel: 5-220-111.
Peninsula—Salisbury Road, Tsimshatsui, Kowloon. Tel: 3-666-251.
Regent—Salisbury Road, Tsimshatsui, Kowloon. Tel: 3-721-211.
Shangri-La—64 Mody Road, Tsimshatsui East, Kowloon. Tel: 3-721-2111.

Expensive—Above HK$400 Per Day

Excelsior—Gloucester Road, Causeway Bay, Hong Kong. Tel: 5-767-365.
Furama—Intercontinental—1 Connaught Road, Central, Hong Kong. Tel: 5-255-111.
Hilton—2 Queen's Road, Central, Hong Kong. Tel: 5-233-111.
Holiday Inn-Golden Mile—50 Nathan Road, Tsimshatsui East, Kowloon. Tel: 3-693-111.
Holiday Inn Harbour View—10 Mody Road, Tsimshatsui East, Kowloon. Tel: 3-721-5161.
Hongkong—3 Canton Road, Tsimshatsui, Kowloon. Tel: 3-676-011.
Hyatt-Regency—67 Nathan Road, Tsimshatsui, Kowloon. Tel: 3-662-321.
Kowloon—19-21 Nathan Road, Tsimshatsui, Kowloon. Tel: 3-698-698.
Lee Gardens—Hysan Avenue, Causeway Bay, Hong Kong. Tel: 5-767-211.
Marco Polo—Harbour City, Canton Road, Tsimshatusi, Kowloon. Tel: 3-721-5111.
Miramar—134 Nathan Road, Tsimshatsui, Kowloon. Tel: 3-681-111.
Prince—Harbour City, Canton Road, Tsimshatsui, Kowloon. Tel: 3-723-7788.
Regal Meridien—Mody Road, Tsimshatsui East, Kowloon. Tel: 3-722-1818.
Royal Meridien Airport—Sa Po Road, Kowloon. Tel: 3-718-0333.
Royal Garden—69 Mody Road, Tsimshatsui East, Kowloon. Tel: 3-721-5215.
Kowloon. Tel: 3-681-111.
New World—22 Salisbury Road, Tsimshatsui, Kowloon. Tel: 3-694-111.
Park Lane—310 Gloucester Road, Causeway Bay, Hong Kong. Tel: 5-790-1021.
Riverside Plaza—Tai Chung Kiu Road, Shatin, New Territories. Tel: 0-649-7878.
Sheraton—20 Nathan Road, Tsimshatsui, Kowloon. Tel: 3-691-111.
Victoria—Shun Tak Centre, Connaught Road, Central, Hong Kong. Tel: 5-407-228.
Warwick—Cheung Chau Island. Tel: 5-981-0081.

Moderate—Above HK$300

Ambassador—4 Middle Road, Tsimshatsui, Kowloon. Tel: 3-666-321.
Astor—11 Carnarvon Road, Tsimshatsui, Kowloon. Tel: 3-667-261.

Carlton—4½ Milestone, Tai Po Road, North Kowloon. Tel: 3-866-222.
Empress—17-19 Chatham Road, Tsimshatusi, Kowloon. Tel: 3-660-211.
Fortuna—355 Nathan Road, Yaumatei, Kowloon. Tel: 3-851-011.
Grand—14 Carnarvon Road, Tsimshatsui, Kowloon. Tel: 3-669-331.
Harbour View—4 Harbour Road, Hong Kong. Tel: 5-201-111.
Imperial—30-34 Nathan Road, Tsimshatsui, Kowloon. Tel: 3-662-201.
International—33 Cameron Road, Tsimshatsui, Kowloon. Tel: 3-663-381.
Luk Kwok—67 Gloucester Road, Hong Kong. Tel: 5-270-721.
Park—61-65 Chatham Road, Tsimshatsui, Kowloon. Tel: 3-661-371.
Shamrock—223 Nathan Road, Yaumatei, Kowloon. Tel: 3-662-271.
Silvermine Bay Beach Hotel—Lantau Island. Tel: 5-984-8295.
Surf Hotel—Tai Mung Tsai Road, Sai Kung, New Territories. Tel: 3-281-4411.

Inexpensive—Above HK$100

Bangkok—2-12 Pilkem Street, Tsimshatsui, Kowloon. Tel: 3-679-181.
Chung Hing—380 Nathan Road, Yaumatei, Kowloon. Tel: 3-887-001.
Galaxie—30 Pak Hoi Street, Yaumatei, Kowloon. Tel: 3-307-211.
King's—473-473A Nathan Road, Yaumatei, Kowloon. Tel: 3-301-281.

Under HK$100

The best bargains are Y's but they are usually quite full. Next come the guest houses especially those in **Chungking Mansions**. (Incidentally, though there are only two listed here, if they are full, there are several smaller ones in the other blocks. (See **Cheap Sleeps**.)

Chungking House—Chungking Mansions, A Block 4th and 5th floors 34-40 Nathan Road, Tsimshatsui, Kowloon. Tel: 3-665-362.
Green Jade House—29-31 Chatham Road, Tsimshatsui, Kowloon. Tel: 3-677-121.
International Guest House—Chungking Mansions, 9th-10th floors 34-40 Nathan Road, Tsimshatsui, Kowloon. Tel: 3-664-256.
YMCA—Salisbury Road, Tsimshatsui, Kowloon. Tel: 3-692-211.
YMCA—23 Waterloo Road, Yaumatei, Kowloon. Tel: 5-319-111.
YWCA—1 Macdonnell Road, Hong Kong. Tel: 5-223-101.
YWCA—5 Man Fuk Road, Waterloo Road Hill, Kowloon. Tel: 3-713-9211.

AIRLINES
(with reservation numbers)

Aer Lingus—See Group Systems Int'l.
Air Canada—1026 Prince's Building, Hong Kong. Tel: 5-221-001.

Air France—21st floor, Alexandra House, Hong Kong, or G07 Hotel Regal, Meridien, Kowloon. Tel: 5-248-145.
Air India—1002 Gloucester Tower, Hong Kong. Tel: 5-214-321.
Air Lanka—505 Bank of American Tower, Hong Kong. Tel: 5-252-171.
Air Malawi—See Jardine Airways.
Air New Zealand—See Cathay Pacific Airways.
Air Niugini—209 Worldwide Plaza, Hong Kong. Tel: 5-242-151.
Alia Royal Jordanian Airline—c/o Deks Air (HK) Ltd., 4th floor, Aurora House, 57-59 Connaught Road, Central, Hong Kong. Tel: 5-442-886.
Alitalia—Hilton Hotel Arcade, Hong Kong. Tel: 5-237-041.
All Nippon Airways—2001 Fairmount House, Hong Kong. Tel: 5-251-306.
Aioha Airlines—See Group Systems Int'l.
American Airlines—202 Caxton House, 1 Duddell Street, Central, Hong Kong. Tel: 5-257-081.
Ansett Airlines—See Cathay Pacific Airways.
Australian Airlines—See Jardine Airways.
Avianca—1025 Swire House, Hong Kong. Tel: 5-269-955.

Bangladesh Biman—c/o Union Travel Company, Grd. floor, 16 Mody Road, Kowloon. Tel: 3-696-760.
British Airways—See Jardine Airways.
British Caldeonian Airways—BBC House, 15/F, 10 Queen's Road, Central, Hong Kong. Tel: 5-260-062.

CAAC Civil Aviation Administration of China—c/o China National Aviation Corporation, Gloucester Tower, Hong Kong. Tel: 5-216-416.
Canadian Pacific Air—Swire House, Hong Kong or Peninsula Hotel Arcade, Kowloon. Tel: 5-225-1001.
Cathay Pacific Airways—Swire House or Lee Gardens Hotel, Hong Kong. Peninsula Hotel or Ocean Centre, Kowloon. Tel: 5-884-1488.
China Airlines—St. George's Building, Hong Kong or Grd. floor, Tsimshatsui Centre, Kowloon. Tel: 5-218-4311.
Continental Airlines—See British Caledonian.
Cubana de Aviacon—See Jardine Airways.
Cyprus Airways—See Jardine Airways.

Dan Air—See British Caledonian.
Delta Air Lines—See Group Systems Int'l. Tel: 5-265-875.
Eastern Airlines—See Wallem Airways.
Flying Tigers—223 New Cargo Complex Office Block, Kai Tak Airport, Kowloon. Tel: 3-769-7564.
Garuda Indonesian Airways—Grd. floor, Fu House, Hong Kong. Tel: 5-235-181.
Gibraltar Airways—See Jardine Airways.
Group Systems Int'l.—900 Chartered Bank Bldg., Central, Hong Kong or 1005 Silvercord, Tower II, 30 Canton Road, Kowloon. Tel: 3-723-7833.
Gulf Air—See Group Systems Int'l.

Hawaiian Air—40 Des Voeux Road Central, Hong Kong. Tel: 5-264-354.
Iberia—Room B, 19/f Chung Hing Commercial Bldg., 62-63 Connaught Road, Central, Hong Kong. Tel: 5-423-228.
Icelandair—See Wallem Airways.
Iraqi Airways—See Wallen Airways.
Jardine Airways—Alexandra House, Hong Kong. Tel: 5-262-245; 112 Royal Garden Hotel, Kowloon.

Tel: 3-689-255. Flight Information: 5-774-626. Reservations: 5-775-023.

Japan Air Lines/Japan Asia Airways — Gloucester Tower, Hong Kong or Harbour Views Holiday Inn Lobby, Kowloon. Tel: 5-230-081.

Kenya Airways — See Jardine Airways.

KLM Royal Dutch Airlines — Fu House, 7 Ice House Street, Hong Kong. Tel: 5-251-255.

Korean Air — St. George's Building, Hong Kong or Tsimshatsui Centre, Kowloon. Tel: 3-768-221.

Kuwait Airways — See Jardine Airways.

Lanchile Airlines — 11th floor, Hua Hsia Buiding, 64 Gloucester Road, Hong Kong. Tel: 5-298-285.

Libyan Arab Airlines — See Jardine Airways.

Lufthansa — 6/F Landmark East, Hong Kong or Empire Centre, East Tsimshatsui, Kowloon. Tel: 5-212-311.

Luxavia — See Wallem Airways.

Malaysian Airline System — 13th floor, Prince's Building, Hong Kong. Tel: 5-218-181.

Mexicana Airlines — See Wallem Airways.

NLM City Hopper — See Wallem Airways.

Northwest Orient Airlines — St. George's Building, Hong Kong. Tel: 5-217-477.

Pacific Western — 505A Bank of America Tower, Hong Kong. Tel: 5-255-668.

Pakistan International Airlines — 1004 Houston Centre, Kowloon. Tel: 3-664-770.

Pan American World Airways — 1st floor, Alexandra House, Hong Kong or Grd. floor, Empire Centre, Kowloon. Tel: 5-231-111.

Philippine Airlines — 305 East Ocean Centre, East Tsimshatsui, Kowloon. Tel: 3-694-521.

Qantas Airways — Swire House, Hong Kong or Sheraton Hotel Lobby, Kowloon. Tel: 5-242-101.

Republic — 231 Caxton House, 1 Duddell Street, Central, Hong Kong. Tel: 5-214-495.

Royal Brunei Airlines — 406 Central Building, Hong Kong. Tel: 5-223-799.

Royal Nepal Airlines — 1114 Star House, Kowloon. Tel: 3-699-151.

Sabena Belgian World Airlines — See Wallem Airways.

SAS — 2407 Edinburgh Tower, Central, Hong Kong. Tel: 5-265-978.

Singapore Airlines — 115 The Landmark, Hong Kong. 17/F, United Centre, Hong Kong. Tel: 9-202-233.

South African Airways — See Jardine Airways.

Swissair — Tower 2, 8th floor, Admiralty Centre, Hong Kong. Tel: 5-292-193, or Peninsula Hotel, Kowloon. Tel: 5-293-670.

Thai Airways International — Shop 123, Worldwide Plaza, Hong Kong or Peninsula Hotel Arcade, Kowloon. Tel: 5-295-601.

Trans Australia — See Qantas Airways.

TWA — 2205 Yardley Commercial Bldg., 3 Connaught Road, Central, Hong Kong. Tel: 5-413-117.

United Airlines — 3606 Gloucester Tower, Hong Kong. Tel: 5-261-212.

Varig Brazilian Airlines — Shop 120, Ambassador Hotel, Kowloon. Tel: 3-690-171.

Vasp Brazilian Airlines — 1401 Tung Ming Building, 40 Des Voeux Road, Central, Hong Kong. Tel: 5-264-353.

Wallem Airways — 1/f, Hilton Hotel, Hong Kong. Tel: 5-237-065.

Western Airlines — See Group Systems Int'l.

IMPORTANT BUILDINGS

On Hong Kong Island

AIA Bldg. — 1 Stubbs Road, Happy Valley.

Admiralty Centre — 18 Harcourt Road, Central.

Alexandra House — 11 Des Voeux Road, Central.

Alliance Bldg. — 130-136 Connaught Road, Central.

Asian House — 1 Hennessy Road, Wanchai.

Bank of Canton Bldg. — 6 Des Voeux Road.

Bank of America Tower — 12 Harcourt Road, Central.

Baskerville House — 13 Duddell Street, Central.

Beaconsfield House — 4 Queen's Road, Central.

Belgian House — 77-79 Gloucester Road, Wanchai.

Capitol Centre — 5-19 Jardines Bazaar, Causeway Bay.

Carrian Centre — 151 Gloucester Road, Wanchai.

Causeway Centre — 28 Harbour Road, Wanchai.

Caxton House — 54-56 Queen's Road, Central.

Central Bldg. — 3 Pedder Street, Central.

Central House — Queen's Road, Central.

Centre Point Bldg. — 181-185 Gloucester Road, Wanchai.

Chartered Bank Bldg. — 3 Queen's Road, Central.

China Bldg. — 29 Queen's Road, Central.

China Fleet Club — Sun Hung Kai Centre, 30 Harbour Road, Wanchai.

China Resources Bldg. — 26 Harbour Road, Wanchai.

Chinese Chamber of Commerce Bldg. — 24-26 Connaught Road, Central.

City Hall — Edinburgh Place, Central.

City Plaza — Taikoo Shing, King's Road, North Point.

Club Lusitano Bldg. — 16 Ice House Street, Central.

Connaught Centre — Connaught Road, Central.

Dina House SA — Duddell Street, Central.

East Point Bldg. — 92 Gloucester Road, Wanchai.

Edinburgh Tower — 18 Queens Road, Central.

Elizabeth House — 250-254 Gloucester Road, Wanchai.

Exchange Square — 8 Connaught Place, Central.

Eurotrade Centre — Des Voeux Road, Central.

Fairmount House — Murray Road, Central.

Far East Finance Bldg. — Harcourt Road, Central.

Fleet House — 6 Arsenal Street, Hong Kong.

Fu House — 7 Ice House Street, Central.

Fung House — 19-21 Connaught Road, Central.

General Post Office — Connaught Place, Central.

Gloucester Tower — Pedder Street, Central.

Great Eagle Centre — 23 Harbour Road, Wanchai.

Hang Lung Bank Bldg. — 8 Hysan Avenue, Causeway Bay.

Hang Lung Centre — 2-20 Paterson Street, Causeway Bay.

Hang Seng Bank Bldg. — Des Voeux Road, Causeway Bay.

Harbour View Mansions — 257 Gloucester Road, Causeway Bay.

Hennessy Centre — 500 Hennessy Road, Causeway Bay.

Hongkong and Shanghai Bank Bldg. — 1 Queen's Road, Central.

Hong Kong Diamond Exchange Centre — Ice House Street, Central.

Hong Kong Exhibition Centre — 26 Harbour Road, Wanchai.

Hopewell Centre—183 Queen's Road, East.
Hutchison House—10 Harcourt Road, Central.
International Bldg.—139-141 Des Voeux Road, Central.
Jardine House—22 Pedder Street, Central.
Korea Centre—119 Connaught Road, Central.
Landmark—11 Pedder Street, Central.
Lane Crawford House—70 Queen's Road, Central.
Liu Chong Hing Bldg.—24 Des Voeux Road, Central.
Melbourne Plaza—33 Queen's Road, Central.
Mercantile Bank Bldg.—7 Queen's Road, Central.
Mercury House—3 Connaught Road, Central.
Minden Plaza—Gloucester Road, Causeway Bay.
Murray Bldg.—22 Cotton Tree Drive, Central.
New Henry House—10 Ice House Street, Central.
New Mercury House—22 Fenwick Street, Wanchai.
New World Tower—Queen's Road, Central.
Overseas Trust Bank Bldg.—160 Gloucester Road, Wanchai.
Pacific House—16 Queen's Road, Central.
Paterson Plaza—22-36 Paterson Street, Causeway Bay.
Peter Building—58 Queen's Road, Central.
Prince's Bldg.—5 Ice House Street, Central.
Printing House—6 Duddell Street, Central.
Queen's Bldg.—74 Queen's Road, Central.
Realty Bldg.—67-73 Des Voeux Road, Central.
Royal Hong Kong Jockey Club—2 Sports Road, Happy Valley.
St. George's Bldg.—2 Ice House St., Central.
Shell House—24 Queen's Road, Central.
Solar House—28 Des Voeux Road, Central.
Sun Hung Kai Centre—30 Harbour Road, Wanchai.
Sutherland House—3 Chater Road, Central.
Swire House—9 Connaught Road, Central.
Tak Shing House—20 Des Voeux Road, Central.
United Centre—95 Queensway, Central.
Watson's Estate—Watson's Road, North Point.
Wheelock House—Pedder Street, Central.
Windsor House—311 Gloucester Road, Causeway Bay.
Wing On Centre—122 Connaught Road, Central.
World Trade Centre—280 Gloucester Road, Causeway Bay.
World-Wide Plaza—Des Voeux Road, Central.

In Kowloon

Bank of America Bldg.—1 Kowloon Park Drive, Tsimshatsui.
Chungking Mansions—36-44 Nathan Road, Tsimshatsui.
Eldex Industrial Bldg.—21 Matauwei Road, Tokwawan.
Empire Centre—Mody Road, Tsimshatsui East.
Hankow Centre—5-15 Hankow Road, Tsimshatsui.
Harbour City—11 Canton Road, Tsimshatsui.
Houston Centre—Mody Road, Tsimshatsui East.
Jordan House—6-8 Jordan Road.
Mirror Tower—Mody Road, Tsimshatsui East.
New World Centre—Salisbury Road, Tsimshatsui.
Ocean Centre—5 Canton Road, Tsimshatsui.
Ocean Terminal—Tsimshatsui.
Silvercord—Canton Road, Tsimshatsui.
South Seas Centre—Mody Road, Tsimshatsui East.
Star House—3 Salisbury Road, Tsimshatsui.
Tsimshatsui Centre—Mody Road, Tsimshatsui East.
Wing On Plaza—Mody Road, Tsimshatsui East.

BUSINESS PUBLICATIONS

Business Environment in Hong Kong—edited by D. Lethridge.
Doing Business in Today's China.
Doing Business in Today's Hong Kong.
Government & Politics of Hong Kong—by N.J. Miners.
Hong Kong Economic growth & Policy—by A.J. Youngson.
Hong Kong Taxation—by David Flux.
Hong Kong Annual Report
Industrial Relations & Law in Hong Kong—by J. England and J. Rear.
Law in Hong Kong—by V.A. Penlington.
Living in Hong Kong.
Who's in Hong Kong—by Kevin Sinclair.

BUSINESS ORGANIZATIONS & GOVERNMENT DEPARTMENTS

American Chamber of Commerce—1030 Swire House, Central District, Hong Kong. Tel: 5-260-165. Hours: 9 a.m. to 12:30 p.m. and 2 to 5 p.m. weekdays and until 12:30 p.m. Saturdays.
Companies Registry—Queensway Gov't. Office Bldg., 13-14/fls., 56 Queensway, Hong Kong. Tel: 5-862-2600/1. Hours: 9 a.m. to 1 p.m. and 2 to 5 p.m. weekdays and until 1 p.m. Saturday.
United Centre—22/f, 95 Queensway, Hong Kong. Tel: 5-299-229. Hours: 9 a.m. to 1 p.m. and 2 to 5 p.m. weekdays and until 1 p.m. Saturdays.
Immigration Department—Mirror Tower, 61 Mody Road, East Tsimshatsui, Kowloon. Tel: 3-733-3111. Hours: 9 a.m. to 5 p.m. weekdays and until 12:30 p.m. Saturdays.
Inland Revenue Department—Windsor House, 311 Gloucester Road, Causeway Bay, Hong Kong. Tel: 5-7959-1111. Hours: 8:30 a.m. to 12:30 p.m. and 1:30 to 5 p.m. weekdays and 9 a.m. to noon Saturdays.
Hennessy Centre—500 Hennessy Road, Hong Kong. Tel: 5-795-6031. Hours: 9 a.m. to 1 p.m. and 2 to 5:30 p.m. weekdays and until noon Saturdays.
H.K. Trade Development Council—Great Eagle Centre, 31/F, 23 Harbour Road, Hong Kong. Tel: 5-833-4333. Hours: 8:30 a.m. to 5 p.m. weekdays, till 12:30 p.m. Saturdays.

SPECIAL CLUBS

Hong Kong has a full complement of societies and clubs that specialize in everything from bird-watching to archaeology. Not many unnofficial visitors drop in on these special interest groups, but they are very hospitable to those who do. Among local clubs and societies are:

Aviation Club—Sung Wong Toi Road, Kai Tak Airport, Kowloon. Tel: 3-713-5171.
Archeological Society—c/o Museum of History, 58 Haiphong Road, Tsimshatsui, Kowloon. Tel: 3-671-127.
Royal Asiatic Society—G.P.O. Box 3864, Hong Kong. Tel: 3-660-174.
Bird Watching Society—c/o G.P.O. Box 12460, Hong Kong. Tel: 0-273-814.
Ceramic Society—G.P.O. Box 6202, Hong Kong. Tel: 5-266-311.
Chess Federation—1202 Luk Hoi Tung Bldg., Hong

Kong. Tel: 5-841-8527.

Contract Bridge Association – G.P.O. Box 1445, Hong Kong. Tel: 5-238-181.

Foreign Correspondents Clubs – 2 Lower Albert Road, Hong Kong. Tel: 5-211-511.

Darts Association – G.P.O. Box 11501, Hong Kong. Tel: 3-743-6776.

Ikebana International – G.P.O. Box 3029, Hong Kong. Tel: 5-508-144.

Union – Kowloon G.P.O. Box 70837, Hong Kong.

Mountaineering Union – Kowloon G.P.O. Box 70837, Hong Kong. Tel: 3-230-102.

Orchid Assn. – G.P.O. Box 9038, Hong Kong. Tel: 3-779-6449.

Press Club – Capital Bldg., 3rd floor, 175 Lockhart Road, Wanchai, Hong Kong. Tel: 5-742-247.

(For information regarding service clubs such as Rotary, Lions, Kiwanis, etc., check with your hotel for the nearest chapter's address.)

FOREIGN CONSULATES & COMMISSIONS
(all in Hong Kong unless marked Kowloon)

Australia – Harbour Centre, 23-24/fls., 25 Harbour Road, Wanchai. Tel: 5-731881. (9:30 a.m. to 1 p.m. and 2 to 4:30 p.m. weekdays).

Austria – Room 2201, Wang Kee Bldg., 34-37 Connaught Road, Central, Hong Kong. Tel: 5-239-716. (9 a.m. to noon weekdays).

Bangladesh – 3807 China Resources Bldg., 26, Harbour Road. Tel: 5-728-278/9. (9 a.m. to 1 p.m. and 2 to 5 p.m. weekdays, half-day on Saturday).

Belgium – 9th floor, St. John's Bldg., 33 Garden Road. Tel: 5-243-111. (9 a.m. to noon and 2 to 4 p.m. weekdays).

Bhutan – 2nd floor, Kowloon Centre, 29-43 Ashley Road. Tel: 3-692-112.

Bolivia – 1101, Far East Exchange Bldg., 8 Wyndham Street, Central. Tel: 5-227-691. (10 a.m. to noon and 2 to 4 p.m. weekdays).

Brazil – 1107, Shell House, 28 Queen's Road Central. Tel: 5-257-002.

Britain – c/o H.K. Immigration Dept., Mirror Tower, 61 Mody Road, East Tsimshatsui, Kowloon. Tel: 3-733-3111. (8:30 a.m. to 12:30 p.m. and 1:30 to 5 p.m. weekdays, 9 a.m. to noon Saturdays).

Burma – Rm 2424, Sun Hung Kai Centre, 30 Harbour Road. Tel: 5-891-3329. (9 a.m. to 12:30 p.m. and 2:30 to 5 p.m. weekdays).

Canada – 15th floor, Asian House, 1 Hennessy Road, Wanchai, Hong Kong. Tel: 5-282-222. (8:30 a.m. to 12:30 p.m. and 1:30 to 5 p.m. weekdays).

Chile – 11th floor, Hua Hsia Bldg., 64 Gloucester Road, Wanchai, Hong Kong. Tel: 5-732-139 (9 a.m. to 1 p.m. and 2 to 6 p.m. weekdays).

China – (People's Repubic of) China Travel Service, 77 Queen's Road Central, Hong Kong. Tel: 5-259-121. (9 a.m. to 1 p.m. and 2 to 5 p.m. Monday to Saturday).

Colombia – Unit A, 6th floor, C.M.A. Bldg., 64-66, Connaught Road, Central. Tel: 5-458-547. (9 a.m. to 1 p.m. weekdays).

Costa Rica – Flat C-10, Hung On Bldg., 3 Tin Hau Temple Road. Tel: 5-665-181.

Cuba – 10th floor, Rose Count, 115 Wong Nai Chung Road. Tel: 5-760-226.

Cyprus – 19th floor, United Centre, 95 Queensway. Tel: 5-292-161.

Denmark – Suite 2101-2102 Great Eagle Centre, 23 Harbour Road, Wan Chai. Tel: 5-893-6265.

Dominican Republic – 813, Peninsula Centre, 67 Mody Road, Tsimshatshui East, Kowloon. Tel: 3-723-1836. (10 a.m. to 1 p.m. and 2:30 to 4 p.m. weedays).

Euacdor – 11th floor, Flat C4, Hankow Centre, 1-C Middle Road, Kowloon. Tel: 3-692-235/6.

Egypt – 9th floor, Woodland Garden, 10 Macdonnell Road. Tel: 5-244-174. (9 a.m. to noon weekdays, till 11:30 a.m. Saturday).

Eire – 8th floor, Prince's Bldg., Central, Hong Kong. Tel: 5-226-022. (9 a.m. to 12:30 p.m. and 2:30 to 5 p.m. weekdays, half-day Saturday).

El Salvador – 1517 Central Bldg., 3 Pedder Street. Tel: 5-228-995. (9 a.m. to 1 p.m. and 2 to 6 p.m. weekdays and 10 a.m. to noon Saturday).

Finland – 1818 Hutchison House, Central. Tel: 5-255-385. (10 a.m. to 12:30 p.m. and 2:30 to 4:30 p.m. weekdays).

France – Admiralty Centre, Tower 11, 26th floor, 18 Harcourt Road. Tel: 5-294-351. (9:30 a.m. to 1 p.m. weekdays).

Gabon – P.O. Box 4599 North Point Post Office, Hong Kong. Tel: 5-724-062.

Germany – 21st floor, United Centre, 95 Queensway. Tel: 5-298-855.

Greece – Rooms 1305-6, Kam Chung Bldg., 54 Jaffe Road. Tel: 5-200-860. (9 a.m. to 1 p.m. and 2 to 5 p.m. weekdays and half-day Saturday).

Guatemala – 2205 Yardley Commercial Bldg., 3 Connaught Road West. Tel: 5-411-300. (9 a.m. to noon weekdays).

Haiti – 7th floor, Botanical Court, 5A Caine Road. Tel: 5-244-306. (9 a.m. to 5 p.m. weekdays and half-day Saturday).

Iceland – 48th floor, Hopewell Centre, 183 Queen's Road East. Tel: 5-283-911. (9 a.m. to 1 p.m. and 2 to 5 p.m. weekdays).

India – Unit D, 16th floor, United Centre, 95 Queensway. Tel: 5-284-029.

Indonesia – 6-8 Keswick Street, Causeway Bay, Hong Kong. Tel: 5-790-4421. (10 a.m. to 12:30 p.m. and 2:30 to 4:30 p.m. weekdays).

Iran – 1901 Alliance Bldg., 130-136 Connaught Road, Central, Hong Kong. Tel: 5-414-745. (9 a.m. to 1 p.m. and 2 to 5 p.m. weekdays and half-day Saturday).

Israel – 1122 Prince's Bldg., Central. Tel: 5-220-177. (10 a.m. to 1 p.m. and 2 to 4 p.m. weekdays).

Italy – 801 Hutchison House, Central. Tel: 5-220-033 (9:30 a.m. to 1 p.m. and 2:30 to 4:30 p.m. weekdays and half-day Saturday).

Jamaica – 23rd floor, Wah Kwong Bldg., 48-62 Hennessy Road, Wanchai. Tel: 5-823-8238.

Japan – 25th floor, Bank of America Tower, Central, Hong Kong. Tel: 5-221-184 (9:30 a.m. to noon, and 2 to 4 p.m. weekdays, except Wednesday which is a half day).

Jordan – 911 World Shipping Centre, Harbour City, Kowloon. Tel: 3-696-399.

Korea (Republic of) – 3rd floor, Korea Centre Bldg., 119-120 Connaught Road, Central. Tel: 5-430-224. (10 a.m. to noon and 2 to 4 p.m. weekdays and half-day Saturday).

Liberia – 703 Admiralty Centre, Tower 1, 18 Harcourt Road. Tel: 5-201-978. (9:30 a.m. to 12:30 p.m. and 2:30 to 4:30 p.m. weekdays).

Malaysia — 24th floor, Malaysia Bldg., 47-50 Gloucester Road, Wanchai. Tel: 5-270-921. (9 a.m. to 12:30 p.m. and 2 to 5 p.m. weekdays).

Mauritius — 7th floor, 1 Lockhart Road, Wanchai. Tel: 5-281-546. (9 a.m. to 1 p.m. and 2 to 5:15 p.m. weekdays and half-day Saturday).

Mexico — Room 2130A World-Wide House, 19 Des Voeux Road, Central. Tel: 5-214-365. (9 a.m. to 1 p.m. weekdays).

Monaco — 33rd floor, Harbour Centre, 25 Harbour Road, Wanchai. Tel: 5-893-0669. (9 a.m. to 1 p.m. and 2 to 5 p.m. weekdays and half-day Saturday).

Nauru — 1st floor, Pacific Star Bldg., 2 Canton Road, Tsimshatsui, Kowloon. Tel: 3-723-3525. (9 a.m. to 1 p.m. and 2 to 5 p.m. weekdays and half-day Saturday).

Nepal — Liaison Office, Headquarters, Brigade of Gurkhas, H.M.S. *Tamar*, 14th floor, Central, Hong Kong. Tel: 5-2893-3111 (10 to 10:30 a.m. weekdays).

Netherlands — 1505 Central Bldg., Central, Hong Kong. Tel: 5-227-710 (9 a.m. to noon and 2 to 4 p.m. weekdays).

New Zealand — 3414 Connaught Centre, Central, Hong Kong. Tel: 5-255-044 (9 a.m. to 1 p.m. and 2 to 5:30 p.m. weekdays).

Nicaragua — 1202 Kincheng Bank Bldg., 51 Des Voeux Road. Tel: 5-246-819. (10 a.m. to 12:30 p.m. weekdays).

Nigeria — 25th floor, Tung Wai Commercial Building, 109-111 Gloucester Road, Wanchai. Tel: 5-893-9444. (9:30 a.m. to 12:30 p.m. and 2 to 5:30 p.m. weekdays).

Norway — 1401 AIA Bldg., 1 Stubbs Road, Happy Valley, Hong Kong. Tel: 5-749-253. (9:30 a.m. to 12:30 p.m. and 2 to 4:30 p.m. weekdays).

Oman — 2210, Alexandra House, Central. Tel: 5-265-664.

Pakistan — 307-8 Asian House, 1 Hennessy Road, Wanchai. Tel: 5-274-623. (9:30 a.m. to 1 p.m. and 2 to 5 p.m. weekdays and half-day Saturday).

Panama — 1212 Wing On Centre, 111 Connaught Road, Central. Tel: 5-452-166. (9 to 11:30 a.m. and 2 to 4:30 p.m. weekdays and half-day Saturday).

Paraguay — 903 Hang Lung Bank Bldg., 8 Hysan Avenue, Causeway Bay. Tel: 5-790-5456. (9 a.m. to 1 p.m. and 2 to 5 p.m. weekdays).

Peru — 10th floor, 'F', Golden Plaza, 745-747 Nathan Road, Kowloon. Tel: 3-803-698. (9 a.m. to 1 p.m. weekdays).

Philippines — 8th floor, Hang Lung Bank Bldg., 8 Hysan Avenue, Causeway Bay, Hong Kong. Tel: 5-790-8823. (9 a.m. to 12:30 p.m. and 2 to 5 p.m. weekdays).

Portugal — 1001-1002, Two Exchange Square, 8 Connaught Place, Central. Tel: 5-225-789. (9 a.m. to 3 p.m. weekdays).

Senegal — c/o Dragages et Travaux Publics, 9-10th floors, 101-102 Gloucester Road, Wanchai. Tel: 5-744-261.

Singapore — Unit B, 17th floor, United Centre, 95 Queensway. Tel: 5-272-212/4. (9:30 a.m. to noon 2 to 5 p.m. weekdays and half-day Saturday).

South Africa — 27th floor, Sunning Plaza, 10 Hysan Avenue, Causeway Bay, Hong Kong. Tel: 5-773-279. (9 a.m. to 12:30 p.m. and 2 to 4 p.m. weekdays).

Spain — 1401-1403 Melbourne Plaza, Central, Hong Kong. Tel: 5-253-041. (9 a.m. to 1 p.m. weekdays).

Sweden — 8th floor, The Hong Kong Club Bldg., 3A Chater Road, Central. Tel: 5-211-212.

Switzerland — 3703 Gloucester Tower, 11 Pedder Street. Tel: 5-227-147. (9:30 a.m. to noon and 2 to 4 p.m. weekdays).

Taiwan — (Republic of China), c/o Chung Wah Travel Service, 10th floor, Tak Shing House, Central, Hong Kong. Tel: 5-258-315. (9 a.m. to 12:30 p.m. and 2 to 5 p.m. weekdays and half-day Saturday).

Thailand — 221-226 Hyde Centre, Gloucester Road, Wanchai, Hong Kong. Tel: 5-742-201. (10 a.m. to noon, 2:30 to 4:30 p.m. weekdays).

Tonga — Room 84, 8th floor, New Henry House, 10 Ice House Street, Central. Tel: 5-221-321. (10 a.m. to noon and 2 to 4 p.m. weekdays, except Wednesday).

Tuvalu — 402 Yuen Yick Building, 27-29 Wellington Street. Tel: 5-225-997.

United States of America — 26 Garden Road, Central. Tel: 5-239-011. (8:30 to 10:30 a.m. and 1:30 to 3:30 p.m. weekdays).

Uruguay — 103 View Point, 7 Bowen Road, Mid-Levels, Hong Kong. Tel: 5-248-792. (9 a.m. to noon and 2:30 to 5 p.m. weekdays).

Venezuela — 805 Star House, Kowloon. Tel: 3-678-099. (9 a.m. to noon and 2 to 4 p.m. weekdays).

NIGHTLIFE SPOTS

The following is an alphabetized address list of the colony's most well-known night spots:

Annie's Bar & Grill — 26-36 Prat Avenue, Kowloon.
Another World — Holiday Inn-Golden Mile Hotel, Kowloon.
L'Aperitif — Peninsula, Kowloon.
Apollo — 18 Silvercord, Canton Road, Kowloon.
Bell Inn — 94 Lockhart Road, Hong Kong.
Better 'Ole — Fanling, New Territories.
Blacksmiths Arms — 16 Minden Avenue, Kowloon.
Bottom's Up — 14 Hankow Road, Kowloon.
Brown's Wine Bar — Exchange Square, Hong Kong.
Bull and Bear — Hutchison House, Hong Kong.
California — 30-32 D'Aguilar Street/Lan Kwai Fong, Hong Kong.
Casablanca Supperclub — Aberdeen Marina Club Bldg., Shum Wan Rd., Aberdeen, Hong Kong.
Canton Discotheque — Harbour City, Canton Road, Kowloon.
Captain's Bar — Mandarin, Hong Kong.
Celebrity — 175 Lockhart Road, Hong Kong.
Chicago Discotheque — 29 Ashley Road, Kowloon.
Chin Chin — Hyatt Regency Hotel, Kowloon.
Club De Luxe — New World Centre, Kowloon.
Coates Wine Bar — Swire House, Hong Kong.
Copacabana — 35 Hankow Road, Kowloon.
Danshaku — 63 Peking Road, Kowloon.
Dai-Ichi — 257 Gloucester Road, Hong Kong.
Den — Hilton Hotel, Hong Kong.
Dickens Bar — Excelsior Hotel, Hong Kong.
Dragon Boat — Hilton Hotel, Hong Kong.
Flying Machine — Regal Meridien Airport Hotel, Kowloon.
Fujiva — 18 Lugard Road, Kowloon.
Ginza — 18 Hankow Road, Kowloon.
Godown — Sutherland House, Hong Kong.
Great Wall — Sheraton Hotel, Kowloon.
Gun Bar — Hong Kong Hotel, Kowloon.
Haley's Rock 'n' Roll Bar — 6-8 Prat Avenue, Kowloon.

Hardy's Folk Bar—35 D'Aguilar Street, Hong Kong.
Hollywood East—Regal Meridien Hotel, Kowloon.
Horse & Groom—126 Lockhart Road and Braemar Hill Road, Hong Kong.
Hot Gossip—Harbour City, Canton Road, Kowloon.
Inn Bar—Holiday Inn Golden Mile, Kowloon.
Jockey—Swire House, Hong Kong.
Kismet—71 Peking Road, Kowloon.
Kokusai—81 Nathan Road, Kowloon.
Latin Quarter—40 Nathan Road, Kowloon.
Lau Ling—Furama, Hong Kong.
London Pride—Landmark, Hong Kong.
Mad Dogs—33 Wyndham Street, Hong Kong.
Makati Inn—Luard Road, Hong Kong.
Mezzanine Lounge—Regent Hotel, Tsimshatsui, Kowloon.
Ned Kelly's Last Stand—11A Ashley Road, Tsimshatsui, Kowloon.
New Lido—36 Hankow Road, Kowloon.
New York—250 Jaffe Road, Central, Hong Kong.
New Playboy—69 Peking Road, Kowloon.
Nineteen 97—9 Lan Kwai Fong, Hong Kong.
Old China Hand—104 Lockhart Road, Central, Hong Kong.
Panda—123 Lockhart Road, Hong Kong.
Pink Giraffe—Sheraton, Kowloon.
Polaris—Hyatt-Regency, Kowloon.
Pussycat—36 Lockhart Road, Hong Kong.
Red Lion—15 Ashley Road, Kowloon.
Red Lips—1A Locke Road, Kowloon.
Rick's Cafe—4 Hart Avenue, Kowloon.
Rock Exchange—21 Luard Road, Hong Kong.
Rotisserie Lounge—Furama, Hong Kong.
Royal Falcon—Royal Garden Hotel, Kowloon.
Rumours—Sunning Plaza, Hysan Avenue, Hong Kong.
Safari—Bar City, New World Centre, Kowloon.
San Franciso—129 Lockhart Road, Hong Kong.
Shakespeare—30 Cannon Street, Hong Kong.
Shesado Discotheque—Bar City, New World Centre, Kowloon.
Ship Inn—4 Cornwall Avenue, Kowloon.
Smuggler's Inn—90A Stanley Main Street, Stanley, Hong Kong.
Spotlight—Hankow Road, Kowloon.
Stoned Crow—12 Minden Road, Kowloon.
Suzie Wong—21 Fenwick Street, Hong Kong.
Talk of The Town— Excelsior Hotel, Hong Kong.
Traps—82 Morrison Hill Road, Hong Kong.
Waltzing Matilda Inn—9 Cornwall Avenue, Tsimshatsui, Kowloon.
White Stag—72 Canton Road, Kowloon.
Wine & Cheese—16 Hennessy Road, Hong Kong.
Yum Sing—Lee Gardens Hotel, Hong Kong.

RESTAURANTS

Cantonese

Floating *sampan* restaurants, Causeway Bay Typhoon Shelter opposite Excelsior Hotel, HK.
Lamma Island seafood restaurants—(various locations).
King Bun—158 Queen's Road Central.
King of Snakes—12 Percival Street, Hong Kong.
Lychee Village—17 Wellington Street, Hong Kong.

North Park—440 Jaffe Road, Hong Kong or Tsimshatsui Centre, Kowloon.
Patek—2-4 Kingston Street, Hong Kong.
Ocean City—New World Centre, Kowloon.
Riverside—Food Street, Hong Kong.
Sun Tung Lok Shark's Fin—78 Morrison Hill Road, Hong Kong.
Tao Yuan—Great Eagle Centre 3/f, 23 Harbour Road, Hong Kong.
Wishful Cottage—336 Lockhart Road, Hong Kong.
Vegi Food Kitchen—Food Street, Hong Kong.
Yip Lam Kee—89 Jervois Street, Hong Kong.
Yung Kee—32 Wellington Street, Kowloon.

Pekinese/Mongolian

American—20 Lockhart Road, Hong Kong.
Genghis Khan—20 Luard Road, Hong Kong.
Kowloon Peking—65 Kimberley Road, Kowloon.
Mongolian Barbecue—58 Leighton Road, Hong Kong.
New American—179 Wanchai Road, Kowloon.
North China—7 Prat Avenue, Kowloon.
Peking—144 Gloucester Road, Hong Kong.
Pine & Bamboo—30 Leighton Road, Hong Kong.
Spring Deer—42 Mody Road, Kowloon.

Szechuanese

Cleveland—Food Street, Hong Kong.
Kam Chuen Lau—68 Granville Road, Kowloon.
Pep 'N Chilli—12 Blue Pool Road, Hong Kong.
Red Pepper—7 Lan Fong Road, Hong Kong.
Sichuan Garden—Gloucester Tower, Hong Kong.
Sze Chuan Lau—466 Lockhart Road, Hong Kong.

Shanghainese

Four Five Six (#1)—340 King's Road, Hong Kong.
Four Five Six (#2)—3 Pilkem Street, Kowloon.
Grand Shanghai—Island Centre 4/f, 1 Great George Street, Hong Kong.
Great Shanghai—26 Prat Avenue, Kowloon.
Yick Heung—Houston Centre, Kowloon.

Sri Lankan

Club Sri Lanka—17 Hollywood Road, Hong Kong.

Chiu Chau

Carrianna Chiu Chow—151 Gloucester Road, Hong Kong.
Chiu Chau—485 Lockhart Road, Hong Kong.
Golden Red Chiu Chau—13 Prat Avenue, Kowloon.
Pak Lok—24 Hysan Avenue, Hong Kong.
Siam Bird's Nest—55 Paterson Street, Hong Kong.
Tsui Lung 12 Saigon Street, Kowloon.

Hakka

Franho—24 Percivel Street, Hong Kong.
Fu Dao—3 Saigon Street, Kowloon.
Home—19 Hanoi Street, Kowloon.
Tsui King Lau—(various locations).

Hangchow

Tien Hung Lau—18C Austin Road, Kowloon.

Maxim's Group

Jade Garden, Sichuan Garden, Peking Garden, Maxim's Palace and Windsor Palace (various locations).

Vietnamese

Golden Bull—9 Hart Avenue, Kowloon.
Perfume River—51-53 Hennessy Road, Hong Kong.
Saigon—66 Lockhart Road, Hong Kong.
Vietnam City—Energy Plaza, Tsimshatsui East, Kowloon.
Yin Ping—24 Cannon Street, Hong Kong.

Japanese

Ah-So—Harbour City, Canton Road, Kowloon.
Benkay—Landmark, Hong Kong.
Hooraiya Teppanyaki—Food Street, Hong Kong.
Kanetanaka—Miramar Hotel, Kowloon.
Nadaman—Shangri-La Hotel, Kowloon.
Nagoya—Hyatt-Regency Hotel, Kowloon.
Okahan—Lee Gardens Hotel, Hong Kong.
Osaka—14 Ashley Road, Kowloon.
Ozeki—Tsimshatsui Centre & New World Centre, Kowloon.
Shiki—Furama Hotel, Hong Kong.
Si Sha Ya—93 Leighton Road, Hong Kong & 9 Chatham Road, Kowloon.
Unkai—Sheraton Hotel, Kowloon.

Korea

Go Gu Jang—Lee Gardens Hotel, Hong Kong.
Korea Barbecue—46 Kimberley Road, Kowloon.
Korea Gardens—New World Centre, Kowloon.
Koreana—Paterson Street, Hong Kong.
Manna Korea—6 Humphrey's Avenue, Kowloon.
Three-Five—6 Ashley Road, Kowloon.

Indian

Ashoka—57 Wyndham Street, Hong Kong.
Cosmo—80 Kwong Fuk Road, Tai Po Market, New Territories.
Gaylord—6 Hart Avenue, Kowloon.
Maharaja—222 Wanchai Road, Hong Kong & 1-3A Granville Circuit, Kowloon.
Maharaja—222 Wanchai Road, Hong Kong.
Mayur—25 Carnarvon Road, Kowloon.
New Delhi—62 Granville Road, Kowloon.
Shalimar—13 Irving Street, Hong Kong.
Viceroy of India—Sun Hung Kai Centre, Harbour Road, Hong Kong.
Woodlands—8 Minden Avenue, Kowloon.

Indonesian

Indonesian—26 Leighton Road, Hong Kong.
Indonesian Satay House—34 Mody Road, Kowloon.
Jaya Indonesian—2 Keswick Street, Hong Kong.
Jaya Rijstaffel—38 Hankow Road, Kowloon.
New Indonesian—26 Yun Ping Road, Hong Kong.
Ramayana Houston Centre—Mody Road, Kowloon.
Shinta—36 Queen's Road East, Hong Kong.
Spice Market—Ocean Centre, Kowloon.

SMI Curry Centre—81-85 Lockhart Road, 1/f, Hong Kong.

Malayan

Cosmo—80 Kwong Fuk Road, Tai Po Market, New Territories.
Malaya—158 Wellington Street, Hong Kong.
Malaynesia—123 Hennessy Road, Hong Kong.
Marseille—25 Leighton Road, Hong Kong.
Merlin Hotel—2 Hankow Road, Kowloon.
Sampaguita—4 Sunning Road, Kowloon.
Spice Market—(see Indonesian above).
SMI Curry Centre—(see Indonesian, above).

Singaporean

Sampaguita—4 Sunning Road, Hong Kong.
Satay Hut—Houston Centre, Kowloon.
SMI Curry Centre—(see Indonesian, above).

Thai

Bangkok Hotel—2 Pilkem Street, Kowloon.
Golden Thai—Harbour City, Kowloon.
Sawadee—1 Hillwood Road, Kowloon.

Filipino

Little Manila—9 Minden Avenue, Kowloon.
Luneta—16 Lan Kwai Fong, Hong Kong.
Mabubay—11 Minden Avenue, Kowloon.

Burmese

Khin's Burmese Kitchen—Wah Kwong Regent Centre 24/f, 88 Queen's Road, Hong Kong.

Western

Annie's Bar & Grill—26-36 Prat Avenue, Kowloon.
Au Trou Normand—6 Carnarvon Road, Kowloon.

Baron's Table—Holiday Inn-Golden Mile Hotel, Kowloon.
Belvedere—Holiday Inn-Harbour View Hotel, Kowloon.
Beverly Hills Deli—New World Centre, Kowloon & 2 Lan Kwai Fong, Hong Kong.
Brasserie, La—Marco Polo Hotel, Kowloon.
Brasserie, La—Regal Meridien Hotel.

California—30-32 D'Aguilar Street/Lan Kwai Fong, Hong Kong.
Casa Mexicana—15 Watson Road, Hong Kong.
Chesa—Peninsula, Kowloon.
Chico 'N Charlie's—128 Gloucester Road, Hong Kong.
Czarina—25 Bonham Road, Hong Kong.

Delicatessen Corner—Holiday Inn-Golden Mile Hotel, Kowloon.
Dutch Kitchen—30-34 Queen's Road (entrance Wyndham Street) Hong Kong.
Gaddi's—Peninsula Hotel, Kowloon.
Hilton Grill—Hilton Hotel, Hong Kong.
Hugo's—Hyatt-Regency Hotel, Kowloon.
Jimmy's Kitchen—1-3 Wyndham Street, Hong Kong or Kowloon Centre, 29 Ashley Road, Kowloon.
La Bella Donna—51 Gloucester Road, Hong Kong.

La Ronde — Furama-Inter-Continental Hotel, Hong Kong.
La Taverna — 1 On Hing Terrace & 57 Wonghaichong Road, Hong Kong, 36 Ashley Road, Kowloon.
Lalique — Royal Garden Hotel, Kowloon.
Landau's — 257 Gloucester Road, Hong Kong.
Le Restaurant de France — Regal Meridien Hotel, Kowloon.
Lyndy's — 57 Peking Road, 1/f, Kowloon.
Louis Steak House — 61 Connaught Road Central, Hong Kong.
Mad Dogs — 33 Wyndham Street, Hong Kong.
Mandarin Grill — Mandarin Hotel, Hong Kong.
Margaux — Shangri-La Hotel, Kowloon.
Mistral — Holiday Inn Harbour View, Kowloon.
Mozart Stub'n — 8 Glenealy Road, Hong Kong.
Napoleon — Miramar Hotel, Kowloon.
Ned Kelly's Last Stand — 11A Ashley Road, Kowloon.
Old Heidelberg — 24 Ashley Road, Kowloon.
Omar Khayyam — New World Centre, Kowloon.
Palm — 38 Locke Road, Kowloon.
Paprika — Ocean Centre, Kowloon.
Park Lane — New World Hotel, Kowloon.
Pierrot — Mandarin Hotel, Hong Kong.
Pizza Hut — Tsimshatsui Centre, Mody Road, Kowloon and Landmark, Hong Kong.
Plume — Regent of Hong Kong, Kowloon.
Rotisserie — Furama Inter-Continental Hotel, Hong Kong.
Rigoletto — 14 Fenwick Street, Hong Kong.
Sammy's Kitchen — 204 Queen's Road, Hong Kong.
San Franciso Steak House — Harbour City, Canton Road, Kowloon.
Sheikh — 89 Kimberley Road, Kowloon.
Spaghetti House — (various locations).
Stanley's — 86 Stanley Main Street, Hong Kong.
Steak House — Regent Hotel, Kowloon.
Stoned Crow — 12 Minden Avenue, Kowloon.
Swiss Inn — 56 Gloucester Road, Kowloon.
Texas Rib House — 15 Watson Road, Hong Kong.
YMCA — 41 Salisbury Road, Kowloon.

SHOPPING PLACES

Clothing

Bonaventure Trading — Kaiser Estate Phase II, Block 2, 11th floor, 51 Man Yue Street, Hung Hom, Kowloon, Tel: 3-622-279; silk items.
Camberley — G4 Kaiser Estate, 51 Man Yue Street, Hong Kong, Tel: 3-337038.
Swire House, Hong Kong, Tel: 5-246-264; leatherware, men's and women's fashions, silk items.
Da Cong — Kaiser Estate, Phase II, J2 11th floor, 51 Man Yue Street, Hung Hom, Kowloon, Tel: 3-336-201; men's sports shirts and fashions.
Delilah — 54 New World Centre, Kowloon. Tel: 3-682-378. For those with a more bizarre taste. Dancers too.
Diane Fries — Connaught Centre, Hong Kong, Tel: 5-227-661; Prince's Bldg., Hong Kong, Tel: 5-810-0378; Ocean Terminal, Kowloon, Tel: 3-721-4342; Harbour City, Kowloon, Tel: 3-723-3790; Tsimshatsui Centre, Kowloon, Tel: 3-723-4588; georgettes, silks, knits, beading, wools, novelties.

Fame — 36 Queen's Road East, Hong Kong, Tel: 5-274-657; Fashion body wear — leotards, tights legwarms, dancewear accessories.
Four Seasons — Kaiser Estate Phase II, Block G, 1st floor, 51 Man Yue Street, Hung Hom, Kowloon, Tel: 3-632-218; silk items.
Genti Donna — Kaiser Estate Phase II, Block G, 7th floor, 51 Man Yue Street, Hung Hom, Kowloon, Tel: 3-335-028, ladies silks & cottons.
K-International — Kaiser Estate, Phase II, 12th floor, Unit I, 51 Man Yue Street, Hung Hom, Kowloon, Tel: 3-626-264.
La Plume — Edinburgh Tower, Landmark, Hong Kong, Tel: 5-240-769. Risqué ladieswear.
Mosaic — Silvercord, Kowloon, Tel: 3-721-6669. Georgette ruffled dresses.
Shopper's World-Safari — Li Fung House, Basement, 2-4 Cameron Road, Kowloon, Tel: 3-662-686; Room 104 Pedder Bldg., Hong Kong, Tel: 5-231-950; ladies', mens' and children's clothes.
Wintex — Kaiser Estate, Phase III, 12th floor, Flat P, 11 Hok Yuen Street, Hung Hom, Kowloon, Tel: 3-634-274; Room 404 Pedder Bldg., Hong Kong, Tel: 5-249-943; ladies' silk items.
Vica Moda — Summit Bldg., 30 Man Yue St., Hung Hom, Kowloon, Tel: 3-348363; G2, 1st fl., Kaiser Estate Phase 2, Tel: 3-765-7333; 1B Bank of East Asia Bldg., Hong Kong, Tel: 5-221-331. Silk, linen, cotton coordinates.

Bedwear

Uluman Trading Co. — 702 Kowloon Centre, Ashley Rd., Kowloon, Tel: 3-721-9937. Sheets, quilt covers in cotton, flannel & poly-cotton.

Brassware

Sum Ngai Brass Ware Manufacturing Company — 195B Kam Tin, Kam Sheung Road, Yuen Long, New Territories, Tel: 0-793-938.

Porcelain

Ah Chow Porcelain Factory — Hong Kong Industrial Bldg., 7th fl., "B" Block, 489-91 Castle Peak Rd., Kowloon, Tel: 3-745-1511.
Mei Ping (Far East) Ltd. — Wilson House, 21st fl., 19-27 Wyndham St., Hong Kong, Tel: 5-213-566.
Yuet Tung China Works — Lot 3726 Tai Wo Ping, Kowloon, Tel: 3-778-1006.

Carpets

Tai Ping Carpet Factory — Taiping Industrial Park, Tai Po, New Territories, Tel: 0-656-5161. Annual sales of Chinese carpets in April and November.

Rattan

Kowloon Rattan — Ching Hing Industrial Bldg., 1st fl., 19-25 Fu Uk Rd., Kwai Chung, New Territories, Tel: 0-294-852.

Jewellery

Amerex Ltd. — 702 Tak Shing House, Hong Kong, Tel: 5-239-145. Pearls.

Continental Jewellry — Kaiser Estate III, 1st floor, 11 Hok Yuen Street, Hung Hom, Kowloon, Tel: 3-626-205.

Lloyd's Jewellery — 68 Sung Wong Toi Road, Unit C, Lower ground, Kowloon, Tel: 3-341-331.

Opal House — Tsimshatsui Centre (Showroom), Kowloon, Tel: 3-724-4535; M2, 5th fl., Kaiser Estate Phase 3, 11 Hok Yuen St., Hung Hom, Kowloon, Tel: 3-341-366.

Opal Creations — Burlington House, "B" Block, 6th fl., 92 Nathan Rd., Kowloon, Tel: 3-721-9933.

Furs

Drama K-Despina — Hay Nien Industrial Bldg., 9th fl., 1 Tai Yip St., Ngau Tau Kok, Kowloon, Tel: 3-756-1398.

Furniture

Luk's Furniture Co. Ltd. — Gee Chang Hong Centre, 25th fl., 65 Wong Chuk Hang Rd., Aberdeen, Hong Kong., Tel: 5-534-125.

Maitland-Smith — 30 Hollywood Road, Hong Kong, Tel: 5-810-4949.

Wah Tung China Co. — Cat Street Galleries, 38 Lok Ku Rd., Hong Kong, Tel: 5-443-446.

Ivory

Kwong Fat Cheong Ivory And Mahjong Factory — 27 Wellington Street, ground floor, Central, Hong Kong, Tel: 5-251-533.

Tack Cheung Ivory Factory — 36 Wyndham Street, Central, Hong Kong, Tel: 5-231-786.

Jade

Fu Hing Jewellery — 4th fl., G1, Kaiser Estate Phase 2, 11 Hok Yuen St., Hung Hom, Kowloon, Tel: 3-626-205.

Major Communist Chinese Stores

Chinese Merchandise Emporium — 92-94 Queen's Road, Central, Hong Kong. The best bet for one-stop shoppers, conveniently located just past Lane Crawford's.

China Products Company — 488 Hennessy Road, Causeway Bay, Hong Kong, 22 Stanley Main Street, Stanley Village, Hong Kong, and 73 Argyle Street, Kowloon.

Yue Hwa Chinese Products Emporium — 301-309 Nathan Road, Yaumatei, 54-64 Nathan Road, Tsimshatsui, both in Kowloon, or opposite Victoria Park at Causeway Bay, Hong Kong.

Chung Kiu — 528 and 580 Nathan Road (mostly arts and crafts) and at 47 Shantung Street, Kowloon.

Chinese Goods Centre — 395 King's Road, North Point, Hong Kong.

Chinese Arts and Crafts — 24 Queen's Road, Central, Hong Kong, and in Kowloon at Star House (just off the Star Ferry Concourse), at 233 Nathan Road, Tsimshatsui and Silvercord, Canton Road, Tsimshatsui. Top of the line, decorative stuff only, including excellent selections of carpets and silk (at somewhat higher prices).

Hifi Showrooms

Accuphase — Dah Chong Hong Ltd., Hang Seng Bank Bldg., 77 Des Voeux Road, Central, Hong Kong.

Advent — Audio Supplies Co., 824 Central Building, Pedder Street, Hong Kong.

Aiwa — A. Dransfield & Co., Harbour City, Kowloon.

Akai — P.H. Shek Ltd., Watson's Estate, Block "A", 9th fl., North Point, Hong Kong.

Bang & Olufsen — Ocean Terminal, Kowloon & Tak Shing House, Theatre Lane, Hong Kong.

Bose — Pacific Audion United Centre, Queensway, Hong Kong.

Hitachi — Tsimshatsui Centre, East Tsimshatsui, Kowloon.

JVC — Shun Hing Electronic Trading Co., Peninsula Centre, East Tsimshatsui, Kowloon.

Kenwood — Kenwood & Lee Electronics, Wan Kee Bldg., 5th fl., 34 Connaught Road, Central, Hong Kong.

Nakamichi — Radio People, 25 Chatham Road, Kowloon.

National — Shun Hing Electronic Trading Co., Peninsula Centre, East Tsimshatsui, Kowloon.

Panasonic — Shun Hing Electronic Trading Co., Peninsula Centre, East Tsimshatsui, Kowloon.

Philips — 225 Landmark East, Edinburgh Tower, Hong Kong.

Pioneer — Shinwa Engineering Co., Hong Kong Mansions, 3-5 Paterson Street, Causeway Bay, Hong Kong.

Quad — Radio People, 25 Chatham Road, Kowloon.

Sansui — Audio Department, Matsuzakaya Department Store, Causeway Bay, Hong Kong.

Sanyo — Tatt Sing Sanyo Electric Co., Wing On House, Connaught Road, Central, Hong Kong.

Sony — Fook Yuen Electronic Co., Harbour Commercial Bldg., Connaught Road, Central, Hong Kong.

Tandberg — Radio People, 25 Chatham Road, Kowloon.

Teac — Dah Chong Hong Ltd., Hang Seng Bank Bldg., 77 Des Voeux Rd., Central, Hong Kong.

Technics — Shun Hing Electronic Trading Co., Peninsula Centre, East Tsimshatsui, Kowloon.

Toshiba — Ma On Toshiba, Queensway Plaza, Queensway, Hong Kong.

Yamaha — Tom Lee Piano Co., 6 Cameron Lane, Kowloon.

Hong Kong Theatres

Cathay — 125 Wanchai Road, Wanchai, Tel: 5-724-745.

Columbia Classics — Great Eagle Centre, 23 Harbour Rd, Wanchai, Tel: 5-738291.

Imperial — Wood Road (off Wanchai Road), Wanchai, Tel: 5-722-883.

Isis — 7 Moreton Terrace (opposite Victoria Park). Tel: 5-773-496.

Jade — Paterson St., Causeway Bay, Tel: 5-778-117.

King's — 34 Queen's Road Central, Tel: 5-225-313.

Lee — 27 Percival St., Causeway Bay, Tel: 5-776-319.

New York — Hennesy Road at Percival St., Causeway Bay, Tel: 5-763-340.

Ocean Theatre – Ocean Centre, Canton Road, Tsimshatsui, Tel: 3-678-091.
Oriental – 1 Fleming Road, Wanchai, Tel: 5-724-907.
Palace – World Trade Centre, 20 Gloucester Road, Causeway Bay, Tel: 5-895-1500.
Park – Tung Lo Wan Road (opposite Victoria Park), Causeway Bay, Tel: 5-705-454.
Pearl – Paterson St., Causeway Bay, Tel: 5-776-351.
President – Jaffe Road at Cannon St., Causeway Bay, Tel: 5-761-937.
Queen's – 37 Queen's Road Central, Tel: 5-706-241.

Kowloon Theatres

Empress – Sai Yung Choi St., Mongkok, Tel: 3-809-570.
Golden Harvest – 23 Jordan Road, Yaumatei, Tel: 3-857-151.
Hollywood – 610 Soy St., Mongkok, Tel: 3-841-144.
Liberty – 26 Jordan Road, Yaumatei, Tel: 3-663-783.
London – 219 Nathan Road, Tsimshatsui, Tel: 3-661-056.
Majestic – 334 Nathan Road, Yaumatei, Tel: 3-847-115.
M2 – 6-22 Saigon St. Tel: 3-841-199.
Ocean – Ocean Centre, Tsimshatsui, Tel: 3-963-110.
Rex – Portland St. (off Argyle St.), Mongkok, Tel: 3-678-091.
Washington – 92 Parkes St. (off Jordan Road), Yaumatei, Tel: 3-310-405.

Appendix B

ACCOMMODATIONS

All rates listed below *exclude* the territory's 10 percent service charge and five percent tourism tax. An asterisk (*) indicates the Hong Kong phone number for booking rooms in that particular hotel.

over $500

Hyatt-Regency – Taipa Island Resort – Taipa Island. Tel: 27000. *5-463-797.
Oriental Av. da Amizade, Tel: 567888, *5-268-868.
Pousada de Sao Tiago, Fortaleza da Barra, Avenida Republica, Tel: 78111, *5-891-0366.
Royal – 2 Estrade de Victoria, Tel: 78822, *5-422-033.

Over $250

Estoril – Avenida Sidonio Pais, Tel: 5-72081.
Lisboa – Avenida de Amizade, Tel: 77666; *5-415680.
Matsuya – 5 Calcada de San Francisco, Tel: 75466, *3-686-181.
Metropole – 63 Rua de Praia Grande, Tel: 88166. *5-444-441.
Pousada de Coloane – Praia de Cheoc Van, Coloane Island, Tel: 28143, *5-455626.
Presidente – Avenida de Amizade, Tel: 71822, *5-416-056.
Sintra – Avenida de Amizade, Tel: 85111; *5-408-208.

Over $150

Bela Vista – 8 Rua Comendador Kuo Ho Neng, Tel: 573821.
Central – 26-28 Avenida Almeida Ribeiro, Tel: 77700.
London – Praca ponte e Horta, Tel: 83388.
Mondial – Rua de Antonio Basto, Tel; 76503. *5-449-283.

Under $150

Empress – 7a Estrada Sao Francisco, 3rd floor, 99-44-115 ptcs.
Hoi Pan – 8 Travessa D. Afonso Henrique; 120-140 ptcs.
Iao Lei – 65 Avenida Infante D. Henrique, 2nd floor; 60-120 ptcs.
Ka Va – Calcada de Sao Jose; 130-140 ptcs.
Oceane – 2 Avenida Dr Rodrigo Rodrigues, 1st floor; 120-130 ptcs.
Tai Fat – 41-43 Rua da Felicidade, 2nd floor; 65-135 ptcs.
Universal – 73 Rua da Felicidade, ground floor; 65-135 ptcs.
Va Lai – 44 Rua da Praia Grande, 1st floor; 130-140 ptcs.

RESTAURANTS

Macanese

Beira Mar – 63 Rua de Praia Grande, Te: 73499. Excellent Portuguese and Macanese food. Open 8 a.m. to 2 a.m.

Bela Vista – Rua Comendador Kou Ho Neng, Tel: 73821. One of the few grand old Macau hotels still operating. Food is so-so, but eating is enhanced by the fine harbour view from the dining terrace. Open noon till 2:30 p.m., 6:30–10:30 p.m.

Belo Restaurant – 43–47 Avenida Almeida Ribeiro. Tel: 73989. Inexpensive home-cooking, with a vast selection (202 menu items). Open 11 a.m. till 10:30 p.m.

Caseiro – 27E Rua Abreu Nunes, Tel: 573323. The name of the restaurant says it all – it translates 'home cooking,' complete with its own bakery. Heavy accent on the seafood – try the crab curry. Open 11:30 a.m. till 3 p.m., 6:30 p.m. till 1 a.m.

Far Siu Lau – 64 Rua Da Felicidade, Tel: 73585. A reputation for great roast pigeon but seems to have suffered a bit in the glare of nearby red lights. Moderate prices. Open noon till 1:30 a.m.

Henri's – 4 Avenida da Republica, Tel: 76207. Try garlic prawns. Open 11 a.m. till 11 p.m.

Fortaleze Restaurante – Pousada de Sao Tiago. Tel: 78111. For a grand night out. Open noon till 3 p.m., 7-11 p.m.

O Pescador – Hyatt-Regency Hotel, Taipa Island. Tel: (2)7000. Excellent seafood but also other Macanese and Portuguese specialities.

Panda – 4–8 Rua Carlos Eugenio, Taipa Village, Taipa Island, Tel: 27338. African chicken is a specialty as are the sardines. Open 11 a.m. – 11 p.m.

Pinocchio – 4 Rua do Sol, Taipa Island, Tel: 07128. spicy fish and fowl in a tree-shaded courtyard. Open noon till 11:30 p.m.

Portuguese – 16 Rua do Campo. Tel: 75445 *Bona fide* home cooking and no-nonsense red wine. Very cheap. Open 11 a.m. till 1 a.m.

Pousada de Coloane – Praia de Cheoc Van, Coloane Island, Tel: 2-8143. Leisurely seaside place. Open 8 a.m. till 10 p.m.

Riquexo (means rickshaw) – 69 Avenida Sidonia Pais (ask for **Park'n Shop**), Tel: 76294. Everything is literally home-cooked because many of the dishes are prepared at home by Macanese housewives and brought here daily. Open 11 a.m. to 3 p.m.

Vasco da Gama – Royal Hotel, Tel: 552222. This eatery has lots more European dishes on the menu – and quite imaginative ones at that – than the other Portuguese restaurants. Stewed lamb is a favorite and for aficionados, real Portuguese, a rarity in Macau. Open noon till 3 p.m., 6-11 p.m.

Solmar – 11 Rua da Praia Grande, Tel; 74391. Boulevard cafe and *bistro*, a local favorite Moderate prices. Open 11 a.m. till 11 p.m.

International Cuisine

A Galera, Hotel Lisboa, New Wing, Tel: 77666. Grill room with live music. Moderately expensive, but half the price of Hong Kong's various hotel grills. Open 12:30 till 2.30 p.m.; 7:30 p.m. till midnight.

A Pousada – Hyatt Regency Hotel, Tel: 27000. The hotel calls it a cafe, not a coffee shop, and the restaurant certainly earns that extra bit of class. Good buffets. Open 7 a.m. till midnight.

Grill Oriental Hotel, Tel: 567888. An opulent and expensive grill room with the usual grill menu plus some Portuguese dishes. Open noon till 3 p.m., 7-11 p.m.

Caesar's Palace – Hotel Lisboa, ground and first floor, Tel: 76996. For 3 a.m. big winners – open 24 hours.

Noite e Dia – Hotel Lisboa, second floor, Tel: 77666. Standard coffee shop. Open 24 hours.

Portas do Sol – Lisboa, second floor, Tel: 77666. A high-roller place with dancing and nightly floor-shows. Moderately expensive. Open till 1 a.m.

Cafe Safari – 14 Pateo do Coto Velo, Tel: 74313. Small, unpretentious, good snacks. Try "daily specials."

Kai Kai – 54 Avenida Infante D. Henrique; Tel: 74202. Chinese-run restaurants with European food. Surprisingly good. Recommended for latenight eating. Open till 1 a.m.

Chinese

456 (Shanghai Restaurant) – Lisboa Hotel, New Wing Tel: 88479. One of the region's best Shanghainese food restaurants, Macau or Hong Kong. Open till 1 a.m.

Chiu Chow – Lisboa Hotel, Tel: 77666. Another excellent Chinese restaurant with a reputation equal to counterparts in Hong Kong. Open 11 a.m. till midnight.

Dynasty – Oriental Hotel, Tel: 567888. First class Cantonese food, including 'dim sum' (which is served only Sundays, 8-11 a.m.). Open 11 a.m. till 3 p.m., 6-11 p.m.

Jade – Central Hotel, Avenida Almeida Ribeiro, Tel: 75125. Especially good for *dim sum*. Wide-ranging prices. Open 7 a.m. to 11 p.m.

Long Kei – 7 Largo do Senado (on the main city square). Tel: 573970. By reputation the best Chinese restaurant in town. Prices moderate and up. Open 11 a.m. till 11 p.m.

Royal Canton Royal Hotel. Tel: 78822. First class Cantonese restaurant which also serves 'dim sum'. Open 8 a.m. till midnight.

Tong Kong – 32 Rua da Caldeira, Tel: 77364. Notable because Hakka-style Chinese cuisine is rare. Open 11 a.m. till 1 a.m.

Italian

Ristorante Italiano Leong Un – 46 Rua de Cunha, Taipa Island, Tel: 2-7061. An Italian bistro with good and filling food. Open 11 a.m. – 11 p.m.

Roma – 34A Rua Nova a Guia, Tel: 81799. A totally Italian eatery, complete with hanging Chianti bottles and red tablecloths. Trattoria-style eating and a rare find. Open 6:30 p.m. till midnight.

Japanese

Ginza – Royal Hotel, Tel: 78822. As befits a hotel belonging to a Japanese hotel chain (Dai-Ichi), the restaurant's cuisine is authentic. Sashimi and teppanyaki. Open noon till 3 p.m., 6-11 p.m.

Furusato – Lisboa Hotel, Tel: 81581. Very expensive, but good. Open till 2:30 a.m.

ART/PHOTO
CREDITS